*Daniel Coit Gilman and the Birth of
the American Research University*

# Daniel Coit Gilman and the Birth of the American Research University

MICHAEL T. BENSON

Johns Hopkins University Press

*Baltimore*

Johns Hopkins University Press
2715 North Charles Street
Baltimore, Maryland 21218
www.press.jhu.edu

Library of Congress Cataloging-in-Publication Data

Names: Benson, Michael T., author.
Title: Daniel Coit Gilman and the birth of the American research university /
Michael T. Benson.
Description: Baltimore : Johns Hopkins University Press, 2022. | Includes bibliographical
references and index.
Identifiers: LCCN 2021045401 | ISBN 9781421444161 (hardcover) |
ISBN 9781421444178 (ebook)
Subjects: LCSH: Gilman, Daniel C. (Daniel Coit), 1831–1908. | Research—United
States—History. | Research institutes—United States—History. | Universities
and colleges—United States—History. | Johns Hopkins University—History. |
Johns Hopkins University—Presidents—Biography.
Classification: LCC LD2626.G55 B46 2022 | DDC 378.0092 [B]—dc23/eng/20211012
LC record available at https://lccn.loc.gov/2021045401

A catalog record for this book is available from the British Library.

Special discounts are available for bulk purchases of this book. For more information, please
contact Special Sales at specialsales@jh.edu.

# CONTENTS

*Preface*   *vii*

*Acknowledgments*   *xv*

Introduction   1

1  Yale and the Life-Giving Springs of New Haven   14

2  The House of Our Expectations in California   43

3  The Three Great Advisers   82

4  Gilman the Recruiter   106

5  Launching Our Bark upon the Patapsco   150

6  Advancing Knowledge Far and Wide   167

7  The Slater Fund and Attempts to Integrate Hopkins   213

8  Allies, Not Rivals   235

Conclusion   258

*Notes*   *263*

*Works Cited*   *317*

*Index*   *339*

In the early months of 2020, as the coronavirus pandemic swept the globe, millions of people visited the Johns Hopkins University website each day in search of the latest data on the crisis. News reports constantly mentioned the university, and researchers and experts from dozens of departments in public health, pathology, pulmonology, emergency medicine, and epidemiology were on cable news and social media explaining both certainties and uncertainties to a fearful public. Suddenly, the deep expertise that is oftentimes taken for granted, discovered and developed in research universities across the globe, was on full display. During this acute crisis, no place was better prepared to disseminate this knowledge than the Johns Hopkins University. How had this institution, founded hundreds of years after the storied Ivy League universities, come to such prominence? At the epicenter of that story is a man who has received much less attention than he deserves: the university's founding president, Daniel Coit Gilman.

In April 2018, while serving as president of Eastern Kentucky University, I was in Baltimore on business. Ever since reading Gilman's 1876 inaugural address and learning the reason for the *s* at the end of *Johns*, I had wanted to learn more about the institution Gilman helped to establish.[1] Having spent my career working in higher education, I have always been interested in the history of institutions, both public and private, and the people involved in the events around their respective establishments. Eager to get my hands on a single-volume account dedicated to the life of Gilman, I visited a campus gift shop and asked where one might find such a book. There happened to be present that day a library employee, who informed me that no such volume existed but that I was more than welcome to take a shot at writing one.

I was shocked to discover that *no* present-day "full-dress" biography of Gilman had been undertaken, nor had anything been written about Gilman for nearly half a century. There was some very good—but very dated—scholarship, with the first volume dedicated to Gilman's life published in 1910 by Fabian Franklin. The most recent, released in 1973, focused on Gilman and his role in shaping graduate education in America.[2] These volumes, together with a smattering of articles detailing Gilman's work as a geographer or librarian, constitute all the literature dedicated to the life of one of the most remarkable figures in the history of American higher education.[3] Scholars of American postsecondary institutions and traditions have all acknowledged Gilman's critical role and his influence at one of the most transformative moments in our post–Civil War history.

I would contend that Daniel Coit Gilman was the most important figure in the shaping of the American research university and that the lack of modern scholarship on his role leaves a significant vacuum along the spectrum of the "new" American system of higher education in the latter nineteenth century.[4] When one hears the word *new* associated with *university*, alarm bells sound, as there is an inherent aversion to change on college campuses everywhere. An examination of Gilman's life and contributions amplifies the uniqueness of the Hopkins approach and how it has impacted university structure and operations from 1876 to the present. What Gilman and his colleagues did—and why it is more relevant today than ever—was to force all institutions to reexamine their own model and to make the requisite changes to adapt, survive, thrive, compete, and contribute.

On the occasion of Gilman's retirement in 1901, one of his former students, speaking on behalf of the hundreds of Hopkins alumni gathered for the occasion, directed this observation at the outgoing president: "If it be true that Thomas Jefferson laid the broad foundation for American universities in his plans for the University of Virginia, it is no less true that you were the first to create and organize in America a university in which the discovery and dissemination of new truths were conceded a rank superior to mere instruction, and in which the efficiency and value of research as an educational instrument were exemplified in the training of many investigators." In so doing, Woodrow Wilson maintained that Gilman's greatest achievement was the establishment in America of "*a new and higher university ideal,* whose essential feature was not stately edifices, nor yet the mere association of pupils with learned and eminent teachers, but rather the education of trained and vigorous minds through the search for truth under the guidance and with the cooperation of master investigators."[5]

While today our country faces looming deficits on multiple fronts, from budget to trade, what Wilson referred to as a "new and higher university ideal"—America's system of higher education, particularly graduate education—remains the envy of the entire world. The United States is the nation of choice for higher education, as evidenced by the fact that twelve of the world's top twenty universities are in the United States, according to the *Times Higher Education* world university rankings for 2022.[6] In its basic form, the present American system combines the best of the British university model (undergraduate instruction as the primary function) with the German university model (research).

Jonathan Cole, a former Columbia University provost, notes that the ambition to excel and the fierce competitiveness of scientists, scholars, and administrators at American research universities have made these entities the engines of America's prosperity. In his book *The Great American University* Cole states, "The laser, magnetic resonance imaging, FM radio, the algorithm for Google searches, Global Positioning Systems, DNA fingerprinting, fetal monitoring, scientific cattle breeding, advanced methods of surveying public opinion, and even Viagra all had their origins in America's research universities, as did tens of thousands of other inventions, devices, medical miracles, and ideas that have transformed the world."[7] If the primary purpose of a university is the discovery, development, dissemination, and application of *new* knowledge for the betterment of society, one would be hard pressed to find a US institution that has contributed more per capita and in a shorter period of time than Johns Hopkins University. At the time of this writing, twenty-nine people associated with Johns Hopkins as faculty members, fellows, residents, or graduates have been awarded the Nobel Prize, including four Nobel laureates currently on the faculty.[8]

Hopkins' $7 million gift in 1873 propelled American higher education to generate life-altering scientific discoveries, and this tradition persists to the present day. According to the latest numbers from the National Science Foundation, for forty-one years in a row Johns Hopkins has led the nation in the amount of institutional dollars spent on research and development. For fiscal year 2019 that number was $2.97 billion. The next institution in the ranking, the University of Michigan, spent more than $1.2 billion *less* on research than Hopkins.[9] A separate listing reveals that Johns Hopkins University recorded $2.25 billion in research funded by federal agencies such as the National Science Foundation and the National Institutes of Health in fiscal year 2018. Spending by the institution following Johns Hopkins, the University of Washington in Seattle, was just shy of $1 billion.[10]

That all this has been accomplished by means of the Johns Hopkins University model, constructed by Gilman and the original Hopkins trustees entirely from scratch, is all the more astonishing. Both Gilman and the board were presented with a completely clean slate as recipients of the largest single bequest ever made to a US university up to that time, with little to no restrictions on its expenditure. Gilman himself would later write, "So far as I can learn, the Hopkins foundation, coming from a single giver, is without parallel in terms or in amount in this or any other land."[11]

When he took the helm of Hopkins, Gilman was one of the leaders of a movement, together with Charles Eliot at Harvard, James Angell at Michigan, and Andrew White at Cornell. These men viewed the university as the sole viable source for advanced scientific training and research.[12] The incorporation of German-style research into the American university model resulted in a sea change for institutions throughout the country. It is no coincidence that this cadre of educational leaders had all done graduate work in Germany. For Gilman and his associates, as they developed the blueprint for their new university prototype, *German* came to mean several things: specialization; research as the first priority, structured around a scientific and systematic approach to knowledge; and the inextricable link between one's primary professional identity and an academic discipline.[13]

Immediately after accepting the position at Hopkins, Gilman undertook a series of deliberate and painstaking preparations in advance of launching the new university. These measures entailed a trustees-financed trip to Europe in 1875, which served dual purposes for Gilman: first, it provided him insight into the structure and operation of great institutions (including Oxford, Cambridge, and the universities of Strasbourg,

Vienna, and Edinburgh, among others); second, it gave him the opportunity to recruit international faculty to add to the ranks of the brightest academic minds available in the United States.[14]

Mirroring Gilman's efforts in Baltimore, others attempted to establish universities and colleges in post–Civil War America, whether they were religiously affiliated institutions concentrated in the Midwest, historically Black colleges and universities (HBCUs) throughout the reconstructed South, or large public and private universities on the West Coast. Wealthy industrialists like John D. Rockefeller in Chicago and Leland and Jane Stanford in Palo Alto endowed their institutions with sizable sums, thus allowing them to cherry-pick faculty and administrators as they pleased. Chicago and Stanford, as well as Clark University in Worcester, Massachusetts, began their endeavors from the ground up.[15] They did not, as was the practice with the older, more established East Coast universities, simply add graduate programs to an existing undergraduate infrastructure. The Yale historian G. W. Pierson described the actions of mature institutions with emerging faith in the scientific method that desired professional programs and PhDs as "built around and on top of and inside of or in place of the old-fashioned college."[16]

But none were as successful as Gilman and the Johns Hopkins University in the final quarter of the nineteenth century. Gilman's commitment to the work and needs of the faculty as the sine qua non of the new enterprise was unqualified, and he was exacting in his selection of professors from America and Europe: they must be committed to both teaching and research. As he stated in his 1876 inaugural address, "The best teachers are usually those who are free, competent and willing to make original researches in the library and the laboratory."[17] Gilman insisted that the dissemination and application of discoveries made were among the primary responsibilities of the university. "It is one of the noblest duties of a university to advance knowledge, and to diffuse it not merely among those who can attend the daily lecture—but far and wide," Gilman asserted.[18] In 1878 the Johns Hopkins University Press was founded; it is the oldest continuously running university press in the United States. The faculty recruited by Gilman formed the vanguard in their respective disciplines, with their work and discoveries being widely distributed through the scholarly journals founded at Hopkins. Several of these journals became the primary organs of their areas of specialization, as five of the original six departments sponsored these publications.[19]

Gilman further insisted that the professors he selected were to be provided with students sufficiently prepared to challenge and motivate them.[20] To attract the best possible student talent, the Hopkins archetype introduced the establishment of fellowships (both graduate and postdoctoral), for which hundreds of candidates applied. As a consequence, aspiring academics from across the United States flocked to Hopkins, the only university promoting advanced scholarship at the time.[21] And what these new recruits found upon arriving in Baltimore was entirely unique: amid the modest structures that made up the Johns Hopkins campus in 1876 (in keeping with both Hopkins' and Gilman's oft-stated commitment to build men, and not buildings), there was a complete absence of "class wars, faculty feuds, moral revolutions, student rebellions, newspaper scandals, or political persecutions."[22] The result? *Study* was the chief student activity.

Others recognized the remarkable cadre of fellows and postgraduates attracted to Hopkins from year one. Gilman invited Thomas Henry Huxley, the renowned scientist and professor of natural history at the Royal School of Mines in London, to Baltimore to deliver the first of many such addresses in September 1876, preceding the official opening of the Johns Hopkins University by a few weeks. The *New York Tribune*, which published the texts of all the speeches Huxley made while in America, prefaced his remarks at Hopkins with the following: "There are already enrolled, as associates, fellows, and resident graduates, 40 young men who have been graduated within the last ten years from American colleges, of whom 12 have pursued prolonged courses in Europe, six have taken the degree of M.D., and six that of Ph.D. The Johns Hopkins University is said to be the only institution in the country which has begun with such a staff of graduates."[23]

Amassing such talent in one place with no constraints whatsoever produced remarkable results in the first twenty-five years of Hopkins' existence. According to the historian of higher education Lawrence Veysey, these early "Hopkins men," as he called them, took enormous pride in the lack of form, ritual, or ceremony. Most, if not all, were experiencing a newfound freedom to devote their energy and substance to whatever course of study engrossed them. A kind of hypercompetitiveness imbued the atmosphere of the "new" university and resulted in unremitting pressure to work hard. Given the small number of students at the outset and the close-range comparison with one's peers, every Hopkins man longed to demonstrate his value and contribute his share.[24]

The productivity spurred by the environment at Hopkins speaks for itself: in the period from 1876 to 1902, Harvard University, with its 240-year head start, produced 320 PhDs. By contrast, Johns Hopkins University from 1878 (the first year doctorates were awarded) to 1902 produced 596.[25] Although Hopkins issued nearly twice as many doctorates, one must not mistake the results for a lack of rigor. In summarizing the early years of Hopkins, Gilman averred that "the multiplication of academic titles and the bestowal of degrees in a careless or wholesale manner receives no encouragement." On the contrary, it was "no easy matter to win the diploma of a Doctor of Philosophy."[26] From the outset, Hopkins was committed to concentration and specialization, and Gilman's expectation was for both faculty and graduate students to "do good work in a limited field."[27]

With the advent of the Hopkins model, an entirely new age of research, discovery, and achievement was initiated. James Burrill Angell, president of the University of Michigan from 1871 to 1909, is credited with helping make Michigan into the institution it is today. Upon Gilman's departure from Hopkins, Angell stated unequivocally, "No one of us has done so much as you to make an epoch in graduate work in America."[28] President Eliot of Harvard would later confess that his own graduate school in

Cambridge "started feebly in 1870 and 1871, did not thrive, until the example of Johns Hopkins forced our faculty to put their strength into the development of our instruction for graduates. And what was true of Harvard was true of every other university in the land which aspired to create an advanced school of arts and sciences."[29]

The faculty Gilman recruited was a veritable who's who of prominent scientists and thinkers in the nineteenth and twentieth centuries. Filling the founding professorships were Henry A. Rowland, a physicist and founder of the American Physical Society; James J. Sylvester, founder of the *American Journal of Mathematics*; Basil Gildersleeve, president of the American Philological Association; Henry Newell Martin, coauthor of *Practical Instruction in Elementary Biology*; Charles D'Urban Morris, professor of Latin and Greek; and Ira Remsen, founder of the *American Chemical Journal* and Hopkins' second president. Three of the seven department heads were under thirty years of age. These accomplished faculty proved to be a tremendous draw, as postgraduate students attracted to Baltimore included Thomas Hunt Morgan, evolutionary biologist and 1933 Nobel laureate; John Dewey, educational reformer and founder of the University of Chicago Laboratory Schools; and Woodrow Wilson, 1919 Nobel laureate and US president from 1913 to 1921.[30]

Committed to recruiting the very best talent to confront society's most unrelenting challenges, particularly in relation to the health sciences, the first physician Gilman lured to Hopkins in 1884 was William Welch, arguably the world's leading pathologist. Welch was referred to Gilman by Dr. John Shaw Billings, one of the primary forces behind the design and construction of the Johns Hopkins Hospital and the structure and establishment of the Hopkins Medical School. The wholly unique personality of Johns Hopkins University and its emphasis on graduate education and research since its founding was powerfully reinforced when the Hopkins Hospital opened in 1889. The nation's first teaching hospital would be inextricably linked to the medical school, which opened in 1893 with eighteen students, three of whom were women.[31]

Like Gilman, Welch was a gifted recruiter who had the ability to recognize and attract talent. Just 34 years old, Welch made a capital selection of young, ambitious colleagues: William Osler (40), the most famous clinical physician of the modern era; William Halsted (37), considered a pioneer in surgical techniques and practices; and Howard Kelly (31), a gynecologist renowned for his advances in radiation therapy. Another of Welch's recruits was Franklin P. Mall (31), a promising anatomist and pathologist then at the University of Chicago, whose program and lab enjoyed the considerable backing of the university's principal donor, John D. Rockefeller. Mall was content at Chicago, but Welch refused to abandon his lobbying efforts to bring the aspiring doctor to Baltimore. Mall finally relented and wired Welch, "Shall cast my lot with Hopkins. . . . I consider you the greatest attraction. You make the opportunities."[32]

Recognizing that all biographies must strike a balance between the poles of beatification and exposé, this work also includes voices critical of Gilman. Some have characterized Gilman as an academic lightweight whose interests were broad—so that he was conversant on a litany of subjects—but whose depth of understanding was superficial. Among those who criticized Gilman for his lack of original scholarship, together with a general absence of gravitas when compared with his contemporaries, was the historian Veysey, who wrote that "Gilman lacked a scholar's temperament. He was the son of a successful businessman, and it was management which always appealed to him." In assessing Gilman's communication skills, Veysey maintained that he "was master of the pleasant platitude. His rhetoric usually confined itself to two moods: stately cheerfulness or ponderous caution. Standing on the same lecture platform as Charles W. Eliot, Gilman could not help seeming rather commonplace by comparison."[33] John Franklin Jameson, the first to earn a PhD in history from Hopkins, in 1882, called Gilman's speeches "extremely neat and disagreeably affable" and described one of his commencement addresses as being "full of the usual taffy."[34] Notwithstanding such critical assessments, a review of the inaugural addresses President Gilman delivered in 1872 at the University of California and in 1876 at Johns Hopkins might persuade the reader otherwise, as Gilman displayed an exceptional ability to inspire on each occasion. More importantly, his oratory translated into action that, in turn, produced results.

One must also address the foundational faculty Gilman personally recruited to Baltimore, one of whom, Gildersleeve, was an unrepentant southern apologist who also happened to be the greatest classicist of his generation. Further, the university's policies relative to the admission of women and African American students during Gilman's tenure, while in keeping with the practices of a southern state like Maryland, are still difficult to explain and impossible to defend (nor should they be defended). All of these aspects of Gilman's life, and much more, are addressed here.

Gilman experienced tremendous personal loss and family crises, which had an enormous impact on his life and career. Family circumstances often dictated Gilman's response to opportunities presented. His unexpectedly short tenure as president of the Carnegie Institution of Washington has led to increased scrutiny of the final chapter in Gilman's career.

His limited contributions to the disciplines of geography and library science notwithstanding, no one can deny Gilman's overwhelming impact on modern American higher education. Those students who choose to pursue degrees beyond the bachelor's—widely viewed as a necessity in today's ever-changing world—will learn at institutions that bear the mark of the Hopkins experiment. Whether in person or online, graduate programs throughout the world have inevitably been modeled on those developed by the Johns Hopkins University nearly a century and a half ago.

Gilman's inauguration at Johns Hopkins occurred on February 22, 1876, a date still celebrated at the university as Commemoration Day. In his address, Gilman noted the many organizations and activities engaged in promoting higher education in the United States and abroad and stated that "the oldest and remotest nations are looking here for light." He then posed a rhetorical question: "What is the significance of all this activity?" In speaking for higher education generally and the new Johns Hopkins University specifically, Gilman answered,

> It is a reaching out for a better state of society than now exists; it is a dim but an indelible impression of the value of learning; it is a craving for intellectual and moral growth; it is a longing to interpret the laws of creation; it means a wish for less misery among the poor, less ignorance in schools, less bigotry in the temple, less suffering in the hospital, less fraud in business, less folly in politics; it means more study of nature, more love of art, more lessons from history, more security in property, more health in cities, more virtue in the country, more wisdom in legislation, more intelligence, more happiness, more religion.[35]

The need for this book has never been more critical. The former Johns Hopkins provost Dr. Lloyd Minor is currently the dean of the Stanford University Medical School. At a conference examining the PhD in America and Gilman's impact on graduate education, Minor noted the debt owed Gilman: his unrelenting belief in the power of research and advanced training in American higher education led to the foundation of the research enterprise that benefits the entire world. "Gilman's contribution," Minor concluded, "was not just as the first president of Johns Hopkins, not just in establishing graduate education in the United States, but in founding the modern university. This is his legacy."[36] And what a legacy it is.

"The establishment of Johns Hopkins was perhaps the single most decisive event in the history of learning in the Western hemisphere," stated the University of Chicago sociologist Edward Shils.[37] Certainly, there will be some who view this statement as hyperbole; I, however, do not. The temerity—one might call it educational hubris—demonstrated by Gilman in establishing the Johns Hopkins University at a pivotal moment in our national experience is something wholly unique in the history of American higher education.

This book chronicles what happened when a donor with a most unusual name—Johns Hopkins—placed his massive gift in the hands of a uniquely qualified administrator. As that 45-year-old geographer concluded his 1876 inaugural address, he imagined this new institution traveling along the river that runs through Baltimore and what might lie ahead. "So, friends and colleagues," Gilman said, "we launch our bark upon the Patapsco, and send it forth to unknown seas. May its course be guided by looking to the heavens and the voyage promote the glory of God and the good of Mankind."[38]

On that February morning so many years ago, no one could fully anticipate what was about to happen: nothing less than the birth of the modern American research university.

# ACKNOWLEDGMENTS

While writing my doctoral dissertation in 1993, I had the good fortune of interviewing David McCullough at his home on Martha's Vineyard. He had just won the Pulitzer Prize for his biography of Harry S. Truman; my older brother, Steve, had won a Pulitzer for editorial cartooning that same year. Our conversation covered a host of topics, including the approach taken by some historians in addressing their subjects. McCullough confessed his particular dismay over the tendency by writers to "suck the warm blood" out of people in trying to recount their life's story.

I've thought much about McCullough's assessment throughout my own attempt to chronicle the arc of a truly remarkable person while allowing the warm blood to still course through his veins. My hope is that Daniel Coit Gilman will spring to life and the reader will recognize the enormous debt owed to him for his contributions, many of which impact us to this very day.

Like each one of us, Gilman was not without flaws, and I have endeavored to cover his life's journey in an open, honest, and transparent fashion. Gilman's foibles and defects should, I believe, give us all hope—hope that we can own up to our mistakes and learn from them while enjoying accomplishment and experiencing failure, with equal measure of magnanimity and resolve.

A project like this is never completed in a vacuum, and many individuals have helped me along the way. I thank the staff at the Johns Hopkins University Press for their belief in this project, especially the editorial director, Greg Britton. From the outset, Greg saw the need for a contemporary contribution to the body of scholarship on Gilman, as did Professor Stuart "Bill" Leslie, who encouraged me from the first time we discussed my taking on this effort, in the summer of 2018. These two never vacillated in their support of the project. My appointment as visiting professor within the Department of the History of Science and Technology at Johns Hopkins University for 2020 proved to be beneficial as well, and I thank the then acting department chair, Professor Sharon Kingsland, for her courtesy and accommodations.

Professor Leslie is completing an institution-sponsored history of the Johns Hopkins University, in which Gilman will certainly feature prominently. Much has been written about the early days of the university; two of the most notable works were written by John French and Hugh Hawkins many years ago. Likewise, the establishment of the Johns Hopkins Hospital and the School of Medicine has been chronicled by Dr. Alan Chesney, dean of the School of Medicine for twenty-four years, who completed an exhaustive, three-volume history of both entities. But the intention of this book is to focus on the entirety of Gilman's life and how experiences prepared him for the task of launching the modern American research university. For Gilman, the Hopkins years were a piece of a larger whole, and the years of preparation for his tenure in Baltimore, together with his volunteer work outside higher education and his post-Hopkins service, are all discussed.

In my work in research libraries, from the David Ben-Gurion Archives in the Negev Desert to the British Archives in London to the Harry S. Truman Library in Missouri, I have never met anyone more knowledgeable about a subject than the archivist Jim Stimpert at Johns Hopkins. From the first time I set foot in the Milton Eisenhower Library in Baltimore to the present day—even during the global pandemic—Jim has always responded to queries and even reviewed the manuscript. Jim is both a credit to his profession and an institutional treasure, and I thank him profusely for all his assistance. My experience within the Hopkins archives is not unique, as countless others have benefitted from its committed staff. Jim's colleague Allison Seyler has also been very helpful. Nancy McCall, director of the Alan Mason Chesney Medical Archives at the Johns Hopkins Hospital, also proved to be an incredible resource, and I'm grateful for her assistance and that of her colleagues. I also wish to acknowledge the very attentive staff in Manuscripts and Archives at Yale University's Sterling Memorial Library.

Sincere thanks to those professors within the Master of Liberal Arts (MLA) program at Johns Hopkins, who had a hand in reviewing this book as I worked on it concurrently with pursuing my degree at the university. Three people in particular—the MLA program director, Laura DeSisto, and professors Duane Cummins and Edward Papenfuse—were particularly helpful. This work is my own, and I readily accept responsibility for any omissions and mistakes, but the finished product was immeasurably better thanks to their critiques and suggestions. Dr. Cummins reviewed the entire work and provided much-needed feedback. Dr. Papenfuse, the retired head archivist for the state of Maryland, also served as my primary faculty adviser for this project, and I thank him for his expertise, insights, and understanding.

To my niece and close collaborator, Natalie Richards-Gebbia: words cannot adequately express my gratitude for her hard work and commitment to coaching, editing, and refining. We began this collaboration in the spring of 2018, and in between her time in France teaching English and her return to Utah to get married and launch her own career, Natalie provided the steady hand so needed for a work like this. Likewise, developmental editors and their role in tightening up one's writing cannot be overstated. Scott Smallwood is the best of the best. His keen eye and crisp edits were just what was needed, and I thank him for the partnership we have enjoyed over the past year. To copyeditor Joanne Allen, who has worked for the Johns Hopkins University

Press for many years, I express thanks for both her breadth of editing experience and her laser-like focus on details.

Special appreciation to the Eastern Kentucky University Board of Regents for granting me a sabbatical year to complete this book. I was provided an office in the John Crabbe Library, and the months of the COVID-19 lockdown proved incredibly productive as I had, literally, the entire place to myself. It would be impossible to overstate how helpful the EKU library staff was throughout this endeavor; the Crabbe Library at Eastern Kentucky is a community treasure. Also, special thanks to my EKU colleague and friend Dr. Tom Appleton, who provided much-needed advice over the past two years. Two Department of History colleagues at EKU—Professors Carolyn DuPont and John Bowes—were extremely helpful in reviewing the manuscript. My longtime friends and collaborators Jim Parkinson, Ken Adelman, and Hal Boyd were also tremendous sounding boards, and I'm grateful for their input.

We are all products of our environment, and I owe a tremendous debt to my family's commitment to learning and exploration. My mother and father, both of whom have passed on, believed in the transformative power of education. I can never repay the sacrifices they made so that my five siblings and I could receive as much education as possible. Everything good that has happened to me is a direct result of my parents' sacrifices. We are trying our best to honor their legacy by providing additional opportunities and access to more education for our own posterity and, on my part, for the students I am privileged to work with every single day.

And lastly, to my wife, Debi, and our children: my unending gratitude for believing I could tackle this project and for supporting me throughout the process. They have listened as I recounted at the family dinner table details about the day's research and writing, and they have lived and breathed all things *Daniel Coit Gilman* as much as I have. Throughout a career that has taken us across the country, my family has always been the North Star, providing unqualified encouragement, motivation, and cajoling. For that, I can never thank them enough. I am blessed beyond measure to have them in my life. This book is dedicated to them.

*Daniel Coit Gilman and the Birth of
the American Research University*

# Introduction

Johns Hopkins was the second of eleven children, born into a tobacco-farming family in Anne Arundel County, Maryland. His family's farm, Whitehall, had been given to his ancestors by the king of England more than a hundred years earlier. For plantation owners at the time, tobacco was extremely profitable—especially when farmed by enslaved people—and Johns' parents, Samuel and Hannah, became quite wealthy. No manumission records registered in Samuel Hopkins' name are extant from this time period, and whether Johns' parents granted freedom to their enslaved workers continues to be debated. We do know, however, that Johns and his siblings were enlisted into service tending to the family's substantial land, and Johns labored on the plantation until he was 17. In 1812, Johns left his childhood home to apprentice with his uncle, Gerard Hopkins, a wholesale grocer in the booming city of Baltimore.[1] Recognizing Johns' innate aptitudes, Hannah sent her son off with this charge: "Thee has business ability and thee must go where the money is."[2] Samuel died in 1814, and Hannah remained on the five-hundred-acre farm until 1840, at which time Johns invited his mother to live with him. Hannah accepted her son's invitation and remained at his residence on Lombard Street until her death in 1846.[3]

Decades earlier, as a teenager, Johns had left the family farm and moved to Baltimore, immediately proving his worth to Gerard. During extended absences from the city, Gerard directed his nephew to "buy goods and do the best ye can." Johns did exactly that, serving as general manager at the age of 19, not only maintaining his uncle's business but increasing it considerably.[4] This improvement in his uncle's business was, however, accompanied by two major disagreements. First, the two men argued over the ethics of accepting whiskey in the place of cash as payment for goods—Johns was for it, and Gerard was against.[5] But even more problematic to Johns' position was his affection for his cousin Elizabeth, Gerard's daughter, and their plans to marry. Owing to the Quakers' prohibition against such a union, the family turned against Johns. Despite their forced separation, Johns and Elizabeth continued their friendship throughout their lives, both remaining single, having vowed to each other never to marry. Some have speculated that Johns focused his energies on making money in part to counter the devastation of losing his first and only love. One of Johns' first business partners and a fellow Quaker, Benjamin Moore, reportedly observed, "Johns is the only man I know who wants to make more money than I do."[6] A chronicler of Baltimore's history noted that some, like Alexander and Napoleon, believed that their course "led them on as conquerors of kings, and the destroyers of empires," while others, such as Gautama Buddha and Francis Xavier, were "preordained to the work of instructing mankind, or saving souls." But, this account concludes, "Johns Hopkins held, we believe, the unique idea that he was *divinely commissioned to make money!*"[7]

Hopkins set off on his own in 1819 and entered into a brief partnership with Moore in dry goods that soon moved into other areas of commerce. When the association with Moore was dissolved, Johns enlisted three of his younger brothers—Mahlon, Philip, and Gerard—as salesmen and formed Hopkins and Brothers Wholesalers. From the mercantile business, Hopkins soon branched out into other pursuits, with a particularly keen eye toward railroads, an interest that sprang from his experience with the challenge of getting goods to market.[8] The Hopkins name became increasingly well known in the 1820s and '30s throughout the region as their wagons, "each crammed with merchandise sufficient to fill a small warehouse, with their spanking teams and jingling bells, were crossing and re-crossing the Alleghenies, to the new states beyond."[9] Hopkins was renowned for his focus on efficiency. He once sent off a load of merchandise weighing four tons to Mt. Vernon, Ohio, a distance of four hundred miles. The wagon returned with three and a half tons of Ohio tobacco, with only a single wagon bow damaged on the trip.[10]

Among the goods Johns and his brothers received in payment for debts was whiskey, which was then bulk-shipped to Philadelphia.[11] The whiskey trade was extremely profitable; Hopkins recalled to a cousin that in the first year of business he had sold two hundred thousand dollars' worth of goods.[12] The decision by Hopkins, a lifelong member of the Society of Friends, to engage in the spirits trade placed him at odds with his fellow congregation members and resulted in his expulsion from one meeting in 1827. Undeterred, Hopkins joined a new orthodox Quaker meeting and contributed to its efforts throughout his life, including donating to a new building fund. Years later, though, Johns admitted to taking the wrong stance regarding whiskey, telling his nephew, Joseph Hopkins, "that he wished he had never sold liquor, and that in so doing he had made the greatest mistake of his life."[13] Regardless, transporting his wares—

whiskey and everything else—over mountain passes and along muddy roads in Conestoga wagons reinforced his view of the transformative power of rail.

## Hopkins and the Baltimore & Ohio Railroad

After the early deaths of the three younger brothers whom he had recruited into the mercantile business, Johns retired at the age of 50 and turned his attention to investments, becoming a leading financier.[14] Hopkins also developed mines in western Maryland and was instrumental in the early days of the Merchants' and Miners' Transportation Company.[15] Extremely careful when it came to allocating finite resources, Hopkins believed that the investment of capital was one thing, "but his precious time was quite another."[16] One enterprise in which Johns invested a great amount of both money and attention was the railroad. At one point, he was the largest shareholder in the Baltimore & Ohio Railroad, serving as chairman of the finance committee from 1855 until his death in 1873. The city's fortunes in the nineteenth century rose and fell with the railroad. When construction on the rails of the B&O began in 1828, Charles Carroll—at 91 years of age the sole surviving signatory to the Declaration of Independence—turned the first spade and told the assembled crowd, "I consider this among the most important acts of my life, second only to my signing the Declaration of Independence, if even it be second to that."[17]

On two occasions, in 1857 and 1873, Hopkins pledged his own private fortune to keep the railroad running in the midst of financial panics, thus ensuring its solvency.[18] In 1858, Hopkins nominated John Work Garrett, then 38, to be president of the B&O. Those representing the state's interests in the railroad countered his nomination by supporting the incumbent executive, Chauncey Brooks. Two of the public-affiliated members had recently begun to lean toward more private control, and their votes would prove decisive: Garrett won on a ballot, 16 to 14.[19] Addressing a deeply divided board, Garrett assured the members, "My ancestry has been identified with Baltimore for many generations and I, born in your midst, have all my interests, my affections, and my future here. I have no greater pride—no greater ambition, than to lend my humble efforts to promote the advancement and prosperity of my native city and my native State."[20] When Garrett assumed the presidency of the railroad, 25,000 miles of rail had been laid; upon his death in 1884 the number had increased to 125,000.[21] Garrett himself would become both wealthy and influential, with several local newspapers advocating for his presidential nomination by the Democratic Party in both 1872 and 1876.[22] The friendship between the two men was immutable, and Garrett would play a pivotal role in helping Hopkins with his philanthropic efforts.

In October 1859, just months into his tenure as B&O president, Garrett would face an unexpected test reflecting Baltimore's deep divide. In the mid-nineteenth century, Maryland, as both a border state and a state where enslaved people were held captive, was caught in the crossfire between its distinct agricultural regions where people were still enslaved and its diverse urban populations. The Mason-Dixon Line was a mere forty miles to the north, and Baltimore considered itself primarily a southern city with deeply held southern traditions and customs. This chasm would only grow wider as armed conflict between North and South appeared imminent. John Brown failed in his attempt to take the federal arsenal at Harpers Ferry in October 1859, a key juncture at the confluence of the Shenandoah and Potomac Rivers, where the B&O had built a bridge to span the Potomac more than twenty years earlier. The Mexican War hero Colonel Robert E. Lee led a detachment of Marines to quell the rebellion, and a militia from Frederick, Maryland, was sent via the B&O, marking the first use of railroad to transport troops to an armed conflict.[23]

By 1860 Baltimore, with a population of 212,000, was the South's largest city; its nearest southern neighbor, Richmond, Virginia, had just 38,000 residents.[24] Of note are the popular-vote results in Maryland in the 1860 presidential election: then vice president of the United States John Breckinridge, of Kentucky and the Southern Democratic Party, secured 46 percent; Senator John Bell, of Tennessee and the Constitutional Union Party, registered 45 percent; Senator Stephen A. Douglas, of Illinois and the Democratic Party, won just over 6 percent; and Abraham Lincoln, also of Illinois but representing the Republican Party, won just 2 percent.[25] In some Maryland counties Lincoln received fewer than five votes; in the state's easternmost county, Worcester, he received none.[26]

Garrett straddled North and South in the months leading up to the Civil War. After Harpers Ferry, Garrett told a Baltimore audience that the B&O was "a Southern line. And if ever necessity should require—which heaven forbid!—it will prove the great bulwark of the border, and a sure agency for home defense."[27] Shortly thereafter, Garrett instructed his agent at Bellaire, Ohio: "Until further order you [are] to take all troops or munitions that offer at regular rates. Our company fully recognizes the present legal authorities State and National under which we live, and as common carriers propose to promptly and safely transport all passengers or freight that those authorities may desire."[28]

Despite being outnumbered in Baltimore, Hopkins remained an unapologetic Unionist, never letting public opinion diminish his resolve for the Northern cause, even as his wealth and prestige continued to grow.[29] In concert with Mayor George Brown, Hopkins even went so far as to lead an effort to secure funds ($1 million in total) from Baltimore banks in defense of the city.[30] Although the secessionists dominated the ranks of the merchants, young professionals, and appointees to the various federal offices in Baltimore, they were also divided among themselves and attracted minimal support from either municipal leaders or the working classes. Whatever cohesion the movement was lacking developed in 1861, when the specter of a federal troop invasion emboldened the secessionists to argue for Maryland's rights. The ten-man delegation sent to Annapolis for the extraordinary session of the state legislature in early 1861 unanimously advocated for states' rights and secession.[31]

Tensions ran particularly high in Baltimore when President Lincoln called for seventy-five thousand troops to quash the rebellion after the fall of Fort Sumter in April 1861. Some national newspapers chose to play down the hostilities, with the *New*

*York Times* claiming that the "local commotion in the South could be put to rest effectually in thirty days" and the *Chicago Tribune* forecasting a fight that would be over in two months.[32] The Baltimore riot on April 19, 1861, was set off when federal troops en route to Washington from Massachusetts and Pennsylvania (and in response to Lincoln's call) had to disembark and march through the streets to catch another train south. Violence ensued, with southern sympathizers hurling rocks at the troops and blocking their path; some soldiers panicked and fired into the angry mob, leaving several civilians and troops dead. On the heels of this event, Maryland governor Thomas Hicks called for a special session of the legislature—not in the state capital of Annapolis but in the pro-Union town of Frederick—at which a vote of secession was to take place.[33] On April 29, 1861, the Maryland House of Delegates voted 53 to 13 against secession.[34]

Two weeks later, Garrett assented to General Benjamin Butler's request to use the B&O Railroad to transport Union troops on their way to Baltimore and their position atop Federal Hill, overlooking the harbor.[35] If there had been any question about which side the B&O might take, the South now knew it could *not* count on Garrett, even though Baltimore was still dominated with southern sympathizers. Although Garrett faced a railroad board of directors filled with these sympathizers, he knew he could count on the support of his friend and mentor Johns Hopkins.[36]

The B&O was the main medium of conveyance for the Union army from Washington, DC, to all points north and west, and the value of Garrett's commitment to the Union, despite the heavy losses inflicted by southern saboteurs throughout the war, is inestimable.[37] Garrett's support for the Union became unequivocal in May 1861, when General Thomas "Stonewall" Jackson commandeered fifty-six B&O locomotives and more than three hundred rail cars for the Confederacy.[38] The South had no use for the engines nor cars, as their rail gauge was different, and most of the equipment was abandoned or destroyed. Jackson also burned twenty-three bridges and tore down 102 miles of telegraph lines. This destructive work kept trains from running between Baltimore and Wheeling, West Virginia, from June 1861 to the end of March 1862.[39] Garrett took the destruction of the infrastructure and the theft of his railroad property very hard—and personally. From that moment forward he was an ardent supporter of the Union and ran the railroad as such.[40]

The Baltimore & Ohio would play a consequential role throughout the war, even conveying President Lincoln from Washington, DC, to Annapolis aboard Engine No. 18 on February 2, 1865. Not wishing to take a carriage through Annapolis to reach the deepwater wharf located on the grounds of the US Naval Academy, Lincoln would walk a mile with a detail of three to Fort Monroe and transport to the famed Hampton Roads Conference aboard the steamboat *River Queen*.[41] Lincoln's trip to Annapolis on Mr. Garrett's railroad was kept so quiet that no one even knew about it: "President Lincoln arrived here on Thursday, by special train from Washington. No one was aware of this distinguished arrival, until it was heralded by the Hospital Band playing patriotic airs of welcome, as he passed from the wharf to the boat."[42]

At the conclusion of the war, and just days after Robert E. Lee's surrender at Ap-

pomattox—in a truly remarkable historical twist of fate—Garrett personally arranged
for a private railroad car to transport General Ulysses S. Grant and his family from
Washington, DC, to Burlington, New Jersey, on April 14, 1865. To ensure privacy for
the general and his family, the train conductor locked the doors to Grant's compart-
ment, and somewhere in northeastern Maryland a man made an unsuccessful attempt
to force his way into the car.[43] Grant would subsequently recount, "I received an
anonymous letter from a man, saying he had been detailed to kill me, that he rode on
my train as far as Havre de Grace [on the southeast bank of the Susquehanna River],
and as my car was locked he could not get in. He thanked God he had failed."[44] Grant
would serve as a trustee for an education fund established in 1867 by another prominent Baltimore resident and titan of industry, George Peabody.

## Hopkins, Garrett, and George Peabody

After the war, Garrett would continue to play a key role in Hopkins' life, perhaps
most consequentially in encouraging his relationship with George Peabody, America's
foremost philanthropist at the time. Like Johns Hopkins, Peabody had been born in
1795, made his initial money in merchandising, and then turned to banking, finance,
and railroads. Neither man ever married. Peabody and Hopkins shared several mutual
interests and were committed, later in life, to a variety of causes. Hopkins would focus
on local charities, while Peabody spent most of his time in London and concentrated
his philanthropy on issues and efforts endemic to Britain, establishing the Peabody
Homes for working people in London and the finance house that became the antecedent to J. P. Morgan Chase. Idolizing the man in England for his philanthropic
efforts and other contributions, the British wanted to have Peabody buried at Westminster Abbey upon his death in 1869, but his will stipulated that his final resting
place be in America. With approval from Queen Victoria, Peabody's funeral was held
in Westminster, where he lay in state.[45] His remains crossed the Atlantic for burial in
Salem, Massachusetts, five miles from his hometown of Danvers.[46] Known as America's first great philanthropist, Peabody on the occasion of the centennial celebration
of Danvers donated funds for a library; the donation was accompanied by a note:
"Education, a debt due from the present to succeeding generations."[47]

Peabody was renowned throughout the world for his generosity throughout his
adult life. By contrast, Hopkins was not known for his philanthropy until he grew
older. He was generous in many ways, one family member recorded, but in small
things he could be "over-careful and economical," while simultaneously being "lavish
and yet penurious" in others.[48] As his holdings approached $8 million, people flocked
to give him advice about what to do with his wealth. On one occasion, Francis T.
King, a close friend and former business partner, told Hopkins, "There are two things
which are sure to live—a university, for there will always be the youth to train; and a
hospital, for there will always be the suffering to relieve."[49]

Hopkins' meeting with Peabody would prove pivotal in determining the recipients
of his historic munificence.[50] The men had met briefly in 1856, when Peabody, on a

year's visit to the United States, founded the Peabody Institute in Baltimore for the encouragement of literature and the fine arts.[51] Ten years later, Peabody crossed the Atlantic again, this time to receive in person the boundless gratitude from Baltimoreans at the institute's dedication of the main building, designed by Edmund George Lind, on October 25, 1866.[52] The brilliant Grecian-Italianate structure had been completed in 1861, but its opening had been delayed by the Civil War. Perched atop Mount Vernon Place, the institute's headquarters were just a few blocks from where the original Hopkins campus would be housed from 1876 to 1916. For the assembled crowd, the gala opening was well worth the wait, and the 71-year-old Peabody used the occasion to convey a message of conciliation. He stated his hope that the Peabody Institute would "be a common ground, where all may meet, burying forever the differences and animosities, forgetting past separations and estrangements."[53]

During this and other visits to America, Peabody often stayed with Garrett and his family at their Baltimore home. On one occasion, Garrett expressed concern to Peabody that his friend Johns Hopkins, who was on his way to amassing a significant fortune for the time, still had not drawn up a will dictating how that money was to be divided upon his death. He asked Peabody to intervene; Peabody agreed. Garrett made plans to host the two magnates at his home for dinner in November 1866. Over the decades, this dinner has taken on an apocryphal air, defined as the singular event that shaped everything Hopkins would do with his trust. One of Garrett's progeny, James R. Garrett, maintained that Hopkins' decision to dedicate his fortune to founding a university and hospital took shape just two days after this dinner with Peabody.[54] Regardless of the exact timing of Hopkins' decision, the meeting between Peabody and Hopkins, two of the wealthiest men in 1870s America, clearly influenced what the latter determined to do with his wealth.[55] Garrett remembered that the conversation between the two men began after his family left the table at 8:00 p.m., "and the conference continued until an hour past midnight. The conversation was remarkable."[56] Garrett recorded parts of the exchange, with Peabody telling Hopkins,

> You are the only man I have met in all my experience more thoroughly anxious to make money and more determined to succeed than myself; and you have enjoyed the pleasure of success too. . . . But, Mr. Hopkins, though my progress was for a long period satisfactory and gratifying, yet, when age came upon me, and when aches and pains made me realize that I was not immortal, I felt, after taking care of my relatives, great anxiety to place the millions that I had accumulated so as to accomplish the greatest good for humanity. . . . I have gone on, and from that day realized, with increasing enjoyment, the pleasure of arranging for the greatest practicable good for those who would need my means to aid their well-being, progress, and happiness.[57]

To illustrate what was possible for Hopkins, Peabody pointed to the institute—the excitement of the recent grand opening still fresh on his mind—as an example. Peabody explained to Hopkins that when creating the institute, after careful consideration he had called on a number of friends in whom he had confidence, proposing that they act as his trustees for his "first scheme of benevolence."[58]

Whatever else Peabody said to spur his fellow multimillionaire into action, it certainly worked. Hopkins subsequently had a will drafted with provisions for his fortune in which he named boards of trustees for both a university and a hospital, and both entities were incorporated in 1867. Hopkins' closest friend and the host of the dinner, John Work Garrett, was appointed to both boards.[59] For both Peabody and Hopkins, the planning of their estates, especially the creation of boards and the selection of trustees, was consistent with that generation of philanthropists and "their rather limited faith in those who might come after them."[60]

Three years later, in recognition of his role as the world's greatest philanthropist, a statue of Peabody in the Royal Exchange in the City of London was unveiled by the Prince of Wales. A replica of the statue, presented to the city of Baltimore by Robert Garrett (John's son, who succeeded him as president of the B&O in 1884), is located in the east garden of Mount Vernon Place, directly across the street from the institute bearing Peabody's name.

## The Hopkins Gift

Hopkins' accumulated wealth, nearly $8 million at the time of his death in 1873, was substantial, but he was far from being America's wealthiest citizen. That designation belonged to Cornelius Vanderbilt (nicknamed "The Commodore"), with an estate estimated at $105 million. But with his accumulated resources, Hopkins' expressed desire to first take care of all his family and then "these two children of mine, a university and a hospital," was certainly achievable.[61] Hopkins did so, dividing more than $1 million among his nieces and nephews and directing generous sums to his servants.

Since Hopkins' grandniece Helen Hopkins Thom published her personal reminiscences of her granduncle in 1929, it has been widely accepted that Hopkins, influenced by his Quaker heritage, was a lifelong abolitionist. However, recent research of mid-nineteenth-century census records by historians has uncovered evidence that Johns Hopkins' household contained one enslaved person in 1840 and four in 1850. No enslaved people appear in the 1860 census of the Hopkins household. At this writing, extensive research is being conducted by the Hopkins Retrospective and by Hard Histories at Hopkins into existing personal files, tax and assessment records, and other official documents to develop a full context for this census data. One might expect this research to validate, enlarge, or correct the interpretation of the newfound evidence, clarifying with thorough accuracy the moral legacy of Johns Hopkins. Indeed, Hopkins' heritage may prove to be multidimensional. The narrative of this volume focuses on the impact of his philanthropy, and specifically upon the gift of a major endowment to found a research university, establish a hospital and medical school open to persons of every ethnicity and socioeconomic status, and construct an orphanage for African American children. The university's historical research will enlarge the knowledge about other aspects of his life and bequest.[62]

In addition to funding a university, a hospital, and an orphanage, Hopkins' largesse benefited a host of Baltimore-area endeavors, including the Maryland Institute,
the Manual Labor School, the Home for the Friendless, and the Baltimore Orphan
Asylum.[63] His giving focused on causes devoted to the care or education of young
people, and he was explicit in enumerating how much stock, real property, chattel, or
other means were to be directed to whom, and for what purposes.[64]

Hopkins' bequest in 1867 for the endowment of a university and a hospital—
$7 million, to be divided equally between the two entities—was the largest to date in
the country's hundred-year history. Other men of means distributed their wealth in
various ways: Cornelius Vanderbilt would bequeath $1 million in 1873 to found a
university in Nashville, and Andrew Carnegie disbursed his wealth to found medical
institutions and build public libraries throughout the country. Decades later, the Stan-
fords and the Rockefellers founded universities of their own—Stanford University
opened in 1891, and the University of Chicago received sizable gifts from Rockefeller
and Marshall Fields in 1890—but at the time of his bequest, Hopkins' gift was in a
category all by itself.

While Hopkins had no formal education, he believed his wealth was intended to
provide such opportunities for others, but the instructions he gave to his twelve trustees regarding this new university were purposely vague. The philosopher Charles
Sanders Peirce, who held a lectureship in logic at the university for five years, called
Johns Hopkins' will "happily free from all definite ideas."[65] The will was drafted by
Charles J. M. Gwinn, a future attorney general of Maryland and one of the most
notable attorneys of his generation. A Princeton honors graduate who studied law
with the Baltimore attorney John H. B. Latrobe, Gwinn became counsel to the B&O
Railroad, was an original member of both the university and hospital boards, and served
as chair of the executive committee of the university's trustees until his death in
1894.[66] Hopkins' directives contained far more details about his desire that the hand-
picked trustees "abstain from all action which may tend to subordinate the Baltimore
& Ohio Railroad Company to any political influence, or management" than about
how to establish or run the new higher education entity.[67] There was no question,
however, about what Hopkins wanted done, or not done, with the fifteen thousand
shares of B&O Railroad stock he was giving to the university: the trustees could not
sell it; instead, only cash dividends, provided they were to be paid out, were to be used
for building and operating expenses. This was the (slightly self-serving) advice Garrett
had given Hopkins as a way to remain solidly in control of the railroad.

The source of the funds for the hospital, the medical school, and even the orphanage was more complex and diversified. Details in Hopkins' will pertaining to what the
university would receive are very straightforward: the Clifton estate (approximately
350 acres) "and all the shares of the capital stock of the Baltimore & Ohio Railroad,
whereof I shall die possessed."[68] While there was an absence of specificity relative to
many university-related aspects of his will, Hopkins was very precise in one area: he
wanted to ensure a "judicious" number of scholarships for students from Maryland,

Virginia, and North Carolina, all southern states where he had made much of his wealth in the railroad.[69] Hopkins wanted the "most deserving of choice, because of their character and intellectual promise; and to educate the young men so chosen free of charge."[70]

In all other areas—capital construction, recruitment of faculty, policies and pro-cedures, degree offerings, admission requirements, establishment of tuition, fees, fellowships—the trustees had unfettered latitude. Hopkins seems to have had an un-trammeled perspective on education, adhering to no particular technique, pedagogy, discipline, or school of thought. In reflecting on the simplicity with which Hopkins approached the task of establishing his university, Daniel Coit Gilman offered this observation: "The founder made no effort to unfold a plan. He simply used one word,—UNIVERSITY,—and he left it to his successors to declare its meaning in the light of the past, in the hope of the future. There is no indication that he was inter-ested in one branch of knowledge more than in another. He had no educational 'fad.' . . . He was a large-minded man, who knew that the success of the foundation would depend upon the wisdom of those to whom its development was entrusted."[71]

The university filed articles of incorporation with the state of Maryland on August 24, 1867,[72] but because the founding of the university was based on a bequest, there were no resources yet available for planning, staffing, or operating the new entity. The trustees met only once while Johns Hopkins was alive, gathering briefly in Baltimore on June 13, 1870, to elect officers (Galloway Cheston as president and William Hop-kins as secretary) and to fill a vacancy on the board. After conducting this business, the board adjourned. It would not officially meet again for more than four years: on February 6, 1874, six weeks after Johns Hopkins' death.

No one could have predicted the educational transformation that Hopkins let loose. An oft-quoted portion of Sidney Lanier's "Ode to the Johns Hopkins Univer-sity" was read by the author at the institution's fourth Commemoration Day in 1880:

> Yet not from Jove's unwrinkled forehead sprung
> But longtime dreamed, and out of trouble wrung
> Foreseen, wise-planned, pure child of thought and pain,
> Leapt our Minerva from a mortal brain.[73]

In the absence of any specific direction from the founder, the model envisioned by the Hopkins trustees was one of the boldest educational undertakings of the nine-teenth century. Not only would these twelve individuals shape the institution to grow out of their home city but they would influence American higher education more broadly for generations to come.

### The Work Begins with a "Full Treasury, a Free Field, a Lofty Purpose"

The original trustees, all citizens of Baltimore, were a formidable group: George Wil-liam Brown and George Washington Dobbin, both judges; Galloway Cheston, a merchant; John Fonerden, a physician; John Work Garrett, president of the B&O Railroad; Charles J. M. Gwinn, attorney general of Maryland and drafter of Hopkins' will; Lewis N. Hopkins, a nephew of Johns Hopkins and tax collector for the city of Baltimore; William Hopkins, a cousin of Johns Hopkins and secretary of the board; Reverdy Johnson Jr., an attorney and son of a former US attorney general; Francis T. King, a merchant who also chaired the board of trustees for Bryn Mawr College; Thomas M. Smith, a merchant, who died a year after the university's opening; and Francis White, the board's longtime treasurer, who had married Jane E. Janney, Hopkins' niece.[74] Seven were college graduates, while three others had attended some college; four were attorneys, one was a doctor, and seven were businessmen.[75] In terms of religious affiliation, six were members of the Society of Friends, four were Episcopalian, one was a Presbyterian, and one was a Swedenborgian. James Carey Thomas, a physician and himself a member of the Society of Friends, took his seat on the board in 1870, replacing Dr. Fonerden, who had passed away the previous year.

Of the twelve university trustees, only Brown, Fonerden, and Johnson did not also serve on the hospital's board. The three "unique" hospital trustees were Richard M. Janney, married to one of Johns' younger sisters, Sarah, and proprietor of a pharmacy company called Janney & Atkinson; Joseph Merrefield, a merchant and treasurer of the hospital and its foundation; and Dr. Alan P. Smith, a surgeon who would become a member of the university's board of trustees in 1881.[76]

Much later, Gilman would describe the original trustees in more detail: "During the Civil War the majority had been, like the founder, Union men; but the temper of all was conciliatory, peace-loving, and disposed to heal the divisions which had rent society in twain. . . . I never knew ecclesiastical preferences to govern the action of a single member of the board."[77] By all accounts and against any standard, Johns Hopkins did an admirable job assembling a capable and committed group—"a capital selection," as they were called.[78]

Johns Hopkins died on Christmas Eve, 1873. The city he had loved and made his home learned of his passing the following morning in a front-page tribute in the *Baltimore Sun*: "The city owes no small share of its prosperity to his enlightened and energetic efforts. . . . In the death of Johns Hopkins, a career has been closed which affords a rare example of successful energy of individual accumulations and of practical beneficence in devoting the gains thus acquired to the public good."[79] The same day, the *Baltimore American and Commercial Advertiser* concluded that Hopkins' "extended commercial enterprises and colossal investments, to say nothing of his magnificent charities, made his name a household word and interested many thousands in his welfare who never saw his face."[80] Hopkins' position as one of the wealthiest men in America at the time of his passing was certainly a long way from where he had come into the world seventy-eight years earlier, just five years shy of the dawn of the nineteenth century.[81]

After the probation of Hopkins' will, the real work of the trustees officially began, and "they took it up with the zeal of discoverers. They had a full treasury, a free field, a lofty purpose."[82] No trustee saw a loftier purpose for this massive undertaking than did George William Brown, the founder of the Maryland Historical Society, former mayor of Baltimore, and chief judge of the Supreme Bench of Baltimore City. Even before the trustees' first "official" meeting, it was clear that Judge Brown had reflected a great deal on the chasm he witnessed between a mature Europe and the youthful United States.[83] In an 1851 speech delivered at his alma mater, Rutgers, Brown bemoaned the lack of general public support for the "highest intellectual culture and of the liberal arts." He believed that public sentiment in America could shift in this regard, "and when it does, it will move onward with a power proportioned to the grandeur of our country, the vastness of our population, and the characteristic enthusiasm of our people." Brown concluded that "there are already many evidences of such a tendency in the matter of education."[84]

Brown would continue his advocacy campaign for higher education for many years. In an 1869 address to St. John's College in Annapolis, Brown declared that "the only successful institution which has yet been established in Maryland for the cultivation of the higher branches of learning and science, as well as of art, is the 'Institute,' founded in Baltimore by the munificence of that good and illustrious man, George Peabody."[85] Brown believed that while America had the best-informed general public in the world, it lacked a high intellectual framework. Extending "the view from the masses to the more highly cultivated classes," observed Brown, "the comparison is not so favorable to ourselves." He concluded, "We then discover that there is something peculiar and unsymmetrical in our civilization; that the base is broad, but that the superstructure is not high; that we have erected a temple without a dome, a column without a capital, a spire without a pinnacle."[86]

A careful reading of this address reveals that Brown, seven years before the opening of Hopkins, had given careful consideration to the branches and methods of learning. Should Greek and Latin be partially or even entirely replaced by modern languages? he asked. Did mathematics and the physical sciences deserve more emphasis? If the curriculum were to be broadened, should electives be introduced? If so, who should be allowed to do the electing?[87] Suggesting that students had exhibited some similar characteristics over the centuries, Brown asked rhetorically, "Will not the majority of students select courses which are the easiest and the shortest?"[88]

A review of the statements, speeches, and correspondence of the board members shows that Brown had given the most thought and attention to fundamental tenets and underlying principles that would imbue the embryonic university. And if one were to name the leading trustee of the first two decades of the Johns Hopkins University, using as a criterion the instilling of lasting qualities of excellence in the institution, "the award would probably go to George William Brown."[89]

As a friend of both Peabody and Hopkins, Brown was aware of the two men's philanthropic intentions and proffered this prediction: "I cannot forbear to add that a great university hereafter to be established in Baltimore, has been planned by the wealthiest of her citizens, a native of this country, and at some future day we may confidently expect that it will be so liberally endowed out of his large fortune as to enable it to take rank among the first and most useful universities in the land."[90] Brown's perspective would prove prescient indeed.

# CHAPTER ONE

# Yale and the Life-Giving Springs of New Haven

William Charles Gilman, born in New Hampshire in 1795, descended from prominent colonial leaders, including Thomas Dudley, a onetime governor of the Massachusetts Bay Colony and founder of Harvard University. After growing up in Boston, 21-year-old William made his way to Connecticut in 1816 and found financial success in manufacturing all manner of goods, from nails to woolen and cotton products.[1] There, in Norwich, he met and married Eliza Coit, the daughter of Daniel Lathrop Coit, a wealthy retired merchant and descendant of the Reverend John Lathrop, an early religious leader in Massachusetts. William and Eliza would have nine children, six daughters and three sons. In the exact middle, born in 1831, was Daniel Coit Gilman.

Born into a well-to-do family at the apex of his father's financial prosperity, Daniel lived very comfortably in a home surrounded by expansive gardens on a hillside overlooking the Yantic River. After completing primary school, Daniel entered the Norwich Academy, described by his brother William as "a school far above the average of schools in inland towns of the day," and fell under the tutelage of schoolmaster Calvin Tracy, a young Dartmouth graduate who was "supposed to know something about everything."[2] One of Daniel's schoolmates was Timothy Dwight, who forty years beyond his days in class with Daniel recalled his experiences in a book of collected essays titled The "How I was Educated" Papers. In reminiscing about Mr. Tracy, Dwight wrote that many of his classmates would think they "did not have the best system of instruction; but somehow or other, either by reason of what he did, or because of nature's gifts and the subsequent advantages which they enjoyed, a goodly number of those boys have had an honorable place in the world." For Dwight and those of his generation, "The man whose happy lot it is to have been born in Norwich, Connecticut, and whose early years were familiar with its beautiful hills, has a recollection of the past, as he passes on in his manhood life, which is full of peace and pleasantness. And so long as the recollection abides with him, he will be thankful for it, and will be glad to think of everything which makes a part of its joyfulness."[3]

When Daniel was 14, his family moved from bucolic Norwich to New York City. William Gilman, Daniel's younger brother, remembered that Daniel initially dreaded the idea of trading the freedom of rural life for a city house with ever-present crowds and the noise of horse-drawn omnibuses rattling over the pavement. Notwithstanding his apprehension, Manhattan opened a new window to the world for the young boy, who was introduced to a diversity of thought, listening to political orators and the best preachers, whether Protestants, Jews, or Roman Catholics.[4] Interspersed with such experiences were visits to orphanages and institutes for the blind, deaf, and dumb, as well as tours of all the public buildings, museums, and government installations and the Navy Yard. Thanks to Daniel's natural curiosity and penchant for exploration, he quickly became more knowledgeable about New York City than 14-year-old boys who had lived there all their lives.[5] As a teenager, he studied with Principal John J. Owen of the Cornelius Institute, a school primarily for candidates for the Christian ministry. Unconvinced that the clergy was for him, in the summer of 1848 Gilman traveled to New Haven, where he sat for entry exams, and he was admitted that fall to Yale. Daniel's journal entry for Monday, September 14, 1848, begins with a simple line of exclamation: "Admitted to College!"[6]

## Gilman at Yale: The Early Years

Yale in the mid-nineteenth century was similar to the traditional colleges dotting the Eastern Seaboard, with a view to molding young minds to enter the ministry, train as teachers, or study law. Sons of patrician families dominated the class rolls, and Daniel would immediately fit in, associating with old Norwich Academy classmates and making new acquaintances. Fellow Calvin Tracy student Timothy Dwight entered Yale three months shy of his seventeenth birthday and preceded Gilman by one year. Andrew Dickson White, who would become Gilman's closest friend and accompany him to Europe for two years upon their graduation from Yale, spent a year at Geneva College (now Hobart and Smith Colleges), in his home state of New York, before making his way to New Haven. Of his initial experience at Yale, White recalled years later, "In January, 1851, I entered the sophomore class of Yale College—and never was man more disappointed at first." Put off by instruction for underclassmen that was "given mainly by tutors, who took up teaching for bread-winning, before going into the ministry," White despised the perfunctory nature of his early experience with "too much 'reciting' by rote." Only by his senior year did things improve, as "the influence of President [Theodore] Woolsey and Professor [Noah] Porter was strong for good. Though 'the system' fettered them somewhat, their personality broke through it."[7]

Despite President Woolsey's best intentions, his attempts to improve the Yale College education failed to get to the root of the problem: "the simple fact that the teaching was atrocious," according to one chronicler of Yale's history.[8] Furthermore, while the Yale faculty boasted many of the foremost scholars in the nation—if not the best of instructors—the institution failed to provide them with the latest in research facilities.[9] For example, to get to his lectures on science the celebrated chemist Benjamin Silliman had to use a ladder to climb out of the subterranean space that served as his laboratory.[10] For White, the American university should be "more stately, more scholarly, more free" than what existed.[11]

Daniel's first letter home to his mother, dated October 5, 1848, marked one week since the commencement of his studies and is replete with the typical observations of a first-year student: the size of the class of 1852 ("the largest class which has entered for several years. One hundred and six have already been admitted to it, and several 'stragglers' are expected") and the daily schedule ("President Woolsey conducts the morning services every day and in the evening different members of the Faculty officiate, each on an appointed night"). This particular letter was interrupted with the disclaimer, "I had hoped to have completed and forwarded this letter, my dear mother, before the last day of the week, but such a succession of matters have occupied both time and thoughts that it has hardly been possible." He picked up where he had left off and finished the missive home the next day with further details about friends and family, notably that "Uncle Kingsley is not well today."[12] Daniel was referring to the noted classicist and member of the American Academy of Arts and Sciences James Luce Kingsley, a relative on his mother's side and a distinguished Yale professor for fifty years. Daniel's family connections at Yale and beyond would prove valuable to him in successive years as he carved out his academic and professional paths.

As one might expect of a college freshman away from home for the first time, Daniel's letters to his family are prolific (if somewhat prosaic), containing the typical details of his daily routine. Occasionally, the news Daniel relayed to his family reminds the contemporary reader of the challenges of living in mid-nineteenth-century America. In the early weeks of summer 1849, Daniel wrote, "There is nothing very new of general interest to report. A few cases of cholera (seven, I think, with three deaths having occurred in the suburbs of New Haven toward West Rock). Uncle Kingsley predicts an increase both here and generally after Fourth of July in consequence both of the fatiguing excitement at that time and of the indulgence in eating and drinking."[13]

After a term of Bible study with Professor Noah Porter, who was also an ordained Congregational minister in New Milford, Connecticut (roughly forty miles from Yale), Gilman and his classmates devised a plan that was emblematic of his pronounced sense of self-awareness. He recounted to his father in June 1849 that a large number assembled for study sessions with Professor Porter, but "he was called away so frequently that the class disbanded. It has seemed almost impossible to revive this class again and a few of us have determined in place of it to teach ourselves by teaching others." What they proposed targeted a mission Sabbath school in one of the most destitute parts of New Haven, at the head of Long Wharf. Daniel and his classmates created and circulated information cards, spreading word that the school was to be held later that afternoon. Expecting at most fifteen to twenty scholars, Gilman was astonished to welcome thirty-six boys and girls to their inaugural session. With one classmate handling the music instruction and another directing the Bible lesson, the students were then dismissed with an urgent request to come again and bring other recruits to the next session. Gilman was guardedly optimistic: "We have hardly a right to expect as many children next Sabbath for many of those present yesterday were Jews and many more Catholics. But even if we have only a few regular attendants, we shall be thankful that they came. The whole region needs some Sabbath school or similar exercises for it is so bad to be called 'Five Points—Sodom Hill, etc.' "[14]

Next, Gilman and his classmates began raising money to purchase books for the students, and Gilman's father, who also had interests in the publishing business, stepped up to help. Within days of receiving his son's letter outlining their plans after their inaugural session, he shipped Sunday school papers and books for the eager students. Daniel concluded, "Thus you see we have been very much prospered at the outset in all of our plans and I do hope that the effort to do good may be successful."[15]

For whatever reason, Daniel could not be with his family for Thanksgiving in 1849, prompting the Yale sophomore to lament to his sister Lizzie, "I may as well confess that I was real homesick yesterday. It is the first time, you know, that I ever spent Thanksgiving away from home and I thought it is no very pleasant era to arrive at. I learnt one thing—that it is a matter of thanksgiving that ours is a great family."[16] The Gilman family was very close, and throughout their lives Daniel and his siblings would rely on one another a great deal, through both tragedies and triumphs. "His deep attachment to his brothers and sisters," wrote Fabian Franklin, "so manifest in the records of his boyhood, was preserved in all its intensity in his manhood and old age; and the love and devotion which pervaded his own immediate family circle formed the chief happiness of his life."[17]

In addition to his mission work, Daniel dove headlong into campus life. He was "a thorough Yale man," recording years later that his curiosity had known no bounds, as he had "never before taken so much interest in entering enthusiastically into all the college requirements."[18] His journal entries for the rest of his first term are fairly pedestrian: "My first sleep over. Was half a minute late at Morning prayers" (October 23); "Initiated at ΔK" (November 11); "Speak at Linonia for first time on the question 'Was the late "Mexican War" justifiable on the part of the U.S.?' " (November 22). His final entry of this first term at Yale is two lines: "Latin to be translated for prizes—

Daniel Coit Gilman, aged 22, senior year at Yale, wearing his Skull and Bones pin, 1852. (Photo courtesy of University Archives, Sheridan Libraries, Johns Hopkins University)

announced" and "Four students dismissed from college for being engaged in breaking the windows of dwellings houses for which they had been arrested by town magistrates and bound over to the proper court."[19]

In keeping with the traditions of Yale's oldest and most secretive society, Skull and Bones, Daniel did not record any of his experiences as a Bonesman, having been "tapped" for membership as his senior year began; Andrew White would be invited to join in 1853.[20] Gilman's association with Skull and Bones extended well beyond his 1852 initiation; his life and career would continue to intersect with those of fellow members at various times around the world. Before his initiation into Bones in 1869, William Welch wrote to his father that "nearly all the members of the faculty are members of this society and keep up their interest in it."[21] Gilman would recruit the world-renowned pathologist Welch to Johns Hopkins in 1884 as the founding dean of the medical school; later, Welch helmed the Hopkins school of public health. Returning to Yale after his European tour, Gilman was instrumental, along with Bones cofounder William Huntington Russell, in incorporating Skull and Bones as the Russell Trust Association in 1856, with Russell as president and Gilman as the first secretary.[22] At the society's convention in July 1858, Gilman presented the society with a bust of Demosthenes, copied from the one in the Vatican Museum, together with a print of an open burial vault that he had brought back from his travels in Germany.[23]

While the majority of Gilman's Yale classmates were eastern blue bloods, one notable exception was fellow 1852 Bones initiate William Preston Johnston, of Louisville, Kentucky. Johnston's father, Brevet Brigadier General Albert Sidney Johnston, was killed at the Battle of Shiloh in 1862, prompting the president of the Confederate States of America, Jefferson Davis, to remark, "When Sidney Johnston fell, it was the turning point of our fate for we had no other to take up his work in the West."[24] General Johnston's only son, William would rise to the rank of colonel in the Confederate army and serve as aide-de-camp to Davis. Both Johnston and Davis were captured in Georgia, and Johnston was kept as a prisoner for a time at Fort Delaware. Following the end of the war, and at the behest of Robert E. Lee (then president of Washington College in Lexington, Virginia), Johnston served as a professor of English on that campus before being named president of Louisiana State University in 1880. He was subsequently appointed the first president of Tulane University in 1884.[25] Another fellow Bonesman and classmate of Gilman and Johnston was Jacob Cooper, later a distinguished professor at Rutgers. In presenting a class portrait of Johnston, Cooper observed,

> It is a remarkable fact, that the founders of three great universities of our country which, like that of Berlin, started out at once as thoroughly equipped teaching powers, were here together at the same time. Two of them, Presidents Gilman and Johnston, were members of the same class; and President White [Cornell], of the next; while all three were brought into the closest companionship by becoming members of the same senior fraternity. We have no other example in our country, nor, in fact, in the world, of three great universities founded severally, and fully equipped, by the genius respectively of three men, undergraduates and companions at one time and in the same college. Nothing at Oriel College [Oxford] in the palmiest days of Whately, Keble, and Newman, can parallel this. . . . Gilman, Johnston, White created their corporations *de novo*, and inspired into them the breath of life.[26]

With his extracurricular activities demanding his time and attention, Daniel took advantage of the elective system at Yale and reported to his mother: "We are now where one of the three daily studies is chosen by the student instead of being assigned to him." The course he settled on—from offerings that included Greek, Latin, German, French, Italian, and Hebrew—was surveying, a choice, he explained in the same letter, that was "not merely for the purpose of being able to survey, but so as to understand surveys when they have been made."[27] Required core courses for his bachelor's degree persisted through Daniel's senior year, but as he noted to his parents, he could put Greek and Latin aside for the time being "except as individual pleasure keeps them up." In place of the classical languages (and in an effort to stay active and outdoors), Daniel took up twice-weekly lessons in botany. After reporting on his studies, he closed his letter by telling his mother that "presentation of the Wooden Spoon is expected to take place soon. The day uncertain."[28]

The Wooden Spoon award, founded in 1847, was presented to that student with the lowest "appointments" (or "grades," in today's vernacular) but soon evolved into an accolade of some renown and was bestowed as more of a "Mr. Popularity" prize. Even though he was extremely popular with his classmates and exhibited a broad range of interests, there was no danger of Daniel being a candidate for the Wooden Spoon. President Woolsey himself vouched for Daniel's record in a letter of recommendation a year after issuing his diploma: "Mr. Daniel Coit Gilman was graduated at this College in July 1852. During his residence here of four years, he bore the character of a young man of exemplary morals, and was a diligent student. In the list of honors made after the examination for the degree of Bachelor of Arts, he occupies a highly respectable place."[29] Daniel's list of accomplishments, affiliations, and memberships while at Yale is impressive: he was president of the Linnaean Society, one of the editors of the *Yale Literary Magazine*, a member of Delta Kappa, Alpha Delta Phi, the Beethoven Society, and the Atalanta Boat Club; and he was elected to Phi Beta Kappa.[30] If college is an experience one makes of it, Gilman had made the most of his days as an undergraduate at Yale. Nearly fifty years later, he would reflect on his days on campus and the "repeated draughts upon the life-giving springs of New Haven."[31]

## The Grand Tour of Europe

Gilman had acquitted himself well at Yale and developed a sterling reputation. Still, he remained uncertain about a definitive career path. When asked what profession his son had selected, his father responded, "Why, I don't know; he is always working rather than professing."[32] Years after his death, a *Time* magazine article summed up this phase of his life as follows: "Daniel Coit Gilman seemed to his friends a young man of great promise who was floundering lamentably in his choice of lifework. He was building better than they knew."[33] A biography of Gilman's colleague and friend William Rainey Harper (who received his bachelor's at 14 and completed his PhD at Yale at 18) was titled *Young Man in a Hurry*.[34] The same appellation could apply to Gilman. While he was not sure what route would help him arrive at his eventual career goal, the prospect of traveling throughout Europe was just what he needed to coalesce his career aspirations with his evolving educational philosophy.

Upon graduation, Gilman stayed in New Haven, taking a "gap" year to read various subjects with several professors. (A wasted year, he later called it.)[35] In 1853 he enrolled at Harvard as a graduate student, attended lectures by Louis Agassiz and Henry Wadsworth Longfellow, and lived with Arnold Henry Guyot, a Swiss American geographer and geologist. French was spoken regularly in the Guyot household, and although he stayed only a few months, Gilman improved his facility with the language, which would prove useful for his next adventure: an extensive tour of Europe with his longtime friend Andrew Dickson White.

Through family and friend connections, Gilman and White were appointed attachés to the former Connecticut governor and minister to Russia, Thomas H. Seymour. Having made arrangements to join the US Legation in St. Petersburg, the two newly minted Yale graduates arrived in England in early 1854. Seymour's post was delayed, though, so Gilman and White were required to wait in London for several weeks. White would recall years later: "I gave myself up entirely to the usual round of sightseeing, but Daniel took his duties far more seriously, his main interest being in education and especially in its development among the poorer classes."[36]

Indeed, what lay ahead for Daniel in the next two years was more than just sightseeing and friend-gathering. Gilman recognized immediately that all these experiences were preparing him for opportunities that would present themselves throughout the span of his life and career. One writer referred to this sweep of interests and diversity of experiences in Gilman's life as having had the potential to create a "dilettante." Instead, they served as his school for "educational statesmanship," the difference for Gilman being his "New England conviction of duty and the seriousness of life."[37] Daniel was anything but the typical college graduate bumping around Europe before heading home and "settling down." For one, Daniel wasn't certain what exactly he would settle into, but he did anticipate that there was something significant in his future, and he was determined to find out what it was.

In journal entries, letters home, and conversations with colleagues and mentors, Daniel displayed a marked sense of destiny and responsibility. Writing to his father from London in February 1854, Daniel confessed, "I constantly endeavor to keep in mind that I am here not for mere enjoyment as a traveler, but for investigation as a student, and in everything I see and in every acquaintance I make, I endeavor to bear in mind that there is work to be done at home, for which these pleasures must be considered as merely preparative." But showing that in one respect he was like most 23-year-olds, Daniel took the occasion to ask his father for more funds: "Still, as I say, in improving these facilities my expenses are greater than I anticipated."[38]

Daniel's initial, entirely self-directed investigations into social and educational conditions in London led him to Richard Cobden and John Bright, founders of what became known as the Manchester school. Ardent supporters of freedom of trade, commerce, contract, and competition, Cobden asked Gilman to address the National

Public School Association at Manchester about improving public schools. Cobden admonished his new friend, "And if you could throw in a word to help us to imitate the wise tolerance of your common school system it might tend to the removal of the religious or rather the sectarian difficulty which has hitherto prevented us from establishing in this country anything deserving the name of national education."[39]

Here Gilman was, not even 23 years old, being requested by one of the most prominent activists in nineteenth-century British politics to speak on important issues. As the day of the Manchester speech approached, Cobden wrote Gilman again. He referenced a recent speech by the Congregational minister and reformer Leonard Bacon (who, accompanied by his son, Leonard Woolsey Bacon, had been on a year-long speaking tour of England), which, he said, had "produced an excellent effect." In spite of Bacon's best efforts, Cobden explained, their difficulty remained "the religious question." Cobden implored Gilman: "Show the meeting how you reconcile the rights of conscience on religious matters and the demands of society for secular instruction. Give us some statistics of what you are doing in the States, and *shame* us out of our intolerance and supineness. Tell the meeting strongly—that you consider in America that all you possess that is most precious in social development and political freedom you owe solely, under providence, to your system of education."[40] Sitting among the attendees, White recorded that Gilman "was received most heartily by the entire audience and at once launched into an admirable speech. . . . He already showed, even then, that straightforward earnestness and devotion to the public interest, which became more and more during his life after so marked a feature of his activity."[41]

These early months were fruitful, but Gilman bemoaned the fact that he needed "two little things" more: "more time and more money to enable me to accomplish all I can reasonably desire!"[42] These desires would shape the entire trip and would be a common refrain throughout his European travels: how to maintain a certain standard of living while accomplishing all he wanted to do and visiting all the places he wanted to see. Gilman was described as being "reluctant to be a burden on his father," so he was perpetually struggling to devise a plan that would adequately cover the costs of his tour. "The thing to be done always came to him. The question was never what? But which?"[43]

Constantly observing, learning, and writing, Gilman recorded his thoughts in notebooks that he always had with him. In another long letter to his father from London in February 1854, Daniel recounted, "I have been here long enough to see that with the introductions I have to persons in high positions, extreme frugality is by no means the best policy, and on that policy I am acting."[44] Before crossing the Channel, Daniel still had pressing financial concerns and wondered how he would make ends meet. He expressed his aversion to resorting to a "rapid, gossiping style of letter writing for the papers (from which I greatly shrink) in order to meet my necessary expenses" and even considered cutting his tour short or "settling down in one place and doing by correspondence what I prefer to do by personal observation" in order to reduce the financial strain. Daniel's preferred plan of action was to visit as many European capitals and universities as possible. Although he assured his father that Colonel Seymour was prepared to employ him and that he would "receive due and definitive compensation," Daniel still fretted. "But that altho valuable, is not enough to warrant my proceeding. A better opening has come."[45]

## Gilman and Goodyear

That new opportunity would come not from the government or an educator but from an industrialist and inventor. Charles Goodyear, a self-educated chemist from New Haven, had through persistence and dumb luck stumbled into a revolutionary discovery fourteen years earlier. At the time, rubber products had a major flaw: they melted in the heat and cracked in the cold. An accident in a Massachusetts factory had led Goodyear to learn that heating rubber with sulfur would solve the problem. This vulcanized rubber, which could withstand extreme temperatures, would transform countless industries. Two years before Gilman arrived in England, "Goodyear's Vulcanite Court" was the talk of the 1851 Crystal Palace Exhibition in Hyde Park. It comprised walls, furniture, jewelry, musical instruments, and inflatable globes all made from rubber.[46] The installation cost thirty thousand dollars to produce, occupied more space than all the other American exhibitions combined, and was awarded the coveted Grand Council Medal. Now, in 1854, Goodyear had approached Gilman about traveling to Russia to observe all he could about the country and show "persons in high positions" what Goodyear was capable of producing.

When Goodyear first suggested that Gilman serve as the inventor's eyes and ears in Russia, the young Yale graduate, still in his twenties, had the temerity to ask for more money for his services. He explained later about his windfall to his father, informing him that "altho I had the opportunity of going under favorable circumstances to Russia, I should not do so unless sufficient inducements appeared. This led to a long conference the result of which was that he offered to pay all my expenses if I will go to St. Petersburg." The contract was for expenses for the six months as Gilman made his way to Russia, in addition to a stipend of £150. "Beyond that time," Gilman explained to his father, "I have no agreement or obligation of any kind, and during that time I am of course visiting *en route* Berlin, Vienna, and Warsaw, acquiring French and German, having so little to do that I may pursue all my educational and other inquiries, and more than that earning enough to make me comfortable next winter in Berlin, or wherever else it may be best of me to stay."[47] This was a remarkable moment for the striving though inexperienced young Gilman.[48] Moving among people far more experienced and much older than him, Gilman proved his maturity and ability time and again, developing a reputation as a very young man marked for opportunities.

Still, Gilman was concerned about how his relationship with Goodyear and the attendant activities might be viewed by others. He worried that some might think he was using his position as a member of the US Legation to further his travels and re-search. He wrote to his father from Paris in the spring of 1854,

> I rely very much upon Prof. Porter's advice, and next to yours there is hardly any which I so much desire to receive. I feel sure that you will rejoice with me that so great an advantage necessarily can be enjoyed without in the least interfering with my first and great aims, the acquisition of modern languages and the becoming familiar with the institutions educational and other of such countries as I may visit. Of course, on every account, I should prefer to have this business [the contract with Goodyear] kept entirely in the family, more especially for fear it should in any way be associated with the Legation—with which it has not the slightest connection. But a mere report that the American embassy were interesting themselves in a pri-vate thing, might be at the least annoying—however false the inference might be. All I have undertaken is in a private capacity, and if needs be I shall drop the title of attaché.[49]

Shortly after conveying the details of his new contract with Goodyear to his par-ents, Gilman left for St. Petersburg, by way of Paris and Berlin, where he reconnoi-tered with Professor Noah Porter and his old Yale classmate Jacob Cooper.[50] Gilman traveled from capital to capital in Europe, connecting with American diplomats, ti-tans of industry, and leading inventors, but he was still undecided about a career path. He wrote about his far-ranging conversation with Porter ("three days long with occa-sional interruptions") in an April 1854 letter to his sister Maria, leaning perhaps at that moment toward the clergy: "I told him that if I should become a minister I should want to preach about every day affairs—not in the style of H.W.B. [Henry Ward Beecher] if I could get above it, but in a more dignified manner—and that instead of dwelling long and regularly upon such points as original sin and the doctrine of elec-tion, I should urge the practical application of the Bible to common events and daily habits."[51] Daniel's older brother, Edward Whiting Gilman, served as pastor of the Con-gregational Church of Bangor, Maine, and it is clear from various correspondence and journal entries that Daniel strongly considered this same professional path. In the end, "Gilman disliked the abstractions of theology, preferring instead the application of Christian values to practical affairs."[52]

But Gilman also felt the strong pull of education and the charge of being at a university, surrounded by endless opportunities to learn about a whole host of sub-jects. Writing to a friend in the summer of 1854, Gilman expressed his desire to be away from the city during the summer heat but said that he wished to be in Berlin the following winter to attend some of "the hundred-fifty lectures which will then be delivered in this university." Gilman concluded with a resolution that he was prepared "to forgo the pleasure of gratifying a traveler's curiosity, so far as making a tour of Europe is concerned, but . . . it will be well to spend the time in gaining as far as possible information which will be of service to America."[53] Whatever thoughts he expressed about career paths in conversations or letters, Gilman repeatedly came back to the primary purpose of his European grand tour. The observations made in his notebooks, the experiences at various universities, the discussions with faculty and administrators about the form, function, organization, and purpose of their institutions— all these and more pointed to Gilman's future in American higher education.

Sustaining his European endeavor was not inexpensive, however. At the outset of his European tour, Daniel had expressed an aversion to making money by writing travelogues for publication. Payments from Goodyear had been delayed, and Gilman resorted to providing a chronicle of his experiences for various newspapers back home, confessing to his father, "Two things are quite certain—one is that I find newspaper letter writing very hard work, and the other is that I must make up my mind to do a good deal more of it whether I find it hard or easy. . . . But my letters when printed always read to me very dry, and I think of adopting another tone which I know will be easier to write and I hope will be easier to read."[54] He was even more direct in another letter: "My great eagerness to go home is a detestation of writing letters for print, and I do not think I can stand another winter of it. It is, as you say, worse than writing book notices, and that is too dissipating for any good mind to follow along. When I return I shall avoid it as much as possible."[55] At one point Gilman was a regular correspondent for four American newspapers, and his dispatches from London, Berlin, and St. Petersburg—some simply signed "G"—appeared in *Norton's Literary Gazette* in 1854–55.[56] Such work was extremely time-consuming, as he noted in his journal in January 1855: "Engaged all day in writing to America."[57]

For the moment, the additional income allowed Gilman to spend extended periods of time in the study of specific subjects, as he did in Germany. Gilman's interest in geography had been piqued during his undergraduate days at Yale, and he pursued the subject while in Berlin, studying with the famed Karl Ritter, considered to be one of the founders of modern geography.[58] Recording his experience of studying in Berlin during the winter of 1854–55 and hearing one of Ritter's lectures, Gilman noted that if one were to compare him to "one of our own countrymen," Ritter was similar in general appearance and manner to the elder Professor Silliman.[59] He also recorded what he had been told about Ritter by others in Berlin: "Now old and does little."[60] During his time as a student in Germany, Gilman also became very good friends with Heinrich Pertz, a historian and director of the Royal Library of Berlin.[61] This relationship would prove extremely fruitful when Gilman returned to Yale and assumed his duties as the college's librarian.

Another associate from this time period who proved particularly helpful toward the latter part of Gilman's time in Europe was Johann Gottfried Flugel, a German lexicographer who had spent years in America perfecting his English and had subsequently been appointed American consul in Leipzig in 1838. Thanks to his reputation in Europe and his fluency in English, Flugel was elected a representative and correspondent for the Smithsonian Institution in Washington and several other leading American literary and scientific institutions. The letter of introduction he provided Gilman and his traveling companion at the time, Professor Kingsley, in March 1855 included the names and titles of thirty-four professors, directors, and administrators at libraries and educational entities throughout the region: Paris, Frankfurt, Munich, Stuttgart, Bonn, Göttingen, Brussels, Heidelberg, Basel, and Zurich, to name a few. Flugel explained in the letter that "the intentions of these gentlemen are to collect general information, to examine the public libraries to make themselves acquainted with their arrangements."[62] Gilman and Kingsley would avail themselves of this introduction by visiting scores of libraries throughout Germany, with Gilman assiduously recording his observations in a book labeled "1855 Europe." One of the first entries, dated "Berlin, January 29, 1855," described a conversation with a fellow American, Thomas Chase, a Harvard-trained classicist who taught at Haverford College and would later become its third president. In 1855 Chase was studying at the University of Berlin. Gilman recorded, "Our conversation turned on journals and methods of keeping them. He [Chase] said so much in their favor, and illustrated his arguments by so many very valuable references and his own experience that I am determined to resume my records, especially as I plan to finish up Berlin sights for this visit, during the course of the next few weeks." And record he did, with subsequent entries describing meetings with the faculty and administrators whose names and contact information Flugel had provided Gilman and Kingsley.[63]

Gilman still had to attend to duties as part of the legation in Russia, and letters to his family are full of specifics relating to both his travels and his time as part of Governor Seymour's staff in St. Petersburg. As attaché, he was invited to all types of government functions, receptions, and gatherings throughout Europe. Being an official representative of the US government in European capitals gave Daniel entrée he would not otherwise have enjoyed. "I am entirely unaccustomed to so much politeness as is evinced," he wrote from St. Petersburg in the summer of 1854, "and although I am perfectly well aware that these special attentions are intended by the authorities as a compliment to the Legation, and through it to the country of which it is the representative, yet I esteem myself particularly fortunate in having the opportunity to go about so fully, in a way which other travelers, if I may judge from their books, have very seldom enjoyed."[64]

## Relationships, Observations, and Critiques

Perhaps it was the novelty of the tour or the unique chances afforded him at such a young age and the entrée he was immediately given as part of an American delegation. But what is most significant about Gilman's inaugural trip to Europe—a sort of educational grand tour, as it were—is the notes he began keeping in journals, detailing his observations of educational practices, faculty, curricula, and facilities. He would keep similarly meticulous records throughout his life, jotting down thoughts about various systems he had both observed and studied during his frequent travels. Interspersed throughout these journals and notebooks are musings on a variety of topics and observations on life experiences that sometimes resulted in a work-related product. For example, in his post as director of the Yale library, to which he was named in

1858, Gilman made use of his thorough notes taken while visiting other libraries and his own research in working with the editors of a student literary magazine to write a comprehensive history of the university's holdings and special collections.[65]

Many of his entries revolved around some aspect of education, from philosophy to pedagogy to organization. One passage (undated but undoubtedly written in later years) detailed the origins of the French "style," as he called it, noting that "the nearest approach to the French idea in the United States is the University of the State of New York, of which the Regents exercise a limited control over all universities, colleges, academies, and schools which are organized by the laws or charters of the State."[66] Gilman's notes contrast this arrangement with what he observed in the United Kingdom: "The great English universities, Oxford and Cambridge, have preserved more of the ancient forms. There are groups of colleges, associated in a University, but each having a great deal of independence in the holding of property and in the training of youth."[67]

While in Berlin during the winter of 1855, Gilman made a point of visiting institutions besides universities and libraries. On a visit to a German prison, he recorded in great detail what he witnessed: the work in which the inmates were engaged ("35 different trades pursued in whole establishment"), their worship schedule ("Sundays they meet in a plain, neat chapel where a sermon is given"), and hygiene ("all must bathe weekly"). This prison visit was followed by a tour of an institute for the deaf and dumb: "Rooms dirty, ill arranged, nothing attractive at all—remarkable however to hear the children talk in reply to simple questions; answers given in simple words very distinctly." Gilman made another entry about his experience touring an Arbeitshaus (workhouse): "My impression is that the whole institution has not the least of a reformatory or improving character, come in bad, go out bad—mentally, morally, and physically—having lived miserably meanwhile."[68] Throughout Gilman's notes were observations about inmates' access to books and educational opportunities.

Gilman also recorded his views on a smattering of topics, often on scraps of paper and pasted here and there, commenting on self-discipline, comportment, and life philosophies. One excerpt was taken from a letter written by the theologian and poet François Fénelon to Elizabeth Hamilton, Countess of Gramont. Under the heading "Rule for a Busy Life" he writes: "Above all try to save your mornings; defend them like a besieged city; make rigorous sallies upon all intruders; clear out the trenches and then, shut yourself up within your keep."[69] Throughout his entire life Gilman's morning activities reflected an immutable commitment to this counsel.

In addition to the writings and observations recorded in his notebooks, Gilman made scores of connections with European academics and with Americans engaged in similar activities. It is impossible to overstate how important these relationships were to Gilman throughout his life or how rare it was for someone in the nineteenth century to maintain and cultivate scores of friendships and connections—across continents and throughout decades—as Gilman so masterfully did. Others certainly went to Europe as a sort of rite of passage, and Gilman had ample examples to emulate, as many Yale classmates and faculty had embarked on similar expeditions. Some even stayed for extended periods—Cooper in Berlin, for example—completing graduate degrees at Germany's finest institutions.[70] But a recurring theme in Gilman's life was his reliance on relationships forged through these overseas experiences and the benefits that would redound to him and to the institutions he led from his careful cultivation of literally thousands of friends and contacts.

### Gilman, Henry Barnard, and Industrial Education

Before Gilman met Richard Cobden or Charles Goodyear or made connections with American diplomats in Russia, he started his European exploration with a powerful tool: a letter of introduction from Henry Barnard, the Connecticut superintendent of schools and principal of the Connecticut State Normal School in the 1850s. Placed alongside Horace Mann as one of the most significant educational reformers of the nineteenth century, Barnard later served briefly as president of the University of Wisconsin, then president of St. John's College in Annapolis, and finally as the first US commissioner of education. Barnard and Mann, known as "common-school crusaders," were staunch advocates of systematizing and improving public education for the primary purpose of fostering civic virtue.[71] Before Gilman's departure for Europe in December 1853, Barnard had provided him with a letter of introduction addressed to "any Officer, Teacher or Friend of Public Education," presenting Gilman as "a graduate of Yale College and a gentleman of the highest respectability" who was "particularly interested in institutions designed to improve the social condition and education of the people."[72]

When Gilman determined to go to Europe, Barnard placed him on retainer as a research assistant and supported his efforts to collect documents and gather data.[73] His instructions to Gilman were explicit: he was to procure every possible document relating to industrial education in Europe, "including particularly Schools of Agriculture, and Schools of Arts, & all Polytechnic Institutions—with as much collateral & incidental information as to the laborer as you can." Barnard also advised, "Don't fail to consult every Commissioner from every country represented in the [Paris] Exhibition, & make him give you as much oral & printed information as he can—& to send home for documents."[74] The two would even travel together when Barnard made a much-publicized visit to Europe and Gilman accompanied him through Saxony. Gilman reported to his father that the famed reformer was working very persistently to complete his educational inquiries in Germany before taking a "somewhat circuitous route to London."[75]

Among Barnard's additional instructions to Gilman was a directive to connect with William A. Gillespie and secure, in duplicate, "the Progamme" of every institution he visited during his tour.[76] Gillespie, a young professor of civil engineering from Union College, had graduated from Columbia College in 1834 and then left for Europe to study in Paris at the École des Ponts et Chaussées (the National School of Bridges and Roads). On this particular trip, from May to September 1855, Gillespie covered five thousand miles visiting technical schools and collecting instruments, models, and drawings.[77] One can assume on the basis of Gilman's twenty-two-page article "Scientific Schools in Europe: Considered in Reference to Their Prevalence, Utility, Scope and Desirability in America," published in 1856 in Barnard's *Journal of Education*, that Gillespie and Gilman collaborated on their findings and research. The article was, in many ways, the blueprint that Gilman would use for decades to come, and it helped shape his own educational philosophies and practices. In turn, his work at the Sheffield Scientific School at Yale, his tenure at the University of California, and his creation of the first bona fide research university at Johns Hopkins in 1876 were all reflections of this founding document.

## Commentary on the European Polytechnic

Gilman's article is worthy of careful examination to see the development of his thinking along the arc of his experiences and observations. Gilman begins the treatise with this statement: "Every American who studies the educational systems of Europe, remarks with surprise the universal prevalence of schools intended for instruction in theoretical and practical science." In contrast to the abundant opportunities for study at these institutions, Gilman noted the relative scarcity, in terms of both options and funding, in America at the time. The material prosperity, asserted Gilman, of many European countries was "manifestly dependent upon the extent and character of their systems of scientific education."[78]

For Gilman, France, with its expertise in manufacturing, architecture, and railroad construction and its superior armed forces, was the gold standard, holding the "foremost place among enlightened nations." France excelled in the "diffusion of elegance and taste, and in the general enjoyment of the comforts and luxuries of civilized life." In his examination, Gilman found one common denominator in all these accomplishments: "the number and variety of those institutions in which scientific investigations are encouraged or applied."[79] After such effusive praise for France, Gilman turns his attention to "the little kingdom of Saxony," owing its success and quality of life to "the fact the Polytechnic School at Dresden, the Forest School at Tharandt, and the Mining Academy at Freiberg, are all institutions of a superior order, the influence of which is not only directly exerted upon the material welfare of the country, but also indirectly, by supplying a multitude of schools of lower grades with properly trained teachers."[80]

Gilman's exposition continues with a country-by-country critique: Belgium ("the workshop of Europe," thus confirming the importance of industrial and scientific education); Russia ("Notwithstanding that the empire is deficient in the means of popular education, a system of technical instruction has been inaugurated in the capital, which is exerting a most important influence upon the development of the country"); and Prussia, Austria, and the lesser powers of Germany (which "likewise unite in testifying that the agricultural and manufacturing prosperity of those countries, other things being equal, has been in direct proportion to the efficiency of their schools of special training"). In contrast to these nations and their wise investments, Gilman describes Spain, Portugal, and Italy as places where scientific education "is still far behindhand." The subject of Gilman's harshest assessment is the land of his ancestors: "England, commercial and industrial England, may be brought up as an illustration of the bad effects of neglecting industrial education."[81]

Gilman's observations on England are further informed by an 1853 report whose title may well be the longest in the history of industrial education: "The Report of the Committee Appointed by the Council of the Society of Arts to Inquire into the Subject of Industrial Instruction with Evidence on Which the Report is Founded." The genesis of the report, it appears, was the aftermath of the Great Exhibition of the Works of Industry of All Nations, organized by Sir Henry Cole and Prince Albert, husband to Queen Victoria, and held in London in 1851. The exhibition's notable attendees included Charles Darwin, Karl Marx, Samuel Colt, and the writers Charlotte Brontë, Charles Dickens, Lewis Carroll, George Eliot, Alfred Tennyson, and William Makepeace Thackeray. The first in a series of world's fairs, all widely celebrated and heavily attended throughout the nineteenth century, the Great Exhibition was where Charles Goodyear had earned the coveted Grand Council Medal. The exhibition was a tremendous financial success, so much so that the money collected from more than six million attendees still funds scholarships today. Proceeds from the Exhibition helped found the Victoria and Albert Museum, the Science Museum, and the Natural History Museum.[82]

While many in England might have expected the Crystal Palace Exhibition to provide a grand stage for British manufacturing, technology, and industry, the reality was quite different. Members of the committee charged with evaluating the public reaction to the exhibition did not hold back: "The committee have found that discussion [sic] on the subject of education and technical instruction have been conducted in this country for many years in an unsatisfactory manner. The promoters of an improved education appealed to theory, and established their case on abstract argument alone. They had but few facts to adduce. Their opponents, on the other hand, pointed to the unrivaled supremacy in trade and manufactures, as the surest test of the soundness of their views." Then the Great Exhibition opened and "dispelled this illusion."[83] The committee averred that the exhibition had had a salutary influence, showing British manufactures "their true position. It brought the truth home, not only to the well-informed few, but to the mass of our ill-instructed population. This could have been done in no other way. No amount of oral testimony, or of written evidence, would have produced such an effect on the public mind."[84] Gilman's deduction was similar: "The practical character of the English was never better illustrated than by the manner in which this humiliating lesson of their industrial inferiority was received throughout the kingdom. There was no denial of the truth, no avoidance of the remedy. The Board of Trade was immediately authorized to organize a Department of Science and Art."[85]

Gilman concluded with a summary of the agricultural institutes he had visited, giving special attention to one just outside Stuttgart that featured a farm of nearly one thousand acres. Divided into two parts, one for practical research and the other for theoretical, the farm "is provided with the necessary buildings for the lectures and the museums, as well as for stables, workshops, beet sugar manufactories, cider presses, etc."[86] Similar arrangements would be attempted in the United States by land-grant institutions as part of their extension mission once federal legislation passed, in the form of the Morrill Land Grant Act of 1862, less than a decade after Gilman wrote his scientific treatise. He summarized his observations by reflecting on the "Fathers of New England" and their commencing "not merely the school for elementary instruction, but the grammar school, and the college, in which more elevated departments of knowledge might be thoroughly taught." He concluded, "In those branches of science which have been discovered since their day, we need to follow their example. The rudiments of science are already taught in various institutions and experimental knowledge is attained in the shop and the field. But, more than this is needed. We need higher courses of instruction, which, alone, will secure our continued advancement, or even our permanent prosperity."[87]

Having traveled thousands of miles to Europe's great capitals, observing mature universities, with their abundant libraries and ample resources, and meeting hundreds upon hundreds of experts and academics, industrialists and policymakers, the 25-year-old Gilman closed his "Scientific Schools" dissertation with a challenge for America that would prove prescient in the coming decades. He envisioned a new type of higher education institution, equipped to compete with the advances he had witnessed, "A school which, rising above those common places which are universally known, should supply an education of the most elevated order, and should stimulate original inquiries and investigations, would confer unspeakable benefits upon every portion of our country, and would not be without its influence upon the progress of humanity."[88]

## The Return to Yale: Gilman as Librarian and Advocate for Public Education

Gilman headed back to the United States having received two years of education unachievable in any other manner and well versed in European educational foundations, facilities, resources, and practices. Inspired by what he had seen and motivated to apply these lessons in whatever capacity he could find, Gilman was determined to make his mark. His first opportunity to do so would be back at Yale.

In the fall of 1855, Gilman agreed to help raise funds and devise expansion plans for Yale's Sheffield Scientific School—named for the New Haven industrialist Joseph Sheffield—on an ad hoc basis. He began by lobbying local Connecticut leaders. In an impassioned letter to the Connecticut speaker of the house, Gilman invited Representative Green Kendrick to a May 1856 meeting "as a representative of the great manufacturing valley of the state, to add a few words upon the importance of good scientific training to practical men of every department."[89] At this same time, Professor James Dwight Dana (about whom Gilman would later write a biography), arguably his generation's foremost expert on volcanic activity, asked Gilman to prepare a plan outlining the organization of a school of science.

Gilman obliged and produced a pamphlet in which he bemoaned the paucity of programs for those desiring to "fit themselves for such practical occupations as Engineering, Architecture, Agriculture, Mining and Manufacturing." Reflecting on his still fresh experiences of travel, research, and observations from overseas, he called out America for trailing "far behind European nations in many important branches of industry. Our agriculture is less productive than that of Europe; our rich stores of mineral wealth are almost unexplored; our manufactures, with the exception of staple goods, are less perfect, durable and varied, while they are also, for the most part, more costly than those of England, France, Germany and Belgium."[90]

While still advocating for the Sheffield School, Gilman was named assistant librarian of Yale College in 1856, his first full-time, paid position in higher education. "The library of a university is its very heart," Gilman would write years later in his book on launching a university. "If the heart is weak, every organ suffers; if strong, all are invigorated. Its impulses send nourishment to every nerve, sinew, and muscle. True it is that stone and wood, however ornamental, do not make a Library, nor does a heap of books, hoarded by an antiquary in some dark loft, ill-arranged, inaccessible and laden with dust. Choice materials well administered in a fitting hall, are the two essentials."[91] From his youth, Gilman was a bibliophile, and he had begun to create his own notable collection. But it was not on the level of his European traveling companion, Andrew White. Having amassed an assortment of scholarly equipment and books that few Americans could match, White "was probably one of the hundred best-educated men in the country" when he returned from Europe, according to the Cornell historian Morris Bishop.[92] While neither could know what was ahead—nor could they imagine the enormity of the roles each would play in shaping American higher education in the mid- to late nineteenth century and well into the twentieth—for the moment Gilman's work was at the library and White's was as a Yale graduate student in history.

Daniel settled into the routine of campus life in his new position at the library, but it was clear that his first European adventure had ignited a passion for travel. Afforded opportunities of which very few in nineteenth-century America ever dreamed, Daniel would venture out across the Atlantic many times throughout his adult life, just as his grandfather Daniel Lathrop Coit had done decades before. In fact, a completely unexpected prospect presented itself just over a year after his return from Russia. Gilman wrote to his father and mother in March 1857, "A gentleman of this town [New Haven], Willie will tell you who it is, wishes someone to do for him in Europe, a somewhat responsible and delicate task."[93] The task, it turned out, was to accompany a 17-year-old boy throughout Europe, which Gilman did, by setting sail from New York on Cunard's best and fastest ship, the *Persia*, on March 18, 1857. With his expenses completely covered, Gilman was also given—"as a sort of compensation for my absence"—five hundred dollars to purchase books for the Yale Library.[94] Again, as he had done during his initial tour of Europe just a few months previous, Daniel wrote home religiously, with letters postmarked from London, Rome, Vienna, and Florence.[95] The volumes Gilman acquired in Europe were brought back to New Haven and added to the burgeoning Yale collection.

Upon the resignation of Edward G. Herrick in 1858, Gilman was named Yale librarian; in addition, he taught geography at Sheffield. Events were certainly impacting the national landscape, and Gilman, like so many others caught up in the outbreak of the Civil War, was spurred by patriotic feeling. Although these sentiments found little expression in his letters or diaries, the *Zeitgeist* influenced many at Yale.[96] In May 1861, just weeks after the shelling of Fort Sumter in Charleston Harbor, Gilman helped muster Norton's Cadets, named for Professor William A. Norton, an 1831 graduate of the United States Military Academy at West Point and one of the founding faculty members of the Sheffield Scientific School. Gilman was responsible for keeping records of the group during their initial formation at "Camp Sheffield." A list of all cadets participating followed this pronouncement: "The undersigned hereby agree to form themselves into a Company for military drill." The commanding officer was Captain W. A. Norton, and Gilman served as "Orderly & Recruiting Sergeant."[97]

Striving to maintain a semblance of normalcy in both his professional and his personal life, and amid the turmoil that the war would unleash on millions of Americans, Gilman married Mary Van Winkle Ketcham, daughter of Frederick Treadwell Ketcham, a New York City merchant, in December 1861. Mary was a close friend of Gilman's two younger sisters Emily and Louisa. The newlyweds settled into the New Haven home of Gilman's cousin Henry Coit Kingsley, and they welcomed their first child, Alice, in 1863. A second daughter, Elisabeth Coit, would be born in New Haven in 1867.

As for his work at the Yale library, Gilman was unrelenting in his efforts to improve the facility and expand the university's collection. Relying on his notes from his visits to European libraries and the research he had done during his two-year grand tour, Gilman produced various appeals to the administration and the Yale Corporation for additional funding for the library. Gilman collaborated with the editors of a student literary magazine to write a detailed history of the university's holdings and special collections. Unfortunately, their collective advocacy for additional resources to expand the number of volumes and extend services fell on deaf ears.[98] Disputes over the lack of a salary increase in 1864 (when all other faculty had received one), coupled with President Woolsey's refusal to appropriate more funds for acquisitions or to invest in the library's infrastructure, led to Gilman's resignation on June 1, 1865. Acknowledging both Gilman's disappointment and his ambition, Woolsey showed little sympathy, stating that the library "does not possess that importance which a man of active mind would naturally seek; and the college cannot, now or hereafter, while its circumstances remain as they are, give it greater prominence. With the facilities which you possess of making your way in the world, you can in all probability secure for yourself, while yet young and enterprising, a more lucrative, a more prominent and a more varied, as well as stirring employment."[99] In his journal, Gilman recorded on July 27: "Commencement Day—terminated my nine years service as Librarian of Yale College."[100]

Gilman, aged 39, with sister Louisa (*left*); first wife, Mary Ketcham (*right*); and elder daughter, Alice, 1869. (Photo courtesy of University Archives, Sheridan Libraries, Johns Hopkins University)

Four days later, Professor Thomas Thacher, a Yale classicist and member of the Connecticut State Board of Education, informed Gilman that he had been nominated secretary of the board. According to Thacher, "There had never been such an opportunity as now presented itself to influence the state," and he believed it was "providential" that Gilman had persisted in his library resignation.[101] This was not entirely unknown territory for Gilman, as he had served as acting school visitor of the New Haven Public Schools. But in this new capacity, Gilman would represent the state's board of education as he traveled throughout Connecticut making a careful examination of the school system. He came to the conclusion, after inspecting the normal schools of Massachusetts, that the Connecticut State Normal School (constructed in 1850 in New Britain) needed a complete reorganization. Just as he approached every opportunity, Gilman completely immersed himself in his new assignment, writing to his brother William in December 1865 that "my new business proves to be very engrossing. I am afraid I am not strong enough to bear it."[102]

By the spring of 1866 Gilman had completed his first annual report to the state board of education during his brief tenure, which was then presented to the state legislature. Among the board's recommendations were to increase the number of good teachers; build up and reform the State Normal School; address the need for more high schools in the state; implement a standard of uniformity for textbooks and registers; and see that "a copy of the last revised edition of Webster's Quarto Dictionary [was] placed as a book of reference in every school district."[103] Having made his mark in Connecticut public education, Gilman would now be afforded the opportunity to develop a more formal relationship with another Yale entity with which he was very familiar.

## Secretary of the Sheffield Scientific School

Gilman had been associated with Sheffield in one form or another since his return to Yale in 1855. He had been appointed professor of physical geography in 1863 (serving in that post even during his work with the public schools), making him the first faculty member in America to hold a teaching position devoted solely to geography and not linked directly with any other subject.[104] Gilman had a broader view of the subject, however, and in his teaching at Yale (and later in his teaching of political economy and physical geography as president of the University of California) he embraced not only geography but economics and history as well.[105] Gilman also served for a time as general secretary of the American Geographical Society, delivering major addresses to that organization as well as a series of twelve lectures at Princeton titled "On the structure of the earth with some reference to human history."[106]

In addition to his faculty appointment, Gilman was elected secretary of the Sheffield governing board in 1866. Founded in 1847 as the Yale Scientific School, the school had struggled financially for years, due to policies at Yale that resulted in "practical" students at the Scientific School (those who wanted to study primarily chemistry, mineralogy, and geology) being separated from those pursuing more traditional disciplines at Yale College and produced substantial inequities in funding.[107] A New Haven railroad magnate and philanthropist, Joseph Earl Sheffield, helped lessen the financial gap when he established a permanent fund for the school in 1858, but the disparity in support and emphasis persisted. The librarian of Sheffield for thirty-three years, the historian Thomas Lounsbury, described the perennial struggle for school funding:

"The college [Yale] had no money to give, but even if it had it is more than doubtful if it would have given it. No one at that time, however enthusiastic, ever dreamed of the supreme importance which the natural sciences were soon to assume in every well-devised system of education. The impression prevailed that chemistry, like virtue, must be its own reward."[108]

The philosophical debates during this time period surrounding the primary purposes and desired courses of study at colleges and universities were not unique to New Haven. During his time in Europe, Gilman had witnessed firsthand the German conflict between the Gymnasium and the new Oberrealschule;[109] and in the United States, the classical curriculum, long the hallmark of the well-established eastern colleges, was being augmented with science and engineering instruction at some institutions (the Lawrence Scientific School at Harvard and the newly established Massachusetts Institute of Technology, for example).[110] As one might imagine, these efforts were often met with stiff resistance from the traditional establishment.[111]

The first technical school in America was founded in 1824 thanks to the largesse of Stephen Van Rensselaer. A Harvard graduate and former lieutenant governor of New York, Rensselaer funded the School of Theoretical and Practical Science to train teachers who would then "instruct the sons and daughters of local farmers and mechanics in the art of applying science to husbandry, manufactures, and domestic economy."[112] At the first meeting of its board of trustees, on December 29, 1824, the new entity was formally established as the Rensselaer School.[113] The early success of Rensselaer helped popularize the idea of scientific education in the United States.[114]

For those wishing to study engineering, there were some southern antebellum institutions that added instruction in the subject as part of a bachelor of arts degree. At the University of Virginia, Charles Bonnycastle, a professor of natural philosophy and mathematics, offered his first full class in civil engineering in 1833, but he had included engineering topics in his science and mathematics courses as early as the late 1820s. Professor John Millington, author of *Elements of Civil Engineering* (1839), was hired by the College of William and Mary in 1835 to initiate a class in civil engineering as a branch of collegiate instruction.[115] Some northern institutions followed suit. For example, Columbia University offered engineering courses as part of a senior-year option embedded in its regular liberal arts curriculum. New York University, in 1836, required all students to complete a series of eighty lectures in architecture and civil engineering, and both Rutgers and the University of Rochester would take a similar approach, offering courses in engineering and civil engineering, respectively.[116] Dartmouth founded the Chandler Scientific School, and Brown University organized a department of practical science, both in 1852. Three years later, a department of mines, arts, and manufactures was established at the University of Pennsylvania.[117]

In spite of all the inherent challenges and the ongoing national debates, coupled with a persistent struggle for funds, Gilman found his work at Sheffield to be enormously rewarding and his colleagues wholly committed to the task of making the school something remarkable. They went so far as to petition the Yale Corporation to reduce their salaries so that courses could be maintained at a level required by the students. Yale's president, Theodore Dwight Woolsey, in reviewing the work of the school would write, "From the first the professors have struggled against probabilities; they have worked by faith, they have aimed to have a school, sink or swim, worthy of the science of this country."[118]

## Connecticut's Land-Grant College

The cumulative, years-long efforts of Gilman and others would soon pay enormous dividends for the Sheffield School. The Morrill Act, which proposed the designation of federal land for colleges specializing in agricultural education, was passed for the first time in 1859. This would mark Justin Morrill's first major effort in the House of Representatives since his election as a Whig in 1854.[119] When first proposed, the bill met stiff resistance, with opponents insisting that the proposal would exhaust public lands and that future settlement of the country would be dramatically curtailed. Morrill's detractors offered withering criticisms: Senator James Murray Mason of Virginia declared the bill "one of the most extraordinary engines of mischief"; Senator Clement Claiborne Clay of Alabama called Morrill's bill "the most monstrous, iniquitous and dangerous measure which had ever been submitted to congress" and "a delusive attempt to do an impracticable if not an impossible thing"; and Henry Mower Rice of Minnesota declared that "the success of this measure would mean a lingering death" for his home state.[120]

As the news of Morrill's proposed legislation spread, Gilman took advantage of the propitious moment by writing a letter to Morrill less than a month before he would introduce the bill formally in the House of Representatives. Gilman informed Morrill that "a few gentlemen of influence in this community have united in the petition which I enclose herewith." Gilman noted that these men had acted of their own accord in drafting their appeal and that "no effort has been made to obtain other signatures although many could be readily obtained here and in other parts of the State, if it should be deemed desirable for the furtherance of the plan."[121] When he brought the bill before the House on April 20, 1858, Morrill attempted to structure his case on the disparity between American and European practices while appealing to his colleagues' sense of philanthropy and their self-interest:

> Many of our wisest statesmen have denounced our general land system as a prolific source of corruption; but what corruption can flow from endowing our agricultural colleges? Here is neither profligacy nor waste, but a measure of justice and benefi-cence. . . . The persuasive arguments of precedence; the example of our worthiest rivals in Europe; the rejuvenation of worn-out lands, which bring forth taxes only; the petitions of farmers everywhere, yearning for a "more excellent way"; philan-thropy, supported by our own highest interests—all these considerations impel us for once to do something for agriculture worthy of its national importance.
>
> By the recent statement of the Land Office, we have 1,088,792,498 acres of land

to dispose of; and when this bill shall have passed, there will then remain about one thousand and eighty-three millions of acres. We shall still be the largest landholder in the world, while confessedly we are not the best farmers. Let it never be said we are "the greatest and the meanest of mankind."[122]

The bill passed both chambers in 1859 but was subsequently vetoed by President James Buchanan, who sided with members of his Democratic Party from the South, contending that education was a state issue, not a federal one. Buchanan's veto message argued "that the measure was unconstitutional, unfair to the western states, and injurious to colleges not receiving federal aid."[123]

The federal government was already giving land to states to encourage the development of railroads (for example, through the Land Grant Act of 1850).[124] Thus, Morrill's proposal to convey federal land—or rights to such land—to the states for the purpose of promoting education, while inventive, was not wholly unimaginable. As John Thelin explains, the grants conveyed to the states "were not literal gifts of land on which a state government would build a college"; rather, "the act established a complex partnership in which the federal government provided incentives for each state to sell distant Western lands, with the states being obliged to use the proceeds to fund advanced instructional programs."[125] Each state received thirty thousand acres per representative and senator; for those states where land was unavailable, scrip was provided to acquire lands elsewhere.[126]

Analysts have noted that Morrill's expertise in Congress was more related to land policy than it was to education, and his views about higher education and its purpose and function would certainly evolve over time. In 1848 he made clear his preference for "practical" education in a response to a notice that he had been elected to the board of Norwich University in Northfield, Vermont: we might as well "lop off a portion of the studies established centuries ago as the mark of European scholarship and replace the vacancy—if it is a vacancy—by those of a less antique and more practical value."[127] Similarly, President Francis Wayland of Brown University observed in 1850 that the United States had 120 colleges, 47 law schools, 42 theological seminaries, and yet not a single institution "designed to furnish the agriculturalist, the manufacturer, the mechanic, or the merchant with the education that will prepare him for the profession to which his life is to be devoted."[128] For Morrill, elevating practical, especially agricultural, education to the level of liberal, collegiate studies was the desired outcome. However, he wisely did not trouble himself with the specifics as to how this was to be accomplished.[129]

The autodidactic Morrill, who had never attended college himself, presented the bill once again in 1862. The political landscape had shifted dramatically with the onset of the Civil War and the absence of members of Congress from the southern states; as a result, the bill passed overwhelmingly. President Abraham Lincoln signed the Morrill Land Grant Act of 1862 on July 2, just weeks before the Battle of Antietam, the single bloodiest day in American history. Over the next twelve months, Gilman and his friend in Ithaca, New York, Andrew White, would both win significant victories for their respective institutions in obtaining these highly coveted federal grants—Gilman for Yale's Sheffield Scientific School and White for Cornell. (After teaching at the University of Michigan, White had moved to New York, served in the state senate, and become president of Cornell in 1866.) Both men would be known for decades and lauded by their respective universities for their adroit and visionary action. Of Congressman Morrill's advocacy of the bill that would bear his name and transform the nation, President White made this observation in 1899: "It is, in my opinion, a service which deserves to be ranked, and which future historians will rank, with those of Hamilton in advocating the Constitution, of Jefferson in acquiring Louisiana, and of Clay in giving us a truly American policy."[130] Scholars have noted that the "received view" of many historians on the collateral impact of the Morrill Act is that by utilizing the only readily resource at its disposal—land—the federal government continued its efforts to democratize higher education "by supporting the shift away from traditional liberal arts education for the elite toward a more practical, useful higher education for the majority of citizens."[131]

Connecticut was the third state to accept the provisions of the Land Grant Act of 1862, and Yale was the first "agricultural and mechanical college" to actually operate under the terms of the act.[132] One of the provisions explicitly stated that no portion of the grant was to be used for the "erection, preservation or repair of any building or buildings," so Connecticut had to either provide land or buildings to draw down the federal funds or make an arrangement with an existing institution. As the state had no intention of founding a new university, Yale was chosen as the designee land-grant institution. President Woolsey was then authorized by the Yale Corporation to execute a contract with the state, and the Sheffield School began immediately to adjust itself to its new status as the land-grant college of Connecticut. This included opening a three-year course in agriculture with an emphasis on French and German. A Sheffield report of 1865 concluded that "the educated farmer should read them with ease."[133]

Tensions between the camps supporting the classical and scientific curricula, respectively, were deepening in America in the first half of the nineteenth century. These tensions would come into even sharper focus when the Morrill Act began granting public lands to states for the founding of colleges teaching agriculture and scientific subjects. The states received broad latitude regarding exactly how the provisions of the act were to be fulfilled. Before the A&M (agricultural and mechanical) land-grant campus came to be associated with the great public universities of the Midwest and the West, private institutions were the recipients of land-grant funds to establish state agricultural programs.[134] A partial list of Morrill Act grantees included Dartmouth in New Hampshire, Transylvania in Kentucky, MIT in Massachusetts, and Columbia's School of Mines and Cornell in New York. But once the possibility of federal funding presented itself, lobbying efforts ratcheted up considerably. Years after the Morrill Act's passage Gilman would note, "There were busy and devoted men in New York, Pennsylvania and Illinois who spared no effort within their power to secure a national appropriation."[135]

## Scientific and Agricultural Education

Gilman's reputation for ardent advocacy of scientific schools generally, and the Morrill Act particularly, was further solidified by the publication in October 1867 of a widely circulated article titled "Our National Schools of Science," first printed in the *North American Review* and reprinted as a pamphlet. Gilman quoted Representative Morrill in summarizing the eponymous legislation:

> The bill proposes to establish at least one college in every State upon a sure and perpetual foundation, accessible to all, but especially to the sons of toil, where all the needful science for the practical avocations of life shall be taught, where neither the higher graces of classical studies, nor that military drill our country now so greatly appreciates, will be entirely ignored, and where agriculture, the foundation of all present and future prosperity, may look for troops of earnest friends, studying its familiar and recondite economies, and at last elevating it to that higher level where it may fearlessly invoke comparison with the most advanced standards of the world. The bill fixes the leading objects, but properly, as I think, leaves to the States considerable latitude in carrying out the practical details.[136]

Yale's history as a classical college focused on the more traditional curriculum led to early and frequent criticism of its designation as the recipient of land-grant funds. These critiques would persist for years, with agriculturalists none too happy with the school's traditional entrance exams, its emphasis on science and languages in the core course, and the fact that Yale had no farm, forcing students and instructors to travel well beyond New Haven for excursions.[137] Many within the Constitution State coveted the land-grant designation. When the US Congress passed the Hatch Act in 1887—recognizing the need for research in developing improved agriculture—the Connecticut State Grange lobbied to split federal funding between the Connecticut Agricultural Experiment Station at Yale (affiliated with the Sheffield Scientific School since 1877) and the newly created Storrs Agricultural Experiment Station. With the passage of the second Morrill Act in 1890, the battle between New Haven and Storrs over federal funding intensified, leading to the establishment of the Storrs Agricultural College (now the University of Connecticut) in 1893. Yale took its case to court to retain the original Morrill grants, as secured by Gilman three decades earlier, but a three-person commission designated Storrs as "the sole beneficiary" of the Morrill Acts and the state's uncontested land-grant institution.[138] Yale received a one-time payment of $154,604.

Sheffield would continue to function without the benefit of federal funds, but its curriculum gradually became completely integrated with that of Yale College after World War I. It ceased to function as a separate entity in 1956. But its 109-year history is emblematic of age-old debates in nineteenth- and early twentieth-century American higher education: first, about the relationship of scientific, mechanical, and agricultural instruction to more traditional disciplines; second, about how Morrill Land Grant monies had originally been appropriated and, in some cases in successive decades, redirected to other institutions.

For his general role as advocate for national schools of science and his specific duties at Sheffield, Gilman developed a national reputation as an expert on the subject. In the summer of 1871 he was appointed by the US commissioner of education, General John Eaton, to visit the various institutions that had been established, "urging that they not allow themselves to become mere trade schools and putting in a good word for Latin."[139] Gilman personally inspected nine of the national schools of science east of the Rocky Mountains, conducted interviews with the principal officers of eight more, and corresponded with faculty and administrators at many other institutions. During this work for the Department of Education, Gilman also represented the Sheffield School and spoke about agricultural education at national conferences in Chicago and Washington, DC.[140]

The impact of the Sheffield School on scientific and agricultural education is impossible to calculate, and it would be looked to for decades as a paragon by schools across the country that were attempting their own curriculum changes. Gilman acknowledged as much in a fiftieth-anniversary celebratory address in New Haven in October 1897, in which he detailed some of the principal actors in the Sheffield School's success, beginning with Professor John Pritkin Norton. An agricultural chemist and student of Benjamin Silliman Sr., Norton had joined forces with Silliman's son, Benjamin Jr., to found the Department of Philosophy and the Arts at Yale. Their department would become the Sheffield Scientific School and ultimately the Graduate School of Arts and Sciences. One of Norton's pupils during his all-too-brief teaching career at Yale (Norton would die at age 30 of tuberculosis) was Samuel William Johnson, considered one of the staunchest proponents of the agricultural experiment station, a building block of today's land-grant universities in America. Norton's successor at Yale was John Addison Porter, who in 1855 married Josephine Sheffield, the daughter of the namesake of the school where Porter would teach for twelve years. An 1842 graduate of Yale College, Porter left for Germany to become a student of the renowned chemist and intellectual forefather of agricultural science, Professor Justus von Liebig, at the University of Giessen.[141] American students who like Porter and Johnson availed themselves of time and experiences in Germany became part of an international fraternity of scientists and researchers with an unyielding commitment to the scholarly values of academic professionalism.[142]

When Porter returned to Yale in 1852, colleges of agriculture or the mechanic arts were unheard of; he set about to change this and invited twenty-six leading agriculturists to New Haven for a conference. The year was 1860. Thirty-seven years later Gilman would observe, "It would not be difficult to show that this unique, primeval example of university extension had a powerful influence in promoting, on right principles, the study of agriculture. It was estimated that five hundred persons from a distance came here to follow more or less these lectures and discussions." The Morrill Act would come two years later, "due in no small degree," asserted Gilman, "to the influences here put forth." Gilman concluded: "From this congressional bounty, Cornell, Madison, Minneapolis, Berkeley and other universities of the Western States derive a considerable part of their revenues."[143]

Gilman's leadership at Sheffield, his relationship with Senator Morrill, and his success in securing federal funds for his institution, together with other advocacy activities in support of education, led to ever-increasing name recognition for him, as well as enhanced attractiveness as a leader in the Northeast and beyond. He had become so well known that the University of Wisconsin attempted to recruit him from Yale in 1867 to be the president in Madison. In turning down the job, Gilman wrote to the Wisconsin board chair, "I cannot deny that a position of so much influence and responsibility in the University of a prosperous and growing state, situated in a town so inviting as a residence, and endowed with the National Grant [Morrill Land Grant monies] for instruction in natural science, looks very attractive. . . . At the same time, I beg you to rest assured that I appreciate the honor of being favorably thought of in such a connection."[144]

At the conclusion of the Wisconsin lobbying efforts, Gilman would write to his friend, Professor Jacob Cooper, that at least for the moment he intended to "abandon all thought of going to the West, my work here being satisfactory, at least to myself."[145] While he may have thought this and written as much to Cooper, Gilman's record of results was gaining more attention than he might have suspected. Before long, he would be the target of other recruiting efforts from even farther west.

# CHAPTER TWO

# The House of Our Expectations in California

Daniel Coit Gilman traveled throughout Europe in his twenties, but as he approached his fortieth birthday in 1870 he had never been west of the Mississippi River. In many respects, getting a steamer from New York across the Atlantic to London was easier for Gilman than making his way from Connecticut to California. But the transcontinental railroad was transforming the United States and shrinking the nation.

News of Gilman's success in securing Morrill Act monies for Yale traveled fast. That accomplishment, along with his increasing national stature, brought Gilman to the attention of those in California. Soon he would be sought out by fellow Easterners, mostly Yale graduates, who were trying to create their own higher education entity in the Bay Area. Called the "New Haven of the Pacific," Oakland had attracted a whole cast of Connecticut clergy and academics to minister to itinerant workers flooding into mining camps and boom towns. This group opened the Contra Costa Academy in Oakland in 1853. Two years later, it was incorporated as the College of California, and it remained a preparatory school until 1860, when it began offering its first college-level courses.

Early supporters of these educational efforts included the Reverend Samuel Hopkins Willey, a Dartmouth graduate. He was joined by the famed Hartford theologian and Yale graduate Reverend Horace Bushnell, who had left the Connecticut church where he had been pastor for twenty-three years and traveled to California in hopes of improving his health.[1] Willey and those who sent him believed that education would be essential to bringing order to the chaos of the violent and materialistic frontier.[2] In effect, they were there to bring "Protestant godliness to the particularly ungodly social environment of Gold Rush California."[3] Assisting Willey and Bushnell were two individuals with direct connections to Yale and Gilman: Sherman Day (Yale class of 1826), the son of Yale's ninth president, Jeremiah Day,[4] and the Reverend Henry Durant (class of 1827), who would later become the first president of the University of California. Indeed, these men—New School Presbyterians and Congregationalists—aspired to establish the "Yale of the West."[5] Gilman was unrestrained in his praise of Bushnell, calling him a "precious heirloom handed down from the Yale of the last century to the Yale of the present. . . . I should place him, in genius, next to Jonathan Edwards."[6]

Some maintain that the emissaries sent to California to establish a private college hoped that a public university would be deemed necessary once their private enterprise had established itself. This may be true; however, in the long run, the College of California and its fortunes were seriously impacted by the failure of denominational interests to support the institution.[7] Nevertheless, Reverend Durant alighted in California in 1853 with one thing on his mind: "I came with college on the brain."[8] And the "college" Durant and his colleagues had in mind was certainly the traditional, New England–style model with which they were familiar. Their efforts would bring into focus the perpetual clash between those advocating for classical curricula and the proponents of a more technical education.

With the passage of the Morrill Land Grant Act, California's land scrip share was 150,000 acres. That California would accept this federal windfall was unquestioned; the problem, however, was settling on its best use. The ensuing debate in one of America's most recently admitted states would mirror similar discussions across the nation as policymakers and educators grappled with the evolving nature of higher education and which institutions should receive this unprecedented largesse. The Morrill Act's stipulation for a college to be established to receive the lands, however, came with a hard deadline: the educational entity had to be instituted by July 1866.[9] The clock was running.

In March 1866 the California legislature, in order "to carry out in good faith the provisions of an Act of Congress,"[10] created what they hoped would suffice: the Agricultural, Mining and Mechanical Arts College. The bill outlined, in thirty sections, exactly how the new state college was to be established, governed, and funded and what subjects it would endeavor to teach. Section 13 elaborated, "The course of instruction shall embrace the English language and literature, mathematics, civil, military, and mining engineering, agricultural chemistry, mineralogy, metallurgy, animal and vegetable anatomy and physiology, the veterinary art, etymology, geology, technology, political, rural, and household economy, horticulture, moral and natural philosophy, history, bookkeeping, and especially the application of science and the mechanical arts to practical agriculture in the field of mining."[11] The final paragraph, section 30, stated explicitly with whom the new institution was *not* to be associated: "The college shall not in any manner whatever be connected with or controlled by any sectarian denominations."[12]

It was then announced that proposals would be considered "for donations of land, money, or buildings from counties, cities, or individuals, to be given to said college in consideration of its being located by the Directors at any place designated by the donors." The last line in section 27, however, appeared to foreclose any private institution from availing itself of federal monies, as the new state college was "not be united to or connected with any other institution of learning in this State."[13] It appeared that California finally had its institution of public higher education, if only on paper. But for the moment, the College of California, despite its persistent growth and development, was not part of the long-term solution.

Durant and his colleagues remained undeterred and looked to other examples of what might be possible in California. Some states had accepted the Morrill Act grant and conveyed it to their most prominent existing institutions (Cornell in New York, Yale in Connecticut), even though some of them were private colleges and universities. Sensing that a similar opportunity might be possible for their own institution, the College of California leapt into action and created a "Mining and Agricultural College" in San Francisco, also referred to as the "Department of Science and the Arts of the College of California." With this new entity now established within the college, they told the state they would happily accept the Morrill endowment as other private institutions in the East had done.[14]

The college's board of trustees notified the legislature of their willingness to hold California's land grant in trust for their emerging enterprise, stating their intention "to promote the liberal and practical education of the industrial classes in the several pursuits and professions of life, especially as miners, agriculturalists, engineers and mechanics, and further, to promote the development of the material resources of the State and the adjoining states."[15] Since many at the College of California were familiar with Yale, the board cited precedent for the legality of such action by referencing the Connecticut legislature's assignment of Morrill Act funds to the Sheffield Scientific School in New Haven. Assisting with the College of California's educational endeavor was yet another Yale graduate, William Phipps Blake (class of 1852), a geologist who had studied under Professor Benjamin Silliman Sr. It would follow, naturally, that a distinguished faculty member from Yale should be invited to California to formally address the college and its graduates. What no one anticipated, however, was the broadside about to be delivered by another member of the Silliman family.

## A Withering Critique

With an official name, a proposed campus, and its accompanying town site in Berkeley atop one of the most coveted parcels of real estate in the state, together with motivated trustees convinced that they were doing God's work amid the rough and tumble of the California frontier, the college invited the esteemed Yale scientist Benjamin

Silliman Jr. to deliver the 1867 commencement address. Silliman, like his father, was a chemist and showed a particularly keen interest in geology. Benjamin Sr. had founded and financed the *American Journal of Science and Arts* in 1818 and was widely acknowledged as the first person to distill petroleum in America.[16] The junior Silliman had become well known in his own right, developing the process that enabled the economical production of kerosene. His traveling across North America lent a certain gravitas to the occasion. This particular commencement, marking the institution's sixth anniversary, was attended by the chair of the board for the state's new Agricultural, Mining and Mechanical Arts College, Governor Frederick Low.

Silliman's address, structured around an unflinching critique of the legislature's lack of a concerted plan for an appropriately developed and adequately funded state university from the year previous, was titled "The Truly Practical Man, Necessarily an Educated Man." Silliman wasted no time in getting to his point: "We live in a practical, matter-of-fact age. The universal cry is for practical men," he declared. "It demands leaders and laborers whose intellectual habits have been moulded in the schools of experience; and the tendency is everywhere seen to subordinate, almost to ignore, those studies and pursuits which do not, to the popular understanding, appear to keep step with what is called the march of improvement."[17] Silliman argued that the self-conceit of the "so-called practical man" cannot be excused as he "conceals his ignorance beneath his empiricism, neither can we pardon the college which has turned out its graduates in arts so artless that his learning fails him when brought face to face with nature and experience."[18]

Silliman suggested that the antidote to such ignorance was "familiarity with Burke and Webster, with Milton, Goethe, and Shakespeare" as he made a full-throated defense of what might be termed the classical curriculum. He had high praise for Superintendent John Swett, the author of *Methods of Instruction and Public Education in California* and widely considered to be the father of California's public school system. Silliman's commendation was effusive: "The People of California in their 'Act to provide for a system of Common Schools' have laid the foundation and set up the framework of the best system of general common school education for the whole people which exists in any State or country where the English language is spoken."[19]

Silliman was not alone in his plaudits toward Swett. Gilman's friend and sponsor Henry Barnard stated in an 1866 article published in his *American Journal of Education*, "His administration of the system of public schools has been marked with vigor and progress, and the Revised School Law prepared by him is a model of codification for this department of public legislation."[20] So revered was Swett that New England newspapers reporting on the National Education Association annual meeting in 1872—held in Boston and attended by Swett, who gave a principal address—referred to the California superintendent as the "Horace Mann of the Pacific Coast."[21]

Silliman balanced his praise of the school system put in place by Swett with a scathing rebuke of the lack of foresight shown by the legislature in its treatment of higher education: "The question of greatest practical importance in the educational affairs of California is, How shall a high collegiate or university system be developed here, and in what respects must it be modified to meet the wants of the situation and time?" With another rhetorical question, Silliman asked: "But what has California done for that higher education which every community must provide for her sons if it would have men properly trained for the learned professions, for statesmen, for arts and sciences?"[22] Silliman had done his homework relative to the prescribed curriculum for the new state institution, and he believed the "courses were deficient, even for an agricultural and mechanical arts school."[23] Citing the state constitution and its provisions for the establishment of one or more universities, Silliman noted that proceeds from the sale of lands had gone exclusively to common schools, when "no University Fund, or lands specially devoted to the uses of a University, exist."[24] Further, Silliman maintained that the agricultural college bill appeared to have been drawn up hastily and failed to cover all the ground implied in its title.[25] Coming from confined spaces in the Northeast with fewer natural resources than were to be found in California, Silliman concluded his remarks with an assessment of America generally that was clearly directed at California in particular: "The ear of the public has been so stuffed with compliments to American enterprise, American self-reliance, and American practical talent, that the public has not yet discovered how incomplete and fragmentary is the practical side of our character. We are swift in all things, but thorough in very few. We are practical, it is true, up to the demands of our most pressing necessities, but beyond that point chaos begins."[26]

Whether Silliman was divining the future or merely expressing a hope for what might be possible should California make the appropriate investment in higher education, he chose to put his listeners on notice:

> Let it once be made clear to the minds of your legislators and men of wealth that there remains for them a great duty to perform, involving the welfare and happiness of the rising generation and of future ages, and the means will not be wanting to make the endowments essential to establish on a firm and sufficient basis either the College of California or a State University. The same wisdom which has framed a law so catholic and ample as the Common Schools system, will not fail when applied to the development of the details of the University system, which is its logical sequence—its indispensable supplement and crown.[27]

Silliman's was a remarkable critique. The state's founders had thought about this very issue when writing California's constitution almost two decades earlier. Despite that promise, for years they had dithered and fought and struggled to create even a shadow of the higher education system that the founders of the state envisioned. Silliman called them out on it, and everyone who heard him knew it.

## The California Constitution

A year after the discovery of gold at Sutter's Mill and a year before the Golden State was admitted to the Union, hope for a California university was expressed at the first state constitutional convention in 1849. The convention, convened by the seventh and last military governor of California, General Bennet C. Riley, met in Monterey from September 1 through October 1, with Riley issuing the constitution and calling for an election to ratify the document. The president and presiding officer of the constitutional convention, Robert Semple, began the proceedings with this charge: "It is to be hoped that every feeling of harmony will be cherished to the utmost in this Convention. By this course, fellow-citizens, I am satisfied that we can prove to the world that California has not been settled entirely by unintelligent and unlettered men."[28] However, with limited resources, there was minimal support for public higher education. Private schools and academies immediately sprang up to fill the vacuum.

The Monterey Convention, as it came to be called, addressed several challenges, such as whether California would be a territory or a state (the vote was overwhelmingly in support of statehood) and whether slavery would be permitted inside its borders. Even though fifteen of the forty-eight delegates to the convention came from southern states, the vote to reject slavery in the Golden State was unanimous.[29]

As the delegates began crafting their guiding document, many looked to their home states as models for the relationship between state government and education. The constitutions of Michigan, Wisconsin, and, most importantly, Iowa and New York influenced the delegates the most, with 66 of the 137 sections in the first constitution originating from Iowa and 19 from New York.[30] Central to any government's efficacy is the generation revenue to fund operations and services, especially with regard to education, and the Committee on the Convention made recommendations on these and other issues. One specific passage was drafted by the committee and became section 4 under article 9 of the constitution. The measure was adopted without any debate and stipulated that the legislature take

> measures for the protection, improvement, or other disposition of such lands as have been or may be granted by the United States or by any person or persons, to this state, for the use of a University; and the funds accruing from the rents or sale of such lands, or from any other source, for the purpose aforesaid, shall be and remain a permanent fund, the interest of which shall be applied to the support of said University, with such branches as the public convenience may demand for the promotion of Literature, the Arts and Sciences, as may be authorized by the term of such grant.[31]

For the improvement and permanent security of all university funds, the legislature was also required to provide "effectual means."[32] President Semple maintained that the fund for educational purposes could not be too large, posing a question and making a suggestion to the president of the state's university: "Why should we send our sons to Europe to finish their education? If we have the means here we can procure the necessary talent; we can bring the president of the Oxford University here by offering a sufficient salary."[33]

### Selecting the Proper Site and Creating the University

Throughout its entire existence, the College of California never officially had a president. Rather, the trustees named Reverend Willey vice president in March 1862, hoping to attract someone of sufficient stature and reputation from the East to take up the office of president.[34] Despite his failing health, Willey was given the further titles and responsibilities of financial agent and manager of the institution, all duties he ably fulfilled. The College of California would gamely persist for several more years until the creation of the University of California in 1868.[35]

As the founders of the college considered possible sites for expansion, one of the names under consideration for the town site was inspired by George Berkeley. An Irish philosopher, poet, and Bishop of Cloyne, Berkeley had visited America in 1729 with plans to establish an educational institution for the evangelization and education of "aboriginal Americans."[36] Finding the time not quite right, the bishop provided the model for King's College, later Columbia University, in New York. In 1732 he deeded his ninety-six-acre Rhode Island farm to Yale as a source for student scholarships.[37] A year later, Berkeley sent one thousand books to Yale and a lesser number to Harvard. Interestingly enough, Gilman, who was an ardent admirer of the bishop's commitment to religion, learning, books, and charity, was the first American writer to publish a full account of Berkeley's library philanthropy.[38]

Before arriving in America, Berkeley had penned a poem titled "Verses on the Prospect of Planting Arts and Learning in America" in 1726. As the College of California board of trustees met on the morning of May 24, 1866, on what would later become known as Founders' Rock, they looked over the San Francisco Bay and the Golden Gate and contemplated an appropriate name for the location. One trustee, Frederick Billings, a University of Vermont graduate, prominent financier, and law partner of the former Union major general Henry Halleck, recalled Berkeley's poem, with specific emphasis on the last stanza, the words of which still hold special meaning for Californians:

> Westward the course of empire takes its way;
> The four first acts already past,
> A fifth shall close the drama with the day;
> Time's noblest offspring is the last.[39]

This confident group of prominent and prosperous men adhered to the Manifest Destiny ideology, which had led to the conquest of California two decades earlier. The Pacific Basin would be the theater in which the next "course of empire" played out to further American expansion.[40] An appropriate and altogether fitting name for this development—and their movement—was paramount to the trustees, and they voted to adopt the name Berkeley for the college site.

But before the state college could consider any additional course offerings, Governor

Low realized that the act of 1866, so roundly excoriated by Silliman, had to be amended to include other departments of instruction. The original legislation that had created the Agricultural, Mining and Mechanical Arts College contained very explicit language relative to mergers with or acquisitions of existing institutions. Undeterred, the governor was very direct in telling Reverend Durant what he was thinking: "We will get a University of the State organized. We will get that created. And we will have the agricultural school a department of the University, and we will have the College of California a department of the University as the College of Letters; and so we will really bring into existence a University. You can reach all the ends you propose in that way. The College of California can accomplish all its ends a great deal better than it could alone."[41]

From mid to late 1867, all those associated with the College of California would mull over the governor's proposal.[42] Two years after initial discussions about the public university and the private college collaborating together, the university's board of regents passed a resolution "to repeat the expression of their profound appreciation of the far-seeing public spirit, devotion to learning and to the good of the commonwealth manifested by the trustees of the College of California."[43] This was in response to the offer extended to the state in October 1867 by the board of trustees of the College of California, by all accounts an offer much too good to pass up. If the state would agree to maintain the college as the liberal arts section of the new university, the trustees would convey their institution and its Berkeley and Oakland properties to state control.[44] What was needed now was enabling legislation. Tasked with drafting the bill were Reverend James Eels, Reverend Henry Durant, Samuel Willey, and a member of the College of California board of trustees, former mayor of Oakland, and recently elected member of the state assembly, John Dwinelle. Originally from New York, Dwinelle had served as the city attorney of Rochester before moving to California in 1849. There he established a successful law practice in San Francisco. His skill as an attorney and his ability to consider all possible eventualities would prove vital in crafting the assembly bill that would create the University of California, known officially as the University's Organic Act.

Cognizant of both California's history in college building and mid-nineteenth-century trends throughout America, Dwinelle and his panel of colleagues had to codify bill verbiage that addressed the concerns of the competing constituencies, and this was no small task. References to practical versus classical studies had to be deftly balanced. At stake was the university's ability to qualify for federal agricultural-college land grants, while allowing for the immediate introduction of courses in letters and pure sciences.[45] Another potential landmine was codification of the governance structure. Included in the language were provisions for the secretary of the regents to fulfill the role of a one-person university extension, with duties that included instruction on practical farming, distribution of agricultural information and samples to California farmers on request, and collection of seeds and cuttings. Further, the governor and respective presidents of the State Agricultural Society and Mechanics' Institute would serve on the board as ex-officio members. With this overt accommodation directed at the scores of practical-education advocates, the bill aimed to provide an even stronger demonstration of the university's secularity. This would be the state's institution, not a college founded by ministers from Connecticut. Such an overture consisted in adding the lieutenant governor, the speaker of the assembly, and the superintendent of public instruction to the board as ex-officio members as well.[46]

The bill was passed by the legislature on March 21, 1868, and signed into law by the governor two days later. Low, who had zealously supported the state university and was instrumental in pushing the measure forward, was denied the opportunity to sign the bill as governor, having been defeated for reelection by Henry Huntly Haight. Although Governor Haight, a native New Yorker and 1844 Yale graduate, had not been prominently identified with the higher education movement before the election, he supported the bill from its inception.[47] Haight was a former Republican who had supported Lincoln, but he had switched allegiances—and political parties—when he lined up behind George McClellan for president in 1864.

In his centennial history of the University of California, Verne Stadtman stresses that the bill signed by Governor Haight created an entirely new institution. It was not, as is sometimes asserted, a merger of the College of California with the Agricultural, Mining and Mechanical Arts College. From the latter, the university inherited the challenge of addressing the popular, ever-increasing demand for practical (as opposed to classical) higher education in California, while also establishing the medium whereby the state could draw down federal assistance. From the College of California, this new university inherited a collegiate tradition, a spectacular setting, and facilities. "But," asserts Stadtman, "these inherited tasks, traits, and privileges were combined into the work and character of a new and distinct institution—the University of California—which the Agricultural, Mining and Mechanical Arts College had never intended to become, and which the College of California, despite two decades of effort, was unable to become."[48]

Per state statute, the regents retained control of and responsibility for everything, and this would certainly factor into the role of the president in the early years of the institution. Their fiduciary responsibilities allowed them to receive lands, moneys, bonds, securities, or other property conveyed to the university and to manage these gifts as stipulated in the provisions outlined by the donors.[49] Furthermore, they were to supervise the general courses of instruction and on the recommendation of the several faculties to "prescribe the authorities and textbooks . . . and also to confer such degrees and grant such diplomas as are usual in Universities, or as they shall deem appropriate."[50] Other statutory responsibilities included electing a president and professors, hiring other instructors and employees, and determining the "moral and educational qualification of applicants for admission to the various courses of instruction."[51] The regents had ultimate control over every single activity and entity associated with the university—and it would remain that way for the next two years.

## The Selection of a President

The regents' first order of business was to elect a president. Foreshadowing the battles to come, their decision quickly became mired in politics. Four nominees were presented at the November 19, 1868, meeting: General George B. McClellan, Dr. Joseph Henry (secretary of the Smithsonian Institution), Reverend Horatio Stebbins (pastor of the Unitarian Church in San Francisco), and Frederick Law Olmsted (landscape architect of New York City). Nineteen of the twenty-two regents were present to cast their ballots, with McClellan garnering twelve votes; Stebbins, five; and one vote each going to Henry and Olmsted. A local paper covered the proceedings and noted that thirteen regents were affiliated with the Democratic Party and were present at the board meeting when the votes were tallied, with twelve of them voting for McClellan.

One might imagine the furor as the public immediately recalled McClellan's opposition to Abraham Lincoln a mere four years earlier, during the 1864 US presidential election. When *The Occident*, a publication of the Old School Presbyterian Church, caught wind of the regents' vote, they responded as follows:

> We have no idea that the regents have really elected General McClellan as president of the University, as several of the daily papers assert; yet, we can but regret the rumor that this is true, as unfortunate. We know little about his literary, and scientific qualifications for the position. Very likely these may be sufficient. But no man should have place, at least in the beginning, who has been prominently identified with either of our political parties, and against whom a large portion of the people have been arrayed. The University cannot afford to encounter political prejudice at the threshold of its career. It will have a mighty work to do if it attains success with all the influence to favor it.[52]

The *Sacramento Union* did not mince words in voicing its view that political affiliation should have been the furthest thing from the regents' minds: "We should have objected as promptly and earnestly to General Pope or General Hooker or General Sheridan or any other general and politician who has been actively a Republican. We should have demurred as strongly against exciting any partisan opposition from Democrats in this matter as from Republicans. It is totally contrary to the purposes of the College to entertain any such proposition. It is in violation of mutual pledges to carry out the spirit and letter of the law."[53]

One of the few newspapers to support the election of General McClellan was the *San Francisco Examiner*, which stated, "We want no narrow-brained, fanatical sectionalist of New England optimism and puritanism to preside over our cosmopolitan University. We want a man of broad views, liberal thoughts and feeling, who does not think the sun rises and sets in one small section of the Union, that no emanation of intellect can be sound unless it proceeds from the vicinity of a certain 'Hub.' "[54] If only they had known that someone like Gilman, with a pedigree as Brahmin as anyone's, would hold the post one day.

But for the present, the regents had to address the fallout from their actions in electing McClellan. Immediately following the vote, former governor Frederick Low resigned from the board in disgust. When notified of the regents' action, McClellan declined the job, but his decision was not read to the regents until weeks later, at the January 5, 1869, meeting.[55] Seven more nominations were then proposed, but no election was held, and the decision was made to elect three regents as an "executive head" of the university until a permanent president could be selected. No further action would be taken until June 1869, when the board offered the position to one of their fellow regents, John Felton, the mayor of Oakland. He declined as well.

Feeling a sense of urgency to move forward with recruiting faculty (and likely assuming that McClellan's answer would be in the affirmative), the board had made its first professorial appointments exactly one week after the McClellan appointment back in mid-November.[56] Their initial selections included John LeConte, professor of physics (he would subsequently serve first as acting president and then as permanent president from 1876 to 1881); Martin Kellogg, professor of ancient languages (and later president of the university from 1890 to 1899); and Robert A. Fisher, professor of chemistry and metallurgy. Two weeks later, Joseph LeConte, John's younger brother, was named the first professor of geology, natural history, and botany.[57] No other faculty appointments occurred until the summer, when the board elected the following: Paul Pioda, professor of modern languages; Ezra S. Carr, professor of agriculture, agricultural chemistry, and horticulture; W. T. Welker and Frank Soulé, both West Point graduates, as professor and assistant professor of mathematics, respectively; and William Swinton, professor of English and history.[58] Carr and Swinton would later play much larger roles in shaping the university's—and Daniel Coit Gilman's—future.

Though the core group of faculty was in place, the university still lacked a president. Turning to the senior faculty member, John LeConte, the regents asked the former Confederate chemist to assume the duties of president in addition to his role as professor of physics. A native of Georgia, LeConte had served during the Civil War as one of the superintendents of the Nitre and Mining Bureau, with responsibilities for "District 6 ½" in Columbia, South Carolina. Professor LeConte's younger brother, Joseph, had also served as a consulting chemist in Columbia during the war.[59] John LeConte accepted the regents' invitation, taking over the responsibilities of faculty and student affairs, while the newly named executive committee remained in place. This arrangement stood for a full year.[60]

## A New President is Unanimously Named

With John LeConte a few months into his time as acting president and eager to recruit a permanent leader, the board of regents drew up yet another list of nominees in June 1870. The new slate included General George Stoneman, General Benjamin Alvord, Dr. John S. Hart (principal of the New Jersey State Normal School), W. T. Lucky (principal of the California State Normal School), General John Gibbon, William P. Trowbridge (faculty member of the Sheffield Scientific School at Yale), Samuel F. Butterworth (regent), Professor Joseph LeConte, and Daniel Coit Gilman (then secretary of the Sheffield Scientific School).[61] Gilman was the shining star on the list, and one particular board member, Edward Tompkins, advocated strenuously for his election. A state senator from Alameda County, Tompkins was a successful attorney originally from upstate New York and brother-in-law to Governor Henry Haight. Determined to cast a wide net that would snag just the right leader for California's first public university, Tompkins reached out to his friend Reverend Henry Whitney Bellows, pastor of the First Congregational Church in New York City, asking him to inquire about Gilman. In turn, Bellows forwarded to Tompkins a note sent to him by Gilman's brother-in-law Reverend Joseph Parish Thompson of New York's Broadway United Church of Christ.[62] This bit of due diligence by Tompkins would prove very beneficial to Gilman as the regents considered their candidates.

At the June 21 meeting, with the roster of candidates before them, the regents tallied their ballots: eight votes for Gilman, three for LeConte, and one for Hart. The motion to elect Gilman was then made, and his election as president was unanimous.[63] Tompkins was ecstatic and immediately wrote Reverend Bellows with news of the board's action:

> I have but a moment to say that the battle is fought and won. Prof. Gilman has this afternoon been elected President of the University of California. Your letter elected him, although there were a far greater number for other candidates. . . . Now, can you not send word to Dr. Thompson at once, so that he will make Prof. Gilman's acceptance certain? The Governor will write him tomorrow informing him of his election, and if by any accident he should decline, *I should be compelled to abscond.* I am inexpressibly obliged to you for all your interest in this matter. That, and the consciousness of the influence for good that you have exercised across a continent ought to give you one more very pleasant memory.[64]

Regent Tompkins followed up his enthusiastic letter to Bellows with an even more voluble missive sent directly to Gilman. This letter is worth quoting at length:

> As one of the Regents of the University of California, I feel a deep interest in your answer to the invitation to become its President. As I was the means of bringing your name before the Board, I am particularly anxious that an unfavorable answer should not be returned, at least until the inducements that the position offers are fully understood. A note from your brother-in-law, Dr. Thompson, to my valued friend Dr. Bellows, was sent me by the latter, speaking of you in terms that led me to learn all that was in my power about you. The result has been to convince me that it will be a misfortune to California, *and I think to you,* if you turn away from the opportunity offered you to shape and form the educational interests of the Pacific Coast. The means are ready to your hand. Neither money nor interest in the matter is wanting. All that is needed is a young man, devoted and earnest, ready to

do his life work in giving the best education to the greatest number, and realizing fully that his best reputation while he lives, and his noblest monument when he is dead, will be best secured, by making the University of which he is *the first President* a grand success. I have become satisfied that you can do all this, and so believing I am not willing to admit the idea that you can refuse to take the lead in so noble a work. Why should you? The lowest consideration, money, will not prevent. We pay $6,000 gold, to which in due season a house will be added. I need not contrast that with any salary paid on your side of the continent. The opportunity *to do good* is vastly greater in a new, energetic, enterprising region, poorly supplied with means of education, than in an old country where colleges and educated men abound. The *promise for the future* is much the greatest on this side of the continent. Where you are, suppose you could be President of Yale. You would get it only after a controversy with "old fogyism," and you would be one of a long line of Presidents. Old ideas, if they did not defeat, would fetter and embarrass you. Here, you would be the founder of a new dynasty, the *first* President, and would forever be "*at the head.*" You would only be asked to *relieve* Regents, who are so hurried that they are glad to be let alone, and thus would shape everything to suit yourself. I concede all that you will claim for the society and surroundings of New Haven, but the educational interests of California are nearly all concentrated at Oakland, a Faculty of a high order is already gathered there, and you would soon be in a position to call around you the best culture in America. I am many years older than you; I know both sides of the continent, and I tell you that such an opening for usefulness and reputation *does not come twice to any man*. I pray you to consider well before you reject such a certainty for anything in the future. The present we *know*. The future can only be read by prophets. My good friend Prof. Brewer (and yours) will *introduce me to you. After that*, you will excuse and believe me cordially your friend.[65]

Others, too, weighed in with lobbying efforts. Professor Martin Kellogg wrote to Gilman, "There is a great opportunity for the first president of this institution to shape the whole educational policy of the State and to stamp success on the University. You seem providentially designated for this work, and I sincerely hope you will not decline it."[66] An 1850 graduate of Yale, Kellogg was one of two faculty appointments at the College of California in 1859 and the only faculty member from the college appointed to the new university's faculty. He would later serve as both the acting and the permanent president of the university in the 1890s.

Despite these intensive lobbying efforts, Gilman declined the offer to come to California, and Governor Haight read Gilman's letter to the board of regents at their meeting on August 16, 1870. The attempt to lure Gilman westward having failed, Tompkins moved immediately to elect Reverend Durant as president. With this action, according to Durant's biographer, William Ferrier, "the Board of Regents hearkened to suggestions within and without and acted as it should have acted in the beginning."[67] Sixty-eight years old and retired, Durant was known for his seventeen years with the Contra Costa Academy and then the College of California.[68] When a regent whose knowledge of the history of educational work in the state was very limited asked who exactly Henry Durant was, Oakland mayor John Felton—a Harvard graduate and an accomplished attorney—immediately responded, "Henry Durant is the Nestor of Education on the Pacific Coast—a man whose shoe's latchet none of us is worthy to unloose."[69] Thus the regents voted for their first official president one more time, with the following results: thirteen for Durant, one each for Lucky and Tompkins, and two ballots left empty.

Once elected, Durant, who lived across the street from the university buildings in Oakland, was immediately swept into service. While there is no record of any inaugural service or formal investiture, one thing was very clear: the regents had become accustomed to the university being managed by their executive committee (now in place two years), sans president, and ingrained habits had been formed. The result was a Durant presidency that was not much more demanding than LeConte's acting presidency had been. Durant would remain in office for two years, retiring at age seventy and opening the door once again for overtures to be made toward New Haven. But the regents' pattern and practice of actively managing the university would be difficult to countermand, regardless of who occupied the president's office.

## Gilman Remains at Yale

Declining the offer to head West, Gilman had many compelling reasons for staying at Yale. First, he stated explicitly in his response to Tompkins his commitment to the "Sheffield College of this University," from which, he said, "it would be very hard for me at present to break away." Second, although not expressly stated in his response (but referenced by Tompkins in his), Gilman was in the midst of campaigning for the presidency at Yale; he was supported by several constituencies, especially students and younger alumni, who ardently advocated for a man of Gilman's youth and disposition. Third, Gilman professed his ignorance of his candidacy in California and emphasized to Tompkins, "I should be very sorry to have you think the letters presented in my behalf were directly or indirectly sent forward at my instance."[70]

Lastly, at this time Gilman was dealing with another personal, and profound, loss: his wife of seven years, Mary Ketcham Gilman, had passed away after a debilitating illness in the fall of 1869. Their elder daughter, Alice, was 6; the younger, Elisabeth, was not yet 2. Among Gilman's personal papers is a scrapbook titled "Alice's Travels: Volume 1, A Trip to the Green Mountains, in June and July 1869." Compiled by Gilman himself, its title page reads:

The Party

Mamma                              Aunt Louisa
Papa                                  Alice

Hattie, the Doll
Preface

This Journal is written for the daily pleasure of a little girl of six years old, who went from New Haven, northward in the summer of 1869. Her mother was in search of health and Alice came with her to be a comfort and a companion to her. Hattie came to be the same to Alice.

Hand-drawn images of the places they visited (completed by Gilman) are interspersed with expressions of hope that the fresh mountain air might improve Mary's condition. The trip lasted nearly two months, and the carefully crafted journal contains this last entry, dated July 29, 1869: "Little Lizzie was fast asleep in her crib but it was not long before Mamma and the rest of us went up to see her as she quietly lay in her little bed. So here ends the story of Alice's Journey to the Green Mountains." The last page of the journal has a simple death announcement: "Mary Ketcham, Wife of Daniel Coit Gilman, Died in New Haven, Connecticut, October 25, 1869, aged 31 years. After many months of weariness and suffering, borne with a beautiful serenity, which was as natural to her as comforting to others, and alleviated by innumerable tokens of sympathy and love, she calmly gave up children, friends, home, with all that made earth dear, and fell asleep, trusting in Christ and hopefully looking forward to the life to come. Thanks be to God, Which giveth us the Victory through our Lord Jesus Christ."[71]

Gilman was devastated. Circumstances would now keep him in New Haven with his two young daughters, close to family. Gilman explained as much in a letter to Tompkins a few months after Mary's passing: "The mother of my two little daughters was taken away from them a few months ago by death and I am not only depressed with bereavement, but I am burdened by the parental responsibility thus thrown upon me." The widower acknowledged his good fortune "in being surrounded by relatives and friends who will aid me in the care of these children but from whom I should be widely separated if I should go to California."[72] Gilman was referring specifically to his younger sister Louisa—"Aunty Lou," as she was affectionately called—who had come to New Haven from the family home in Norwich shortly after Mary's passing in 1869. At her brother's request, Louisa lived with the family for many years and was a mother to Alice and Elisabeth during their childhood.

Trying desperately to overcome this personal loss, Gilman threw himself into the work of incorporating the Sheffield Scientific School. He crafted the articles, made the requisite filings, and shepherded the institution through the process to its completion on February 8, 1871.[73] Per the request of Mr. Joseph Sheffield, Gilman joined Professors Brush and Trowbridge, along with Messrs. John S. Breach, William Walter Phelps, and Charles J. Sheffield, to create a "body politic" for the purposes of incorporation. The group was subsequently named the Board of Trustees of the Sheffield Scientific School and would later add three ex-officio members to their ranks: the governor of Connecticut, the president of Yale, and the chairman of the trustees of the Peabody Museum. This was a significant achievement and yet another contribution to Gilman's alma mater and his legacy in New Haven. Ever since his arrival as a freshman in 1848, Yale had represented Gilman's entire higher education orientation, except for his brief studies at European universities in the mid-1850s. Now before him was the chance to become president of Yale. This was Gilman's dream job. It was the only school he knew, and he loved it.

For his entire time at Yale, the university president had been Theodore Dwight Woolsey. An 1820 graduate of Yale, Woolsey had left New Haven to spend a year in legal study in Philadelphia, followed by two years of theological training at Princeton. Like Gilman, he had spent considerable time abroad, attaining expert command of Greek, with additional study in Leipzig, Bonn, and Berlin. In 1846, just before Gilman would arrive on campus as a freshman, the Corporation needed to choose a new president. Despite being one of Yale's preeminent scholars, Professor Benjamin Silliman Sr. was ruled an unviable candidate on the grounds that he was not an ordained minister, as all the previous presidents had been, nor had he even studied theology.[74] The Corporation turned its attention to Woolsey, who was licensed to preach but had not yet been ordained. A solution was found as Woolsey was examined on October 20, 1846, and found fit for the ministry. Woolsey was ordained the following morning and then inaugurated as president of Yale that afternoon.[75]

Twenty-five years later, the question who would succeed Woolsey as Yale's eleventh president was sparking tremendous interest, and speculation ran wild. Local newspapers reported the jockeying and lobbying by various candidates and their blocs of support. The agitation reached its apogee in the first half of 1871, with undergraduates holding debates on the Yale curriculum, a movement among young alumni demanding (and receiving) representation in the Corporation, and faculty advocating schemes for equalizing departments, investing in more graduate programs (Yale was the first American college to grant an earned PhD, in 1861), and raising a substantial endowment.[76]

*The Courant* of Hartford reported on the eve of the election that the race was down to three candidates but two schools of thought: "These are the two heads—old school and new school. Professor [Noah] Porter, who has advocated old school principles in his recent work, as well as in his conversation and lectures, is the candidate of that side. On the other are Professor Gilman, who is supported largely by the state, and also Hon. Wm. E. Evarts of New York [former US secretary of state and attorney general]. The latter has lately been presented as a candidate in accordance with President Woolsey's wishes, it is said."[77] The next day, July 11, 1871, Porter would be named president. As one Yale historian described it, "A group of old men, presided over by an old man, they [the fellows of Yale College] chose the old way and an old professor."[78] For Gilman, the disappointment of being passed over for president stung. Remaining in New Haven was no longer an option.

With a growing reputation built around his experiences at Yale, observations of technical education in America and abroad, scholarly work, and the successful acquisition of federal funds for the Sheffield School, Gilman was in high demand. He was asked to travel the breadth of the country under the auspices of the US commissioner of education in the summer of 1872 to study scientific schools and ascertain whether progress had been made in America relative to its European counterparts. This particular trip, marking Gilman's first visit to California, was a follow-up to his work for Commissioner John Eaton the previous summer investigating scientific schools in the Northeast.[79]

While Gilman was in California, representatives from the board of regents informed him of Dr. Durant's intention to retire and informally asked whether he might be interested in the presidency this time.[80] Again family concerns shaped his decision. His daughter Elisabeth, then 4 years old, had been struck with meningitis in the spring of 1872 and was tended to daily by Aunt Louisa. "All my activity is paralyzed by the sudden and alarming illness of our dear little child, four years of age, who has been the joy of our household these last sad years," Gilman wrote to Andrew White in April 1872.[81] Little was known about the illness, and Gilman sent to Europe for additional information. What he did know, however, was that the local doctors believed the California climate was just what Lizzie needed.[82] Described by a family friend and medical doctor as "tough as a pine knot," Elisabeth would lead a long and full life, passing away in 1950 just eleven days shy of her eighty-third birthday.[83] Convinced that the California climate might help ameliorate Elisabeth's health, Gilman let the regents know he was interested in the job.

The timing for Gilman was close to ideal, and he felt ready for a new challenge. This opportunity in Oakland was just what Gilman had been waiting for: the chance to put into practice all the educational theories and leadership principles he had developed through travel, observation, experience, and discovery over the past two decades.

## California Comes Calling Again

Not tied to any past tradition and free from ecclesiastical prerequisites or sectarian affiliations, the University of California board of regents met on July 30, 1872, to cast their ballots for a new president. The result was twelve for Gilman, with five ballots left blank. The five unmarked ballots reflected some regents' desire that a Californian be elected, and they initially threw their support behind such a candidate. However, when this alternative candidate learned that Professor Gilman was finally willing to be propositioned for the presidency, he bowed out. The other candidate was Edward Tompkins, the regent who had advocated so strongly for Gilman two years earlier.[84] Gilman was elected as the new president.

When Gilman returned to New Haven from his cross-country tour for the National Schools of Science in late July 1872, Governor Newton Booth, an ex-officio board member, was among the many to wire congratulations. Booth told Gilman that his selection had "elicited favorable comments from the newspapers that reflect the best public opinion," and he closed with a comment hearkening back to the first offer made two years prior: "I should regard your declination as a calamity to the University and to the State."[85] Other messages soon followed: "You have the strongest endorsement of our press and people, and we assure you the hearty cooperation of the regents and professors," read a telegraph from regents Hager, Ralston, Hammond, and Booth. Gilman responded to board secretary Andrew J. Moulder in the affirmative on August 2, 1872: "Regents' telegrams and yours received. After the promised letters come, I leave immediately for San Francisco prepared to accept the great responsibility."[86]

Gilman would leave New Haven just eight days later, but he elected to make a few important stops along the way. First, he visited Cornell and his longtime friend Andrew White before continuing west. He stopped in Indianapolis to discuss the plans of the developing Purdue University with Governor Conrad Baker. Next, he detoured to Urbana-Champaign to visit with the first president of the University of Illinois, Dr. John Milton Gregory, and a young professor of engineering and mathematics who would later serve as the university's business agent and comptroller, Samuel Walker Shattuck.[87] On the other side of the Rocky Mountains, it had only been three years since the "golden spike" was ceremonially driven into tracks at Promontory Point, near the Great Salt Lake, thus joining rail lines coming from both directions, east and west. Gilman's final stop before California included a visit with the territorial governor of Utah, Brigham Young, and his associates. He finally arrived in San Francisco at the end of August.[88]

Gilman's stay in California was purposely brief, and he turned back toward New Haven, writing to Andrew White from Connecticut, "Safe home again, with a head full of new experiences and aspirations. . . . I expect to begin my new duties *out there*, about November first."[89] The transcontinental railroad had connected the continent only since 1869, but Gilman made great use of the routes during the summer and early fall of 1872. Upon his return to Yale, Gilman tendered his resignation to President Porter in a letter dated September 12, 1872:

> Since the close of the last college term I have been chosen President of the University of California, and have been to San Francisco that I might personally become acquainted with the Regents and their plans. The prospects of the new institution are full of hope, and the opportunities for usefulness in its service are ample. Family considerations had predisposed me to regard with favor a change of climate. Under all the circumstances, I have come with great reluctance to the decision that duty requires me to relinquish my work in the Scientific School and to sever the ties which have bound me to New Haven uninterruptedly since I came here as a student.[90]

Gilman had arrived as an undergraduate at Yale in 1848 and was leaving as the newly named president of the University of California, twenty-four years later. Gilman was now more a peer than a subordinate, and Porter sent the new president on his way with a letter much warmer in tone than the President Woolsey had offered upon Gilman's resignation as the Yale librarian seven years earlier: "Your connection with the great university on the Pacific will add a new bond of interest and sympathy to the many which connect Yale College with that land of enterprise and hope. Accept my grateful acknowledgments for your many acts of personal kindness and for the friendly feelings which you have so uniformly manifested to myself."[91]

## The University of California Inaugural Speech

Gilman traversed the continent once again, arriving back in Oakland in late October, this time with his daughters and Aunt Louisa. He set about preparing for his inauguration, which was to be held on November 7, 1872, at Oakland's Congregational Church. The significance of the event's location was not lost on one scholar who observed: "California's state university was a devoutly nonsectarian institution but not a godless one."[92] Afforded the chance of a lifetime to lead a university in what would become America's most populated state, Gilman understood the weight and uniqueness of the opportunity. This was his chance, before a broad audience, to demonstrate his knowledge of and familiarity with the issues facing higher education in the nation, applying them specifically to California. Gilman's collective life experience—the international travel and observations of some of the world's oldest and finest institutions, his advocacy for the scientific disciplines, his broad range of contacts and associations, and his emerging international reputation—had all brought him to this moment.

After an invocation by Reverend George Mooar, the program featured Nathan Newmark, representing the students; retiring President Durant, on behalf of the academic senate; and an address by Edward Tompkins, who presented Gilman with the charter and keys of the university. It was then Gilman's turn to speak. Writing about Gilman's speech, the historian Verne Stadtman said, "If Gilman had not spent another day as president of the University of California, his contributions on the day of his inauguration would have earned him a significant place in the institution's history."[93]

"Grateful for the kindness with which I have been met," Gilman began, "and full of hope for the future which opens before us, I enter upon this trust, imploring for the University of California the generous support of all good men within the commonwealth, and seeking the divine blessing upon our united efforts for the diffusion of knowledge, the promotion of science, and the furtherance of the welfare of our fellowmen. . . . My theme will therefore be the Building of the University."[94] Gilman was a gifted orator, and his address includes a wide array of elements: examples of his own life experience, observations from his global travels, institutional lessons from other states, quotations from the Bible, statements from Emerson, Shakespeare, Berkeley, Newman, and others, and a charge for the new university.

Since the university's founding, Gilman noted, inaugural ceremonies had been held in historic seats of learning (Cambridge, New Haven, Princeton) as well as in "newer, freer and hardier circumstances" (Ithaca, Ann Arbor, Minneapolis, St. Louis) and in other locales "which are neither old nor new." "Here," he continued, "the voice of Experience, and there the voice of Hope, has been heard in the eulogy of learning and culture, and in the earnest pleas for progress and support."[95] Noting the "venerable shrines at Oxford and Cambridge, before which every scholar loves to bow," Gilman reflected on his detailed examination of Teutonic institutions, where one might "see scholastic Germany—the United States of the Old World—now engaged in the foundation of a new university at Strasburg." This was Gilman's opportunity to draw the parallel between Germany's newest university and what he intended to build in Oakland, an institution to rival anything extant in America at that time. Gilman cited Strasbourg as "a university which, in its comprehensive faculties, its liberal structure, its probable power, approaches the University of Berlin, and may well serve as an example to those in California who desire completeness, and who want it quickly."[96]

To accomplish such a task would require resources, to be sure. In describing the inherent advantages of California and its abundance, Gilman's rhetorical flourish, with local examples, shines through: "Now comes the turn of this new 'Empire State.' California, queen of the Pacific, is to speak from her golden throne, and decree the future of her University. California, the land of wonders, riches and delights; whose hills teem with ore; whose valleys are decked with purple and gold, the luscious vine and life-giving corn; whose climate revives the invalid and upholds the strong; whose harbors are the long-sought doorways to the Indies . . . whose citizens are renowned for enterprise, patriotism, and vigor; whose future no seer can foretell." It is a University for California, "not the University of Berlin nor of New Haven which we are to copy," Gilman continued. "It is not the University of Oakland nor of San Francisco which we are to create; but it is the University of this State."[97]

With this in mind, Gilman turned to the foundation upon which to build, surmising that the charter was good, "not perfect—and what instrument is perfect—but carefully drawn, on the basis of good models, with strict reference to this community, and with a perception of the needs of this age."[98] Administered by an "earnest Board of Regents," the university had inherited from the College of California "a good name, good books, good collections, and good-will. Honor to those who founded it, and honor to those who enlarged it!" Perhaps in response to editorial writers from four years previous who had expressed their ardent opposition to "a narrow-brained, fanatical sectionalist of New England optimism and puritanism to preside over our cosmopolitan University," Gilman issued this retort with high praise for the College of California founders who had arrived twenty years before: "Those pioneers, who in the earliest days of this State established a college, were worthy children of the pioneers of the Atlantic, who founded a college at Cambridge when the country was still a wilderness. Here the task was no less difficult than there."[99] One commentator described Gilman and his rhetoric as "a railroad agent singing the praises of the entrepreneurial people who had populated the Golden State."[100]

Reminiscent of the time fifteen years earlier when Reverend Durant and Captain Simmons had stood upon the proposed college property in Berkeley, Gilman reflected on his own experience of taking in the entire panorama and the appropriateness of the locale: "When I first stood at Berkeley, and looked at the mountains and the bay, the town and the distant glimpses of the open sea . . . when I listened to the story of how this spot was chosen, of the rides and walks which were directed by an observing eye over the hills and into the valleys of this charming region, with a prophetic anticipation of the coming day when the college germ, already planted, would require a site worthy of this growth."[101] Gilman even quoted the Oxford antiquarian Anthony à Wood's observations about those elements required to make a suitable university: "a good and pleasant site, where there is a wholesome and temperate constitution of the air; composed with waters, springs or wells, woods and pleasant fields; which, being obtained, those commodities are enough to invite students to stay and abide there."[102] According to Gilman, "All this, and much more, is included in your site."[103] Recognizing the ever-present tension between the classical curriculum and those advocating more scientific and technical pursuits, Gilman deftly acknowledged California's pathbreaking work in both areas, concluding: "When such science and such literature flourish, the day of the University has certainly dawned."[104] Little did Gilman suspect the battles he would face in trying to strike a balance between those advocating for their respective interests or the toll it would take on him.

Gilman's foray into public higher education was completely new territory for him. His entire experience—as a student, faculty member, and administrator—had been at a relatively small, private institution with a corporation as its governing body and responsible to no government entity. The Sheffield Scientific School was an even smaller subset of a larger, institutional whole in New Haven. Gilman would learn soon enough that the University of California was a completely different animal. No longer able to take quick and decisive action on a degree program, policy, capital project, or anything else, Gilman would run headlong into the political machinations of the Grange, the vested interest of elected and appointed board members, the shifting tide of public opinion, and the vicissitudes of state budget priorities and funding.

Gilman turned his speech to the heart of any great university: an accomplished faculty. "It is on the Faculty more than on any other body that the building of a university depends," he proclaimed. As important as apparatus, halls, library, and regents all were, "*the genius loci*, the spirit of the place, will be the spirit of the Faculty."[105] Gilman then recognized the role of the regents—"the power behind the throne"—who had remained invisible during the daily work of the institution "but never for a moment unfelt." The challenges Gilman would face in the future were, at the moment, completely unforeseen. Such observations about elected officials render Gilman's views from later in life even more telling: "The state authorities, executive and legislative, have also a great part to perform in the support of this university, not by over-much legislation, nor by hasty action in respect to its development, but by steady, munificent, and confiding support. 'Quick to help and slow to interfere' should be their watchword."[106]

It was to this future that Gilman directed the final third of his speech. First, he named the individuals upon whom he intended to rely: ministers of religion ("they are interested in all that promotes intelligence and truth"); the press ("it can quicken or retard the establishment of a complete university by its favoring or censorious attitude"); and men of wealth ("It is true the state has been, and is likely to be, liberal in its appropriations; but a great university requires almost unlimited means for its support. . . . We must look to men of wealth to provide the richer and more complete endowments which will place our university by the side of her older sisters in the East").[107] Returning to an earlier theme, Gilman then described the foundation upon which the university was to be built, with equal parts devoted to the new education ("in the development of its mines, manufactures, agriculture and commerce") and to the more traditional curriculum: "We may say that there is no distinction between new and old education—there is only the wise adaptation in each generation of the experience of the past to the wants of the present."[108]

In a section he titled "The Outlines of the Foundation," Gilman then proceeded to explain the place and function of the fundamental disciplines: natural sciences, history and social science, languages, and religion.[109] Relative to religion, Gilman observed, "I hail it as an omen for good, both for religion and learning, that the site of this university bears the name of Berkeley, the scholar and the divine." Recalling that the Bishop of Cloyne "could not do as we would; he therefore did as he could" for the "American aborigines," Gilman encouraged his listeners, "Let us emulate his example. In the catholic love of learning, if we can not do what we would, let us do what we can. Let us labor and pray that his well-known vision may be true." Gilman then quoted Berkeley's stanza from "Verses on the Prospect of Planting Arts and Learning in America," just as the College of California trustee Frederick Billings had done six years previous on Founders' Rock. Gilman concluded with a rhetorical "What for?" in reference to the fundamental purpose of the institution and offered responses, including the following: "It is to hand down to the generations which come after us, the torch of experience by which we have been enlightened. It is wisdom that the university promotes; wisdom, for individuals and nations, for this life and the future; a power to distinguish the useless, the false, the fragile, from the good, the true, and lasting."[110]

News of Gilman's remarks on the West Coast reached the East, with the New York *Daily Tribune* reporting:

> Professor Gilman, late of Yale . . . put particular and determined emphasis upon the need of Science in the University's course, advocating the most thorough study of modern scientific truths and theories as well as of the scientific professions. His recognition of the fact that California has special wants in the way of special studies is a hopeful note for the future . . . in California's case, the mathematical, physical, and natural sciences. Of course, he also prescribes the other elements of liberal culture, but while recounting their necessary claims he does not give to them that exclusive rank which they have hitherto held in a country preeminently an industrial one.[111]

In the weeks following his inaugural address, the response to Gilman was universally favorable. "His enthusiasm was contagious; his personality was magnetic. Within a few months of his arrival in California, he had no trouble at all in gathering together a group of leading citizens, regents, and professors who enjoyed stimulating discussion and conversation."[112]

### "To the House of Our Expectations"

The honeymoon continued for Gilman over the first months of his tenure, with one local paper exclaiming that "the prospects of the university were never so good as now" and noting that every constituent group—the public, high-school teachers, the governor and other state authorities, the faculty and the board of regents—was to a person "alive to the importance of the great undertaking . . . to make a great success of the university."[113] Aligning himself with literary, social, and cultural societies throughout the Bay Area, in particular the Berkeley Club, gave Gilman exposure to learned company and influential people from all strata of society, engendering broad support for him throughout the region. So impressed were the regents with the peripatetic Gilman and his ebullient nature that they invited him to attend their meetings and participate in the board's deliberations—a first. They even went so far as to pass legislation to revise the Political Code in 1873 such that they could name Gilman an ex-officio member. He would take his seat on the board in this capacity on July 1, 1874.[114]

Presaging what would later distinguish Johns Hopkins University, Gilman was keen on expanding professional education and hoped to found a law school in California. For the present, however, the first opportunity was medical education. In the early months of 1873 the Toland Medical College in San Francisco, founded by Dr. Hugh Huger Toland, transferred ownership to the university.[115] A native of South Carolina and a graduate of Kentucky's Transylvania University, Toland had moved to San Francisco in 1851 and become one of the state's leading surgeons. His medical college would subsequently become the university's Medical Department and its first professional school. Three months later, the university brokered another affiliation, this time with the California College of Pharmacy. In a few short months Gilman had succeeded in formulating a medical component of the professional-school cluster he aspired to.

In July 1873, Gilman presided over the university's first commencement. The 1868 Organic Act had provided for the university to be housed temporarily in Oakland, with intentions to expand the campus in Berkeley. But as the moment approached to begin building the Berkeley campus, debates materialized over whether the structures should be built of wood, stone, or brick; three different standing committees claimed oversight for campus planning. Some distressing news emerged to further complicate matters: the income from the college land grants and state endowment was insufficient to complete the capital projects. As a result, a series of construction projects staggered along until all building was halted in January 1871. Shortly before Gilman was named president in 1872, the legislature appropriated three hundred thousand dollars for Berkeley campus construction, and activity resumed in June.[116]

With construction ongoing, the university's first commencement exercises took place in the still unfinished College of Letters. The exercises took place over a five-day period, with the actual Commencement Day being held in Berkeley. The 1873 graduating class had a particular fondness for President Gilman, as he had personally taught two of their courses: Political Economy and Physical Geography. Imbuing the event with even more meaning, the former College of California trustee Frederick Billings presented the university with a portrait of Bishop Berkeley completed by John Weir of Yale University.[117] During the presentation, it was noted that during his undergraduate days at Yale Gilman had been one of the recipients of the Berkeley Prize, thus benefitting from the generous gift Berkeley had made before returning to England nearly a century and a half earlier.[118]

The academic procession began at the university buildings in Oakland and made its way to the new Berkeley campus, a distance of five miles. As one graduate recalled, "The students, about one hundred strong, marched in uniform led by their drum corps, three in number, and preceded by a number of carriages filled with distinguished guests, including our own professors."[119] As the new president began his remarks, and with a stylistic display that was his practice, he proclaimed: "Although the sound of the hammer is still heard upon the walls, and the grounds are not yet graded, we have come up hither to the house of our expectations, that the class of 1873, the first to complete a four-year course in the university, might receive their diplomas dated from Berkeley."[120]

For the assembled crowd of more than one thousand, many of whom came from Oakland and San Francisco to be part of the historic day, the setting was unlike anything they had ever seen. Those who recorded the events of the first Commencement Day recalled the perfect weather conditions: bright sunshine and not a breath of wind. Admission to the ceremony was by ticket only, and the majority of attendees could not cram into the College of Letters. From his vantage point—and with Dr. Willey and Durant on the platform—Gilman remarked, "As we survey this site in all its richness, let us pause for a moment to render a tribute of gratitude to the perseverance and foresight of the College of California which secured for all time this beautiful possession."[121]

When the university had begun its work four years earlier, nearly to the day, on the college grounds in Oakland, twenty-four students enrolled as freshmen. Twelve remained and stood as the first graduates of the university.[122] To those twelve, Gilman delivered this parting message: "Young gentlemen, as we part, I invoke upon you the blessing of Almighty God; I bid you welcome to the responsibilities and the opportunities of educated men; I warn you against dishonesty, selfishness and sloth; and in the name of this band of instructors, who have watched for four years the unfolding of your characters, and who will ever be your friends, I bid you, with mingled hopes and fears, an affectionate farewell."[123] Governor Newton Booth, caught up in the emotion of the stirring scene before him, left the assembled crowd with this charge: "The buildings dedicated today to their high purpose inspire us with hope rather than with pride. They are not so much the visible sign of what has been done as the pledge of what shall be done—the assurance that this institution shall keep abreast with the most advanced thought. . . . All Hail the hereafter!"[124]

This commencement ceremony and moving the campus to the Berkeley site the following September marked the high points for Gilman during his tenure at California. These events had created a sort of aura around Gilman, and he was now regarded as somehow larger than life, even stronger and more irreplaceable than the institution he led.[125] In reflecting on the events since Gilman's arrival in California, the *Overland Monthly*, in an article titled "The Gain of a Man," extolled him:

> There are some men who have a talent for turning everything touched by them to gold. All ventures turn out fortunately. There is a better gift than this. It is the half unconscious power of influencing other men to bestow their wealth wisely and beneficently—the faculty of enlisting the interest of others in a good cause. When the University of California found such a man, it was started on a new career of prosperity. . . . The hearts of many have warmed toward the University as never before. Perhaps the President could not explain how men have been drawn to him as the head of the institution, neither is it necessary now. The fact is better than the explanation.[126]

## Opposition Emerges

Unquestionably, Gilman was at the apogee of his influence and reputation in the fall of 1873, one year into his tenure as president. His accomplishments were not inconsequential: he had outlined a bold and exhilarating vision for the university in his inaugural address; helped negotiate the establishment of professional schools in San Francisco; presented the first graduating class with their diplomas; engendered immeasurable goodwill for the incipient university; and welcomed new students to the sparkling edifices in the idyllic Berkeley setting. The press continued to fawn over Gilman and his Midas touch, cheering the new president on as he pushed the institution forward with his irrepressible enthusiasm. Just below the surface, however, roiled a controversy that was poised to derail everything Gilman had envisioned. Somehow, the university would not be more damaged than it was, as critics and enemies arose on every hand. There was one particular set of charges, however, that threatened the very existence of the university: questions surrounding the emphasis placed on the literary, agricultural, and scientific departments and the use of the funds for the institution's maintenance.[127]

Leading the assault against the regents and Gilman was the labor economist and owner and editor of the San Francisco *Daily Evening Post*, Henry George. Although George was light on higher education experience, he deeply understood federal land policy, and the *Post* would not hold back in its unflinching criticism of congressional actions, the university, and Gilman.[128] In 1871, as Senator Morrill was making an active push for "endowments" to the first Land Grant Act in Washington, DC, George took the occasion to call the original legislation "one of the worst acts by Congress . . . owing to the dense ignorance of the American people on all economic subjects, and their habit of regarding the public lands as surplus property possessing an intrinsic value of its own, and Congress as the grand almoner, which in such gifts as these draws upon some mysterious fund belonging to nobody in particular, instead upon the earnings of the workers of the country."[129] He would continue this refrain with a January 1872 article aimed directly at the university's board: "The original idea was that the university should be a college of industry. . . . But the regents, to whose care the institution was entrusted, have perverted the university from its original design into a college of the classics and polite learning."[130]

Coming from the ivy-covered cloisters of Yale, Gilman was unaccustomed to the vehement opposition he was now facing. He would admit as much in a note to the board of regents after a particularly brutal legislative session: "For university fighting I have had no training; in university work I delight."[131] Gilman had witnessed such ideological battles before and undoubtedly realized that no state or legislative body—or specific institution, for that matter—had the corner on these perennial struggles. Similar debates raged all across the country, attesting to the importance of this issue within the context of post–Civil War America and the dawn of the industrial age.[132] What Gilman had not previously experienced at this level, however, was the ferocity with which he would be opposed by those on his own campus. He had never before been the target of such personal attacks.

Henry George was joined in his efforts against the university by two faculty members, both of whom had been appointed by the board of regents in the summer of 1869: Ezra S. Carr, professor of agriculture, agricultural chemistry, and horticulture, and William Swinton, professor of English and history. Both men had interests that would keep them active in various circles beyond campus. Carr was the leader and historian of the Granger movement in California, first organized in 1873. Founded after the Civil War, in 1867, as America's first agricultural advocacy group, the national Grange actively lobbied Congress for lower railroad transport rates and free rural mail delivery by the US Post Office. Carr was also a close friend of the famed naturalist John Muir. Swinton, the brother of John Swinton, the New York labor leader and journalist, was a published author and had been a Civil War correspondent for the *New York Times*.[133] George's biographer, Charles Barker, noted that Swinton's relatively short time in California had earned him the reputation as a "malcontent on the faculty," concluding that "it is easy to guess he encouraged George to criticize the university."[134]

Carr and Swinton, two of the fourteen professors then teaching at the university, took particular umbrage at Gilman's Yale pedigree, his autocratic approach toward the faculty, and—from their vantage point—his lack of knowledge of, interest in, or sympathy toward industrial education.[135] With the backing of the Grangers and Mechanics, Carr, Swinton, and George set about launching a frontal assault against Gilman and his plans, with George reporting at the end of 1873 from Sacramento what the imminent legislative agenda would entail: "Investigations, this session, will be the order of the day."[136]

### Legislative Inquiries Begin

When the legislative session convened in early January 1874, legislators immediately authorized its Assembly Committee on Public Buildings and Grounds to investigate the university's management of construction work in Berkeley. The first investigation focused on the construction of the College of Letters (North Hall), where just a few months previous Gilman had sent off the first graduating class of the university. The board had entrusted the oversight of North Hall's completion to one of their own, Dr. Samuel Merritt. Originally from Maine, Merritt—a practicing physician who left funds for a health sciences university to be founded in his name—arrived in California in 1852 and subsequently served as mayor of Oakland. Multiple investigations into the building's cost overruns were launched that winter: the original one; one conducted by the state senate; and a third, a "reopened" assembly committee investigation.[137] At the conclusion of days of testimony, Samuel F. Butterworth, a regent and former law partner of Edward Tompkins, offered this statement: "We have the testimony of President Gilman that the building is, in every respect, admirably adapted to the use and purpose for which it was intended. With these facts before you, gentlemen, we are content to leave you to report to the Legislature where we have been guilty of neglect, and whether the State has been defrauded or lost any money in the erection of this College of Letters. In any event, we shall remain satisfied with what we have done."[138] The sworn testimony before the committee runs 464 pages.[139]

The Assembly Committee's official report determined that while the regents might have been satisfied—as attested by Butterworth—the committee felt otherwise, concluding that the building had cost $24,024.12 more than it was worth.[140] The majority of the blame was placed squarely on Merritt, but the rest of the regents did not escape excoriation: "The Board of Regents should, as soon as charges of fraud, mismanagement, and corruption had been made against Dr. Merritt, have called upon him to defend himself therefrom, while they held themselves aloof that they might be better able to pass a cool and unbiased judgment upon the testimony offered on both sides. Instead of this, they have rushed to his defense, and exhibited a clannishness in his behalf that, in the opinion of your committee, deserves the severest condemnation."[141] Merritt would resign from the board of regents in June 1874 and reimburse the university $867, the profit his Oakland Lumber Yard had made in the construction of North Hall.[142]

On the heels of the first legislative inquiry into the university in 1874 came the second, with the Grange driving an investigation pointed squarely at Gilman and the university. The Grange movement had steadily gained political strength since its founding, and now was the chance to demonstrate its influence. The second review, specifically charged with investigating the university's use of Morrill Land Grant monies, was launched early March, just one week after the close of the College of Letters inquiry.

The California Grange had a simple complaint: federal money was supposed to support agricultural and technical training, and the University of California barely supported either one. The Grange's formal memorial added even greater detail, maintaining that of the university's monthly appropriations ($6,000), "only one twentieth is now devoted to the Agricultural Department, and that one professor is discharging all the duties of instruction on the subjects specially related to it. No technical instruction in the mechanic arts has thus far been given."[143] Further, the Grange called out the regents, claiming that they had sold land well below market value to friends. Another charge held that the management of all the federal land grants in California (some eight million, with six million earmarked for education) was riddled with fraud and corruption. In the memorial, the Grange went so far as to propose legislation to abolish the board of regents and replace it with a fifteen-member state board of education. The proposed board would have authority over the university, the state normal school, public elementary schools, and a handful of new secondary schools, with the head of the state Grange serving as an ex-officio member.[144]

In response to the Grange's memorial, the Joint Committee of the Senate and Assembly released its own resolution detailing exactly what it intended to investigate and what information it required from the board of regents and the university.[145] In concert with faculty, the secretary to the regents, and the university's land agent, Gilman prepared his forty-one-page response to the legislative inquiry.[146] He first emphasized that the agricultural land grant received from the federal government was only one of six sources of the university's original funding endowment. Other sources included the old Seminary of Learning grant, property donated by the College of California, a smaller public building grant made by the federal government, various grants from the California legislature, and gifts from private donors.[147]

Gilman and his associates certainly presented a strong case for the defense. It was now the prosecution's turn, represented by two star witnesses, Carr and Swinton.[148] Carr had to walk a tightrope in supporting the charges made by the Grangers and the Mechanics—which formed the basis of the inquiry—while being very careful not to openly criticize the university, for fear of losing his job. Therefore, "his testimony was masterfully noncommittal."[149] In addition to the personal animosity existing between Gilman and Carr, the two men differed enormously in their pedagogical approaches.[150] Carr believed that an agricultural curriculum to teach young farmers the technical and vocational elements of day-to-day farm management was best accomplished with hands-on experiences. Nothing could replace actually working the land and developing a farm operation outside the classroom. Gilman's philosophy was built on the tradition of the great universities: study within the classroom and laboratory—with ample opportunities to engage in research—together with exposure to the classical liberal arts curriculum.[151] That the proportion of agricultural students then enrolled bore no relationship to the number of farmers in the total population of California was a disgrace, according to Carr. By contrast, Gilman's orientation would prove to be the foundation of extension activities built into every American land-grant program: the entire state benefited if only *one* student enrolled in the university's agricultural course so as long as that student was learning how to uncover and disseminate new truths and practices that all the state's farmers could use.[152]

Gilman expounded on the topic in an 1874 article about agricultural education in which he referred to the "trial of experiments, not at Berkeley only but in other localities, all over the state, at Marysville and Visalia, at Los Angeles and the Russian River valley; experiments as to the conditions of growth under different skies and soils, different fertilizers, different culture." His estimation was that once the university had trained a score of observers capable of conducting these experiments and collating the data, the results would be published to the world, thus doing "more to promote the right principles of agriculture, to increase the wealth, and elevate the work of the agriculturist, than it will accomplish by teaching a thousand boys to plow." Drawing a final distinction between his position and that taken by Professor Carr, Gilman concluded, "Any boy can learn to plow on the farm at home; when he comes to college he wants to learn something which he cannot learn at home."[153]

The second faculty critic, Professor Swinton, had a personal axe to grind with the president. On Gilman's recommendation, the regents had twice refused to allow Swinton to take an extended leave of absence (five months) to edit a selection of school geographies slated to be published in New York.[154] As a result, Swinton resigned his position on March 2, 1874, the day before the legislature's investigation began.[155] Free to speak his mind with no fear of retaliatory action, Swinton did not hold back when summoned before the Joint Legislative Committee on University Affairs ten days later. When asked by the committee how he might improve the university, Swinton responded, "As a measure of economy, I should say that the abolition of the office of president would be a desirable measure. I should be happy to respond in writing, more fully." Asked about his relations with the president, Swinton confessed, "They have always been chilly. I think he is not as good a president as the University of California deserves."[156] Swinton argued that the president had encouraged the board to become antagonistic toward practical education. Further, Swinton gave his assessment of how the students felt toward Gilman: "I do not think there is that feeling of confidence, on the part of the students toward him, that is necessary to the successful working of the University for any considerable length of time."[157]

Upon learning of Swinton's claim, the students wrote to the legislature and declared, "President Gilman is our true friend."[158] Pressed for a timeline showing when his feelings toward Gilman had formed, Swinton admitted that he had never held the president in high esteem because of what he had heard from the East: "I did not entertain a very high regard for his abilities before he came here. My observation did not increase my regard for his fitness. That feeling has been growing ever since."[159]

Amid the hearings and the committee's investigation, the third part of the troika aligned against Gilman, Henry George, came forward with another angle of attack: that the president was not scholar enough to lead the university. Writing in the *Daily Evening Post* on March 16, 1874, George said: "We think, as we said at the time, that the election of President Gilman was a mistake, as he was unknown here, and has never made any mark in the world of literature or science such as has been made by several of the gentlemen who were already connected with the university." George continued with what he and others of his persuasion had thought they were getting when the legislature of California was motivated to "so liberally supplement the first endowment [the Morrill Land Grant monies]." "It was not to found a college like Yale, or Harvard, or Oxford, or Cambridge, great as they are, and useful as they are, that these donations were made," he wrote; "but to found a College of Agriculture, Mining and the Mechanic Arts; not a college where lawyers, and doctors, and divines might be made; but a college whence should issue men who would bring to the practical work of the farmer, miner and artisan, all the advantages which science can give." Reflecting the prevailing view of the Grangers and other vocal opponents to Gilman, George concluded: "What have we over at Berkeley? A very good, old style college, but certainly not a college of agriculture, mining, or the mechanic arts."[160]

Included in Carr and Swinton's 1874 book on industrial education in California (meant as a defense of their positions and an exposition of their ideas on mechanical and agricultural practices and policies) is an article titled "The New Education." Originally published under the pseudonym Columella (the name of a prominent agricultural writer in the Roman Empire), the author is revealed to be "The Honorable G. W. Pinney" of Oakland. His monograph runs thirty pages and charges that Gilman had disappointed the hopes of the university's founders, because the number of its students was so small: "And he offers this as a reason why our university should await the result of some more fortunate experiment. In the meantime our agricultural and mechanics students are to be fed upon such shreds and crumbs of knowledge as at the smallest possible expense can support a claim to the increased but conditional endowment of Congress."[161] The case for the prosecution had been heard, Gilman had offered his defense, and now it fell to the legislators to weigh in.

## A Final Verdict

The Joint Committee considered the Grangers' and Mechanics' memorial, reviewed the regents' case statements, studied the testimonies from Professors Carr and Swinton and others, and prepared its final report. The committee concluded that given the infancy of the state, the regents and faculty of the university had done as well as any reasonable citizen could expect without realizing any great results as of yet: "We do not gather ripe and luscious fruit from very young trees—they must have time to grow; so with our institutions of learning."[162] The committee members ended their report with a very telling, somewhat acerbic line noting "the impatience of our people in all matters—a people not ready or willing to wait very long for good results in anything, but more inclined to jump to the conclusion that everything is a failure that does not, to use a California expression, 'pan out' good results at once."[163] For all intents and purposes, the case was closed. Gilman and the university had been exonerated.

With the legislative hearings and queries behind them, Gilman and his colleagues could focus on lobbying efforts to defeat reform proposals put forward by Carr and Swinton.[164] Gilman was successful, as all the Grange's proposed remedies were defeated in late 1874. But the entire episode—the inquiries, the personal attacks, the lack of support for his vision—all had an impact on Gilman. In June, Gilman wrote to his sister Louisa that he was "happy and contented," but he worried aloud that "our best work may be overthrown in an hour by a capricious legislature,—and that makes me question constantly whether I ought to remain here." His approach was to continue on, but he left the door ajar to other options: "I have an impression also that I ought not to be indifferent to opportunities elsewhere and I should listen favorably to any call to work at the East."[165]

For the time being, however, Gilman remained sanguine. He wrote to White in May that "we seem to have come out in still waters—and have a smooth prospect for the next two years, but I should not like to go through such a tussle again." Recounting the actions of Professors Swinton and Carr, Gilman noted to White that their "plotting mischief, within our own ranks, one of them eager to sell books and the other to hide his own incompetency, were too much for any institution to carry."[166] The supreme irony of this entire period in his educational career is that contrary to Swinton's, Carr's, and George's assertions, Gilman, as the record shows, was never remotely antagonistic toward agricultural or technical training. In fact, Gilman was a vocal and ardent supporter of these disciplines and their place within the University of California.

If there was any fault on Gilman's part, it might be ascribed to the fact that his worldview had been shaped by his East Coast experiences and perspectives. Additionally, he arrived on the West Coast with absolutely no idea of the persistent tension between the Grange and others. Gilman's stirring 1872 inaugural speech, with its soaring rhetoric and lofty ambition, certainly resonated with some, but it must have worried, perplexed, or even offended others. If the goals that Gilman outlined were too opaque for those who wanted practical education immediately to be implemented, the language he employed did not help assuage their concerns. "Science," Gilman had implored, "though yet you have built no shrine for her worship, was the mother of California. It was her researches, her summings-up of the experience of the world, her studies of nature, which have made possible and fruitful the work of practical men. Science stands ready to do far more for the community than ever yet, if only you will encourage her wholesome efficiency."[167] The Grange elements who heard this call were certainly thinking of more applied, experiential learning in the fields, mines, and factories, not the science as conducted on the opposite coast at Yale, MIT, Cornell, and Harvard—all institutions Gilman had in mind, given his experience and orientation.

Still, from Gilman's post-European-trip monographs on America's need to invest in scientific schools to his incessant petitioning on behalf of the Morrill Land Grant Act and the Sheffield School at Yale, he had proven his adroitness in navigating both worlds, and he would deal with constituent groups from both sides throughout his career.[168] In early 1887, he delivered an address before the Industrial Education Association that was eventually published under the title "A Plea for the Training of the Hand." In pointing to New York as a paragon, Gilman commended the city for its "three great educational lessons," through the establishment of the Astor Library (which combined with the Lenox Library and the Tilden Foundation in 1895 to become the New York City Public Library), Central Park, and the great museums of natural history and the fine arts. Gilman believed that entities such as the School of Mines at Columbia College, the College of the City of New York, the Auchmuty Trade Schools, the Cooper Institute, the Adler Schools, and the Metropolitan Art Schools "are all held up to other cities as examples of good foundations" in helping teach America a vital lesson: "the right method of promoting physical, manual, industrial, and technical education."[169]

Gilman's bona fides in support of technical, scientific, and agricultural education had long been established. Something else, then, must explain why this eminently qualified and irrepressibly motivated president had such a short tenure in California. It certainly was not the old problem of the new education versus classical education, which Gilman knew firsthand and with which he had dealt so nimbly at Yale while advocating for federal funds.[170] His battles against the bulwarks of educational conservatism in the East were quite different from what he faced in California. Gilman was pitted against those who believed that *their* position—advocacy for agriculture and a mechanic arts college—was the only one that aligned with both the spirit and the letter of the Morrill Act. In the end it really did not matter how forcefully Gilman may have supported technical training and education. Regardless of the level of Gilman's support, the Grange would have always viewed it as insufficient. Gilman wasn't really on the other side of the debate; the Grange had simply decided that he was not the proper medium for their message, and they were bent on ridding themselves of him.

In many ways, this entire chapter in California was a microcosm of a larger, national issue. A collateral impact of the Morrill Land Grant Act was that it bifurcated purpose, complicated questions of identity, and gave rise to a bitter conflict about how to reconcile practical and classical studies, vocational and liberal pursuits. It would result in opposite educational philosophies and schools of thought throughout the United States: those supporting German intellectualism versus those advocating American populism. For as much as some may have despised Gilman, his patrician background, and his philosophical approach to education, he ran headlong into a systemic issue that was larger and more complex than the Grange, the board, the faculty, or even the president himself. This clash of ideas outlived his brief tenure in California and continues to bedevil boards, faculties, legislatures, and administrators to the present day.

## "Release Me from the Post I Hold"

The nadir for Gilman came in the spring of 1874 and led him to submit his resignation in April. He delivered it directly to the regents, who then quietly persuaded Gilman to reconsider.[171] Governor Haight wrote Gilman on April 14 that "the regents will not suffer you to leave if they can help it."[172] To better understand Gilman's state of mind and how he reached this point in his tenure, portions of his resignation letter are worth citing. In many ways, he offers his own conclusion as to why his tenure was coming to a premature end:

> I believe that the real controversy which has been carried on during the last few months arises from a deep and radical difference of opinion as to the scope of the University of California. On the one hand are those who insist upon it that the chief object is to maintain an Agricultural College, or, as it is sometimes more liberally stated a College of Agriculture and Mechanic Arts. They call for a large increase in the "practical" elements of instruction, often going as far as to insist that instruction in carpentry, blacksmithing, and other manual and useful trades should be given in the University. On the other hand are those who insist upon it that the constitution and the laws of the State, the condition of the endowments, and the highest interests of California demand a true University, in which indeed there should be maintained at least one college of agriculture and the mechanic arts, but where the best of every sort of culture should likewise be promoted. These claim that the most practical service which the University can render to the state is to teach the principles of science, and their application to all the wants of men—and at the same time to teach all that language and history have handed own as the experience of humanity.[173]

Gilman concluded,

> The honorable post which I hold by your appointment was not of my seeking. I came to it with hesitation, when your invitation was renewed after an interval of two years from its first proposition. I have tried to the utmost of my ability to conciliate the various conflicting parties and beg them to sink the points on which they differ for the sake of those on which they agree; to make a University of the most liberal, elevated and comprehensive sort, worthy of California, worthy of the 19th century, worthy to train up the future citizens of this great State. You have as a Board and as individuals strengthened me in this effort,—encouraged me amid many difficulties, conquered many obstacles, and remained true to the University idea. You have received the cooperation of multitudes of the most intelligent and far-sighted persons in the community. You have had the satisfaction of attaining great results within a short time, which have attracted the attention of intelligent people at home and abroad. Notwithstanding all this, and notwithstanding that my record as an advocate of technical instruction is clear and decided, it is probable that some one else will better serve you in the present complexities. . . . I therefore beg of you to release me from the post I hold, at the earliest day you can consistently do so. I only ask leave to present more fully for your consideration at another time the embarrassments to which I have been subjected from within as well as from without the University circle.[174]

The regents persuaded Gilman to reconsider, and he relented, remaining in office. But news of the criticism he was facing was beginning to spread and became very well known around the country. "I am glad," White wrote Gilman, "to find all Californians I meet thoroughly in sympathy with you and ashamed—with a patriotic shame—of the attacks upon you and your work."[175] Gilman had withdrawn his resignation, but his heart really wasn't in the job anymore.

As the 1873–74 academic year drew to a close in California, Gilman recounted the difficult days of inquiries and unremitting criticism in a letter to White. These were incredibly trying times—unlike anything Gilman had ever experienced—and he confessed to his friend that he had entertained serious thoughts of leaving his post during the winter months. However, Gilman concluded that "the legislature did so well, and the Regents stood firm, that I cannot resign here without some very strong reason presents itself for doing so."[176] Just such an opportunity would now arise.

### Overtures from Baltimore

Gilman's younger brother, William, had conversed with White about a unique possibility in Baltimore for his brother Daniel. Upon learning of this discussion, Gilman wrote White in June 1874: "I would give *all my pile* just now for a talk with you; the provocation being a single line from my brother that you have been talking with him."[177]

Shortly after the 1874 fall term began in California, Reverdy Johnson Jr., chair of the executive committee of the trustees representing a brand-new venture, The Johns Hopkins University, reached out to Gilman. The timing was certainly propitious. Coming off a brutal legislative session in California, this incipient university in Baltimore was the polar opposite of what Gilman was facing in Berkeley in terms of direction, board influence, legislative meddling, capital construction, faculty appointments, fundraising, and budgetary constraints. Johnson's initial letter to Gilman spelled out all of this in enticing detail: "I believe you are apprised of the existence and character of the Institution which I represent. It is the recipient of a fund of some three and a half millions of dollars—with no shackles of state or political influence, and with no restriction but the wisdom and sound judgment of the Board of Trustees. Not denominational—freed from all sectional bias, and entirely plastic in the hands of those to whom its founder has entrusted its organization and development."[178]

In early November 1874 Gilman acknowledged the receipt of Johnson's earlier communication, which had engaged his "most serious consideration." The fact that nothing on the scale proposed in Baltimore had ever been attempted in America was not lost on Gilman: "The guidance of such a trust as you represent seems to me one of the most important educational responsibilities in our country, and I regret exceedingly that the distance between us is so great that I cannot propose a personal conference at an early day on a subject of so much moment." Gilman asked for a few days' time to consider the proposition and concluded by telling Johnson, "As I look at the opening sentences of your letter and read that this munificent gift is free from any phase of political and ecclesiastical interference, and is to be administered according to the judgment of a wise and judicious body of Trustees; when I think of the immense fund at your control; and when I think of the relations of Baltimore to the other great cities of the East, and especially of the relations which this University should have to the recovering states of the South, I am almost ready to say that my services are at your disposal."[179]

Again seeking direction from his closest confidant, Gilman wrote White in early November:

The Baltimore overtures have reached me an hour ago. I suppose my family are half way across the continent; but if I can stop them coming on I shall do so, and shall ask leave to go East and see for myself. I feel much gratified by the confidence which so many of my friends have shown in me by saying a good word, at the opportune moment; but I must be very careful that the interests here do not suffer. We are apparently over the crisis; that answer to the Grangers has silenced them; our large increase of scholars, and general quiet and serenity surprises us all; if I am to resign at all within two years, now is the moment. No legislature for thirteen months; and then the tidal wave of what sort of democracy? . . . I think I shall resign,—resignation to take effect at a time to be mutually agreed upon. Then being free, I shall go East and look at the situation. It would be unwise to accept such a post without having first a personal interview.[180]

The correspondence during this time period between Gilman and White is revealing indeed and highlights their unique friendship, which sustained both men throughout their lives and careers. White responded with the advice that Gilman had to be the judge of his relations with the board and his duties at the University of California but that he saw no reason why he could not "take up the Baltimore work" by year's end. White encouraged him to meet with the trustees in person to ascertain exactly what the work entailed: "My general opinion is that this chance is a grand one—that there can be built up there a University in the highest sense—and I know no one who can do it as well as yourself."[181]

Gilman determined that the possibilities in Baltimore indeed required a face-to-face meeting with the Hopkins board of trustees. Always eager to travel, he telegrammed Johnson in early December, informing him of his willingness to visit Baltimore. Arrangements were made for Gilman to head east once the fall term had concluded in Berkeley. Knowing that such a journey could not be kept secret and that his standing in California was about to change for good, Gilman committed to telling his current employer of his plans. He wrote to Governor Newton Booth on December 9, 1874: "It is my intention to inform the Regents at their next meeting that I have received letters from an institution of learning in the East looking to my acceptance of the Presidency of the same. The overtures are so attractive that I feel bound to consider them and in order that I may honorably do so, I shall present my resignation to the Board."[182]

The original author of the Organic Act, which had brought the University of California into being, John Dwinelle, had stepped down from the board of regents three months prior. In a letter to Gilman just days after learning of his intention to resign as well, Dwinelle confessed, "I sleep much better than I did when I shared the cares of the University, and wonder now how I endured them so long."[183] Two months later, Dwinelle wrote Gilman again:

> If I have not said, before now, what I now say, it is because I thought the time and the place had not come when it would be perfectly proper to say it. Of course you will accept the Baltimore appointment. First: We have not furnished you the entertainment to which you were invited. We are on the eve of a contest where the Board of Regents is to be assailed by falsehood, malice and every kind of nastiness from the outside, aided by treachery from within. We did not invite you to this, and you have a right to retire from it, particularly when the mode of retirement comes in the form of accepted reward of well-doing—promotion. Secondly: You have a great opportunity at Baltimore, that of organizing the first real American university. That you will do it successfully, and thus place yourself at once at the head of your profession in America, I have not the least doubt. God bless you in this great mission![184]

Dwinelle was prophetic concerning the chance Gilman would have to leave a profound and lasting mark on higher education. The former regent was not alone in his assessment of Gilman, his abilities, and the loss to the state that his resignation would bring. Upon Gilman's arrival in California in 1872 the *Overland Monthly* had hailed him with an article titled "The Gain of a Man." Reeling from the news of his imminent departure, the magazine appropriately titled its farewell article "The Loss of a Man," stating:

> Only one man, but we cannot imagine any other that the State could worse afford to be without at this momentous period of her educational development. . . . We are glad for the sake of the Johns Hopkins University, glad for the sake of American education, glad not least for the sake of D. C. Gilman; but we are sorry for the sake of the University of California, sorry for the sake of Californian education, sorry for ourselves, for we have lost a man . . . a man of surpassing talent for organization, of extraordinary insight and sympathy as to the strong and weak points of colleagues and students, who can do more with poor materials than most men can with good.[185]

The Board of Regents accepted Gilman's resignation on March 2, 1875, nearly a year after his first effort to step down. Immediately thereafter, Professor John LeConte was once again called upon to serve as acting president.[186] The board then unanimously adopted a resolution: "From the first, President Gilman has displayed insight into academic life and discipline, a fertility of resource and enterprise in organization, a tact and practicability in administration, which have won the constantly increasing respect, confidence and admiration of the Regents." The document concludes, "The sense of regret and loss personal and public which the Regents feel, is relieved only by the conviction that wherever he may be, his good and well trained abilities, his high and honorable character, will be devoted to the best human interests and that his work will be a contribution to the treasury of indestructible good."[187]

Gilman wrote to Johnson on March 3 with news of the regents' formal acceptance of his resignation and offered to begin at Johns Hopkins on May 1. "The more quietly I begin, the more confident I shall be," he wrote.[188]

## The Final Days in California

As the final discharge of his duties, the regents requested that Gilman prepare a report on his presidency chronicling the development of the university. He did so, submitting the *Statement of the Progress and Condition of the University of California* on March 23, 1875. The completed document runs fifty-six pages and is subdivided into eighty-three numbered sections. In a relatively short time period Gilman had placed the university on a solid foundation, and the exhaustive report outlines in great detail the progress made during his tenure.

Upon his arrival in 1872, Gilman had trained his attention on the basic institutional structure, and one of his first tasks had been to organize the university into seven "courses," or colleges. Agriculture and Letters had been established in 1869 with the university's founding; Engineering had been added in 1871. To these, courses in Mechanics, Mining and Chemistry (all within the College of Science) were added. Letters was then separated into Classics and Literature.[189] Gilman included details of the two degrees the university offered: a bachelor of philosophy within the College of Science and a bachelor of arts within the College of Letters. Gilman took the occasion to offer one more pointed salvo at those still engaged in the perpetual struggle between the classical curriculum and those advocating for more "practical" instruction:

> While prominence is given to technical and scientific instruction, the University of California is so organized that literary, historical, and philosophical studies are not neglected. The Regents have been impartial in their plans for the development of all departments of the University, fully recognizing the responsibility which the law places upon them to maintain a "College of Letters" as well as "Colleges of Science." All scientific students connected with the University are expected to devote a part of their attention to literary subjects, just as all the literary students receive instruction in the natural sciences. Important as technical instruction may be, the State of California cannot afford to neglect the study of man; and its University would be unworthy of the name of university, if ample provision were not made for the study of language, literature, morals, history, and art, or if the methods of accumulating material wealth were represented to her youth, in the highest educational institution of the Pacific Coast, as more important than the methods of forming character and promoting culture.[190]

Another notable accomplishment was something Gilman would implement and perfect at Hopkins: graduate fellowships. The board of regents had, in the summer of

1874, determined "to appoint as assistant instructors several young men who had recently graduated." It was thought that these graduate fellows would be able to pursue advanced studies under the direction of the faculty. The plan, nearly equivalent to the creation of graduate scholarships, was working well.[191] Gilman also highlighted the founding of the Agassiz-endowed chair in Oriental Languages, as well as another scheme he would pursue at Hopkins: visiting lectureships.[192]

Another significant achievement was that women had been eligible for admission to the University of California since its formation, and "its doors were freely opened to all properly qualified students above a certain age." In summarizing how these female students had done, Gilman observed, "Among the regular students the proportion of ladies who have been good scholars has been greater than that of young men."[193] A decade after the university opened its doors, there were 62 female students, out of a total undergraduate enrollment of 244, and a California Supreme Court ruling in 1879 extended female students the right to enroll in graduate programs.[194] In giving women access to higher education, California was far ahead of institutions in the East in terms of both practice and codified policy. With a few notable exceptions—Oberlin in Ohio, Berea College in Kentucky, the University of Michigan, Cornell in New York—the records of the more established colleges and universities were not exemplary. At the universities where Gilman had worked—California excepted—the opportunities for men had been much greater than those for women. Gilman would preside over a university on the East Coast that, had it not been for a donor-mandated change to the School of Medicine's admission policies in 1893, would have foreclosed opportunities for graduate study to women even longer.

Apart from the final report submitted to the regents, few records exist detailing Gilman's last days in California, with the Faculty Senate simply noting "the recent resignation of President Gilman and his speedy departure to a distant field."[195] Farewell gatherings were organized, the first on March 24, put together entirely by the students as a complete surprise to Gilman; the second on April 2, announced in the press and attended by friends of Gilman's from Oakland and San Francisco.[196] Notes among Gilman's personal papers—not numbered and not always in order—outline some of his thoughts. It is impossible to know whether he ever delivered them publicly or communicated them to others in smaller settings or in private letters. But Gilman began his reflections with the following, the tenor of which is similar to that of his letter of resignation (refused by the regents) from the year before: "It is with great reluctance that I take the final steps which will sever my connection with the University of California. I came with much hesitation; I have stayed with increasing satisfaction; I go with sincere regret. Whatever the future may bring forth, Berkeley will be remembered with delight. It seems as if even friendships ripened quicker than elsewhere beneath these favoring skies."[197]

Some have concluded that the most injurious result of the university's involvement in political controversy in the early 1870s was the resignation of President Gilman.[198] Notwithstanding his abbreviated tenure, Gilman had put a solid foundation in place, and the institution would now realize astounding growth, made possible by those committed to ensuring that California had a first-rate university. The people who advanced the University of California forward in the next twenty-five years, some of whom had been recruited personally by Gilman, shared the president's vision and worked in unison for those common ideals.[199] What resulted was a university that in its first quarter century of existence was among the top ten in the country in enrollment, number of faculty, income, and graduates; in its first fifty years it was in the top fifteen.[200]

One can certainly posit that Gilman was too thin-skinned during his first experience of working at a public university with an appointed board, elected officials, and an irascible faculty. What Gilman experienced certainly impacted his faculty recruitment at Hopkins. But in the end the naysayers won and ran him off. The biographer of Henry George—as one of Gilman's harshest critics George was relentless—surmised that a "liberal editor" of a prominent paper might have recognized that in Gilman the university had just the man "to nurse along together in tender transplantation the scientific and the humanistic vines of learning in the new California environment." Likewise, a new president might have chosen to refrain from commenting on social and political questions not relevant to his office, as Gilman was inclined to do, and would have been hyperattentive to the possible press reaction to university policy and expenditure.[201] As has been amply shown, there was a chasm as big as the bay between the two camps: on the press side in San Francisco and on the university campus in Berkeley.

Although his presidency ended prematurely, Gilman left an indelible mark on California. He was still a young man, in his mid-forties. As he boarded a train for Baltimore, he was prepared for an opportunity that represented his "third attempt to define an American university."[202] But before a chronicle of Gilman's tenure at Hopkins can be undertaken, how the trustees arrived at their unanimous decision to hire the first president must be examined.

# CHAPTER THREE

# The Three Great Advisers

While Gilman was struggling through the early months of 1874 in California, members of the newly formed Johns Hopkins University Board of Trustees—twenty-eight hundred miles away in Baltimore—were trying to learn as much about higher education as possible, as quickly as they could. Some on the board were familiar with colleges dotting the East Coast, but none was a professional educator, nor were any of them particularly near the mainstream of college and university life. At best, they were only well-informed amateurs, and they knew it.[1] Recognizing the benefit of seeing campuses firsthand and meeting with administrators, faculty, and students, they paid visits to some of the nation's finest institutions—Harvard, Yale, Cornell, the University of Michigan, the University of Pennsylvania, and the University of Virginia.[2] The Baltimore businessman James Carey Coale, who knew all of the trustees personally, reported to William Gilman in November 1874 that two Hopkins trustees had "just returned from Europe where they went to examine English and Continental institutions."[3] William would prove to be a useful go-between, relaying information to his brother Daniel about conversations with various people involved in the new Hopkins enterprise, including Andrew White. Coale's assessment of the trustees was that "they are all among our best people in every position of life . . . cautious and conservative, going to 'make haste slowly' and we are going to place the Concern in the top rank, if money, experience, and hard work on their part will do it."[4]

The celebrated Harvard biologist Louis Agassiz expressed his views on American higher education and its governance in an 1872 report prepared by the US commissioner of education. Agassiz's opinion was shared by many, and the report was circulated widely, with parts of it published by the *New York Times* in August 1874, including this statement: "The very fact that there is no university in the United States the intellectual interests of which are managed by professors, but always by a corporation outside, shows that we do not understand what a university is. The men who are in it must know better what are the wants of an institution of learning than outsiders." Agassiz concluded, "I believe there is no scientific man who will concede that there can be a university managed to the best advantage by anybody but those interested in its pursuits, and no body of trustees can be so interested."[5]

If this was indeed a popular perspective, the Hopkins trustees showed that they were up to the task of proving it wrong. The hand-picked board members made a collective commitment to ensuring that *their* new university was going to be markedly different from those criticized by Professor Agassiz. In addition to touring campuses, the trustees dove headlong into their self-directed primer on higher education. "Here was something unique in university history," noted former Hopkins librarian John French, "a reading course for trustees, prerequisite to the assumption of their duties."[6] Acting on behalf of the executive committee, Reverdy Johnson purchased a substantial list of titles, everything from university histories to scholarly reflections to treatises on educational reform.[7] Dr. James Carey Thomas subsequently wrote to his oldest daughter, M. Carey Thomas (who would later serve as the second president of Bryn Mawr College), that he was "engrossed and deeply interested in reading up on university subjects."[8] While they were visiting campuses throughout 1874 and into the early months of 1875, the board members were pursuing their own research and reading.

The time came to solicit input directly from university presidents. Reverdy Johnson was deputized by the executive committee "to continue correspondence with heads of institutions, looking to formal interviews in Baltimore."[9] Although it is impossible to determine the exact number of presidents contacted for information or interviews, it is known that some, such as Noah Porter at Yale and James McCosh at Princeton, never responded to the trustees. McCosh, the Scottish metaphysician who had been named president of Princeton University in 1868, would write Gilman in January 1876, "I believe I gave unintentionally some sort of offense to the Trustees by overlooking so far a letter which came near Commencement time. I do not believe I would have aided them in any way. Every thing is safe in your hands. But if I can aid you in any possible way you may command me remembering that you aided me."[10] While Porter never submitted anything in writing to the board, he hosted the trustees in New Haven in September 1874 and shared his perspectives with them in person.[11]

Three presidents responded affirmatively to the trustees' invitation to meet with the board and offered their assistance free of charge: James Burrill Angell, president of the University of Michigan from 1871 to 1909; Charles William Eliot, president of

Harvard from 1869 to 1909; and Andrew Dickson White, president of Cornell from 1867 to 1885.[12] There were some common denominators among the three: all were in their forties; each had graduated from an Ivy League institution (Angell from Brown, Eliot from Harvard, and White from Yale); all had spent time in Europe studying and observing educational institutions; and with all three, the respective academic disciplines—modern languages and international law for Angell, chemistry for Eliot, and history and literature for White—were subordinate to their administrative responsibilities.[13]

Frederick Rudolph described this group (along with John Howard Raymond of Vassar and William Bartram Rogers of MIT) as the new leaders who "seized the initiative in American higher education after the war in the way that John D. Rockefeller seized it in oil, Andrew Carnegie in steel, Washington Duke in tobacco." "For the new leaders and the new institutions that rode the wave of reform," according to Rudolph, "the old ways and the old curriculum were too narrow, elementary, or superficial. There was insufficient attention to the German-university ideas of free teaching, study, and research. There was insufficient attention to the technical and the practical. The colleges were too sectarian, too undemocratic. Their psychology was faulty; their philosophy, wanting."[14]

## The Presidents Weigh In

That the trustees recruited arguably the three most respected and best-known higher education voices in the latter part of the nineteenth century to tutor them is telling. It certainly speaks to the importance of their new academic endeavor and underscores the seriousness with which they took their positions and assignments. These presidents have entered into the Hopkins tradition as the "three great advisers to the trustees," committed to "rescuing American higher education from what they considered outmoded and trammeling customs."[15] All three men were innovators in education who represented three different types of American educational institutions: a large, publicly funded midwestern university; a brand-new private institution that had been designated New York's land-grand university; and the nation's oldest and arguably most prestigious university, in a major metropolitan area. In consulting with each one privately, the trustees hoped to reach some consensus as to what form the Johns Hopkins University should take.[16] On the dedication page of his 1906 book, *The Launching of a University*, Gilman inscribed, "In grateful recognition of the encouragement of James B. Angell, Charles W. Eliot, and Andrew D. White."[17]

Reverdy Johnson's letters of entreaty to these three presidents contained an invitation to Baltimore to meet the board in person. Angell and Eliot committed to doing so in the summer of 1874. White, owing to extenuating circumstances and despite multiple attempts to find an amenable time, was unable to make the trip. He was, however, the first to respond in writing. His letter outlining perspectives on a litany of issues runs thirty-two handwritten pages.[18]

The records of the two in-person meetings are a fascinating snapshot of what the trustees were considering (and how their campus visits and readings had informed the questions they asked), as well as how these presidents were grappling with their own challenges—and what lessons could be deduced from them. The transcripts from the discussions with Eliot and Angell are expansive: Eliot's record of his exchange with the board runs fifty-four typewritten pages; Angell's session runs forty-seven handwritten pages of transcript. In recalling his perspective of the experience to Gilman months later, Eliot wrote, "If you will ask Mr. Johnson for the report of what I said to the Trustees last June, you will never need to talk to me any more. I talked to them seven hours, and told them all I knew and a great deal more."[19] After his time in Baltimore with the board, Eliot wrote Johnson that his "brief visit was a very pleasant one and I hope that it may perhaps prove not wholly useless to your Trustees." Nevertheless, he concluded, "Sometimes it is almost as profitable to learn what not to do as to be shown what to do."[20]

On the occasion of the twenty-fifth anniversary of the Johns Hopkins University's founding and the inauguration of Ira Remsen as its second president in 1902, Angell recalled his experience of a quarter century earlier: "I was shut up in a room with these Trustees and a stenographer, and what few ideas I had in those early days were squeezed out of me remorselessly."[21] Some of the trustees had had experience as board members at smaller colleges such as Haverford, Guilford, or Bryn Mawr, but nothing on the scale of what they were proposing. The depth of the trustees' research and the breadth of their readings and campus visits were all revealed as they discussed the following with their presidential advisers: capital investment in academic buildings, dormitories, discipline, religious affiliation, requirements for admission, preparatory schools, student finances, coeducation, faculty (hiring, rank advancement, and tenure), presidential qualifications and salary, curriculum, libraries, the elective system, professional schools, fellowships, graduate training, and more.[22]

## White of Cornell

Daniel Coit Gilman's closest and most trusted friend since their days at Yale, Andrew Dickson White, had followed a circuitous educational path to becoming president of Cornell in 1866, when he was just 34. While in Europe with Gilman in the mid-1850s, White had studied at the Sorbonne, the Collège de France, and the University of Berlin. His experiences there had caused him to reflect in his two-volume *Autobiography* on studying history at Yale, where "lectures were few and dry. Even those of President [Theodore Dwight] Woolsey were not inspiring; he seemed paralyzed by the system of which he formed a part."[23] Contrasting his time in New Haven with what he experienced in France and Germany, White recalled the European faculty "lecturing to large bodies of attentive students on the most interesting and instructive periods of human history." Deciding that higher education was his calling in life, White posed the question, "Why not help the beginnings of this system in the United States?" "I had long felt deeply the shortcomings of our American universities, and had tried hard to devise something better," he wrote; "yet my ideas as to what could really

Cornell University president Andrew Dickson White, 1885. (Photo courtesy of Andrew Dickson White Papers, #13-6-2497, Division of Rare and Manuscript Collections, Cornell University Library)

be done to improve them had been crude and vague."[24] As with his friend Gilman, the charge against White—at least from the Cornell historian Carl Becker—was that his profession was not scholarship. Becker held that White was essentially a crusader and promoter of good causes, "primarily interested in changing the world rather than in understanding it."[25]

Upon his return to America, White returned to Yale to earn a master's degree in history. He declined an offer of a teaching position in the Department of Fine Arts. A longtime devotee of the arts, especially architecture, in which he would maintain a keen interest throughout his life, White felt that he could be of more use to society by turning his energies to improving the instruction of history. Despite encouragement from friends and mentors that a teaching opportunity would present itself at Yale, White grew uneasy and unhappy as there was not a clear path forward. This all changed for him at Yale's 1856 commencement. White was mingling with his classmates in the college yard when, serendipitously, he heard that President Francis Wayland of Brown University was addressing the graduates in the Hall of the Alumni. White made his way to the hall. Looking in, he "saw at the high table an old man, strong-featured, heavy-browed, with spectacles resting on the top of his head." White had never seen Wayland before, nor would he ever see him again. The president's remarks lasted all of ten minutes, but for White, "it settled a great question for me." Wayland's observations to the newest alumni included this: "The best field of work for graduates is now in the West; our country is shortly to arrive at a switching-off place for good or evil; our Western States are to hold the balance of power in the Union, and to determine whether the country shall become a blessing or a curse in human history."[26]

At the conclusion of Wayland's remarks, White knew exactly what he would do next. Drawing on his extensive pool of friends and contacts, White sent out letters declaring that he was the ideal candidate "for the professorship of history in any Western college where there was a chance to get at students." He received two offers: one from a southern university, which he could not consider because of his antislavery opinions; the other from the University of Michigan, which he eagerly accepted.[27]

Arriving in Ann Arbor in October 1857, White was appointed professor of history and English literature. Teaching on a variety of historical subjects, White earned the privilege of delivering a series of lectures to seniors and students from the law school in the university's old chapel. The first of the lecture series was titled "Development of Civilization during the Middle Ages." White decided to take a novel approach to the subject matter and lecture without manuscript or even notes. Full of trepidation, he expressed his unease to the man seated next to him, who had been invited especially to introduce the professor to the capacity crowd on the first day of class: President Henry Tappan. A seasoned extemporaneous speaker, Tappan leaned over and exhorted White, "Let me, as an old hand, tell you one thing: never stop dead; keep saying something."[28]

During his six years in Ann Arbor, White would glean many more useful lessons from Tappan. Above all else, Michigan differed from the leading institutions of the East in that it was utterly *unsectarian*, an adjective White preferred to *nonsectarian*. Further, various courses of instruction were established at Michigan, and students were allowed to choose among these elective courses. On these accounts, maintained White, the University of Michigan held "a most important place in the history of American higher education; for it stands practically at the beginning of the transition from the old sectarian college to the modern university, and from the simple, single, cast-iron course to the form which we now know, in which various courses are presented, with free choice between them."[29]

Family and business took White from Ann Arbor back to upstate New York in 1863.[30] From there, he served in an unofficial diplomatic capacity, traveling to Europe to enlist the support of France and England for the Union cause in the Civil War—and urging both nations not to aid the Confederacy. Upon his return to the United States, White received a telegram informing him that he had been nominated for the New York State Senate.[31] White was subsequently elected the youngest senator and chairman of the committee on education. In January 1864 White took his seat in the Senate chamber in Albany, "and there, as if by the Providence of God, was Ezra Cornell."[32] Cornell, twenty-six years White's senior, was chairman of the committee on agriculture. Their service as legislators marked the beginning of their friendship and launched a years-long collaboration that eventually led to the founding of Cornell University as New York's land-grant institution.

The Morrill Act had served to place emphasis on long-neglected subjects and aspects of higher education, and Cornell was a model of what was possible in terms of emphasis on vocational, scientific, and literary subjects, as well as nonsectarianism and coeducation.[33] Cornell was also the most contemporary example among those examined by the Hopkins trustees, having welcomed its inaugural class to Ithaca, New York, just six years earlier, in the fall of 1868. Ezra Cornell stated his ambition for the eponymous university: "I hope we have laid the foundation of an institution which shall combine practical with liberal education, which shall fit the youth of our country for the professions, the farms, the mines, and manufactories, for the investigations of science, and for mastering all the practical questions of life with success and honor."[34]

Striking the delicate balance among vocational, scientific, and literary subjects, Cornell was also a leader in nonsectarianism and coeducation, in keeping with Ezra Cornell's decree that the institution bearing his name would be one "where any person could find instruction in any study."[35] Cornell was doubly astute in purchasing the university's land scrip, locating valuable timberland in Wisconsin. These lands were held in pledge to the nascent university as their value appreciated, resulting in $5 million for the institution. This represented a windfall of nearly ten times the average price per acre received by other land-grant schools.[36]

The trustees were just a few weeks into their higher education primer (and the probating of Hopkins' will)[37] when President White sent his responses to the board's queries by way of a letter to Dr. Thomas dated March 13, 1874. White began, "You have, indeed, imposed upon you one of the greatest and noblest works of these times. Indeed, I can recall no other instance of so great an endowment placed at once and fully in the hands of trustees for the establishment of a great university."[38]

White's first recommendation was that the trustees expend only a modest amount of the new endowment upon buildings "and that you expend none of it upon building of dormitories," maintaining that two or three buildings could be constructed for the general purposes of the institution from the income of the endowment. This,

White concluded, would be sufficient for all purposes. Such a view would be echoed subsequently by Gilman in his oft-quoted axiom that in its formative years Hopkins was about men and not buildings. Leaning in on his view of dormitories, White asserted that the erection of such structures "is one of the greatest mistakes which a university or college can make." White's perspective was that dormitories resulted in little or no return on the investment and that they "increase the labor of the Faculty ten-fold." White took his opinion one step further by asserting that "three-fourths of the difficulties in governing American colleges and universities arise from the dormitory system."[39]

Again White spoke from experience: while at Michigan he had observed that the gradual abolition of the dormitory system had been followed by a "very marked elevation in the tone and character of the students." Based on what he saw in Ann Arbor, White suggested to the Hopkins trustees that students be placed "in the families of various, approved persons," which in turn would break up "the main opportunities for caballing and mischief and also brings each student directly under the influences to some extent of a home circle." White concluded with this admonition: "The sooner our university authorities learn that the proper duty of a university is to *educate* students and not to lodge or feed them, the better for all parties concerned."[40]

White then turned his attention to the organization of disciplines, urging the trustees to "give great weight to the technological side; that is, to science at its application to various industries."[41] He specifically cited civil engineering, mechanical engineering, and chemistry, "applied to the arts, especially including agriculture, mining engineering and architecture." Referring to himself as a "lover of classical and general literature," White stressed that the board must "not fall into the error of making any separation between the students in various courses." He concluded, "I think it of very great importance to place all good studies on a full equality."[42] White had observed what happened at both the Sheffield Scientific School at Yale and the Lawrence Scientific School at Harvard. Separation of the scientific disciplines from the rest of the university community was not the preferred course, nor was it reflected in White's organization of Cornell.

On the question of religious affiliation—perhaps bearing in mind that a majority of board members were Friends—White adjured, "More earnestly do I hope that while your institution promotes Christian civilization it will not be allowed to lapse into the hands of any single religious sect or body. Nothing can be more unfortunate." Citing Cornell's founding documents and their provision that no candidate for any position be accepted or rejected on account of any religious or political ideas, White then proceeded to outline just how ecumenical the Ithaca institution was, providing a list of donors, their respective religious affiliations, and the amounts of their gifts since the university's founding less than a decade earlier: Ezra Cornell "is a Friend" ($500,000); Henry Sage "is a Congregationalist" ($300,000); Sage's elder son, Dean, was "a Congregationalist of a non-conservative type" ($30,000 to endow a religious lectureship); John McGraw "has, it is understood, religious sympathies with the Baptists" ($150,000); Hiram Sibley "is connected to some extent with the Protestant Episcopal Church" ($90,000); and Professor Goldwin Smith, whom White had recruited away from Oxford to join his educational experiment in central New York and who in turn had donated his entire personal library to Cornell in 1869, "is a member of the Church of England."[43]

Brief reference was made to an original report that advocated a plan for nonresident professorships, but White chose to focus even more intently on graduate fellowships, which he had been attempting to establish at Cornell since 1871. More than on any other factor, the success of Johns Hopkins as a graduate institution hinged on finding a way to aid students financially. It was abundantly clear that no contemporary American university had solved the dilemma of how to both attract postgraduate students and retain them as productive members of the campus community while allowing them to specialize within their chosen disciplines.

The recommendation from White was that the trustees consider funding fellowships—"ten to twenty, each one yielding a sum sufficient to maintain a young graduate at the University in a reasonable degree of comfort while he pursues a more extended course of study under the general direction of the Faculty." These fellows would also be required to "discharge some duty for the university, say to the extent of one hour per day through the university year." Possible positions White envisioned included serving as a board of examiners for testing scholarship, given that such duties placed a "terrible labor upon professors who could better employ their time in less irksome and more important work." White spoke of his own classroom experience at Cornell, relating that he had entrusted "to recent graduates of talent" the responsibility of grading examination papers and "found that with comparatively little labor they made more thorough and more perfect examinations and estimates than I had patience to make myself."[44] Throughout his tenure as president at Cornell, White taught history, with a series of his seventy-three lecture outlines being published in 1872.[45]

White's position on fellowships was unequivocal, and he stressed this distinctive investment forcefully with the Hopkins trustees: "In no way can your University render a greater service, when it is established, with an equal expenditure of money than by establishing *fellowships* to be held by students who graduate in high standing in any particular department." This would be one of the recommendations the trustees both endorsed and funded, thus differentiating Johns Hopkins from every other institution in America. Of the three presidents, White was the one who forthrightly advised the trustees to plan for graduate work, and he did so before either Eliot or Angell had been contacted. Two years after the founding of Hopkins, White told his own board of trustees at Cornell, "Johns Hopkins University has carried into practice a policy I have so often recommended to this board and which has been held in abeyance only on account of our lack of means, i.e., the policy of establishing a number of Fellowships for Post Graduate study."[46] It was not until 1884 that White's own university created a fellowship fund producing seven annual awards in the amount of four hundred dollars each, placing graduate studies at Cornell on a firm foundation a full decade after his advice to the Hopkins trustees.[47]

Curriculum offerings were addressed next, with White urging the establishment of very thorough courses in subjects to which American universities had not yet given sufficient attention: history and political and social economy. White came to this view from his own experience, having taken the route of teaching history at Michigan as a personal quest to address what he believed to be a pedagogical vacuum in the United States. Asserting that the want of knowledge in these areas was "most disheartening," White held "that some of the worst mistakes that have been made in our country are directly traceable to the lack of this kind of knowledge among the men to whom we entrust our legislation." White's categorization of the social sciences was especially broad, as he bundled into this large group the study of "crime, disease, including diseases of the mind, and sanitary science."[48]

While White had strongly advised against the spending of earnings on anything but the most basic of capital projects, he did urge the proper "fitting up" of laboratory space not only for chemistry but also for geology, botany, physics, and physiology. His argument for such an outlay was that "it is a great thing to get students at studying *things* in addition to what men have written about things." White returned briefly to the subject of capital investment, this time in terms of faculty housing, and relayed to the trustees what Cornell had done in terms of "long leases at merely nominal rates" to professors who agreed to "erect cottages in accordance with plans approved by the Executive Committee of the Trustees."[49] White also encouraged the trustees to consider borrowing books from already established libraries in Baltimore. If that were not possible, then the board should appoint "one person using lists provided by men who know well the literature in the various arts and sciences" to go out and procure volumes. The same went for securing the latest laboratory equipment. Only in this way, White contended, could Hopkins build up a "nucleus in the way of books, collections, and apparatus to induce first-rate men in science and literature to congregate themselves about a university. And such collections will often prove more tempting than a larger salary."[50]

Attracting faculty to Baltimore was White's next area of focus. He suggested that faculty be elected to five-year professorships with "somewhat larger" salaries but that at the end of the five-year term the faculty member must stand for reappointment on a vote of the board. Citing the limitations of the annual income provided by the original endowment at Cornell, White admitted that such a structure had been "urged upon me very strongly" by Professor Agassiz. "The only reason why it was not tried was that our means did not allow it," lamented White.[51] Further (and this was included in the postscript to Thomas), White suggested an arrangement of nonresident professorships whereby subject-matter experts were brought in to deliver lectures. Such a diverse group would have a positive impact "not only on the students but also on Professors" as the visiting faculty would "come from great cities and centers of thought generally." Having this cohort of professors as part of the university community, White argued, would tend at Cornell to "break up provincialism and clannishness." Such a system "constantly infuses new life and prevents monotony and humdrum sluggishness—the bane of so many colleges."[52]

White ended his letter by apologizing "for taking so much of your time," but he took the opportunity to urge that the university hire a first-rate treasurer or business manager, "whether it be a member of the board or not." White cited this omission at Cornell and admitted that "our experience here was at first to me a very trying one for the lack of this, and the lack of it cost us more than the salary of the very best sort of man for this business." White had addressed this shortcoming by hiring "an admirable man," which resulted in savings to the institution "many times his salary."[53] (Shortly after completing the contract terms with their new president, the Hopkins trustees met formally on March 1, 1875, and elected Francis White as treasurer, authorizing him to appoint a bookkeeper "who shall, under his direction, keep full books and accounts.")[54]

Andrew White then extended to the board members a standing invitation to visit the Cornell campus. "We are still far from the realization of our ideal," he acknowledged, "but believe that we are working steadily toward it." James Carey Thomas, along with several other trustees, would take White up on his offer, traveling to Ithaca in late September not only to examine the institution carefully but also to hear directly from its head whom he thought they should hire as president.[55] The first of the troika of advisers having registered his view, they were now prepared to meet with President Eliot.

## Eliot of Harvard

An 1853 Harvard graduate in chemistry, Charles William Eliot was appointed tutor in mathematics the following year and pursued additional studies under Josiah Parsons Cooke, the chemist known for his pathbreaking work in the area of atomic weights. When he failed to secure the coveted post of Rumford Professor of Chemistry, Eliot left for Europe, where he spent two years investigating the impact of education on national life, especially in Germany. His view of Great Britain was not like Gilman's; in his view the English were "the most ignorant and uncivilized people he had ever seen, 'if you except the poor whites and slaves of the South.'"[56] Finding Germany much more to his liking, he settled in at the University of Marburg, in Hesse, to work in the laboratory of the eminent chemist Hermann Kolbe. His work in the lab, however, was secondary to his close-range observation of how a German university and a laboratory like Kolbe's were administered and how the students were treated. On visits to other universities Eliot called upon chemists whom he knew by reputation and their publications to see "what manner of men they were in the flesh."[57] Upon his return to the United States in 1865, Eliot was appointed professor of analytical chemistry at the newly founded Massachusetts Institute of Technology, where he remained until his appointment as Harvard's twenty-first president in 1869.

Eliot met with the Hopkins trustees on June 4, 1874, at the Mount Vernon Hotel.

Harvard University president Charles William Eliot, ca. 1875. (Photo courtesy of Harvard University Archives, HUP Eliot, Charles W., 22a, olvwork260224)

In his March letter to the board White had made no reference to any previous communication containing questions or topics for which the board wanted answers, leaving historians to speculate what might have been asked. This was not the case with Eliot. In his letter of invitation and introduction, Reverdy Johnson provided an initial view of his fellow trustees' orientation: "The large majority of our Board favor Harvard as the type at which we should aim in future development; though we are wise enough to admit, that for the present we must adapt ourselves to the less developed character of the field in which our operations lie."[58]

In his opening remarks, Eliot referred to this communication from Johnson and a request to address four main areas: (1) the relative "merits and advantages of the Old

System and more advanced systems of Education"; (2) the elective system; (3) "to what extent should we advance our course, looking to the defective character of our preparatory schools—and if desirable to use a special preparatory school"; and (4) "the relative advantages of the commons and dormitory system and that of the students living separate."[59]

Relative to the first point, Eliot referred the board to an article he had written for the *Atlantic Monthly* in 1869, while teaching chemistry, detailing the difficulties of effective scientific education in America.[60] Eliot had noted in the article that the challenges were not inherent "but accidental," given that many still believed the old classical method "to be superior to the modern scientific method" and that the bachelor of arts was considered more valuable than the bachelor of science. In Eliot's view, the underlying challenges stemmed from the paucity of trained and capable faculty: "There is in this country," Eliot stressed, "already, a very considerable body of teachers who know how to teach Latin and Greek, and the elements of language; but if you are in search of teachers to teach botany, chemistry, physics and so on, you cannot find them. They do not exist."[61] The lack of educators capable of teaching the scientific method resulted in a faculty "who teach science by the method appropriate for language, or by the method appropriate for mathematics." Either of these two methods, Eliot averred, was "utterly inappropriate for scientific instruction." In his *Atlantic Monthly* article, Eliot had been even more direct, maintaining that "spasmodic and ill-directed genius cannot compete in the American community with methodical, careful teaching by less inspired men." Eliot's solution held that the best conditions would be attained only "when genius warms and invigorates a wise and well-administered system."[62] The lack of trained teachers was a serious problem, and it would continue to be a problem for years to come. It was exacerbated by the lack of books. A chasm still existed between the means of instruction then available for the sciences and those resources for instruction in the ancient languages and mathematics.

Eliot mentioned the requirement of both Latin and English prior to admission to Yale's Sheffield Scientific School; at Harvard, admission required Latin, English, and either French or German. Both schools believed "that if you omit this ingredient from the preliminary education of a youth he will suffer for the lack of it all his life; and that whatever else you give him, as mathematics or elementary science, you should give him a fair training in the elements of at least two languages besides his own."[63] Observing the proliferation of scientific schools in the Northeast, Eliot urged caution so as not to "overstock the market with engineers," citing the great demand for scientific teachers. He again held up the Sheffield School as the most successful example of "one and the same institution [carrying on] the classical course and the scientific course . . . to advantage." Presaging what the trustees would observe in a few weeks' time during their visit to Yale, Eliot admitted that Professor George Brush (one of the founding trustees, along with Gilman, of the Sheffield Scientific School) had been the person responsible for building up the school. "Of course," Eliot concluded, "the President of Yale College is the head of the whole Institution but he has not taken much interest in the Sheffield Scientific School. Professor Brush is the real head of the school."[64]

At this point in the conversation with Eliot, a trustee asked about offering graduate degrees with opportunities for more specialization. Eliot seized upon this, stating that "it was about the most important matter in the education in the United States. It was the most important point of all." Eliot saw a pressing need for institutions to yield "men thoroughly instructed in something." At the time, he said, higher education was "producing an average man, a low average quality of attainment, and . . . we want to work out of that and give more attention to the special capacities and powers of individual men and carry those individual men to higher levels."[65] Further discussion about proposed graduate programs would continue throughout the exchange, but Eliot took this question as a segue into his addressing Johnson's second area of focus, the elective system.

At Harvard, Eliot summarized, once undergraduates completed a broad range of preparatory study they could "devote themselves to the one or more subjects for which they are best adapted," thus allowing the university "to develop largely the variety of instruction offered to the older students." Introducing too great a variety of subjects into a fixed four-year course, Eliot warned, would result in too little time for each subject, ultimately producing a superficial course of training. Reflecting a very traditional mid- to late nineteenth-century view, Eliot outlined what happened "before the youth is eighteen years of age" with the "best schools" doing the preparatory work in languages, mathematics, science, and history. But even with this system in place, remediation was required "to devote the greater part of our Freshman year to Latin, Greek and Mathematics, in order to perfect the foundation, a broad foundation on which we afterwards build." The second year was a mix of both required and elective courses; the third year had very few required courses; and the fourth year was entirely left to the student for specialization. "In that mode," Eliot noted, "we are breeding men who are far advanced when they graduate, in some one or perhaps two subjects. They cover with great thoroughness a certain field." Eliot then detailed the process, following the model of the more traditional colleges, whereby after a year's residence and examinations the bachelor's degree could become a master of arts. "The grade of Doctor of Philosophy is awarded after two years residence and an examination."[66] For Harvard and Eliot, this was relatively new ground, as they had awarded their first PhD in mathematics to William Elwood Byerly in 1873, one year before Eliot's meeting with the Hopkins trustees.

Next, attention was given to how the elective system at Harvard might apply to what was being proposed at Hopkins. Eliot's unvarnished view was that a comparable system in Baltimore was not possible "for the reason that the Preparatory Schools from which you would draw are not so good as those in the neighborhood of Cambridge." Eliot drilled down even more: "Young men will not come to you from abroad at first, you will have to supplement the defects of the scholars you receive from the

Preparatory schools until you can bring the scholars up to a level which suits you better."[67] Eliot admitted that he was not familiar with the condition of schools in Maryland, Virginia, North Carolina, Tennessee, and adjoining states, but this did not stop him from opining.

One trustee, George Dobbin, took great exception to Eliot's suggestion that the quality of schools was inferior in the South, not during Eliot's interview but one month later when the subject was raised in President Angell's session.[68] In Eliot's view, one of the best things the proposed university could do was "to build up and improve the School System of Maryland. . . . If you could improve the schools through the action of the university you would do a good work for a much larger number of children than you would ever bring under your direct influence."[69]

This led to the trustees' third query, relative to the establishment of a special preparatory school, which Eliot maintained "should be apart from the college and have a distinct set of teachers." He cited examples of New England institutions such as Dartmouth, Amherst, and Wesleyan, all of which had "intimate relations with academies." When pressed by a trustee about whether it would be wise for the university to publish its terms of admission and "let the academies of Baltimore and such schools as would be likely to fit young men, mould their course according to our needs," Eliot concurred that such action would indeed be wise but added that "three years is the shortest time in which preparation can be made." Eliot offered a suggestion: that the Hopkins trustees determine the prerequisites for admission and then send someone familiar with college admission examinations to make a thorough investigation into the state of preparatory schools in Maryland and the surrounding states. The university could then determine the initial standards, and "these requisitions might be constantly raised year after year."[70]

Johnson's last item for Eliot to discuss was dormitories, and the latter's exposition on this topic runs fourteen pages. Eliot, interviewed in person just a few weeks after the receipt of White's letter, focused much of his discussion on the subject of dispersing the incoming Hopkins students in private houses around campus. Eliot's statement that "the city is sure to grow out to your Estate" was based on the assumption that the new Hopkins campus would be constructed at Clifton, some three miles northeast of downtown. This, of course, did not happen; the Homewood Campus did not become operational until the School of Engineering moved there in 1914, followed by the School of Arts and Sciences in 1916. For nearly four decades the Hopkins campus was a modest collection of buildings on and around Howard Street.

The trustees' reaction to Eliot's views on dormitories was undoubtedly framed by White's immovable view of the deleterious effect of such residential facilities. Reading White's perception of the role of dormitories most certainly impacted the trustees before President Eliot met with them in person, as evidenced by the response of the Harvard president to a view expressed by one trustee in particular: "I think it possible that Judge [George] Dobbin has an exaggerated apprehension of the evils of the dormitory system."[71] Eliot's conclusion was that they had been essential in Cambridge, "and we like them." His experience, however, had run the gamut from seeing no dormitories at German universities to seeing some "quite insufficient" ones in terms of capacity for young men at Oberlin College, where "for women a large hall is provided."[72]

The trustees asked a range of questions about housing, from an inquiry about Eliot's perspective on the viability of constructing "moderately priced houses in which eight to ten students could be accommodated" to the question "how far do you undertake to supervise the morals of the Students at Harvard?"[73] Eliot's 1874 approach to in loco parentis was this: "If we find a young man is doing nothing, not studying, does not pass his examinations, we tell him and his father, after sufficient warning 'you must go away, we cannot have you here.' "[74] Harvard's position, as summarized by Eliot, was simple: "With regard to their going in and out, going to bed, going to the theatre or studying at certain hours, we exercise no supervision whatever. We believe in freedom." Recognizing that the majority of their incoming freshmen were 18- and 19-year-old young men, Eliot then went through a whole host of rules, including "students are forbidden to make a noise or throw a snowball"; "any violation of decorum on Sunday, or on a public day shall be considered an aggravated offence"; and "no undergraduate shall lodge in any house or board in any family disapproved by a vote of the Faculty."[75]

Having covered dormitories quite thoroughly, a trustee then asked Eliot about the desirability of establishing a medical school. Citing the state of medical education in nineteenth-century America, Eliot held that "medical schools everywhere in this country are exceedingly poor" and that the trustees' opportunity "for the founding of a proper medical school in this community is a very precious one." Dependent almost entirely on student fees and "the gratuitous labor of faculty" for their subsistence, Eliot maintained, the pecuniary condition of medical schools had to be addressed or else "it will be difficult to raise them out of the slough." Eliot recounted to the trustees Harvard's efforts to address the funding mechanism and to cull its medical student ranks from 300 to 170. He then noted the inherent benefits of Hopkins and its location: "You have a large fund which you may apply in part to this object. You have the whole south to draw upon, and an opportunity which any man desiring to serve his country might envy." The chemist turned president then summarized part of the examination structure: three years' residence ("not three winter sessions, but actual three years study") followed by an oral examination schedule that covered nine subject matters. If the candidate passed in the majority of the nine subjects, he was to be admitted as a doctor.[76] Clearly, such a system was not producing the best results. In a rather matter-of-fact admission, Eliot observed that the shortcomings and mistakes of an ignorant young minister or a young lawyer "are not so fatal to the community; the ignorant young doctor kills people, that is just the long and short of it." To illustrate, Eliot recalled a recent example in a town near Cambridge of a "single ignorant doctor holding a degree of a reputable college." While he had passed the examinations Eliot described, "he was grossly ignorant of *material medica* and killed three people in the period stated, with overdoses of morphine."[77]

Eliot could have cited other examples of woeful inadequacies in both faculty qualifications and students' training. One of his own faculty members, a professor of pathological anatomy, confessed in 1871 that he did not know how to use a microscope.[78] After the episode of the inappropriate dosages of morphine and resultant deaths, Eliot pushed hard for reform but met stiff resistance from an intransigent faculty. One of these faculty, Professor of Surgery Henry Bigelow, protested loudly to the Harvard Board of Overseers that Eliot "actually proposes to have written examinations for the degree of doctor of medicine. I had to tell him that he knew nothing about the quality of the Harvard medical students. More than half of them can barely write. Of course they can't pass written examinations. . . . No medical school has thought it proper to risk large existing classes and large receipts by introducing more rigorous standards."[79]

After a brief discussion of legal education and what had been attempted at Harvard, Eliot turned to what he believed should be the natural progression of developing the proposed university and recruiting its faculty. It was on the subject of faculty, perhaps more than any other, that Eliot completely failed to grasp the kind of institution the trustees and their hand-picked president envisaged.[80] This may have been no fault of Eliot's, but as the Hopkins model continued to develop, it became clear that it was entirely distinctive from what Eliot had described at Harvard and what was de rigueur in America at the time.

For Eliot and his colleagues at traditional colleges and well-established universities, graduate work was a natural continuation of undergraduate study at the same institution. In his view, the university must organize the "whole of the College course"; in other words, it should begin at the undergraduate level—which would take a minimum of five years, in Eliot's estimation—and then add selective graduate programs. Given this timeline, Eliot admonished the trustees: "The post-graduate course is a matter far off for you."[81] The trustees chose not to listen to Eliot on this point. When Hopkins opened in the fall of 1876, the model was based on the graduate course—an entirely novel approach.

Eliot's views on this subject were inextricably linked to the Harvard model, which had four sorts of teachers, starting with tutors. The recently graduated tutors were to be "men who have not only received the ordinary training of Cambridge but have also studied in England and Germany." Eliot believed that it was "dangerous to breed in and at universities" and that the university should "add the training of other institutions whenever you can."[82] When asked by a trustee what the duties of the tutors were, Eliot outlined the Harvard faculty structure, which progressed from tutor (three-year appointment) to assistant professor (five-year appointment) to full professor (appointment for life). "We have no retiring age and no retiring compensation," Eliot stressed. "We expect to pay our professors as long as they live when we have once accepted them, but we try to be sure of the man before we appoint them."[83] The fourth category was instructors, equivalent to modern-day adjunct faculty. "For provisional, temporary or exceptional work, instructorships are convenient; there is no regular salary for this grade," Eliot concluded.[84]

Next Eliot described the examination process at Harvard before moving on to fellowships. In his opinion, "post-graduate fellowships which give a complete support to the incumbent are of doubtful utility unless rigidly guarded and vigilantly watched." Harvard leaned more toward need-based aid than toward the British practice of making awards according to scholastic merit. White's advice, it should be remembered, was for the board to establish "ten or twenty" fellowships—a wholly innovative idea. If such a system had been in place before the Civil War, efforts to develop graduate work in America might have had very different results.[85] The Hopkins trustees would follow the advice proffered by White, thus initiating an entirely unique approach to attracting postgraduate students to Baltimore and then allowing them to specialize within their chosen disciplines.

A trustee then directed questions to Eliot on how to select a president and at what salary. Eliot's advice was to find "a young man, bred in the profession . . . somebody who thoroughly understands this community. . . . He need not necessarily be an instructor. . . . He should be at least thirty-five years of age." Eliot offered his own salary as a benchmark ($5,000 and the use of a house and stable) but also encouraged the board to consider the "salaries of the Judges of the Courts of the City of Baltimore" as well as those of "the ministers of influential churches."[86] When pressed as to how to avoid exposing themselves "to a flood of applications from incompetent persons," Eliot suggested that the trustees go directly to those institutions from which they would be willing to take a president (his list included Columbia, Harvard, and Dartmouth, among others) and bring that individual before the board "to see that person and hear him talk."[87] This was exactly what the trustees would do.

Brief discussion of tuition and fees and the cost of building construction marked the latter part of Eliot's presentation (which began at 4:30 p.m. and lasted until nearly midnight), which also included a description of Harvard's book holdings and how it had built a collection of 150,000 volumes in its main library, with an additional 50,000 volumes in the specialty libraries of "divinity, law science and medicine." Eliot's advice was that "judicious buying for a great library must be the work of many persons."[88] Relative to overall campus facilities, Eliot was succinct: "In the construction of the buildings care should be taken to guard against conflagration. The libraries should be absolutely fireproof."[89]

In response to a question from a trustee relative to Columbia College, Eliot noted the difficulty, at least from his perspective, of locating a university in a large metropolitan area, citing the nation's two largest urban areas in the 1870s and their respective universities, New York City (Columbia) and Philadelphia (the University of Pennsylvania). At the time, Baltimore was among America's largest cities, with a population approaching three hundred thousand. "I think a good deal depends upon the atmosphere in which the institution is planted," opined Eliot. "I mean the intellectual and moral atmosphere. New York City is as hard a place as you can imagine in which to maintain a university. Absorbed in business on the one hand and pleasure on the other, and too heterogeneous for the efficient action of the best public opinion, the city hardly gives standing room for an institution of learning."[90]

The final question from a trustee focused on the admission of women. Throughout this exchange about coeducation at American universities, Eliot demonstrated that he stood, ultimately, on the wrong side of history. "As to the co-education of the sexes," Eliot began, "I am not a believer in that doctrine. It seems to me a thoroughly wrong idea which is rapidly disappearing, but there are those who think it all important." Eliot then cited the experience of various institutions: Boston University ("admits women into all its departments"); Oberlin ("young men and women have always been taught together"); and Cornell ("they are just introducing this system"). Eliot concluded that coeducation of the sexes would "work very well in any community which is very homogeneous, where there are no diversities of pecuniary condition, and where the standard of scholarship is low."[91] Not willing to leave it there, Eliot ended with this flourish: "In short, not to go into long explanations, I believe what is called the co-education of the sexes is not possible in highly civilized communities; and that it is contrary to the natural instincts of most persons, whether male or female who are at once vigorous and refined."[92]

When asked how best to educate women, Eliot maintained that "co-education of the sexes is on the wane; of this I am perfectly certain." Buttressing his argument, Eliot provided examples of successful institutions created especially for females: Vassar College at Poughkeepsie and Wells College at Aurora, just north of Cornell. "The creation of separate places for the higher education of women is to my mind both wise and just," Eliot concluded.[93] The exchanges with the three advisers show that the Hopkins trustees were divided on coeducation. But the university ultimately followed Eliot's advice on this score, and as a consequence, women wouldn't be admitted to Johns Hopkins as undergraduates for nearly a century.

## Angell of Michigan

A native of Rhode Island, graduate of Brown University, and former president of the University of Vermont, James Burrill Angell was appointed president of the University of Michigan at the age of 42. He is hailed as the father of the modern public state university. Angell's thirty-eight-year tenure in Ann Arbor was groundbreaking in many ways, but he might be best known for a statement that has been cited by his successors to this day: the University of Michigan's primary purpose, he said, was "to provide an uncommon education for the common man."[94]

When contacted by Reverdy Johnson in April 1874 about meeting with the Hopkins board, Angell responded, "While I do not think that a visit from me could be of much service to your Committee, still, as a College Man, I should be willing to do anything I well could by meeting them in Baltimore or elsewhere." "As to remuneration," he told Johnson, "I should be unwilling to receive anything beyond my expenses, unless possibly the expenses of my wife should be included, if she should

University of Michigan president James Burrill Angell, 1903. (Photo courtesy of University Archives, Sheridan Libraries, Johns Hopkins University)

choose to accompany me. She used to spend much time in Baltimore with friends."[95] Angell ended up making the trip from Ann Arbor to Baltimore by himself—more than four hundred miles each way—and submitted a simple note requesting reimbursement for his train ticket: $110.52.[96] Other communications were exchanged between Johnson and Angell before the in-person meeting. Parts of Hopkins' will were shared with all three advisers. Angell responded, "Nothing, it seems to me, could be more timely than this splendid provision for higher education in your state, which with her unsurpassed natural advantages and her brilliant destiny has yet lacked a first-rate college or university." Angell further insisted that the trustees should begin with a plan sufficiently large and flexible "to allow for the inauguration of a college, a Polytechnic School, a Law School, and a Medical School. Your situation invites and requires all these."[97]

Angell met with the board of trustees on July 3, 1874.[98] He began by repeating an observation he had made to Johnson earlier, that "with your fund, you might be able to develop a plan looking to the largest work that any of our institutions now have. It seemed to me your plan should contemplate that as an ultimate object." Angell urged caution, allowing plans to develop as the institution progressed: "You will find the work growing upon your hands. I have known some Institutions to err from being obliged, by their announcements, to begin work before they were quite ready, and a little delay now is of consequence in the history of your institutions, in making no mistake in your organization."[99]

Judge George Dobbin was the first to ask a question. It is clear that he was still agitated about President Eliot's assessment of local schools and the quality of education one might find in and around Baltimore. "We have here very respectable Common Schools," Dobbin asserted. "We have in this City a system of Public Schools not surpassed anywhere. They are extensively patronized and adequately supported. The teaching is respectable, and is growing better, and we are now about building a City College."[100] Dobbin's question suggests that some trustees feared being criticized for founding a weak college.[101] At its core, therefore, Dobbin's query had to do with the "ultimate aim of our institution" and what Johns Hopkins intended to be: "If we propose to have a large, populous Institution, where a great number will get an education, it will be different from that intended to cultivate only high scholars." Angell understood what Dobbin was asking and advised that "at the outset you do not take so high a start as to break your connection with your constituency." Even if their numbers were initially low, Angell favored "starting with a high purpose." In keeping with the "rising tide raises all boats" axiom, Angell maintained that the character of schools throughout Maryland would benefit from such a course: "The elevating power of such an Institution over all the Schools within its influence is very great."[102]

Angell explained that he had walked about Baltimore before their meeting and seen a "great mechanical, industrial, and manufacturing interest here"; he then stressed the importance of the practical applications to sciences and arts. In considering what form this model might take, Angell emphasized the importance of having "The Literary" at the center. Judge Dobbin then asked how they should begin—"with a general plan, or take it up, branch by branch a part, each in succession?" Angell suggested beginning incrementally with more than one course of study based on demand, with both a "classical department" and an element of the "scientific school" from the outset.[103]

In one of the most interesting exchanges, Angell described his student body at Michigan, which contrasted sharply with students at Cornell and Harvard, even with prospective students at Hopkins: "A very large proportion of our students are boys who work their way, who grow up on a farm, teach school—earn a little money this way and that, then take a college course. Many of these young men look for Civil Engineering, which is more attractive to them than other pursuits." There was still demand at Michigan for the more classical curricula, however: nearly half of the recent graduating class of seventy-four students had pursued a full Latin and Greek course.[104] Angell emphasized the importance of developing close relationships with the preparatory schools throughout Michigan, telling the trustees that they should not establish their own school, which would only "awaken the jealousy and opposition" on the part of other schools throughout Maryland.[105]

When the topic of dormitories was raised, Angell recounted that two large halls had been constructed before his tenure but that students had overrun them. The administration was faced with the decision whether to construct new dormitories or "turn the students into the town." They opted for the latter, with students flooding the local houses: "No family has more than eight or ten students at a time. Almost everybody takes one or two." When asked about discipline, Angell noted that the students "never forget that they are citizens of the community. We allow the police to arrest them and send them to jail, if necessary, and are glad to have them do so."[106]

Johnson had taken Angell on a tour of Clifton, again based on the assumption that the campus would be built on the former Hopkins home site. "If, with the advantages of the ground which you now have, you could attract persons, who could build houses enough to provide in part or in whole for the students, it would be better still. The population now in the vicinity of the estate is not so desirable as I could wish."[107] One might assume that Angell was suggesting Johns Hopkins erect its own dormitories and tolerate them as a necessary evil, given the dearth of other housing options in and around Clifton.[108] Noting that the university site in Ann Arbor was forty acres and that Hopkins had more than three hundred at Clifton, another trustee, James Carey Thomas, asked what an ideal plot of land would encompass. Angell said a one-hundred-acre parcel would be sufficient.

The next topic was coeducation of the sexes. Angell began by stating that the system in Michigan had been in effect for four years and "was forced on the Institution by public opinion," having "originated in the Public Schools, most of them located in Detroit."[109] Angell cited the "custom in the West to educate boys and girls together" and noted that Methodist colleges, such as Oberlin (which admitted women in 1837—the first in America to do so), had been doing so for years. Only in the clinical schools were ladies taught separately, and Angell was pleased overall with the coeducational arrangement: "I think, so far as we are concerned, there has been no practical embarrassment arising out of the system." Johnson then asked, "Do these boys and girls sit in classes indiscriminately?" Angell's response hinted at the vestiges of a sectarian eastern college that lived on at a new western university: "In the chapel the students sit by classes. The front seats are occupied by the girls, who sit together."[110]

A trustee then asked Angell how professors were appointed. Angell responded that it was on a one-year basis, since "it is impossible to tell until a man is tried" whether he is suited to teaching. If, after that trial period, the instructor was not a successful teacher, "he will be at liberty to withdraw at the end of the year. . . . Almost any honorable man is willing to put himself in that position." To Judge Dobbin's question "what class of people" the members of the board of regents were, Angell responded that they were "a better class than you would suppose, being elected by the people" to eight-year terms, meeting quarterly, and only having their expenses paid. "The position is considered very honorable," Angell concluded. "The parties seem to have felt the responsibility of putting in respectable men, who have held responsible positions and are men of weight and character."[111]

Angell also addressed—and he was the only one to do so—without a prompt from any of the trustees the issue of hazing. He gave as an example "pumping" freshmen, or dousing them with cold water. Apparently, this form of hazing—almost a type of college sport—had become extremely popular. The activity had become such a nuisance that the faculty attempted to end it with swift, forceful action, suspending three freshmen and three sophomores.[112] Protests ensued, with other students admitting their guilt as a show of support for their accused classmates. In all, eighty-one students were dismissed for the remainder of the year, resulting in a great deal of publicity for the university and its president. Angell admitted "receiving letters from a number of Presidents of Colleges about our treatment of the case, though we had no idea of becoming famous."[113]

The penultimate issue Angell addressed included a stern warning to the trustees about college newspapers published by students: "It would be well to keep your eye on these in the beginning. . . . These papers now take the high function of informing us how our Institutions should be administered." They seemed to be proliferating, Angell bemoaned, "in every college in this country. . . . We all feel that they are a nuisance in many respects. You can easily see that the time of some of the best students is absorbed there which might be spent more profitably in study."[114]

Finally, Angell spoke about denominational matters, confessing that he personally conducted the voluntary morning chapel session, which had been instituted upon his arrival at Michigan. Students opened the service with song, "and they sing admirably," he observed. A scriptural passage was then read, followed by "an extempore prayer," and the service was always closed with the Lord's Prayer. The same went for Sunday services, held both in the chapel and in the hall. Attendance was entirely voluntary, with ministers and members of the faculty conducting the services. Student attendance was "from two-thirds to three-quarters. As examinations approach, the attendance falls off considerably." Angell added that an interdenominational Young Men's Christian Association (YMCA) had been organized and was highly subscribed.[115]

With that, the trustees concluded the last in-person session. They had a trove of testimony from three sitting presidents on how best to structure their new enterprise.

## The Advisers Suggest a President

Not wanting to miss the opportunity to meet Andrew White in person, members of the board visited Cornell at the president's invitation in September 1874, making stops in Cambridge and New Haven on the way. The day of their visit, White sat down to recount his impressions in a letter to Gilman: "We have here today the Johns

Hopkins Trustees—eight or ten of them, and they have made a very thorough inspection, having first visited Harvard and Yale. They seem to be a very fine body of men—men of cultivation and gentlemen. They go from here to Ann Arbor, and will make I suppose an inspection of other institutions in the West."[116] White also conveyed to Gilman the trustees' thoughts on Yale and made a point to note President Porter's "reticence in regard to the scientific department and scientific studies," mentioning further the trustees' surprise "that none of them were invited to attend a lecture or recitation" while on campus.[117]

White would add his endorsement of Gilman's emerging candidacy at Hopkins in his letter: "Between ourselves, I think that you are to be called there, for I find that Elliot [*sic*], Porter and myself thoroughly agreed upon you as the man to organize the Institution for them."[118]

During the trustees' tour of Cornell, White was asked to communicate publicly to the entire group what he had conveyed to two or three of them privately regarding Gilman. It happened that White's remarks endorsing his longtime friend took place on the steps of Sibley Hall. In his letter, White reminded Gilman of a prior experience on that very spot in June 1871: Gilman, then still at Yale's Sheffield Scientific School and just a year shy of being named president of the University of California, had been invited to speak at the dedication of the hall, which housed Cornell's School of Mechanical Engineering, on the study of scientific disciplines in American colleges and universities.[119]

White wrote Gilman that from questions asked by the trustees following the endorsement of his friend's candidacy, "I judge that your organizing faculty, your knowledge of educational matters at home and abroad, your catholicity in regards to all departments of knowledge and your liberal orthodoxy in religious matters gives them a great deal of confidence in you. I think that before you are much older you will hear from them. I told them that you would require nothing in the way of absolute power but a great deal of liberty of action." White closed his report to Gilman by saying, "Of course, this is confidential. Let me hear from you, and let me know how the year opens in California."[120] Gilman would indeed discreetly keep his friend apprised of developments. And just as White had predicted, Gilman would hear from the Hopkins trustees within a few weeks' time.

Although the question was never posed during the in-person meetings, Reverdy Johnson wrote to each of the three advisers asking whom they might consider to preside over such a new university. The same question was asked of Porter during the trustees' visit to Yale. To a man, they recommended Daniel Coit Gilman.

# CHAPTER FOUR

# Gilman the Recruiter

After their respective experiences with the Hopkins trustees in the summer of 1874, both Andrew White and Charles Eliot reached out to Gilman to describe their impressions and to offer advice. White wrote Gilman that he should give the upstart university careful consideration, although doing so would thwart White's succession plan at Cornell: "Your doing it [going to Hopkins] would break down one of my most desirable hopes—the hope of having you carry on my work to greater heights here."[1] Eliot was even more direct, writing, "Don't you want to go to Baltimore and start the Johns Hopkins University there? 300 acres of land within 2½ miles of the heart of Baltimore, $3,500,000, personal property which cannot be encroached upon, and a good board of private trustees. They wanted some advice from me last month and I went there to look into their affairs a little. I should say that the chance of doing a useful work was a good one."[2] Both men hinted at what Gilman might hear from the Hopkins trustees shortly. The back and forth between Gilman and Reverdy Johnson led to the former taking yet another transcontinental trip to investigate the Baltimore possibilities in person.

The meeting between Gilman and the Johns Hopkins University Board of Trustees was set for December 29, 1874, in the Bible House, at 25 North Charles Street. Recollecting the experience of meeting the entire group for the first time, Gilman noted that the board was a "very sedate, perhaps they might be called a very solemn, body."[3] These were serious men focused on serious work. After each trustee was afforded the opportunity to speak, Gilman was called upon to give "his impressions of the situation." Writing in the third person after the interview, Gilman recorded that he was not interested in establishing "another college, or to aim only at local benefits," but that if the board "would seize the opportunity to establish a university which should extend its influence far and wide, throughout the land, it would be a privilege, as well as an honor, to be associated in the work; without regard to their political, sectional, or ecclesiastical belongings, the best professors should be brought together, and the most advanced students should be invited to follow their instructions." The trustees heartily responded to this bold vision, and in a meeting the next day, "when the candidate was not present, they chose him to be their leader."[4]

About meeting the trustees in person, Gilman was very circumspect in what he said and to whom. But in a letter sent to his sister Louise back in Berkeley, Gilman confessed, "I have fallen into the hands of the most excellent persons—intelligent, sensible, cautious, cooperative. . . . They unanimously invite me to come, and I think I shall accept; but I keep back the formal words until I can confer with the Californians."[5] The meeting had gone swimmingly, and the trustees proceeded straightaway, voting on December 30 to tender the presidency to Gilman. Reverdy Johnson was authorized to transmit the official offer letter to Gilman. Dated January 4, 1875, it stated that the communication was "mere formality" following the "recent full and satisfactory interview between yourself and our Board." Johnson outlined a base salary of eight thousand dollars (seven thousand dollars once a proper home was supplied)[6] and this charge: "With entire confidence in your ability and energy in developing those purposes, we invite you as our leader and guide."[7]

The subsequent correspondence between Gilman and Johnson reveals some of the issues percolating throughout the Baltimore community. Upon his arrival in California in 1872, Gilman had been caught unawares by the deep-seated issues and debates that would eventually unsettle his presidency and cut short his tenure. He was determined not to let that experience repeat itself. While the issues were entirely different in nature and origin, there is no doubt that Gilman discussed circumstances in Maryland with the Hopkins board. Johnson followed up the offer letter with another communication the same day, under separate cover, alerting Gilman to some of the strong feelings on the part of many on both sides as a result of the Civil War and Baltimore's position throughout the conflict. Johnson explained that sensitiveness remained "even to this day . . . namely, the absence of all sectarian bias, and of political spirit on the part of the President of the University."[8] The trustees—and Gilman—had to strike a delicate balance.

Even those attempting to help the South recover after the war, such as George Peabody, did not escape criticism from ardent abolitionists bent on making the southern states pay for their role in America's costliest conflict. Maryland was a border state and never seceded, but this did not dissuade some from full-throated condemnations of the state and its citizens. Referring to the establishment of the institute that would bear Peabody's name, William Lloyd Garrison roundly criticized Peabody for his gift "made to a Maryland institution, at a time when the state was rotten with treason."[9] Peabody had attempted a public defense earlier, stating: "I wish publicly to avow, that during the terrible conflict through which our nation has passed, my sympathies are still and always were with the Union."[10] It was evident that feelings were still raw and exposed nearly a decade after Appomattox, and Gilman would make clear his ecumenical position on this and other issues in subsequent transmissions to the board. Johnson's communications with Gilman reveal Johnson's attempts to try and inoculate the new president against the inevitable charges that the board had brought a Connecticut "Yankee" into a southern state like Maryland.

The South was still very much in the throes of Reconstruction in 1875, and Johnson was direct in his counsel to Gilman: "In coming into this community from a different section of the land, our President should enter cordially and with sympathy, into relations with those who, as individuals or communities, occupied a position hostile to those of his own native section." Relative to the latter point, Johnson invited Gilman to express himself in the "broadest and most emphatic sense in unison with the sentiment of the Board," promising that he would be happy to convey to the rest of the trustees what Gilman shared with him.[11] It then fell to Gilman to transmit his answer, which he did in a letter dated January 30, 1875, sent from Oakland: "Deeply sensible to the responsibilities I am to assume and confidently relying on the wisdom of your counsels and the certainty of your devotion to the trust, I accept your invitation and will enter upon your service as soon as arrangement can be made to relieve me from my present duties. I have reason to hope that this will be at an early day." He concluded his acceptance letter with an assurance "that the Johns Hopkins University shall be forever free from sectarian bias and from political partisanships, and that all its resources shall be consecrated to the advancement of knowledge and the promotion of Christian civilization."[12]

## "My Most Zealous Cooperation"

Just as Johnson had done with his second letter, Gilman wrote a reply—this time addressed to Johnson in his role as chair of the executive committee—the same day, also under separate cover, detailing his views relative to the two issues Johnson had raised. In a succinct and articulate response, Gilman provided his unvarnished perspective on what constituted a university and his unwavering commitment to academic freedom:

> The institution we are about to organize would not be worthy the name of a University if it were to be devoted to any other purpose than the discovery and promulgation of the truth; and it would be ignoble in the extreme if the resources which have been given by the Founder without restrictions should be limited to the maintenance of ecclesiastical differences or perverted to the promotion of political strife. As the spirit of the University should be that of intellectual freedom in the pursuit of truth and of the broadest charity toward those from whom we differ in opinion

it is certain that sectarian and partisan preferences should have no control in the selection of teachers, and should not be apparent in their official work.[13]

In anticipation of hiring the faculty, Gilman pledged to choose those "so catholic in spirit, so learned as to what has been discovered and so keen to explore new fields of research, so skillful as teachers, so cooperative as builders, and so comprehensive in the specialties to which they are devoted,—that pupils will flock to their instruction, first from Maryland and the states near to it,—but soon also from the remotest parts of the land." Gilman closed by promising "that in seeking this result the Board may rely on my most zealous cooperation."[14]

Communications between Johnson and Gilman during this interval reveal a delay in responses because the mail was unpredictable, resulting in uncertainty on the part of the new president about his standing with his future employer. Johnson had written a letter dated February 12, 1875, reporting to Gilman that his acceptance of the position had been communicated to the board. However, the letter did not arrive until weeks later. When it did, Gilman responded with obvious relief: "I am glad to feel that the matter is settled, for were the question open, I should find it almost impossible to break away from this place. Indeed, if I had foreseen, two months ago, what earnest remonstrations should be made against my leaving by the Regents, the Faculty, and the students, I do not think I could have resisted their request to remain here."[15] Indeed, the expressions toward Gilman upon learning of his imminent departure had been so generous and effusive—from every constituent group—that he may have experienced some second thoughts, given what he could reasonably expect in the future at Berkeley compared with the complete unknown at Baltimore.

Not that Gilman was experiencing serious buyer's remorse, but additional issues began to present themselves to the president-elect. One in particular was the sine qua non for him and the new institution: what exactly was to be the core mission of the university? Gilman wrote to Johnson,

> I refer to the possibility of building up in Baltimore an institution of *national* influence. The more I reflect upon the remarks which were made by the various members of your Board, the more do I rejoice that the gift has fallen into the hands of such enlightened men and the more confident I am that their administration of the trust will be marked by wisdom and prudence and by a liberal determination to advance the highest educational welfare of the country. I should like to show you the letters which are pouring in upon me, from far and near, expressions of interest and confidence in the Baltimore foundation.[16]

At this same time, letters not so complimentary of Gilman's educational philosophy or his tenure at Berkeley started to reach the Hopkins trustees from the Grangers, accompanied by clippings from California newspapers. Johnson informed Gilman of the deluge of mail, to which Gilman responded from his office in California, "I am not surprised that you are favored with Granger squibs. Here they are utterly empty, because they are well known to emanate from those 'eliminated' professors and their immediate belongings, aching through the prejudices of the Grangers and the columns of a communist newspaper. I have never directly nor indirectly answered one of these attacks because the Faculty, the Regents, the students and the Parents have stood so united, and because the best of all answers is the very remarkable progress of the University during the last two years."[17] Gilman encouraged the trustees to seek the opinions of California governors (past and present), members of the board of regents, or even the parents of students if they had further questions or concerns.

Johnson reassured Gilman that Maryland had no Grangers, but the national stature and elemental character of the university—and its relation to the local community— would prove to be a persistent point of debate (and some notable division) among the board. At one end of the spectrum were the views espoused by John Work Garrett, particularly his belief that Johns Hopkins himself (whom he knew better than any other board member) wanted the university to be focused primarily on Baltimore residents and their endemic issues, especially relating to vocational and practical pursuits. Because Mr. Hopkins had not been formally educated, Garrett contended that the university bearing his friend's name should be oriented toward the local students and applied subjects, and less concerned with building a national reputation. Garrett's view was not supported by a majority of the board, but this particular disagreement would not be the last time a position taken by his fellow trustees provoked the anger of the railroad magnate.[18]

If John Work Garrett purported to represent Johns Hopkins' implicit desires for his namesake university, George Brown, another trustee, strenuously argued the opposite view. Brown described what he believed the primary purpose of the university (and higher education as a whole) should be: "To bring together a competent corps of professors, some of whom, if possible, should be teachers in the largest sense, that is, should have the ability and the leisure too, to add something by their writings and discoveries to the world's stock of literature and science."[19] This particular observation was made five years before Gilman arrived in Baltimore, and history shows that Brown's belief in the potential of the Johns Hopkins University to take its place among the most prominent institutions on the national and international stage would carry the day. Brown's persistent and unyielding commitment to creating a unique, radically innovative university enabled Gilman to propose his initial plan. And while Hopkins' first president most assuredly deserves high praise for creating America's first research-oriented university, he must certainly share some of that credit with George Brown.[20]

## The "Plan of Procedure"

Always eager to learn as much as he could from whomever he might consult, Gilman wrote to M. Dwight Collier, a Yale-trained attorney, about his plans to stop in St. Louis en route to Baltimore, and Collier graciously replied offering to host Gilman at his home.[21] Eager to investigate what the Hegelians had done in advocating new educational ideas, Gilman met with William Torrey Harris, then serving as superintendent of the St. Louis public schools and editor of the *Journal of Speculative Philosophy* (Harris would also serve as US commissioner of education), and William Greenleaf Eliot, cofounder and the first chancellor of Washington University and grandfather of T. S. Eliot.

Gilman arrived in Baltimore on May 10, 1875, and shortly thereafter received a letter from one of his closest work associates and the first director of the Sheffield Scientific School at Yale, Professor George J. Brush: "All hail Mr. President. May health and strength be given you as twenty years of solid successful work on the Johns Hopkins foundation!"[22] Brush would be shy by only five years in his salutation, as Gilman would helm Hopkins for a quarter century. Gilman too was a man in demand, as his reputation and his experience made him a sought-after speaker even during this presidential transition. Just a few days after arriving in the East, his good friend William Watts Folwell, the first president of the University of Minnesota, invited Gilman to Minneapolis to address the graduating seniors. But owing to the incessant demands on his time and attention, Gilman had to respectfully decline his friend's offer.[23]

The work commenced immediately for Gilman, as the trustees had arranged for numerous social events for the new president, plus visits to the Baltimore City College, the State Normal School, the local high schools for girls, and the Peabody Institute. Another central question was something quite basic: where would classes be held? The board had discussed with the three presidential advisers various proposals for using the sprawling Clifton property, but they were on such a scale as to be impossible, at least in the short term. So the trustees decided to begin "the organization and practical operation" of the university in downtown Baltimore while proper facilities were designed and constructed at the former Hopkins estate. Two attached dwellings were purchased just north of the new Baltimore City College on Howard Street; these "temporary" structures would prove to be much more permanent, housing university functions well into the twentieth century. Also established was the Committee on Organization, made up of trustees Dobbin, Johnson, and Thomas. This group deferred many decisions until Gilman arrived, but they did settle upon a firm date for opening the university to students: fall 1876. They had just over a year to put everything in place and make the university operational.

In reflecting on the development of the Hopkins plan, Gilman noted just how novel their approach was. "We did not undertake to establish a German university, nor an English university, but an American university, based upon and applied to the existing institutions of this country. Not only did we have no model to be followed; we did not even draw up a scheme or programme for the government of ourselves, our associates and successors."[24] Having no formal bylaws, Gilman and the three trustees devised an initial blueprint for the university and its primary functions; this template would serve as a road map from the university's inception. Gilman, its principal author, presented the outline to the board at its May 27, 1875, meeting. The elements of the "Plan of Procedure" were as follows:

Instruction was to be given in the buildings on Howard Street recently purchased by the trustees, but this was "regarded as only a temporary arrangement until plans can be formed for the permanent buildings of the University." Other events would take place in September (such as Professor Huxley's much-celebrated speech), but actual instruction was to begin in October 1876.

The organization of the departments of medicine and law was to be postponed. Attention was to be directed "to the departments of literature and science." No portion of the corpus of the Hopkins endowment could be used for buildings, so the trustees established a Reserved Accumulating Fund, in which unappropriated revenue could be deposited and then deployed for capital improvements. The literary and scientific classes were to proceed gradually, and outlays for instructional costs were set and budgets appropriated for three academic years: $60,000 for 1876–77, $75,000 for 1877–78 and 1878–79; and $90,000 for 1879–80. These were generous amounts, and the proposed salaries for Hopkins faculty were above the national averages. Prospective faculty were to be presented to the committee, which in turn was to "report to the Board, next autumn, the names of such persons as they recommend for appointment." The recruitment of the original six faculty would prove to be a tremendous undertaking and require a significant investment of time and energy on the part of both the president and the board.

The committee was to consider the appointment of three classes of teachers and devise their own nomenclature. "Class I" was made up of permanent professors, "on whom shall rest the chief responsibility of instruction and government, and who will be expected to give to the University their time and strength. . . . Among the number should be some who can be especially helpful in the organization of the University, and in influencing the character of young men." "Class II" comprised "Professors and Lecturers, resident or non-resident in Baltimore, who will give but a limited amount of time and service to this University, and who will not be expected to take part in the administrative work. . . . Professors in other colleges may thus be called to the Johns Hopkins University for a portion of the year, and possibly men from other lands." And "Class III" was made up of "Adjuncts and Assistants, who will be usually appointed for periods varying from one to five years. . . . The efforts should be made to secure young men of ability and promise from whom the staff of permanent teachers may be in time reinforced."

Reflecting Johnson's concern about the delicate political issues a decade after the Civil War, a section titled "Sectarian and Political Tests" included the following: "In the appointment of the Faculty care shall be taken to avoid sectarian and political influences, and the effort shall be made to bring together a staff of teachers who are known and esteemed in different parts of the country."

Academic departments included Ancient Languages (Greek, Latin, and comparative philology); Modern Languages (English, French, German, Spanish, Italian, etc.);

Mathematics (pure and applied); Physical Sciences (chemistry and physics); Natural Sciences (geology, mineralogy, zoology, and botany); and Moral and Historical Sciences (ethics, political economy, history, international and public law).

Students had to be at least 15 years of age and show that they were "proficient in those preliminary studies required for admission to the best colleges and schools of science in the country."

Examinations for degrees "shall be strict and comprehensive." The bachelor of arts degree was to be given for proficiency in classical studies, and the bachelor of philosophy for proficiency in scientific studies (later changed to the BA as well). The second degree, a master of arts and doctor of philosophy, "shall be given on examination only, at an interval of at least two years subsequent to the first degree."

In an effort to extend the benefit of Hopkins "to distant parts of the land," graduates of other colleges would be allowed to attend, "with or without reference to professional work or to the taking of a second degree." It was also believed that many residents of Baltimore would surely be "glad to avail themselves of such opportunities." Finally, scholarships—as specified explicitly by Johns Hopkins in his cursory instructions to the university trustees—"shall exempt the holder from any charge for tuition."

While the final sections of this Gilman-authored "Plan of Procedure" specify provisions for undergraduate study, it is also abundantly evident that Gilman and the committee placed a substantial emphasis on graduate education.[25] This would be the distinguishing characteristic of the university. Gilman, Brown, and most of the other trustees refused to be parochial in their vision. They clearly wanted an institution whose reach extended well beyond Baltimore, one that would become a university of national and international influence.

The broad strokes of the original framework provided both Gilman and the board the latitude they needed as they turned to faculty recruitment. This task fell squarely on Gilman. "I was encouraged to travel freely at home and abroad," the new president wrote. And travel he did, first along the Eastern Seaboard, followed by an extended period visiting campuses and potential faculty throughout the United Kingdom—in Oxford, Cambridge, Glasgow, Dublin, and Manchester. He combined these visits with extended European stops as well—Paris, Berlin, Heidelberg, Strasbourg, Freiburg, Leipzig, Munich, and Vienna.[26]

## Recruiting the Six Faculty Who Built Hopkins

A portion of Gilman's 1872 inaugural speech in California bears repeating, as it explains his view of the faculty's role within the university: "It is on the Faculty more than on any other body that the building of a university depends. They give their lives to the work. It is not the site, nor the apparatus, nor the halls, nor the library, nor the Board of Regents, which draws the scholars—it is a body of living teachers, skilled in their specialties, eminent in their calling, loving to teach. Such a body of teachers will make a university anywhere."[27] In the intervening years Gilman's opinion had not wavered, and he now began the process of recruiting faculty to Baltimore with this immutable belief firmly in place.

From the outset of his recruiting efforts, Gilman faced dual dilemmas: first, a large number of candidates had been suggested by the trustees, but few of them had distinguished themselves as investigators or teachers.[28] Even the board grew weary of the incessant importuning by people, especially former officers of the Confederate army, who had heard that the trustees favored "Southern men" only to be told that the university was more inclined to "New Englandism."[29] At a meeting of the board's executive committee in early April 1876, Gilman presented the application materials for 198 candidates.[30] To their credit, the board embraced Gilman's primary criterion for prospective faculty, which was that they had produced original work. And true to their word, the trustees "kept themselves aloof from all dangerous entanglements, and were determined to make their selections with sole regard to the welfare of the University."[31] The trustees would have to ratify all of Gilman's faculty recommendations, but the task of bringing them forward was the singular responsibility of the president.

Gilman had in mind exactly the kind of faculty he wanted, and now he realized the monumental task before him of personally enlisting these men in the new endeavor. In the dedication of Sibley Hall at Cornell University in 1871, Gilman had warned that a dearth of qualified faculty did not bode well for the future of higher education. Gilman argued that American universities should make primary research and investigations a priority. "Professors should not be so engrossed by class-room duties, or so fettered in their domestic economy that they have no time for original work," Gilman advised. "Again it should be remembered that the supply of first rate men of science, fitted either to investigate or to teach is limited. This is true abroad and at home."[32]

The pool of qualified candidates was not as deep as Gilman had hoped. Compounding the challenge was the press to get these faculty in place before the university's opening in just over a year. Gilman was prepared to scour the United States and Europe to assemble just the group he desired. While keen on finding professors who were good teachers, Gilman was particularly intent on landing faculty who had demonstrated primary-research ability and could attract students advanced enough to propel the faculty to do their best work. In turn, the results—in keeping with Gilman's maxim that one of the university's "noblest duties" was not only to advance knowledge by means of lectures on campus but to diffuse it "far and wide"—would be manifested in the form of published results.[33]

A second challenge for Gilman was that his original proposal had predicted $155,000 per year for instruction at the outset, hoping for four professors at $6,000 each and twenty other faculty positions with salaries between $4,000 and $5,000. These proposed compensation levels were higher than other institutions were paying and Gilman was afforded latitude to make adjustments throughout the recruitment process to land the professors he wanted. Actual budgets, however, necessitated his settling for instruction costs of $60,000 in the first year, with incremental increases of $15,000 the next two years.[34]

Gilman wasted no time in launching his efforts. Writing in the *North American Review* a few years after his trip to Europe, Gilman made allowance for the different kinds of faculty necessary to construct Hopkins and the role of the preeminent researcher in the new kind of institution:

> It is clear that, while universities require as professors many good teachers, they also afford careers for minds of a different order. Men who have no skill in training youthful students, who have no sympathy with their difficulties and no patience in the requisite routine of collegiate instruction, may yet be most serviceable in the prosecution of scientific research, and very capable of giving aid to those who are already strong enough to walk alone. There is a sense in which it is true that the best of all teachers is the original investigator. His methods are not adapted to beginners. His followers may be few. But if his mind is endowed with rare qualities which have been assiduously cultivated under favorable circumstances, he will exert a powerful influence upon those who are able to follow him; he will incite his fellow teachers to constant activity; he will draw around him other superior minds; he will bring enduring renown to the university of which he is a member.[35]

If Gilman's objective was to recruit faculty who would bring renown to the university, the first six were a superb selection, and his efforts in personally hiring the founding core are of particular note. They were a talented and eclectic group: three Englishmen and three Americans, the first of whom was a homegrown talent discovered in Hopkins' backyard.[36]

Getting them all to Baltimore within a very constricted window of time was an accomplishment in and of itself. Writing years after the "anxieties and perplexities" of the recruitment process, Gilman recalled, with a nod to William Wordsworth, "It is enough to remember that Sylvester, Gildersleeve, Remsen, Rowland, Morris and Martin were the first professors. As a faculty, 'we were seven.' Our education, our antecedents, our peculiarities were very different, but we were full of enthusiasm, and we got on together without a discordant note."[37]

Shortly after the "Plan of Procedure" was considered and ratified by the trustees in May 1875, Gilman began his efforts locally, calling on distinguished men of science and medicine in Washington, DC, one of whom, Dr. John Shaw Billings of the Office of the Surgeon General, would play a significant role at Hopkins for the next fifteen years.[38] After a brief visit to Yale at the end of the month, Gilman made his way to the United States Military Academy, where he had been appointed to the board of visitors, to address the graduating class. It had only been a decade since the end of the Civil War, and Gilman told the graduating class that records showed that a very large percentage of the academy's graduates had been "absorbed sooner or later into civil life." Many graduates had chosen to become professors: "West Point is now teaching at colleges—in Cambridge, at New Haven, in New York, Pennsylvania, California and I know not in how many other places."[39]

Following two weeks at West Point in early June, Gilman made additional visits to Cornell, Swarthmore, and the University of Virginia. His traveling companion on some of these trips was Reverdy Johnson, and he took him north again, making stops at Amherst and Smith. The largest of the Seven Sisters colleges, Smith opened in the fall of 1875 with fourteen students and six faculty. Gilman and Johnson alighted at Harvard at the end of June to visit with President Eliot and to continue their Hopkins goodwill tour while discreetly sizing up potential faculty. In preparing for their visit and for attending Harvard's graduation, Gilman had written Eliot to thank him profusely for his endorsement of his Hopkins candidacy. Eliot responded, "I beg that you will get rid immediately of all sense of obligation to me. I did mention you as a suitable person for the work; but a dozen other people probably had the same idea and expressed it as I did. The Trustees asked me a question, and I answered it to the best of my judgment. That was all. I shall be very glad to see you here at Commencement. Make use of my house by all means, though I shall be rather a preoccupied host."[40] While Eliot was busy attending to matters at Harvard, Gilman roamed about the entirety of Cambridge and the rest of the Northeast in search of the right faculty to populate the Hopkins ranks. The new president at the upstart Baltimore university was equipped with better salaries to offer prospective faculty members, and according to Eliot's biographer Henry James, "Gilman fished in all waters, casting his lures wherever he saw the man he wanted."[41] So even though Gilman did not get all the resources he originally requested, he was willing to pay the first cohort of faculty more than was being offered elsewhere.

Knowing of his recruitment efforts, Eliot wrote to his friend shortly after Gilman's inauguration that he appreciated the difficulties the president faced in recruiting more seasoned and established faculty members, given that Hopkins was "new, and therefore without traditions and associations." Eliot concluded: "Please don't think that I feel in the least annoyed at proposals made by you to Harvard men. On the contrary, I should have thought it very odd if there had been no men here whom you care to try for. Of course I am glad to be early informed of anything decided upon by your Board which may affect our administration; but I have not rights or dues in the premises."[42] For all the Harvard men who would turn down overtures from Gilman—Gibbs, James, Child, Lane, and Trowbridge—he still managed to land a handful of established names. Gilman's singular success, however, was in persuading those who wanted to make their own reputations with him in Baltimore. And it all started in upstate New York.

### Henry Augustus Rowland

During his time at West Point, Gilman made a thorough examination of its operations and spoke with numerous faculty members, becoming especially well acquainted with Professor Peter Smith Michie. A former Union officer who had served as chief engineer of the Army of the James under General Benjamin Butler, Smith taught at West Point for thirty years and would prove to be a tremendous resource for Gilman as the process of recruiting the inaugural class of professors began.

When asked by Gilman whom he might recommend to chair the the not-yet-founded Hopkins physics department, Michie named a 27-year-old wunderkind on the faculty at Rensselaer Polytechnic Institute, Henry Augustus Rowland. Michie then wired Rowland asking him to come to West Point; Rowland responded immediately and made the 120-mile trip south to meet Gilman.

Impressed that Rowland had just published an article in the highly regarded *Philosophical Magazine*, Gilman inquired why it had not been submitted for publication in the *American Journal of Science*, founded by Yale's Benjamin Silliman. "Because it was turned down by the American editors," Michie told him. Upon rejection by the American journal, Rowland had sent his piece to Professor Clerk Maxwell, the famed Scottish physicist, who had forwarded it to the English periodical.[43] Apparently the Yale professors in charge of reviewing articles for the *American Journal* had rejected submissions by Rowland not once but three times on account of his age and inexperience.[44] Gilman made the following brief notation in one of his notebooks after his visit with the upstart physicist: "Rowland of Troy. . . . Sent papers to N.H. [New Haven] thrice rejected—'too young to publish such.'"[45]

Gilman recognized an uncommon talent in Rowland as the two walked in Kościuszko's Garden, overlooking the Hudson River, and discussed the professor's plans and considered the possibilities in Baltimore. The new Hopkins president would later record, "It was obvious that I was in confidential relations with a young man of rare intellectual powers and of uncommon aptitude for experimental science. When I reported the facts to the trustees in Baltimore, they said at once, 'Engage that young man and take him with you to Europe, where he may follow the leaders in his science and be ready for a professorship.'"[46] Four days later, on June 25, 1875, Rowland traveled to Baltimore and became Gilman's first hire at Hopkins.[47] During the next year, Rowland earned two thousand dollars and had the official title of "assistant in the Department of Physics," with authority to purchase the apparatus he deemed necessary.[48]

In his first annual report to the board of trustees, on January 3, 1876, Gilman noted that while "no appointments of professors have been made by the Trustees," Rowland was pursuing studies in Europe as well as actively acquiring equipment for the "construction and management of physical laboratories." The president also highlighted the papers that Rowland was having published in scientific journals, which marked the "first contributions to science which have been made under the auspices of this University, and may be regarded as an indication of the work which the Trustees are ready to encourage."[49]

The new president and his first hire set sail for Europe from New York on July 7 on Cunard's SS *Bothnia*. Both men were in search of ideas, scholars, and equipment, but they were also intent on spreading the good news of Hopkins far and wide. Gilman's travels throughout the Continent yielded fewer faculty than he would have liked, but he took advantage of the opportunity to apprise the trustees of his progress. His observations over the next few months came in the form of long letters (most of which were addressed "Dear Sirs") postmarked from Geneva, Freiburg, Vienna, Munich, and Rugby, England.

Unbeknownst to the trustees, Gilman was using these communiqués as a type of "tutorial," describing the best practices and facilities in some of the world's finest universities with the intent of emulating them at Hopkins. Gilman was artfully attempting to build a rapport with the trustees by directing certain comments at individual members' interests. Gilman knew that to accomplish what he envisioned at Hopkins, he needed the unflagging support of the trustees. He closed one particularly long missive with the following: "I am afraid that my story has been too long but I have endeavored to make it include points of interest to different members of the Board, and I remember that no one need read the next chapter if the first is tiresome."[50]

In addition to extended stays in London and Oxford, Gilman was eager to examine two institutions in particular. The first was the University of Strasbourg, which he visited after ten days in Paris "so busily occupied that I found but little time for letter writing."[51] Of special interest to Gilman at Strasbourg was the library collection; starting with 150,000 donated volumes, its holdings had grown to more than 350,000 in only five years. Gilman recounted his tour of "the laboratories and lecture rooms, which are excessively plain, but which abound in the convenient apparatus for good scientific work."[52]

Gilman visited the second institution of specific interest to him, Owens College, toward the end of his trip. The details of Gilman's college review were sent directly to the board chair, Galloway Cheston: "Manchester is of special interest to Baltimore, for it is the seat of Owens College, which was founded by a wealthy man whose name it bears, about a quarter of a century ago, and from a very modest beginning it has attained great prominence among the scientific and literary institutions of Great Britain."[53] John Owens, a successful textile merchant, had provided about one hundred thousand pounds in his will to found the institution, which is now part of the University of Manchester. From its inception in 1851, the college was located on Quay Street in the home of Richard Cobden, Gilman's local host in Manchester upon his arrival in England twenty-one years earlier.

During his tour of the Owens facilities, Gilman was especially impressed with the various "ingenious contrivances which relate to heating, ventilating, supply of gas, water, light, and removal of all offensive gases" and noted that both the chemical laboratory building and the medical college building were "brick, and of very respectable aspect—but not at all showy in their architecture."[54] Gilman had graduated from Yale, with its Gothic structures akin to what he saw at Oxford and Cambridge; toured throughout the Continent and seen some of the grandest, most historic universities in existence; and helped oversee the construction of the first buildings at the University of California. His belief in "build[ing] men, not buildings" manifested itself in the physical plant before the Hopkins campus moved to its location at Homewood in 1914. While he made note of building functions and the latest technology for laboratory and research spaces in Europe, Gilman's first task was to attract top-tier professorial talent.

As he traveled throughout England, Gilman was especially pleased with the reaction of faculty to the news of Henry Rowland as the first Hopkins hire. "They predict for him a great career," Gilman wrote to the trustees. "Two of his articles appear in the last two numbers of the Philosophical Magazine, and all dated from the Johns Hopkins University. In this engagement I am sure we have made no mistake."[55] In order to cover more ground, Gilman and Rowland parted company in early August, a few weeks after arriving in England. Writing to Gilman from Bristol shortly thereafter, Rowland reported on his equipment-procuring activities and stated his intentions upon returning to Baltimore: "I would like to commence *at once* when I get back and what can I do without apparatus?"[56]

Rowland's quest to procure the best equipment for his lab at Hopkins would take him throughout England, France, and Germany, and he would eventually compile a list of ninety-six pieces of apparatus suitable for his planned physics department. Some of the specifics were spelled out in great detail in a letter dated August 25, 1875, as Rowland attended the meeting of the British Association for the Advancement of Science. Included on this particular wish list (along with approximate prices) were a "Thomson reflectometer, Resistance coils, Dividing engine, Optical circle with attachments, Apparatus for comparing scales."[57] Rowland's requisition amounted to $6,429, and he received authorization to purchase everything in it. For purposes of comparison, Rowland's trustee-approved starting salary at Hopkins was $1,600 (it would later be bumped up to $2,000). Once the university's original structures on Howard Street were secured and remodeled, the next largest expenditure approved by the trustees was for "fitting up" the lab of a 20-something physicist who got every single piece of equipment he requested. Gilman would recall that everything was left to Rowland's discretion: "Those were the days when the scientific lecture-rooms in America gloried in demonstrations of 'the wonders' of nature: the birth light, the loud noise, the bad smell.' Rowland would have none of this. Instruments of precision he would have, and would have them in abundance, and of the best makers, no matter about the cost."[58] Indeed, when Rowland began his teaching and research at the Johns Hopkins University in 1876, he had, according to one appraisal, the best-equipped physics laboratory in the United States, and it was among the best equipped in the world.[59]

Rowland remained in Europe for several months after Gilman's return to Baltimore, availing himself of the singular opportunity to work in the Berlin laboratory of Hermann von Helmholtz, the esteemed German physician and physicist. Together, they focused on measuring the magnetic efforts of a rotating, electrified disk. Rowland had conceived of the experiment as a way to determine whether magnetic effects were produced by an electrified body in motion.[60] Rowland's manner of both planning and executing the research, all completed in such a short period of time, impressed the director of the laboratory so much that he not only had it presented immediately to the Berlin Academy but also offered to cover all the attendant expenses of the experiment.[61]

Rowland embodied the kind of faculty member Gilman wanted: an exceptionally focused professor committed to producing original research. But Rowland was also renowned for his occasional but legendary inattention to students. When asked by his fellow physicist Professor Thomas Corwin Mendenhall what he intended to do with the new crop of students in his lab, Rowland responded: "Do with them? Do with them? Why, I shall neglect them, of course!" Mendenhall included in his memoir of Rowland this postscript to Rowland's comment: "To be neglected by Rowland was often indeed more stimulating and inspiring than the closest supervision of men lacking his genius and magnetic fervor."[62]

Rowland is considered one of the founders of physics in America. Among his many contributions was the Ruling Engine, which divided the visible spectrum of light into constant, reproducible components. Elected to learned societies all over the world, Rowland was the recipient of the Rumford Prize, awarded by the American Academy of Arts and Sciences in 1883. Upon his tragic death at age 52 from complications of diabetes, the Johns Hopkins faculty eulogized their colleague: "In losing Henry Augustus Rowland, we have lost a great light, a great force, a great example. . . . Rowland's eminence as a physicist is indisputable. There is no danger of an overestimate. The only danger is that we who stood so near him have not taken the full measure of the man as he will appear to after times."[63] Today, his name is forever linked with Hopkins by virtue of the place where he made his mark most profoundly: the Henry A. Rowland Department of Physics. During his time at Hopkins, he trained more than one hundred PhDs, including more than thirty who became department chairs at universities all over the United States.[64]

## James Joseph Sylvester

While Rowland was busy with equipment procurement and laboratory work during the summer and fall of 1875, Gilman continued with his faculty recruitment. Thanks to his broad networks, Gilman received many suggestions. However, one name kept emerging: James Joseph Sylvester. At age 61, Sylvester had already enjoyed a circuitous, varied, and unusual career. Because of Sylvester's Jewish heritage, opportunities at British universities were foreclosed to him, although he did matriculate at St. John's College, Cambridge, in 1831 at the age of 17. Unable to subscribe to the Thirty-Nine Articles of the Anglican Church, Sylvester was denied a degree from the university even though he had successfully completed all the examinations. This profession of faith remained a requirement at Cambridge until 1856. At Oxford, assent to the Thirty-Nine Articles was required just to matriculate up until 1854.[65] Sylvester was eventually granted both his bachelor's and master's degrees by Cambridge four decades after his admission. The college record notes in Sylvester's profile: "Being a Jew, did not take his degree until 1872."[66] Institutions like Oxford and Cambridge, still "steeped in port and prejudice," as Sir William Osler described them,[67] refused to give the brilliant mathematician any sort of faculty appointment. Offered the chair of mathematics at the University of Virginia, Sylvester came to America in 1841.

In Charlottesville, Sylvester found some wild and rambunctious pupils. Before leaving for America, Sylvester was warned by friends to be guarded in what he said, especially as it related to his vehement opposition to slavery. While the "elite students" of Thomas Jefferson's famed academic village gave Sylvester a warm welcome (complete with fireworks and bonfires), there were others who strongly objected to him both as a Jew and as a foreigner.[68] The year prior to his arrival, Professor John A. Davis, of the law school, had been shot to death by one of his own students. Just a few weeks into his tenure in Virginia, Sylvester was threatened by another student, and he was appalled at the university's perfunctory response.[69] When the university declined to sanction the student in any way, Sylvester chose to leave campus immediately for New York—after only four and a half months in Virginia. Once in New York, he became close friends with the Harvard mathematician Benjamin Peirce. An attempt to gain an academic affiliation with Columbia College was denied Sylvester, based once again on his being a Jew.[70]

Returning to England, Sylvester tutored math privately, ventured into actuarial science, and displayed his customary alacrity and brilliance by taking up legal studies. He was admitted to the bar but never practiced law.[71] Sylvester finally settled into an academic appointment at the Royal Military Academy in Woolwich in 1855, but he was forced to step down in 1869 owing to the academy's compulsory retirement age of 55.

Sylvester dabbled in areas in which he had perpetual interest, such as poetry and music. His fecund mind remained engaged on a host of topics, leading to a highly regarded lecture in early 1875 on the mathematization of the mechanical theory of linkwork.[72] A few months later, during Gilman's final days in London, the new Hopkins president was introduced to Sylvester by Professor Peirce, Joseph Henry of the Smithsonian Institution, and Sir Joseph Dalton Hooker, then president of the Royal Society of London and director of the Royal Botanical Gardens, Kew. In his book *The Launching of a University* Gilman recollected much of the idiosyncratic behavior for which Sylvester was legendary but concluded: "I must not blind the reader to the extraordinary strength and fertility of Sylvester's mind. From every point of view he was a marvel—first and foremost as a mathematician, as all the world has acknowledged; then as a teacher of gifted scholars, not by any means a drill-master, but an inspirer; then as a man of letters."[73]

The initial exchanges in London between Gilman and Sylvester went well, but no accord was struck, and Gilman began to feel the press of getting back to Baltimore, having been away from the university since early July. Perhaps sensing some anxiousness from Gilman in his letters to the trustees that his faculty recruitment had not netted the numbers originally desired, the president of the board, Galloway Cheston, wrote to Gilman in early September that "my purpose in dropping you this line is to make you feel perfect freedom in extending the time of your absence, until you can come in contact with those men you would most like to meet whether in England, or on the Continent."[74] Gilman would remain a short while longer, setting sail for America on October 16, 1875.

After his initial meeting with Sylvester and before returning home, Gilman had begun soliciting reference checks on the eccentric mathematician on account "that he was hard to get on with."[75] Gilman sent out letters of inquiry to those familiar with Sylvester's work, reputation, and disposition. He received favorable responses from Hubert A. Newton of Yale and Albert E. Church of West Point, as well as multiple communications from Director Hooker of Kew Gardens.[76] While still in England, Gilman wrote to Benjamin Peirce. The eminent mathematician, who taught at Harvard for fifty years, provided this ringing endorsement of Sylvester in his response to Gilman:

> If you inquire about him you will hear his genius universally recognized, but his power of teaching will probably be said to be quite deficient. . . . But as the barn door fowl cannot understand the flight of the eagle, so it is the eaglet only who will be nourished by his instruction. But as the greatness of a university must depend upon its few able scholars, you cannot have a great university without such great men as Sylvester in your corps of teachers. . . . I hope you will find it in your heart to do for Sylvester what his own country has failed to do—place him where he belongs—and the time will come when all the world will applaud the wisdom of your selection.[77]

The other endorsements echo these refrains: Sylvester's abilities as a teacher were wanting, but he had no equal in terms of intellectual capacity and original discoveries. The "firsts" attributed to him and his work are worth noting. The contributions of Sylvester, who referred to himself as the "mathematical Adam," to the modern-day mathematical lexicon—*matrix, determinant, graph, Jacobian*—are familiar to all science students.[78] Gilman was determined to land what would be considered the biggest faculty catch for Hopkins, as there was no telling what Sylvester's fame could bring the newborn university.

With Gilman in Baltimore and Sylvester in London, contract negotiations—conducted via cable and in long, handwritten letters, with Hooker serving later on as a go-between—involved several weeks of circuitous dialogue, cryptic messages, fits of intransigence, and periods of impatience.[79] The trustees finally voted on November 27 to offer Sylvester a $5,000 salary plus moving expenses. Sylvester then countered with three conditions of his own: that his salary be paid in gold, that the university provide him housing, and that he be allowed to appropriate student fees.[80] The practice of student fee appropriation funded many medical school faculty positions at the time, and Sylvester had successfully employed a similar scheme during his brief tenure at the University of Virginia. Sylvester had augmented his base salary of $1,000—as a department chair in 1841—with $25 from every student who enrolled in mathematics, resulting in an annual salary of well over $2,500, a fairly substantial sum for the time.[81] Writing from London a week before Christmas, Sylvester ended his letter containing his counterproposals with one more request: "When the Trustees have come to a decision, I should feel much obliged if at my expense you would cable me the result (whether favorable or otherwise) not sparing words to make the meaning clear."[82] Two weeks later and still awaiting a response, Sylvester revealed his impatience in a January 4 cable to Gilman: "Wrote 17th December. Anxious for reply. Sylvester."[83]

Gilman, knowing the importance of landing someone like Sylvester, with his international reputation, shifted into high gear, meeting with members of the executive committee and writing letters to others in early January. "Mr. Cheston has been in to express his views in respect to Mr. Sylvester," Gilman wrote to Mayor George Brown. "He would prefer to send him a telegram offering him 'gold but not fees nor residence.' . . . Will you express your assent or dissent?"[84] Gilman met with the executive committee and then relayed the trustees' response to Sylvester on January 8, 1876, via a very terse telegram: "Gold without house or fees. Answer." The president followed up with Sylvester in a longer letter of the same date: "I hope we may receive from you a favorable response, so that the formal action of the Trustees on the 17th inst. may complete our negotiations."[85] Two days later, Sylvester cabled Gilman a counter to the trustees' counter, backing off slightly from his original position: "House from 1877 or equivalent—with gold—without fees. Ultimatum answer."[86] When Sylvester's cable arrived in Baltimore, it was met with silence on the Hopkins end. In the absence of any formal response from either Johnson or Gilman, Sylvester cabled this message on January 26, 1876:

> Untried institution uncertain tenure
> favorable home prospects stipend
> crowning career inadequate against
> risk incurred regret thanks decline
> Sylvester.[87]

Undoubtedly disappointed that the negotiations with someone of such global acclaim as Sylvester had failed, Gilman was now prepared to cast an eye toward the field of American mathematicians. Headlining the list was Simon Newcomb, the Harvard-trained protégé of Benjamin Peirce, head of the Naval Observatory in Washington, DC, and editor of the *Nautical Almanac*.

The Sylvester rejection, combined with his failure to recruit talent from Harvard or Yale, prompted Gilman to lament in a letter to Cecil Franklin Patch Bancroft, principal of the Phillips Academy: "We can't have a great University without great teachers; and great teachers won't come to us till we have a great University! What shall we do?"[88] At this point, the winter of 1876, he had hired just one professor, and his inauguration was two weeks away. In the closing of his letter to Bancroft, one can sense the disappointment and frustration Gilman was experiencing: "On the 22d of Feb. I am to explain our position, and I should be delighted to have you among the hearers."[89]

Sylvester was intent on adding a final point to his interaction with Hopkins and penned what he certainly thought would be his last note to Gilman and the trustees: "I feel it my duty, too long I feared delayed, now that our official correspondence is terminated to express to you and to the Trustees of the Johns Hopkins University my full sense of the compliment conveyed to me in their offer and of the extremely courteous terms in which it was conveyed." Sylvester had been advised throughout the process by associates in England and asserted that the course he had taken "was not founded on selfish consideration solely and throughout received the approval of Dr. Hooker, Mr. Spottiswoode, and Mr. Herbert Spencer."[90] This troika of advisers was formidable indeed; in addition to Dr. Hooker, William Spottiswoode was a fellow mathematician and president of the Royal Society, and Herbert Spencer was the famed political theorist and anthropologist who first introduced the phrase *survival of the fittest* in his 1897 work *Principles of Biology.*[91]

Ten days before Sylvester's letter was sent to Baltimore, Joseph Dalton Hooker— Sylvester's closest confidant and the man who had brokered the original meeting between Sylvester and Gilman in London—determined that he might be able to help the two sides reach a solution. Sylvester had shown Hooker the correspondence between him and the university, and the latter decided that a gentle push to the trustees from him might make a difference. Stating his regret in hearing that the negotiations had ended, Hooker confessed to Gilman that he would "have been personally proud of having aided in carrying a cornerstone to an institution with as promising a future as The Johns Hopkins." Hooker said that what the Hopkins trustees had proposed did not properly recognize Sylvester's "eminence, age, experience, and the fact that his tenure of office could not but be brief and that it would not saddle the University with a prolonged, exceptional expenditure."[92]

Hooker recommended an increased salary or even a housing allowance as an inducement. The executive committee weighed Hooker's letter and, after careful consideration, offered an additional $1,000 for Sylvester to use for accommodations. The offer was delivered from Gilman directly to Hooker, via telegram: "For house, offer one thousand dollars gold, annually. Answer."[93] With this latest offer in hand, Sylvester cabled Gilman five days before the new president's inauguration at Hopkins: "Accept offer. Hookers telegram. Thanks. Sylvester."[94] In a meeting on February 19, 1876, the trustees approved Sylvester's annual salary of $6,000 in gold, together with $2,000 for moving expenses, also in gold.[95] This was far and away the most expensive faculty hire in American higher education in the 1870s.[96]

Gilman had done it. He and the board had succeeded in securing for Hopkins one of the greatest mathematical minds in the world. Sylvester's hire would have inestimable impact far beyond his time in Baltimore. Although his tenure at Hopkins was short, just seven years, Sylvester's impact on the institution was of tremendous consequence, leading one journal to attest, "The importance of his work there can hardly be exaggerated. He practically originated the study of mathematics in the United States."[97] Before Mr. Johns Hopkins made his gift to establish the university, before Daniel Coit Gilman assumed his role as the first president, and before James Joseph Sylvester came to head up its mathematics department, "the United States was a virtual mathematical wasteland," according to the science historian Karen Parshall.[98] Apart from "isolated researchers" such as Benjamin Peirce at Harvard and Josiah Willard Gibbs at Yale, there had been no mathematicians of note in the nation's first one hundred years.[99] The Mathematical Seminary, founded by Sylvester in 1878 at Hopkins, amounted to a research school for mathematics, the first in America, and those who participated in it went on to promote mathematical research elsewhere. Another first was Sylvester's editorship of the *American Journal of Mathematics*, which continues to thrive today.[100] This was a bold move, as until then no specialized mathematical journal launched in the United States "had lasted more than eight years, and most had died within a year or two of their founding."[101]

Gilman's successful hiring of Sylvester undoubtedly helped with other potential hires. Thomas Craig, a 21-year-old high-school teacher in New Jersey, was recruited intensively by Gilman to come as a graduate student, and the new president used the Sylvester hire as a hook with the mathematics wunderkind: "Have you heard that our Professor of Mathematics is to be Prof. J. J. Sylvester, of London, one of the most famous mathematicians of his times? We expect him at the beginning of our work and with your proclivities should think you would be fortunate to come under his guidance."[102] Gilman reported Craig's reaction to Sylvester: "It did me good to see the sparkle in the eyes of a mathematical candidate when I told him you were to be here. He knew your writings & could not believe it possible that it was *the* Sylvester who was to be here next year."[103]

Before Sylvester set sail for America in early April 1876, Gilman wrote to him, "A good voyage to you, a safe arrival, a cordial reception, and a great career!"[104] When Sylvester, then in his early sixties, arrived on campus—such as it was, within the humble structures on Howard Street—many did not know what to expect in terms of his level of engagement, activity, productivity, and collegiality. But the environment at Hopkins was just what the aging genius needed, and he thrived at what he often referred to as "our university." Speaking at the annual Commemoration Day festivities in 1877 to mark the university's first anniversary, Sylvester (who shared the podium that day with the professor hired just weeks before his appointment, Basil Gildersleeve) declared,

> I hesitate not to say that, in my opinion, the two functions of teaching and working in science should never be divorced. I believe that none are so well fitted to impart knowledge (if they will be recognized as existing, and take the necessary pains to acquire, the art of presentation) as those who are engaged in reviewing its methods and extending its boundaries—and I am sure that there is no stimulus so advantageous to the original investigator as that which springs from contact with other

minds and the necessity for going afresh to the foundations of his knowledge, which the world of teaching imposes upon him. I look forward to the courses of lectures that I hope to deliver in succession within the walls of this University as marking the inauguration of a new era of productivity in my own scientific existence; nor need I consider any subject too low for me to teach.[105]

Sylvester's influence would also be profoundly felt in another area, the education of women at Hopkins. Emily Nunn appealed to the executive committee in October 1877 to be allowed to attend the biology lectures of Dr. William Keith Brooks. She was denied.[106] That same year, M. Carey Thomas applied for admission to the master's program and the Greek seminary. A Cornell graduate, and daughter of the trustee James Thomas, she was admitted with this condition: "to have the direction of studies without class attendance in the University." Professor Gildersleeve agreed to take Thomas on as a student, and she was free to consult with other faculty, but she was barred from graduate seminars.[107] Without the advantage of class lectures or interaction with her fellow students, she grew increasingly frustrated in spite of completing her first-year examinations with commendation. As was true for all female students in the early years, no records were kept in official university publications nor was her name listed in the *Circulars*.

Before leaving the university, Thomas wrote a letter to the Hopkins trustees that expressed thanks but also the hope that things might be different for future candidates: "I make this explanation to you in order that my withdrawal may not be prejudicial to any other applicant and because, so far as I have been informed, the only official recognition of my relations to the University exists upon your minutes."[108] Thomas would go to Germany for further study, first at the University of Leipzig and then at the University of Zurich, where she became the first woman and the first foreigner to earn a PhD in linguistics in 1882. While the Thomas experience had been less than ideal, Sylvester's advocacy on behalf of the next prospective female student would make all the difference.

In 1878, another woman of extraordinary intellect, Christine Ladd, requested admission to study with Sylvester. An 1869 graduate of Vassar, Ladd had published widely on various mathematical subjects, and these articles had impressed Sylvester so much that he urged President Gilman to admit her.[109] The executive committee acquiesced, but on the condition that Ladd attend *only* Professor Sylvester's lectures and no others. The committee notes were explicit: "It was agreed to admit Miss Ladd to attendance at the lectures as a candidate for second degree of Professor Sylvester, refusing her application to attend other branches of instruction in the University."[110] The task of informing Ladd of the trustees' decision fell to Gilman. He wrote: "As this is an exceptional recognition of your mathematical scholarship, no charge will be made for tuition and your name will not be enrolled on the annual Register."[111] After demonstrating her keen ability, Ladd was granted permission to attend other lectures. She was also awarded a fellow's stipend, but without the title. This arrangement persisted for three years, but it is clear that the trustees preferred to keep the situation as quiet as possible. Ladd's original application was signed "C. Ladd," and her name is absent from both the university *Circulars* and the official school rolls.

"C. Ladd" was the first woman to successfully meet the requirements for a PhD at Hopkins. She completed her studies in 1882, the same year that she married fellow student and Gilman biographer Fabian Franklin. Her thesis adviser, the renowned Charles Sanders Peirce, who has been called the first American experimental psychologist, published her work in the journal *Studies in Logic*.[112] Sylvester had to wait thirty-eight years to receive his degrees from Cambridge on account of his being Jewish; Ladd would have to wait even longer, not receiving her PhD from Hopkins until February 1926, on the occasion of the university's fiftieth anniversary, because she was a woman.[113]

Hooker's prediction to Gilman that Sylvester might not remain long at Hopkins was correct, but not on account of any dissatisfaction on the professor's part, as he continued to enjoy his colleagues, students, teaching, and research. Appreciated far more at Hopkins than he had ever been at Woolwich, Sylvester was enjoying "the high summer of his career."[114] During his first semester at Hopkins Sylvester wrote to his friend Barbara Bodichon, "It is impossible to imagine a more generous and appreciative mode of treatment by any institution of its professors than that which we experience here."[115]

But Sylvester's native England would come calling in 1883 upon the death of Oxford Professor Henry Smith, of Balliol and Corpus Christi Colleges. Offered the prestigious Savilian Professorship of Geometry at Oxford, Sylvester, aged 70, returned home to join the ranks of the educated English elite, by which at one time he had been shunned. This was the capstone of Sylvester's career, and he would hold the position until his death in 1897. Sylvester was the first Jewish professor in the history of Oxford. Contemplating his tardy embrace by the community, he wrote to his good friend Arthur Cayley, "She is a good dear mother our University here and stretches out her arms with impartial fondness to take all her children to her bosom even those she has not reared at her breast."[116]

Sylvester's annual Oxford salary was seven hundred pounds, with the possibility of increasing to nine hundred. While the Hopkins trustees had refused to accede to his demand for housing during the contract negotiations, at Oxford accommodations were made for Sylvester, who was single, to live within New College.[117] However, before Sylvester left for England, the Hopkins trustees, in recognition of his immeasurable impact on the university, honored him with a title they had never bestowed on anyone before: professor emeritus. This was a fitting acknowledgment of what Sylvester had accomplished in seven short years, taking the mathematics group at Hopkins "from suspect, unknown, and untried to successful, recognized and vital."[118]

Leaving Baltimore in a blaze of glory—a gold medal was even struck in his honor—Sylvester took from America "the initial, driving force which had propelled it into research level mathematics." Lost too was the research momentum; another twenty years would pass before the early Hopkins challenge of the 1870s would be met by institutions such as Harvard, Yale, and Princeton.[119] Sylvester had certainly reached the mathematical mountaintop with his new position at Oxford, but he always had a genuine fondness for Gilman, Baltimore, and the Johns Hopkins University. At the conclusion of the first academic year in England, Sylvester wrote Gilman: "If you miss me as you are good enough to say at the Johns Hopkins, I miss you no less." The professor further admitted to telling associates at Oxford and throughout England that the Johns Hopkins was "the first university in the world for what it can do for its students and the true university spirit which animates the place."[120]

### Basil Lanneau Gildersleeve

During his time at Harvard with Reverdy Johnson, and just before leaving for Europe with Henry Rowland, Gilman had reached out to other potential faculty members to gauge their interest in coming to Hopkins. One in particular, William Watson Goodwin, the Eliot Professor of Greek Literature at Harvard since 1860, had known Gilman for years. Both he and Francis James Child, professor of rhetoric and oratory (and the leading expert on Anglo-Saxon literature and Chaucer in America), topped Gilman's recruiting list. Eventually, both would decline offers from the new president to join him in Baltimore. In the case of Child, the reasons he cited were "domestic," but he later conveyed thanks to Gilman that his aggressive lobbying to wrest him away from Harvard had provided some leverage whereby Child was now "wholly relieved at last from the burden of correcting undergraduate compositions."[121]

Goodwin consulted with Child about the Hopkins offer but wrote to Gilman, "He feels very much as I do,—much attached to Harvard." Goodwin was scheduled to meet Gilman in Cambridge on July 3, 1875, but he was unable to make their appointment. Shortly thereafter, in his letter of refusal, Goodwin confessed being amenable to exploring other options, given the uncertainty of Greek's future in the Harvard curriculum: "If the President [Eliot] succeeds in making the Faculty reduce seriously the influence of Greek in the course of preparation for College or in the Freshman year, I shall feel that self-respect requires me to pull down my flag and go somewhere where I can work under more favorable conditions."[122] Goodwin would not have to go elsewhere, remaining at Harvard until his retirement in 1901—a forty-one-year tenure.

Disappointed at being turned down by both men, Gilman did, however, receive a recommendation from Goodwin about another potential candidate for the Department of Ancient Languages: Professor Basil Gildersleeve, of the University of Virginia. A native of South Carolina, Gildersleeve described himself as "a Charlestonian first, Carolinian next, and then a Southerner—on my mother's side a Southerner beyond dispute."[123] In fact, his maternal grandfather, Belize Lanneau, had been among the Acadian refugees expelled by the British in 1755 who made their way to the Lowcountry of South Carolina. An orphan left to fend for himself in Charleston, Lanneau would go on to help found the Huguenot Church there.[124] Basil was extremely precocious as a child and first attended the College of Charleston, followed by Jefferson College in Pennsylvania, before entering Princeton at age 18 as a junior and graduating fourth in his class in 1849. After a brief stint as a classical schoolmaster in Richmond, Virginia, Gildersleeve headed to Germany for graduate school, enrolling at Berlin and Bonn before completing his PhD at the University of Göttingen in 1853. Of his experience overseas in the early 1850s, Gildersleeve recounted, "To see Germany, to enter a German University, to sit at the feet of the great who had made and were making German scholarship illustrious, was a prospect to stir the blood of aspiring youth."[125] Gildersleeve and those who followed had been preceded decades earlier, however, by a group of Americans whom Charles Franklin Thwing, president at Western Reserve University for thirty-one years, called the "First Quartette."[126] Lectures had begun at Göttingen in 1734, making it younger than three American colleges. "Its situation and environment had none of the historic charm of Heidelberg," observed Thwing, "but its teachers were of the greatest."[127]

Upon his return from Germany, Gildersleeve landed a professorship at the age of 25 at the University of Virginia, where he would teach for the next twenty years. The university did not close during the Civil War, and Gildersleeve remained in Charlottesville, instructing the maimed and wounded who had returned from the battlefront, as well as those boys too young for military service. He spent the summer vacations of 1863 and 1864 with the Twenty-first Virginia Infantry and the First Virginia Cavalry. In the summer of 1864, during a skirmish in the Shenandoah valley, Gildersleeve was carrying orders on behalf of General John B. Gordon when a bullet broke his thighbone and nearly resulted in the amputation of his leg. From that day forward he walked with a pronounced limp.[128] Of the experience, Gildersleeve recalled, "I lost my pocket Homer, I lost my pistol, I lost one of my horses, and finally I came near losing my life from a wound which kept me five months on my back."[129]

Recalling the recruiting efforts directed first toward Sylvester and then toward Gildersleeve, Gilman summarized this time period (October–December 1875) in his first annual report to the board of trustees, January 3, 1876, noting that the executive committee had "entered upon one of the most delicate and difficult tasks which will ever come upon them." Further complicating the task, explained Gilman, was the absence of guidelines with regard to the distribution of subjects or the kind of instruction to be given; he concluded that the plans of the trustees depended on the character of the teachers whom they recruited to Baltimore.[130] But Gilman had given the following advice when the board asked him how to begin a great university: "Enlist a great mathematician and a distinguished Grecian; your problem will be solved."[131] Having landed the great mathematician, Gilman was now focused on securing a distinguished Grecian.

Gilman and Gildersleeve met for the first time in Washington, DC, on December 8, 1875. During a wide-ranging conversation that stretched into the early morning hours, the new president offered the Virginia professor a position at Hopkins as chair of ancient languages. Three days later, Gildersleeve conveyed his letter of acceptance to Gilman, telling him that "your generous appreciation for my work as a teacher has afforded me the greatest gratification. To such confidence you have reposed in me my whole nature responds with all its earnestness and I shall enter into my new duties with heightened interest because my success will be in a measure yours."[132] The offer and acceptance still needed to be ratified by the board, but after two decades in Charlottesville, Gildersleeve had cast his lot with Hopkins and was prepared to leave for Baltimore. Gilman presented Gildersleeve's name to the board for approval (the executive committee had already sanctioned the action) at their meeting on January 3, 1876, contingent on Gildersleeve officially accepting, with an effective start date of July 1. Board minutes reveal that the offer was accepted and the final vote of approval recorded on February 7, 1876, making Gildersleeve officially the very first faculty member appointed at the Johns Hopkins University.[133]

Gilman had forwarded to Gildersleeve a copy of his first annual report to the Hopkins trustees from a few weeks prior, to which Gildersleeve responded, "If such wise and prudent management be continued the University cannot be considered an experiment. Its success is assured."[134] Gildersleeve attended Gilman's inauguration on February 22, 1876, and wrote an even more effusive message afterwards: "My visit to Baltimore was not only a rare enjoyment but a powerful incentive to hard work for the Johns Hopkins and I certainly did not dream that so much enthusiasm was left in me. . . . With many thanks for your kindness and renewed assurances of my earnest desire to bear my part in the furtherance of your plans."[135]

In spite of his impeccable curriculum vitae, Gildersleeve posed a significant challenge because of his Confederate past, the incendiary editorials he had written for the *Richmond Examiner* from October 1863 to August 1864, and the record of his personal views. The editor of Gildersleeve's papers, Ward Briggs, noted a certain mellowing over time. In contrast to the writings produced in the midst of the war (with the impending fall of Richmond ever present), in the essays the classicist would pen in later years "the anger, prejudice, finger-pointing, and despair in 1863 [had given] way to an elegiac, sometimes lyrical, nostalgia of 1895."[136] Be that as it may, Gildersleeve's views, regardless of when he wrote them and especially when read today, are nothing short of jarring.

Gildersleeve is perhaps best known for "The Creed of the Old South" which originally appeared in the *Atlantic Monthly* in 1892. The periodical's editor, Horace Scudder, a native Bostonian and graduate of Williams College, had solicited a piece for publication from Gildersleeve "to make more intelligible to the educated man of the North . . . those springs of conduct that send the young Southerner into the field with untroubled conscience and high sense of duty." In obliging Scudder's request, Gildersleeve offered a quintessential Lost Cause apologia: "They cannot understand the serenity of our confidence in the justice of our cause. . . . The cause was one for which I wrote, prayed, fought, suffered but in the long agony I never was haunted by a doubt as to the righteousness of the course which we followed and even if there had been a doubt as to the justice of our cause, the command of the State would have sufficed."[137]

Gildersleeve's "Creed" was popular and widely read, and he would follow up that publication with an article titled "A Southerner in the Peloponnesian War." This piece, also written for the *Atlantic Monthly*, appeared in September 1897 and further demonstrated Gildersleeve's stance as an unapologetic defender of the Confederacy even years after the Civil War. The Johns Hopkins Press republished the two articles in one volume in 1915, on the occasion of Gildersleeve's retirement from the university after thirty-nine years.[138]

Both essays elucidate Gildersleeve's views on a host of issues, including his opinion that the "peculiar institution" of slavery was a "crushing burden" inherited from the forefathers of the South that he and his generation were "supposed to be defending with the melodramatic fury of pirate kings." Gildersleeve continued, "We were born to this social order, we had to do our duty in it according to our lights, and this duty was made indefinitely more difficult by the interference of those who, as we thought, could not understand the conditions of the problem, and who did not have to bear the expense of the experiments they proposed."[139] Gildersleeve would later argue that "the slavery question belongs ultimately to the sphere of economics."[140] He would further assert that the idea that the "cause we fought for and our brothers died for was the cause of civil liberty, and not the cause of human slavery, is a thesis which we feel ourselves bound to maintain whenever our motives are challenged or misunderstood, if only for our children's sake."[141] Such a view reflected a school of thought, then prevalent in some circles in the United States, that the southern enslavers had been presented as victims of a system—victims of history, as it were—and that both sides had fought with nobility and honor. Not only was this theory historically wrong but it refused to cite slavery as the root cause of the most catastrophic event in American history. The Union general Ulysses S. Grant, in his critically acclaimed *Memoirs*, put it as clearly as can be written: "The cause of the great War of Rebellion against the United States will have to be attributed to slavery."[142] While it may have been popular in the late nineteenth century to ignore the primary factor that propelled the nation to war, and as the nation sought to mend, some continued to ignore the historical facts and saw no reason to confront the distorted Lost Cause myths. Gilman might very well have been influenced by the popular trend of "healing the breach" by seeking reconciliation. He therefore could morally justify employing Gildersleeve, although he never recorded any feelings or justifications for his action.

There is no evidence of anti-Semitic views in Gildersleeve's writings before the Civil War, but he was equally spiteful and malevolent in the attitude he expressed toward Jews during the conflict. This is somewhat surprising, given the way he wrote about his Jewish friend and tutor Jacob Bernays, who had taught Gildersleeve in Germany in the early 1850s and later became chair of classical philology at the newly founded Jewish Theological Seminary of Breslau. Bernays had suggested the subject of Gildersleeve's doctoral dissertation while Gildersleeve was studying under him at Bonn (Gildersleeve successfully defended his dissertation, *De Porphyrii Studiis Homericis Capitum Trias*, in March 1853).[143] Their relationship notwithstanding, Gildersleeve's latent anti-Semitic views found their voice a decade later, directed at the Jewish Confederate secretary of war, Judah P. Benjamin. In a December 1863 editorial for the *Richmond Examiner* titled "The Angel Gabriel," Gildersleeve wrote the following:

> This journal was, perhaps, the first to call attention to the spread of Judaism in the Confederacy. The fact is now so evident that proof and illustration are unnecessary. We know that the Jews have the chief seat in every Main street and Broad street throughout the land. They tell us themselves that they constitute a large proportion of the army, and perhaps it is their presence that makes our banners trail in the dust. If so, let the Hebrew census of the army of Northern Virginia, and of the shifting army of the West, be taken at once, and let Lee lose his undeserved prestige and Bragg be exonerated from the charge of imbecility. . . . But a larger development is now demanded, and, not to be behind the times, we shall have a column in Hebrew as soon as we can get the types; and, to show our sympathy with the new order of things, we shall print the state of the marke's in the "holy tongue," with all the "poin's."[144]

Upon the passage of an bill by the Confederate Congress just a few weeks after the above editorial appeared, Gildersleeve did not hold back in calling out Jewish soldiers as cowards in a January 4, 1864, piece titled "Anti-Substitute Bill": "Thousands will soon withdraw in righteous indignation of the jesuitry of our legislators. The children of Israel will decamp in companies of fifties and hundreds, and hasten back to the fleshpots of Egypt, weary of the insubstantial manna of Confederate notes, and frightened by the fiery serpents of conscript officers."[145]

Throughout his career, Gildersleeve's unabashed role as a southern apologist was manifested time and again. In "The Creed of the Old South," Gildersleeve used the rhetoric of Greek statesmen in their defense of the Peloponnesian War to justify Southern secession as a states' rights issue: "To us submission meant slavery, as it did to Pericles and the Athenians. . . . Submission is slavery, and the bitterest taunt in the vocabulary of those who advocated secession was 'submissionist.'"[146] Other writings are even more unvarnished, such as an editorial published in April 1864 titled "Sambo the Ass," in which Gildersleeve contended, "The ass is the American citizen of African descent. . . . The whole Yankee nation is in love with the ass, and the best of prospective provender is lavished on the poor creature." He continued, "If, however, these African brethren wish to put to the test the sincerity of the professions which have been made so profusely, let them try, while their hands are warm from Massa Lincoln's cordial grasp, to put so much as a little finger into the Federal plum pie, and they will see what they will see." With the presidential election just months away, Gildersleeve concluded,

> Sambo may perfume their saloons; Sambo may take to his sooty bosom their daughters and their sisters; Sambo may eat at their tables; Sambo may lord it over the Irish and the Dutch; Sambo may even buy, as at Beaufort, his old master's deserted mansion and hold it until the Confederates come again; but as for a substantial share in

any of the present or future profits of the Great National Speculation, Sambo may indulge his native genius in whistling for it. In the meantime Sambo is the favorite, and until the next election is over, every possible distinction will be showered on the winning donkey.[147]

It is impossible to square these malicious views with the sterling reputation Gildersleeve cultivated as a scholar and man of letters. How could one of such an allegedly broad outlook and generosity of spirit—according to those who knew Gildersleeve best—hold such contempt for certain groups? Why would Gilman, worried about the aspirations of a new university and the trustees' concerns about being perceived as sectarian, make such a person the very first faculty hire at Hopkins? The precise motivations behind Gilman's hiring of Gildersleeve are unknown. The president did not offer any defense of the action, nor did he write about Gildersleeve's overtly racist views, which the professor espoused for years after arriving at Hopkins. One is left, therefore, to speculate.

Perhaps Gilman's work with the Slater Fund and the Peabody and Rockefeller endowments, which spanned more than twenty-five years of his life and were especially directed to improving educational opportunities in southern states, served as a ballast, in his mind, against what Gildersleeve represented and expressed. Or it might be that Gilman was able to compartmentalize the most distasteful and bigoted views expressed by Gildersleeve in exchange for his reputation as America's greatest classicist. But at what price did such a Faustian agreement come? That Gildersleeve continued to express these views after such a long tenure at the university is troubling. Even more disconcerting is that the university's press gave voice to Gildersleeve's racist writings— as a way to honor the professor's nearly four-decades-long tenure in Baltimore—by republishing "The Creed of the Old South" twenty-three years after it first appeared in the *Atlantic Monthly*.

Gilman wrote that the original seven faculty were "very different, but we were full of enthusiasm, and we got on together without a discordant note."[148] Given that the initial professoriate was so small, they would have interacted with one another on a regular basis. The first two hires, Sylvester and Gildersleeve, were asked to share the podium at the university's celebration of its first anniversary in 1877. Another participant in the events of that day was James Russell Lowell, one of the Fireside poets, who wrote to his wife of the experience: "We had first a very excellent address by our President Gilman, then one by Professor Gildersleeve on Classical Studies, and by Professor Silvester [*sic*] on the Study of Mathematics, both of them very good and just enough spiced with the personality of the speaker to be taking."[149] From all accounts, the relationship between Sylvester and Gildersleeve was one of mutual respect and genuine friendship. While traveling in Europe in the fall of 1878, Sylvester wrote Gilman: "I hear with great satisfaction of the success of our fellows on their several courses and of Mr. Gildersleeve's lecture on Colleges and Classics. I rejoice in having such a man for my colleague."[150]

Gilman was certainly an idealist when it came to vision, broad thinking, and university building, but he was also a practical administrator and must have known that benefits would redound to Hopkins if he were to recruit Gildersleeve from Charlottesville to Baltimore. Scholars writing on the history of the institution have concluded as much that it could be argued that Gildersleeve was not hired *in spite of* his views and southern apologia but *because of* them. The university librarian and author of the 1946 history of Johns Hopkins, John French, maintained that Gildersleeve's hire as the first professor "was a tactful, and as events proved, a very wise choice. . . . His literary taste and skill, his nimble, if sometimes caustic, wit, his sound judgment and breadth of outlook made him an admirable senior professor; and Gilman found in him a trusted friend and adviser."[151] Such an assertion was corroborated by Hugh Hawkins, who wrote that Gilman "must have realized that in Baltimore a faculty with only Northern scholars would be vulnerable," as there was a rumor afloat in the city that the South "was to be fairly and numerously represented in the Faculty" in spite of the Northern sympathies of its new president.[152] In what might be termed an even more benign summary, Hawkins averred that in 1876 Gildersleeve would have called to mind the South and the intellectual opportunity the Johns Hopkins University offered to the region: "Out of the poverty into which the war had plunged it, the South could rise to intellectual and spiritual riches, and Gildersleeve as much as any man from his section accomplished this ascent."[153]

Gildersleeve's reputation as a scholar and reformer of classical education in American universities, coupled with his forty-five-year editorship of the *Journal of American Philology*, is incontestable. The tributes from colleagues and other classicists bear this out and even border on deification.[154] On the eve of his ninety-second birthday, in 1923, the *New York Times* ran an article titled "St. Basil of Baltimore," in which it called Gildersleeve "probably the most eminent and authoritative of classical scholars as yet produced by America."[155] In 1912, the National Institute of Arts and Letters published its list of "Forty Immortals." Included on the register were names like Woodrow Wilson, Theodore Roosevelt, John Muir, John Singer Sargent, Henry Adams, Nicholas Murray Butler, Henry James, Henry Cabot Lodge, Henry Van Dyke, and Basil L. Gildersleeve.[156]

The relationship between Gilman and Gildersleeve was a complicated one, but there is no question that their friendship was sincere and the commitment to each other immutable. Gilman was restrained in describing "the immense influence" of both Professors Gildersleeve and Ira Remsen in his 1904 *Launching of a University*, given that both men were at the time still living and "serving the university with increasing ability and increasing influence." Gilman did, however, conclude, "For more than twenty-five years they were the chief counsellors of the President, and the authorities upon whose wisdom and knowledge the Trustees relied for advice."[157]

A more thorough examination of Gildersleeve's influence on Hopkins may very well be undertaken by a future investigator. But for now, the explanation provided in May 2020 by the Department of Classics, which he helped found in 1876, offers the best counsel for how to gauge Gildersleeve and his writings. Describing him as "a classicist who, despite his noteworthy contributions as a scholar, teacher, and educational innovator, repeatedly lent material and moral support to the forces of racial oppression," the department wrote:

> Today, the Department of Classics at Hopkins repudiates the racist views of Gildersleeve and pledges its efforts to bring the benefits of discovery to the world. We are committed to diversity in all of its forms, and we educate our students to think both critically and creatively about the past, including about the history and mixed legacy of the discipline of Classics itself. We continuously search for new ways to recruit a diverse body of students and faculty, and we actively oppose racism, sexism, homophobia, and other forms of discrimination in higher education and beyond.[158]

## Ira Remsen

Ira Remsen was only 30 years old when Gilman offered him the chair of chemistry in 1876. He would remain at Hopkins longer than any of his founding faculty colleagues, serving as professor of chemistry for twenty-five years and then as Gilman's successor as president for twelve years. In a very literal sense, Remsen is still on the Homewood campus, as he holds the distinction of being the only person to be buried at the university. His ashes are behind a memorial plaque in the building bearing his name, Remsen Hall.

A native of New York City, Remsen came from a family of "men and women of stalwart character and abundant vigor, endowed with intelligence and imbued with deep religious convictions."[159] Ira earned his medical degree at the age of 21 from the city's College of Physicians and Surgeons (which formally became part of Columbia University in 1891) and practiced as a physician for a brief period—to satisfy his family—before heading to Germany to pursue studies in the subject that was his first love, chemistry. After a year in Munich, Remsen transferred to Göttingen and completed his PhD under the tutelage of the famed Wilhelm Rudolph Fittig. The German mentor was so fond of Remsen that he took him as his assistant to the University of Tübingen in 1870.[160] After two years with Fittig, Remsen returned to the United States to become professor of chemistry and physics at Williams College.

Gilman was convinced that the best configuration for Hopkins was to have chemistry and physics unified into one with Wolcott Gibbs, a professor at Harvard, as the chair. Like Remsen a native New Yorker, Gibbs earned a bachelor's degree at Columbia College before completing the requirements for his medical degree in 1845. In keeping with the habit of many of the prominent students of science of the age, Gibbs went to Europe to study in Berlin and Giessen; before returning home in 1848, he attended lectures in Paris.[161] Gibbs would serve as professor of chemistry in the College of the City of New York for fourteen years before beating out Eliot for the Rumford Chair at Harvard in 1863 and overseeing the laboratory of the Lawrence Scientific

School for eight years. A founding member of the National Academy of Sciences, Gibbs would later serve as its president.

Gibbs and Harvard's president Charles Eliot had a history together. Shortly after Eliot returned to Harvard in 1869, he transferred all classes in chemistry and some in physics to the College Laboratories, thus relieving Gibbs of instruction in chemistry and moving him and his assistant into a private chemical lab. None too pleased, Gibbs became persuaded "that he must expect something less than considerate treatment from the teacher whom he had formerly displaced and who had now become his President." According to Eliot's biographer, Henry James (who won the Pulitzer Prize for History for his account of the Harvard president's life), this "incident furnished the first and I believe the only occasion for accusing Eliot of having treated a man vindictively or unfairly."[162]

Knowing of Gibbs' discontent over this slight, Gilman pressed the distinguished chemist to join him in Baltimore, where he would find an "attractive climate" and would be "well supported by adjuncts and assistants, independent of other departments of the Univ, & from established routine, encouraged to develop a strong school of chemistry and physics."[163] After giving the proposition his full consideration, Gibbs told Gilman that he was much too old "to begin again in a new place." He did, however, offer this thought: the president should recruit "young men and not fossils like myself"; and he suggested that Gilman tap John Trowbridge, of the Lawrence Scientific School, to head the joint department, with Henry Rowland and Ira Remsen as his associates.[164]

As he had done in other instances and with different candidates, Gilman now began lobbying Trowbridge to leave Harvard for Hopkins with the enticement of rank as a full professor and chair. The young chemist also would turn Gilman down, but acknowledged that in doing so he might well be "consigning myself to the position of assistant professor for an indefinite period of years." Willing to run this risk, Trowbridge decided to remain in the community "which has known me from boyhood and endeavor to make a scientific reputation irrespective of my college position. My mother and sister are also opposed to my going to Baltimore. I therefore decline your kind offer."[165] Trowbridge would indeed make a reputation for himself at Harvard, following the man who had recommended him to Gilman. In 1888, Trowbridge succeeded Wolcott Gibbs as the Rumford Professor of Physics at Harvard, teaching and researching in Cambridge until his retirement in 1910.

Having failed to recruit either Gibbs or Trowbridge, Gilman abandoned the idea of a combined department of physics and chemistry. At the same time, he was growing ever more impressed by the rising stature of Henry Rowland. Elected to the American Academy of Arts and Sciences in 1876, Rowland would be elected to the National Academy of Sciences five years later at the "unprecedentedly early age" of 33.[166] But with Rowland's official appointment as professor and chair of physics ratified by the Hopkins trustees on April 17, 1876, Gilman still needed a chemist.

He determined to follow up on Gibbs' recommendation of Remsen, knowing him by reputation and by the success of his 1877 textbook, *Principles of Theoretical Chemistry*. Remsen's text received immediate recognition and was soon translated into German and Italian, with his methods of presentation being largely followed up in many elementary books.[167] Remsen had grown increasingly frustrated that Williams College did not place any sort of emphasis on original research or invest in equipment for experimentation. When he petitioned for a small room in which to carry out some of his research, he was admonished by President Paul Ansel Chadbourne: "You will please keep in mind that this is a college and not a technical school. The students who come here are not to be trained as chemists, or geologists or physicists. They are to be taught the great fundamental truths of all sciences. The object aimed at is culture, not practical knowledge."[168] Remsen's modest request was perfunctorily denied. A masterful teacher and very popular with the students, Remsen persisted at Williams but also wished to pursue his research interests, as he had done in Germany. Alerted about what was planned in Baltimore, Remsen wrote Gilman in December 1875 to inquire about prospects at Hopkins.[169]

Four months later, on the same day that Rowland was approved as the third Hopkins faculty member, Remsen was appointed as the fourth: professor and chair of chemistry. In a letter dated a week later from Williamstown, Massachusetts, Remsen told Gilman, "Last Monday I received the telegram you were kind enough to send me. In doubt whether I should consider the telegram as an official announcement of my election or whether it would be followed by a letter, I have carelessly neglected to acknowledge its receipt. In accordance with what I have already written you, I am prepared to formally accept the position whenever I receive the offer."[170] News of Remsen's acceptance of the Hopkins position spread across the Williams campus, and the student reaction was published in the first issue of the *Athenaeum* to appear after the announcement of his resignation: "The present policy of the trustees of the Johns Hopkins University gives evidence that we shall have at least one institution of learning which shall rival the best universities of Germany. We have only one cause of regret in connection with the success of the institution and that is that they should take away one of our ablest professors, Professor Remsen, who occupies the chair of Physics and Chemistry."[171]

Remsen remained in residence at Williams through the summer but began inspecting laboratories throughout the Northeast—in Boston, New York, New Haven, Princeton, and Easton, Pennsylvania. Writing to Gilman that his tour had "not proved as profitable as I hoped it might," Remsen did note that he had "obtained some valuable hints which I shall make the most of in due time." Among Remsen's ideas, which he outlined in this same letter with schematics and square-footage requirements—was a larger footprint for chemistry space. "It was necessary to take a little more ground than I originally calculated upon," he wrote.[172] In response to some pushback from the executive committee relative to his capital request, Remsen wrote Gilman two weeks later: "I hope the Committee do not think I have given orders for an unnecessarily expensive building. I do not see exactly why it should be materially more expensive than that indicated by my rough plan shown to the gentlemen of the committee. I am not at all anxious to have it expensive, and if anything can be done to lessen the cost and, at the same time, not lessen the essential accommodations furnished by the buildings, I should say by all means—let it be done."[173] Remsen would get his laboratory, but not right away—it did not open until 1877—and the complex would be built in stages.

The teaching and laboratory building Remsen envisioned called for a "fitting up" with the appropriate apparatus and chemicals. Along with the rough estimate he forwarded to Gilman—totaling five thousand dollars—he sent this final request: "In addition to the above sum, I shall also want about one thousand dollars for books for the Chemical Reference Library."[174] As with Rowland and his physics laboratory, Remsen was provided with every piece of equipment he needed, and each of his requests to outfit his lab was approved.

Remsen also required an able assistant, and he suggested that Harmon N. Morse, an Amherst graduate with a PhD from Göttingen, be considered. Morse had called on Remsen shortly after Remsen's appointment at Hopkins became known bearing a letter of introduction from Ralph Waldo Emerson. Remsen recalled, "This letter led me to take more than ordinary interest in the bearer."[175] Hopkins had already made Morse a fellow, but in response to Remsen's entreaties, Gilman agreed to raise his status to associate with a base salary of one thousand dollars.[176] Together these two men established a new standard for chemical education in America over their long association. As Remsen would remember it years later, they arrived in Baltimore for the fall term 1876 and

> began our work together for better or for worse. We had no laboratory. We had less than a handful of students. What was to come of it? I need not go into the story thus suggested, except to say we were absolutely untrammeled and left to work out our own salvation. Morse and I were of one mind as to the object to be attained and there were no discussions as to the methods to be adopted. They were not original, but they had never been tried in this country. There had never been an opportunity. The opportunity that many of us had hoped for, had dreamed of, was furnished by the bounty of Johns Hopkins and the wisdom of his trustees and of President Gilman.[177]

Morse would remain at Hopkins for his entire career, first as an associate professor in 1883, becoming a full professor of inorganic and analytical chemistry in 1892 and director of the chemical laboratory in 1908, and retiring in 1916. Remsen too enjoyed a distinguished career, which included founding the *American Chemical Journal*, a periodical he edited for thirty-five years.

Remsen's summary of what he and his fellow faculty members found upon arriving at Hopkins and the reaction of their students when they realized that they were participating in original research is worth quoting:

It would be difficult, not to say impossible, for anyone who has not had the same experience to form any conception of the hope and joy which came to us young men in the message of President Gilman that in the new university an effort would be made to provide for the needs of those who wished to carry on researches. Here was an opportunity of which many had been dreaming. It is needless to say that I accepted the offer with alacrity. President Gilman's injunction was simply this: "Do your best work in your own way." What could be finer? I bought all the apparatus I wanted and all the books I wanted. A simple laboratory was built. I had but three or four students and we went to work. Now I am well aware of the fact that chemistry was not revolutionized as a result of our efforts, but we made a start in a new direction. Research became an essential part of the training of graduate students and soon they began to come in larger and larger numbers. There was great enthusiasm among these students. I have often been surprised and delighted to see how generally, advanced students of chemistry (no doubt it is the same with other subjects) become deeply interested in abstruse problems the moment they begin to feel that what they are doing is going to be a contribution, even though a slight one, to the knowledge of the subject.[178]

## Henry Newell Martin

During his faculty recruiting trip to Europe in 1875 Gilman had become friendly with the famed British biologist Thomas Huxley, whom he would invite to address the university community in September 1876. But Huxley's lobbying on behalf of his protégé Henry Newell Martin would begin months earlier in a letter to Gilman: "I do not think you could possibly have a better man than Dr. Martin—he is thoroughly well trained in Physiology and general Biology; a fellow of his College in Cambridge; young, energetic, ever pleasant in manner and a thorough gentleman in all his ways."[179]

Martin was yet another prodigy among the original six faculty. The eldest of twelve children, he was admitted to University College London at age 15 and later matriculated at Christ's College Cambridge. While still in his early twenties, Martin cowrote with Huxley *Practical Instruction in Elementary Biology*. This commendable track record notwithstanding, Gilman conducted his own research on Martin and sent notes of inquiry, not dissimilar to the letters he sent when vetting James Sylvester, to associates who were more familiar with the fields of physiology and biology than he was. He sent one such letter to the Yale professor Sidney Irving Smith, who provided an honest assessment of Martin but confessed to knowing the British physiologist only by reputation and through the *Manual of Biology*. Smith's response included the view that "Professor Huxley's commendation is certainly very strong and would seem sufficient evidence of Dr. Martin's fitness as a student and as an instructor." Nonetheless, Smith's letter concluded with this observation: "Whether he has executive ability for such a place, and whether he possesses the faculty—rare in most foreigners to this country—of getting on pleasantly with American students, are questions which only a personal acquaintance can answer." Smith's brother-in-law, the noted zoologist Addison Emery Verrill, added a postscript to Smith's letter: "With what Professor Smith has said, I heartily agree and have nothing more to add."[180]

That Gilman was inclined to inquire of British scientists regarding this position speaks to his concern relative to the state of American departments of biology. Except at Harvard, physiology was barely addressed in the United States. Owing to the dearth of viable American candidates, and with Huxley's strong endorsement of his former assistant, Gilman decided on Martin. He offered the young scientist a starting salary of twenty-five hundred dollars to come to Baltimore and organize a laboratory and school of biology "on a plan similar to that of Prof. Huxley at So[uth] Kensington" for two groups of students: those preparing to become physicians and those wanting to pursue careers as naturalists.[181] This offer was certainly in keeping with Gilman's philosophy of building an energetic and ambitious group of faculty who would "have twenty years before them rather than twenty years behind them."[182]

Martin initially declined Gilman's offer, "chiefly for the reason that, others being at present partly dependent upon me, I cannot afford the pecuniary loss which acceptance of your offer would entail." Of additional concern to him was the skeletal laboratory space Gilman described: only a single room for the time being. "I could not undertake to direct the whole biological teaching of the University," Martin argued, "as well as the encouragement and assistance of the more promising students in original research, with such scanty accommodation."[183] In this one instance Martin highlighted two aspects of Gilman's original offer that were wanting, and for which the new president would passionately advocate: appropriate space (with ample equipment and apparatus) for original research and the promising students capable of pushing professors to do their best work.

Begging permission to counter Gilman's offer—"on the advice of my scientific friends in England"—Martin stipulated three conditions: first, a starting annual salary of four thousand dollars for two years, increasing to five thousand thereafter; second, that the university should "build and fit up" a proper biological laboratory; and third, that he be afforded the title of professor, providing Martin "a direct voice in the arrangements of the curriculum and studies of the University."[184] Gilman acceded to all three conditions, and Martin then became the university's fifth professor, with the board of trustees ratifying his appointment on September 3, 1876.

Upon hearing the news, Huxley wrote Gilman: "I have great regard and esteem for him [Martin] and it is a great pleasure to know that he has secured so excellent a position."[185] Martin wasted little time. He secured passage to New York from Liverpool—traveling with Professor Huxley, who was beginning a speaking tour—on July 27, 1876, just a few weeks after his twenty-eighth birthday.[186] The university honored all its pledges to Martin, announcing in the August 1876 *Circular* that the "laboratory will be very completely fitted up, and so far at least as regards physiology will present facilities for work unequalled, it is believed, in this country, and excelled by but a few laboratories abroad." The notice further announced an additional room for the study of physiological chemistry "to supply material to those wishing to investigate the anatomy of special groups of animals or plants."[187]

Martin would become known for many things during his tenure at Hopkins, including being named the first professor of the medical faculty in 1883 and his path-breaking research in experimental procedures in physiology, which led to new techniques for studying the isolated mammalian heart. The year 1879 was particularly busy for Martin, as he taught courses in general biology and animal physiology, instructed medical students in physiology, delivered twenty public lectures, and continued his Saturday classes in biology.[188] The Saturday classes were directed at schoolteachers and patterned after similar instruction that Martin had done with his mentor, Thomas Huxley, in London.[189] Martin described the purpose of the Saturday sessions to Gilman: "Our object is not so much to teach Physiology as to teach how to teach it, and it is therefore more important, I venture to think, that this course be made as perfect an example of science teaching as possible, than it is in the case of any other course in the University."[190] Further adding to his activities that year, Martin married Hetty Cary, the widow of the Confederate army general John Pegram, thus facilitating his entrée into Baltimore society.

What Martin accomplished in his first decade at Hopkins is remarkable: he initiated a successful program for the training of advanced workers in biology, undertook and supervised important original research in a host of areas within physiology, and built up a well-appointed laboratory. He was now looking forward to playing a significant role in the development of the Hopkins medical school. However, Martin's second decade in Baltimore "would be characterized by the subtle erosion of much that he accomplished" in his first ten years.[191] The decline began, ironically, with the opening of Martin's new laboratory in 1883. One of his star students, William Henry Howell, recorded years later that from the time the new laboratory opened, "a kind of apathy became apparent in his work. . . . But as a matter of fact Martin's verve and inspiration were dying out. . . . The cause of this decline in energy and ambition is difficult to understand. It is only partly explained, I think, by the fact that in his later years he became distinctly an alcoholic—but before that misfortune came to him, there had been some diminution in the driving force that characterized his first years in the University."[192]

Martin described the new facility as "unrivaled in the United States, and not surpassed in the world,"[193] but he was taken aback by the reaction to its opening and the personal attacks leveled by antivivisection activists. Among those most vocal in their criticism of Martin and his activities were Henry Bergh, founder of the American Society for the Prevention of Cruelty to Animals, and a fellow Hopkins faculty member, J. Rendel Harris. Martin expended tremendous energy in responding to the criticism, recalling the way opposition had severely stunted physiological labs in Great Britain. Even Gilman expressed, in 1906, how hard it was to imagine "what prejudices then prevailed in respect to 'biology.' "[194] Fearing that the criticism would impede what he was doing with physiology at Hopkins, Martin developed guidelines for animal experimentation that were eventually adopted by the executive committee.[195]

In addition to the incessant condemnation of his work, Martin also faced the departure of many of his star pupils as they began populating departments of physiology across the United States. Henry Sewall, the first person in America to earn a doctorate in physiology, graduated in 1881 to become head of physiology at the University of Michigan, and William T. Sedgwick, a graduate of the Sheffield Scientific School at Yale and recipient of a PhD in biology from Hopkins, took up an appointment at the Massachusetts Institute of Technology in 1883. While Martin was pleased for his pupils, these departures left him exasperated. As he wrote to Gilman, "Of course this recognition at the hub is in one way very gratifying; in another it is extremely annoying as it leaves me to go into a new Laboratory without an associate and no chance of getting a man who is competent to take the course of lectures which I had got Sedgwick trained for. . . . I shall have to take the lectures on both General Biology and on Physiology next year and try to get [William Henry] Howell or H. [Henry Herbert] Donaldson or some one into training for Sedgwick's place."[196]

The successful placement of Hopkins graduates in universities of renown was certainly a point of pride for the institution. However, the disruption caused to Martin's lab and his ongoing research by the departure of these gifted and capable students is impossible to calculate. Sewall, Sedgwick, and their fellow student Frederic S. Lee, who would go on to a forty-three-year career at Columbia, all earned PhDs with Martin. There was, nevertheless, a marked drop-off among the students who would follow Martin's first cohort. The cardiologist and medical historian W. Bruce Fye notes that "none of the degree recipients after 1885 would achieve the distinction in physiology of Martin's earlier pupils."[197]

Martin was also expected to take on a larger role in the development of the Hopkins medical school. Appointed to the medical school faculty in June 1883, at the same time as his colleagues Ira Remsen and John S. Billings, Martin was to teach physiology. A confluence of anxiety-inducing events—the turnover among his staff and students, the ongoing attacks of the antivivisectionists, and the additional responsibilities associated with the medical school enterprise—were further compounded by the illness of Martin's wife, Hetty.

The granddaughter of the writer Virginia Randolph Cary, Hetty came from proud Virginian lineage. Hetty and other members of her family were professed secessionists who helped sew the first three Confederate battle flags. Hetty married General Pegram on January 19, 1865, in Richmond, Virginia, at a ceremony attended by the Confederate president, Jefferson Davis, and his wife, Varina. Eighteen days later, Pegram was killed by a Minié ball while leading a charge in the Battle of Hatcher's Run. Exactly three weeks to the day, in the very church where Pegram and Cary had been married, the general's funeral was conducted by the same pastor, with many of the same attendees sitting in the pews.[198] For a time, Cary taught at the Southern Home School in

Baltimore, for girls, and during a trip to Europe she met Martin, who was twelve years her junior. They were married in Baltimore in 1879. After a protracted illness, probably tuberculosis, Hetty died at home in 1892.[199]

Martin's own health continued to worsen as a result of his perpetual struggle with alcoholism. He developed peripheral neuritis, which in turn led to a morphine addiction. Martin was attended to by his faculty colleague William Osler, who then referred him to his close medical colleague S. Weir Mitchell in Philadelphia. Recognizing that Martin was in no condition to teach or help with medical school development, Gilman urged him to resign. Martin did so in April 1893. He then spent time at the Homewood Retreat in Ontario, Canada, a hospital established in 1883 for the treatment of alcoholism and drug addiction. Martin would return to Baltimore one more time, spending nearly two months at the Johns Hopkins Hospital before being discharged on December 29, 1893, with diagnoses of neurasthenia and alcoholism.[200] In 1894 Martin set sail for England, where he would briefly resume his physiological research in Huxley's laboratory before passing away on October 27, 1896. He was 48 years old.

One can only imagine what further advances Martin might have made had his life not been cut short by his debilitating addictions. Gilman observed what Martin and his career meant to biology and medical education:

> To this study, Dr. Martin had a noteworthy impulse, and the methods he introduced were soon followed in other parts of the country. In the Johns Hopkins University it was soon determined that no one should be encouraged to enter upon the study of medicine without a careful previous training in a physiological laboratory. The improvements now common in medical schools are largely based upon the recognition of the principle that living creatures, in their normal and healthy aspects, should be studied before the phenomena and treatment of disease, and credit should always be given to Dr. Martin for the skill with which he introduced among Americans the best methods of study.[201]

### Charles D'Urban Morris

Gilman had his first-rate Greek scholar in Gildersleeve. He was now prepared to fill the last of the six original faculty slots with a professor of Latin and Greek, demonstrating just how important both the president and trustees considered classical studies to be. Further emblematic of the classical flavor of American higher education of the age, there were more applications for this position—twenty by the end of March 1876—than for any other.[202] Ralph Waldo Emerson had contacted Gilman on behalf of a candidate, and the president responded, respectfully, "We shall not fail to bear in mind what you say; but ought perhaps to add that in no department of learning have we so many promising candidates, 'all honorable men,' as in Latin."[203]

As early as late fall 1875 Gilman had reached out for recommendations to one of America's luminaries in the field: Harvard's George Lane, the Pope Professor of Latin for twenty-five years. In his response to Gilman, Lane offered four names: Walter Blair of Hampden-Sidney College in Virginia; James Greenough, Lane's colleague at Harvard; Henry John Roby, a fellow of St. John's College and future member of Parliament; and Basil Gildersleeve.[204] Lane served as the go-between with Roby and conveyed the Englishman's response to Gilman at the end of January: "At this time of life (45), he would not think of leaving England, and even if he did think of it, he is bound down by such articles of partnership that to leave is an impossibility, much as he would prefer study to 'spinning cotton thread.'"[205] Roby's tenure as first secretary and then commissioner for the Endowed Schools Commission had come to an end with the body's dissolution in 1874. Roby had then became a partner, together with his father-in-law, in a cotton manufacturing firm just outside Manchester.

Learning that Lane himself might be interested in the position, Gilman made overtures to Cambridge. Lane responded in mid-February: "Your proposition about Baltimore takes my fancy amazingly and I thank you very much for thinking of me. . . . I have been here so long that at first thought it seems almost impossible to go. I know just what kind of work is expected of me and I can do it successfully: and at Baltimore I must forego one thing which has more attractions than almost anything else—the Library."[206] Hopkins being brand-new, its library was far from an established institution like Harvard's. This would pose a significant recruitment hindrance for a classicist like Lane, who had access to one of the nation's most expansive collections. Gilman's plan from the start was to partner with the Peabody Institute in hopes that its resources—and its ability to expend considerably more on rare books and other materials—might suffice as Hopkins expanded its own holdings. For the time being, as Gilman explained to Gildersleeve, the trustees proposed "to buy those books which professors or students will require for future use—placing those of general interest in our Reference Room—those of special importance in the various class rooms."[207]

Lane noted that his tenure at Harvard had been twenty-five years and his salary had never been sufficient. "I have been obliged to eke it out by sidework of the most laborious and distasteful kind. The community has taken no interest in the professors or their welfare, and though the President's ideas are liberal, I cannot see any prospect of hope for the future." Lane pined for "the prospect of living without the galling anxieties of a Cambridge life" but worried aloud to Gilman about whether he would be successful and asked what was to be expected of him. Nonetheless, Lane left the door to further consideration ever so slightly ajar, concluding that before "deciding irrevocably, I should like to hear further particulars. Gildersleeve is a great attraction. If it is proper to ask it, is Sylvester coming?"[208] Lane's suggestion that the prospect of working alongside colleagues like Gildersleeve and Sylvester was irresistible served as evidence that Gilman's recruitment efforts were bringing attention to the fledgling Baltimore enterprise. The new president was attracting a first-rate faculty, and people were taking note.

Gilman continued to press for his Latin scholar and even traveled to Harvard to meet Lane in person. All these efforts notwithstanding, Lane finally declined in late

March, although he did cite many of the job's attractions—"the pleasant city, the hospitable people, the prospect of work in a new field, and the companionship of my old and valued friend, Gildersleeve." Lane and Gildersleeve had been housemates in Germany in the summer of 1851, and Lane's son, Gardiner Martin Lane, married Gildersleeve's daughter, Emma Louise, in 1898.[209] But Lane, because of his stage in life and his station at Harvard, remained fixed in his decision, allowing that "if I were twenty years younger I should not have any hesitation."[210]

Gilman now had to move on to other prospective candidates, and this time he used another go-between. Assisting Gilman with his recruiting efforts was the founder and first editor of *The Nation*, Edwin Lawrence Godkin. Godkin would write Gilman with another recommendation just a few days after Lane's decision. Gilman and Godkin had known each other since the former's tenure at the Sheffield Scientific School. Gilman had submitted his first article to Godkin's publication, titled "The Life of Percival," which ran on November 1, 1866. For his efforts Gilman was paid ten dollars.[211] Multiple articles by Gilman, on a wide variety of subjects, would find their way into print in *The Nation* over many years. After an interview with Gilman in January 1875, Godkin even published the new president's initial plans for the Johns Hopkins University (months before Gilman would officially begin in Baltimore). The article summarized the proposed emphasis on advanced scholarship and the training of graduate students, while leaving the instruction of undergraduates to other universities.[212]

For the moment, however, both men were focused on landing the right candidate, as the first Hopkins classes were set to begin in just a few months. Godkin wrote to Gilman telling him about a "very excellent man in New York who wants a professorship of Greek or Latin . . . Chaz D. Morris."[213] Gilman did his homework on Morris and fretted that what he had in mind at Hopkins might be below Morris's expectations and what he could command given his years of experience and his age. Gilman wrote to Godkin, asking him to find out whether Morris would come for a three-year appointment and a starting salary of three thousand dollars, adding, "I think it would not be well that he should even know of this."[214] A few days later, Godkin wrote Gilman again, expressing his belief that Morris was "among the half dozen best Classical Scholars in England or America, and an admirable tutor of College students. He has, through a series of unfortunate accidents, been wasted on boys, and likely on reprobates."[215] Morris had extensive experience with younger, less mature students, in addition to fulfilling Gilman's criterion of producing meaningful research. The author of two textbooks, *Latin Grammar and Reader* and *Attic Greek Grammar*, Morris had developed original views on the proper methods for teaching elements of the ancient languages.[216]

A graduate of both Lincoln and Oriel Colleges at Oxford, Morris accepted Gilman's offer and was assigned to oversee the required chapel sessions and serve as faculty adviser to the thirty-five undergraduate students who matriculated in the fall of 1876. At first, Gilman visualized Morris in the post of adjunct professor of Greek and

Latin rather than as a full professor of Latin, and Morris appeared somewhat hesitant to leave New York without getting a pay raise. Over the next few weeks of correspondence between the two, however, the position continued to evolve, and Morris became increasingly enthusiastic about how Gilman saw his role at Hopkins. Morris wrote to Gilman in June: "I cannot help confessing I have a hunger for the sort of work you offered me."[217] While the first five hires—Gildersleeve, Sylvester, Remsen, Rowland, and Martin—represented the nucleus of a great research faculty, Morris "was Gilman's connection with the collegiate world which assured its continuation."[218] This was certainly in keeping with the "Plan of Procedure" that Gilman had outlined to the board and that the trustees had subsequently ratified. From the outset, the emphasis at Hopkins was unquestionably on graduate education, but Gilman viewed this last appointment—especially given Morris' background, experience, and orientation—as an explicit recognition of the college idea within the institution. The college idea was something of inestimable value in the life of the university as a whole.[219]

Since Gildersleeve's hire as the first faculty member in February, Gilman had repeatedly asked him to weigh in with thoughts on candidates that the president was vetting. In the month of June 1876 alone, Gildersleeve would write five lengthy letters to Gilman with a whole range of opinions on prospective hires. He was, however, particularly pleased to hear of the trustees' support for his own discipline: "I am glad to learn from your letter that the board is so liberally disposed toward Philology."[220] On the subject of Morris becoming a faculty colleague, Gildersleeve wrote the president: "I have formed a favorable opinion of Morris and judge from some points in his books that he would not be indisposed to work with me—a vital matter so far as my usefulness is concerned."[221] Learning of Gilman's continued recruitment efforts, he wrote a few weeks later, "Morris is full of sap and vigor and he will prove a valuable acquisition."[222]

Morris would eventually agree to the modified position proposed by Gilman, and the contract terms were negotiated over the summer months. Morris' appointment was officially ratified on September 4, 1876, just a month before the official launch of formal instruction. Upon learning of the news, Morris wrote Gilman that he was "now at the command of the university" and hoped that the president might give him "some hints which might shorten my labours of search" in finding accommodations in Baltimore. Gilman was so invested in hiring his original six faculty that he even assisted them in finding the appropriate housing.[223]

Morris' original appointment was as "associate professor of Greek and Latin," though this would be changed later on to "Collegiate Professor of Latin and Greek." His starting salary of three thousand dollar (the same as Ira Remsen's) was one thousand dollars more than Rowland's, although all three men's salaries would be bumped up to four thousand dollars for the academic year 1880–81.[224] In effect, there was no distinction among the faculty appointments and salary rankings of the original six professors between those who taught graduate students and those who taught underclassmen. Gilman's change to Morris' title made his status scarcely distinguishable from those of his colleagues who had more interaction with advanced students.[225]

The last of the original six faculty to be selected, Morris was also the first to pass away, in February 1886 at age 59. While his time at Hopkins was short, his influence was profoundly felt, and Gilman lauded Morris for bringing "the best traditions of an English university," noting that "among other valuable suggestions he made was the appointment of advisers to small groups of students, so that every one of them might be guided in the choice of his studies by a qualified friend."[226] Gilman noted that given the diminution of interest in classical studies among Hopkins undergraduates, the number of students who elected Morris' courses was never very large. Nonetheless, in a moving tribute at the university memorial service at the time of Morris' death, Gildersleeve read a resolution in honor of his colleague: "As a teacher, he carried into the classroom the strength and warmth of thorough conviction. Enthusiastic devotion to his subject, confidence in his methods, an ardent desire to impress and to impart, gave him a hold on his pupils that is given to few, and his instruction will ever be memorable to those who had the privilege of his inspiration and guidance."[227]

It was not until Morris' passing that his appointment as "collegiate" professor revealed the many dean-like functions that he had masterfully performed during his tenure. This commitment to the traditional model was evidenced by Morris and his early role as the de facto dean of undergraduate students. One of the customary roles of such a position is the disciplining of students when required. As there was no such position designated for postgraduates, the role of dean of graduate students fell to President Gilman. The historical record reveals that this arrangement was very much a work in progress, and what to do with certain students was determined on an ad hoc basis. Allowances for "special cases" were made; some worked out, while others did not. Gilman's personal correspondence contains letters to parents about their sons' academic performance. In a letter directed to a Mrs. Child of Richmond, Virginia, he wrote: "Madame, I am sorry to be obliged to say to you that your son has been so insensitive to his duties to the university that there is great doubt he can retain his place among us."[228] The student in question was Charles Tripler Child, who had come to Hopkins in 1885 as a special graduate student (despite not having earned a bachelor's degree) in physics and mathematics under the tutelage of professors Rowland, Clark, and Franklin. He was also a member of the inaugural class in electricity, under the direction of Dr. Louis Duncan. Hopkins did not appear to be the right fit for Mr. Child, but it was not for lack of effort on the part of Gilman and his faculty colleagues. Nor was Child lacking in intelligence, as he left Baltimore in 1887 and enjoyed a distinguished career as an electrical engineer and technical editor for several engineering publications. He died tragically at age 35 from malaria.[229]

By 1889 the Hopkins faculty had grown to fifty-five members, fifteen of whom (including Rowland, Gildersleeve, and Sylvester's replacement, Simon Newcomb) had no direct connection with undergraduates. Conversely, Ira Remsen took tremendous pride in the fact that he taught beginning chemistry.[230] Morris was replaced by John Henry Wright, a young Dartmouth graduate whose appointment at Hopkins included the dual roles of "Dean of the College Board" and professor of classical philology. Shortly after his arrival at Hopkins, Wright gave an address to begin the school year titled "The College in the University and Classical Philology in the College," in which he praised Morris for bringing "to the service of this university, in the most important years of her existence, the best and manliest culture of England, a pure heart, a tender conscience, and an unselfish devotion to the welfare of his fellowmen."[231] While his time at Hopkins was very brief—Wright announced less than a year into his tenure that he was leaving Baltimore to become professor of Greek at Harvard—he would go on to develop a reputation as one of America's most eminent nineteenth-century classical scholars.

Desiring someone with a bit more experience who would remain at Hopkins longer than one year, Gilman and the board appointed Edward Herrick Griffin dean of the college faculty and professor of the history of philosophy in 1889. This appointment, according to Frederick Rudolph, was evidence of the university's support of a "full-blown undergraduate program," with Griffin serving, in effect, as an undergraduate dean teaching undergraduate philosophy.[232] Within the Hopkins faculty, Griffin was "the sole representative of a type then already beginning to disappear, the clergyman-teacher who carried urbanely the best traditions of New England culture into other parts of the land."[233] The "gentle Dean," as Griffin was affectionately known by his former students, came to symbolize—within an environment aggressively oriented to the purposes of scientific German (or specialized) scholarship—the persistence of the collegiate way and the humanist spirit still extant at Hopkins.[234]

## "We Were Seven"

Gilman had scoured the American and British educational landscapes to land the founding core of his Hopkins faculty. The original six—"we were seven," Gilman reflected years later—were an eclectic and accomplished group that would chart the innovative course for the university as it moved into its first decade. Some would have truncated careers at Hopkins, either because they went somewhere else or because they died prematurely, while others would remain for much longer and take on additional administrative functions beyond the classroom, seminar room, and laboratory. Of the five "research" professors, all but Sylvester were younger than Gilman. They were provided what no other university offered: a limited number of students with exceptional capacity; an entirely free hand in conducting their original research; and the means whereby their work would be disseminated to the world.

Each brought a unique perspective along with prodigious accomplishments. Rowland was the epitome of the emerging genius with nothing but limitless opportunity ahead; Sylvester was renowned worldwide; Gildersleeve came with the sympathy and respect of the South; Remsen was the ardent advocate of the ideal of the German research university; Martin was vilified for his science but remained resolute in defense of the means to his pathbreaking ends; and Morris embodied the classical college element within the overtly graduate-oriented institution.[235]

In recruiting this cohort, Gilman had proven his tenacity, while articulating a clear and unimpeded vision of the uniqueness of the model Hopkins was creating. Nowhere in the annals of American higher education is there a similar story of a new president personally recruiting his own faculty in this manner. Gilman had made an extraordinary investment of time, attention, resources, and energy. And it had paid off. "Opportunity is one thing," the medical historian Richard Harrison Shryock wrote, "the ability to make the most of it something else again." Likewise, "traditions have their values but can also impede progress: The Hopkins had neither antiquated notions nor obsolescent staff to handicap it at the start. Most of its faculty was relatively young, which was no small advantage in itself."[236]

Heretofore research had been a personal pursuit for the faculty, ancillary to their central duties. But Gilman and the trustees proposed to make original research the university's fundamental and initial concern.[237] Gilman also put every other institution on notice that what was being launched in Baltimore should be viewed not as the exception but rather as the rule for the modern American research university. While it would take decades, the new university's innovation resulted in tectonic shifts relative to the form, function, and mission of institutions everywhere.

# CHAPTER FIVE

# Launching Our Bark
# upon the Patapsco

In February 1876, a little more than a year after accepting the job, Daniel Coit Gilman sat in the Academy of Music building in downtown Baltimore to be officially inaugurated as the first president of the Johns Hopkins University. While it had none of the history or tradition of America's foremost universities in 1876, Hopkins launched itself with pomp and circumstance, which so many of them, started as small religious academies, never could have done. The date—February 22—was set purposely to coincide with George Washington's birthday in the centennial year of America's independence.[1] National and state officials attended, and the *Baltimore Sun* reported that the ceremony was "dignified by the presence of nearly all the more prominent and influential citizens of Baltimore . . . and by many cultivated women."[2] A friend who regretfully could not attend was Senator Justin Morrill of Vermont, who wrote to the new president, "I congratulate you upon reaching a position at last where you will have ample room for your laudable enthusiasm in behalf of higher education."[3]

The attendees had come to hear Gilman and to learn whether he intended the focus of the institution to be national or local; its nature nonsectarian or religious; its emphasis on graduates or undergraduates. Gilman recognized that many in the audience, and some among the board of trustees, held widely divergent views. Months earlier, when Gilman's broad perspective and ambitious plans for the university had been revealed, some locals had resisted. They firmly believed that the primary role of the institution should be to benefit the largest possible number of Baltimore residents, with particular emphasis on agriculture and the mechanic arts, rather than serving as a graduate school designed for the few. This pushback reminded Gilman of the provincialism and anti-intellectualism he had encountered while at the University of California. Undeterred, Gilman advocated for a national and international role and vision for the newest of universities. He would refer to this commitment throughout his remarks.

The large crowd settled in and enjoyed music provided by the Peabody Conservatory Orchestra, followed by an invocation delivered by Dr. Alfred Magill Randolph, rector of the Emmanuel Protestant Episcopal Church. Reverdy Johnson Jr. then offered brief remarks noting the significance of the date, as the birthday of both the United States and the father of the nation: "We may say that the University's birth takes place today, and I do not think it mere sentiment, should we dwell with interest upon its concurrence with the centennial year of our national birth, and the birthday of him who led the nation from the throes of battle to maturity and peace."[4]

Johnson then introduced the featured speaker. That the president of Harvard University, Charles Eliot, was showcased so prominently in the program was an unmistakable reminder that this was not the launch of just any new college in 1876. Eliot began: "The oldest university of the country cordially greets the youngest, and welcomes a worthy ally—an ally strong in material resources and high in purpose." The chemist turned president got straight to the point: "The splendid benefaction of Johns Hopkins must be unsectarian . . . but the absence of sectarian control should not be confounded with lack of piety." Eliot then congratulated the mayor and the city of Baltimore, for he believed that in a few generations "she will be the seat of a rich and powerful university" holding aloft the "high standard of public duty and public spirit" and enlarging "that cultivated class which is distinguished, not by wealth merely, but by refinement and spirituality."[5]

President of an institution founded 240 years earlier, Eliot reminded his colleague that he should be prepared for the long haul: Gilman might not see the real fruits of his efforts in the early days, "for to build a university needs not years only, but generations; but though 'deeds unfinished will weigh on the doer,' and anxieties will sometimes oppress you, great privileges are nevertheless attached to your office."[6] The new Hopkins leader was not unaware of what the position entailed, having experienced presidential peaks and valleys during his tenure in California. Eliot finished his brief comments where he had begun, appealing to a loftier mission and goal for the newest of institutions: "Universities, wisely directed, store up the intellectual capital of the race, and become fountains of spiritual and moral power. . . . Here may the irradiating light of genius sometimes flash out to rejoice mankind; above all, here may many generations of manly youth learn righteousness."[7]

## "We Launch Our Bark Upon the Patapsco"

It was now Gilman's turn. The years of experience, the relationships cultivated, the travel to some of the world's finest universities and libraries to study with some of the most renowned faculty, the turbulent tenure in California, the research on the structure, form, and function of the modern university, even the opportunities passed over in anticipation of something else—all these had brought Gilman to this moment and place. Acknowledging that his entire academic career had been spent on opposite coasts at two very different institutions—"one full of honors, the other of hopes; one led by experience, the other by expectations"—Gilman spoke of his hope that "the lessons of both, the old and the new, be wisely blended here."[8] While Gilman may have been a remarkable orator, no other speech of his has lived on as his inaugural address has. Parts are still quoted in the twenty-first century as expressions of the ideal of what a university can aspire to be, while aspects specific to Hopkins and its ambitions are masterfully woven throughout.

Gilman's speech is, in so many ways, the gold standard of university inaugural addresses. In anticipation of a significant milestone for the Johns Hopkins University in 2001, Ross Jones—a fifty-year employee of Hopkins and chair of the 125th Anniversary Committee—noted the colossal task of capturing in a single volume all that Hopkins had accomplished since its founding. The result was the book *Johns Hopkins: Knowledge for the World, 1876–2001*. The book is organized around the themes Gilman expounded in his inauguration. The idea came from Mame Warren, the creative editor of the project, who described her rationale for the work's organizational structure as follows: "President Gilman described an array of activities—many of them unprecedented—that he believed the university would pursue. Over the next 125 years virtually every development Gilman foretold became a reality."[9] The twelve themes are not addressed in the order in which they were presented in his speech, but a brief outline of the book is noteworthy, as each chapter title is a direct quote from Gilman:

— "By One For All"
— "We Launch Our Bark Upon the Patapsco"
— "Listen, Ponder, and Observe"
— "The Best Investigators"
— "Relations to Society"
— "Genius, Talent, Learning and Promise"
— "Strong, Bright, Useful and True"
— "The Morning has Dawned"
— "A Good Service"
— "An Academic Grove"
— "The Best Opportunities"
— "A Generous Affiliation"

For all the sense of expectation as the new president began his remarks, Gilman would launch into his address in a most unusual way: by tamping down expectations for the new university. The Hopkins gift was remarkable, he told the crowd, but it wouldn't build monumental structures or pay for generous salaries. "And so it happens that dreams of monumental structures and splendid piles and munificent salaries flit through the mind which can never become real. Do not forget how much wealth is accumulated by older colleges—in repute, experience and influence, and also in material things."[10]

In rehearsing for his audience the income-yielding endowments of Harvard and Yale (and Cornell too, with a fleeting reference to Northwestern University in Evanston, Illinois), Gilman bemoaned the stark reality that Hopkins must subsist on an endowment producing an annual budget of two hundred thousand dollars, with this ominous footnote: "But all our revenue is not at once available; for as the capital cannot be spent on buildings, some income must be reserved for this."[11] In Gilman's estimation, this amount was little more than half what Harvard operated on annually. After a brief summary of the challenges in accruing enough money to begin construction, Gilman apologized that his remarks might seem "a little ungracious." However, he continued, "our friends are so very generous in their expectations that I feel compelled, at the very outset, to utter a word of caution." Until the original bequest was supplemented by other gifts or Baltimore's growth increased the value of the university's investments, Gilman adjured, "we must be contented with good work in a limited field."[12] The phrase *good work in a limited field* would be a guidepost for the university in its early days.

But then Gilman pivoted. He had not come to focus on the university's limitations. Instead, he outlined the "five-fold advantages" Hopkins enjoyed that no other university could claim. First, the trustees had complete and unrestricted latitude to perform their duties. Second, because the institution had been founded in the absence of any political or ecclesiastical control, it would "doubtless serve both church and state the better because it is free from the guardianship of either." Third, Johns Hopkins' location in a large town, an old state, at the crossroads of North and South, East and West, provided the university geographical advantages, the very advantages that had resulted in excellent high schools, a city college, and good private schools. Fourth, the promise of a hospital linked to the university and a medical school would mean that their remedial and preventive agencies were extended "to thousands who may never come within its walls, but whose ills will be relieved by those taught there." This alignment of the hospital and the medical school was a unique approach and would transform medical education in the United States. Finally, Gilman acknowledged the propitious "timeliness of our foundation": "We begin after the national bounty has for fourteen years, under the far-reaching bill of Senator Morrill of Vermont, promoted scientific education; and after scores of wealthy men bestowing many million dollars for the foundation of new institutions of the highest sort."[13] If there was ever an ideal time for launching a university in Baltimore, this was it. Gilman hammered home that no institution could lay claim to such an advantageous moment and place—with all the attendant benefits—as could The Johns Hopkins University.

A keen student of history and American higher education institutions, Gilman was very familiar with the "numerous experiments, some with oil in the lamps and some without." Hopkins could learn from these costly ventures and "reap the lessons, while others bear the loss."[14] The university was unequivocally committed to not re-peating the mistakes of those that had preceded it. Gilman and his colleagues recog-nized that pre–Civil War reformers had "left a great deal of unfinished business, but they set the agenda for change."[15] It was now their opportunity to drive that agenda for change at Hopkins.

### "Listen, Ponder, and Observe"

To provide context for the Hopkins experiment, Gilman launched into a summary of educational discussions happening at the time, emphasizing the debates within Ger-many. Gilman advised against jumping headlong into wholesale adoption of the German model "lest we accept what is there cast off; lest we introduce faults as well as virtues." It would behoove Hopkins to "listen, ponder, and observe; and above all to be modest in the announcement of our plans." Still, the "oldest and remotest na-tions" were at that very moment looking to the United States for light; Gilman re-ported that American higher education was being held up as an example in China, Lebanon, Egypt, and the Hawaiian Islands.[16]

"What is the significance of all that activity?" Gilman asked. His answer became the most well known and most often quoted portion of his speech:

> It is a reaching out for a better state of society than now exists; it is a dim but an indelible impression of the value of learning; it is a craving for intellectual and moral growth; it is a longing to interpret the laws of creation; it means a wish for less misery among the poor, less ignorance in schools, less bigotry in the temple, less suffering in the hospital, less fraud in business, less folly in politics; it means more study of nature, more love of art, more lessons from history, more security in prop-erty, more health in cities, more virtue in the country, more wisdom in legislation, more intelligence, more happiness, more religion.[17]

From this appeal, Gilman turned to the five institutions founded in modern soci-ety for the promotion of superior education: universities, learned societies, colleges, technical schools, and museums. For purposes of illustration, Gilman asserted that wherever a strong university was maintained, the other agencies revolved around it: "It is the sun and they are the planets. In Baltimore you have hitherto had a College, an Academy of Sciences, Professional Schools and a Scholars' Library, but you have not had such an endowed University as that which is now inaugurated." Noting that most institutions are not free to build anew ("traditions and conditions impede their progress"), Gilman laid out what might be widely accepted in management parlance today as a mission and vision statement for Hopkins. "Our effort will be to accept that which is determined," proclaimed Gilman, "to avoid that which is obsolescent, to study that which is doubtful,—'slowly making haste.'"[18]

One might detect a certain resignation in Gilman's final phrase, suggesting an ac-ceptance of the status quo, while moving the university forward ever so deliberatively into those areas where it chose to wade. But Gilman was merely preparing his audience for the "Twelve Points Determined," a rallying position for the Hopkins community. They clearly delineate both his own personal convictions as well as suggest the direction the university would take under this leadership, and are worth quoting:

1. All sciences are worthy of promotion; or in other words, it is useless to dispute whether literature or science should receive most attention, or whether there is any essential difference between the old and the new education.

2. Religion has nothing to fear from science, and science need not be afraid of religion. Religion claims to interpret the word of God, and science to reveal the laws of God. The interpreters may blunder, but truths are immutable, eternal and never in conflict.

3. Remote utility is quite as worthy to be thought of as immediate advantage. Those ventures are not always most sagacious that expect a return on the morrow. It sometimes pays to send our argosies across the seas; to make investments with an eye to slow but sure returns. So is it always in the promotion of science.

4. As it is impossible for any university to encourage with equal freedom all branches of learning, a selection must be made by enlightened governors, and that selection must depend on the requirements and deficiencies of a given people, in a given period. There is no absolute standard of preference. What is more important at one time or in one place may be less needed elsewhere and otherwise.

5. Individual students cannot pursue all branches of learning, and must be allowed to select, under the guidance of those who are appointed to counsel them. Nor can able professors be governed by routine. Teachers and pupils must be allowed great freedom in their method of work. Recitations, lectures, examinations, laboratories, libraries, field exercises, travels, are all legitimate means of culture.

6. The best scholars will almost invariably be those who make special attainments on the foundation of a broad and liberal culture.

7. The best teachers are usually those who are free, competent and willing to make original researches in the library and the laboratory.

8. The best investigators are usually those who have also the responsibilities of instruction, gaining thus the incitement of colleagues, the encouragement of pupils, the observation of the public.

9. Universities should bestow their honors with a sparing hand; their benefits most freely.

10. A university cannot be created in a day; it is a slow growth. The University of Berlin has been quoted as a proof of the contrary. That was indeed a quick success, but in an old, compact country, crowded with learned men eager to assemble at the Prussian court. It was a change of base rather than a sudden development.

11. The object of the university is to develop character—to make men. It misses its

aim if it produces learned pedants, or simple artisans, or cunning sophists, or pretentious practitioners. Its purport is not so much to impart knowledge to the pupils, as to whet the appetite, exhibit methods, develop powers, strengthen judgment, and invigorate the intellectual and moral forces. It should prepare for the service of society a class of students who will be wise, thoughtful, progressive guides in whatever department of work or thought they may be engaged.

12. Universities easily fall into ruts. Almost every epoch requires a fresh start.[19]

Some of Gilman's twelve points were unique; others were amalgamated perspectives pieced together by a 45-year-old man long on experience, optimistic in outlook, and eager to get started. Gilman surmised that "if these points are conceded, our task is simplified, though it is still difficult."[20]

### "What Will Be Its Scope?"

The second portion of Gilman's address—in which, the *Sun* reported, "President Gilman came out strongly and left a good impression"[21]—was focused on the question that had brought everyone together that February morning: "The Johns Hopkins University: what will be its scope?" Regarding its organization, Gilman delineated the disciplines and areas of focus for the faculty: the hiring of medical school professors was not to be long delayed, jurisprudence to come in time (this, of course, did not materialize, nor did theology). Fundamental to the entire enterprise was Gilman's commitment to finding the "fittest teachers" and expecting them "to do their very best work." He then spoke of distinct disciplines: medical sciences and biology, modern humanities, national surveys (Gilman's definition here was broad and included astronomical, geodetical, topographical, meteorological, geological, zoological, botanical, and economical), and applied mathematics. Gilman conceded that fleshing out plans for the hospital and the medical school would take time. Before their codification, however, the president recognized a unique opportunity to "provide instruction antecedent to the professional study of medicine." His perspective fashioned after the practices at the Sheffield Scientific School, Gilman insisting that a premed student "should acquire enough of French and German to follow with ease European science, and enough Latin for his professional needs."[22] Elements of the then classical American education with which Gilman was very familiar made their way into the technical and scientific areas of focus, even at Hopkins.

Gilman then addressed the task of recruiting faculty to Baltimore, admitting that it was not an easy task "to transplant a tree which is deeply rooted"—a reference to his inability to persuade European professors to join him at Hopkins. "Many are reluctant to cross the sea," he admitted. The answer lay in "young Americans of talent and promise—there is our strength, and a noble company they are!" Gilman gave examples of academics, scientists, lawyers, and presidents who had achieved renown and acclaim at a young age. This was what he proposed at Hopkins. Gilman's approach was to secure a strong retinue of young men, "appointing them because they have twenty years before them." He was speaking not only of faculty recruitment but also of the fellowship system at Hopkins, which in turn produced graduates, some of whom stayed at the university to join the ranks of the full-time faculty. The proposed model Gilman outlined had elements of both the English and German fellowship systems. Nevertheless, although this approach would eventually become de rigueur throughout American higher education, in 1876 it was unique.

Gilman described another novel approach: visiting professorships. Crediting the trustees with working out the details, Gilman explained that Hopkins planned to invite "distinguished professors from other colleges to come to us during a term of years, each to reside here for an appointed time, and be accessible, *publice et privatim*, both in the lecture room and the study."[23] Public lectures were an expectation of this program, but these presentations were required of full-time faculty as well. In Hopkins Hall, an auditorium added on the back of the Howard Street building, ten lecturers gave approximately twenty lectures in the first academic year. Three of the series were published in book form. Prominent visitors delivering lectures in the first year included Thomas M. Cooley, professor of law at the University of Michigan and judge of the Michigan Supreme Court; Simon Newcomb, of the Nautical Almanac Office; Francis A. Walker, noted Yale economist and statistician (and later president of MIT); Francis J. Child and James R. Lowell, both of Harvard, who gave lectures on Chaucer and Dante, respectively; and John W. Mallet, professor of chemistry at the University of Virginia.[24] These visiting lectures were so important in the early days of the university that detailed records of attendance were reported annually to the trustees. In the first three years, turnout ranged from twelve (John M. Cross, ten lectures on the New Testament) to 258 (Hermann Eduard Von Holst, twenty lectures on the German Empire).[25]

Gilman next turned to what Hopkins would look for in students and what plans were in place for buildings. As to the former, Gilman admitted that the standard for admission "is not yet fixed" but said that the university was committed to finding the best "at home, in Baltimore and Maryland" and then radiating outward with a "hope that our influence will be national." Relating to the latter, buildings would be "temporary, but commodious; in the heart of the city, accessible to all; and fitted for lectures, laboratories, library and collections." In due course, the permanent Hopkins home would migrate to Clifton and be modern in nature: "not a mediaeval pile, I hope, but a series of modern institutions; not a monumental, but a serviceable group of structures. The middle ages have not built any cloisters for us; why should we build for the middle ages?"[26] The move to the Clifton property would never happen, but standing on stage in February 1876, Gilman could not predict the persistent financial struggles the university would face. He saw the temporary university quarters and the initial university offerings being augmented through affiliations with the Peabody Institute and its extensive library, the Academy of Sciences, the City College, and the Department of Education at both the state and city levels.[27] These would all help nurture the young institution along in the beginning stages. Speaking to the resources just miles south in Washington, DC, Gilman predicted "perpetual advantages" resulting from access to the many government institutions that had already evinced "goodwill toward their new ally in Baltimore."[28]

Broaching the next subject—the education of women—was a bold step for Gilman, as it posed peculiar challenges given the setting, the orientation of several trustees, and the accepted norms of the day. Gilman chose to use the example of Girton College, established just seven years prior as the first women's college in Cambridge, England. Not prepared to tackle this issue solo, Gilman used veiled language, referring to what someday might produce "a good solution of a problem which is not without difficulty." The subject of educating women had been robustly discussed by the trustees during the presentations of three sitting presidents, but no formal action had been taken by the board, as no woman had asked to study at Hopkins. At least not yet. Gilman told his audience—which, as noted above, the *Baltimore Sun* said was full of "cultivated women"—that the board's conclusions would "depend very much upon the way in which the subject is brought forward."[29]

To Gilman's mind, introducing women into the residential environment ran the risk of "exposing them to the rougher influences which I am sorry to confess are still to be found in colleges and universities where men resort." Apparently, the special Saturday courses in physiology established by Dr. Henry Newell Martin in 1877 for schoolteachers, the majority of whom were women, did not pose such a threat.[30] Gilman said that he hoped some donor might endow Hopkins' version of a women's college—"for the establishment in Baltimore of such a hall as Girton I shall confidently look." Unfortunately, no such proposition ever materialized.[31]

The board's position on the admission of women would be thoroughly examined a year after the university opened in the cases of Emily Nunn and Martha Carey Thomas and in 1878 in the case of Christine Ladd. It is worth noting here the organization in 1890 of the Women's Fund Committee. The committee was made up of four Baltimore women, all daughters of Hopkins trustees: Martha Carey Thomas, Mary Elizabeth Garrett, Mary Gwinn, and Elizabeth King. As a result of their insistence that the Hopkins medical school admit women, three of the eighteen students in the inaugural class were women. A few years later, in 1893, a geologist, Florence Bascomb, became Hopkins' first female PhD. Then, in 1907, three decades after Gilman's inauguration speech, his successor, President Ira Remsen, declared that women were to be admitted as graduate students, as a matter of "justice and common sense."[32] But women would have to wait until 1970 to be admitted as undergraduate students, *nearly a century* after Gilman first broached the subject publicly in his inaugural.

Gilman adroitly addressed the issue of academic freedom both for the faculty and for students in the context of allowing those who chose to study at Hopkins to choose their own course of study as well. But these students "must have been matured by the long, preparatory discipline of superior teachers, and by the systematic, laborious, and persistent pursuit of fundamental knowledge." For professors, their freedom was for the express purpose of discovering and advancing "truth and righteousness" so as to "promote the good of mankind." Gilman stated his aversion to the traditional four-year class system of American colleges, citing Virginia, Harvard, Cornell, and Michigan as examples of the enlightened institutions where the "collegiate rather than a university method" had been either modified or abandoned. Years, if not decades, before proficiency examinations would be required of students before entering a university, Gilman was advocating for "attainments rather than time" as the condition for promotion: "I would encourage every scholar to go forward rapidly or go forward slowly, according to the fleetness of his foot and his freedom from impediment."[33]

## "Enter the Armory and Equip Yourselves"

His remarks drawing to their logical end, Gilman prescribed a bold course whereby Hopkins would not be restricted by its walls nor limited to those listed on its class rolls. As an extramural influence, Gilman proposed that the university do three things: (1) as an examining body, confer degrees or other academic honors on those who might have been trained elsewhere; (2) as a teaching body, provide educated persons, "whether enrolled as students or not," access to public lectures and symposia; and (3), as a publishing body, encourage professors and lecturers to disseminate to the world the results of their research.[34]

Speaking directly to the local citizens, Gilman insisted that they were *not* to view the undertaking as solely the trustees' responsibility. The entire community had a stake in this new enterprise.[35] Portending his role as the chief fundraiser for the university, Gilman implored his audience to proffer their own means to "enable the trustees to administer with greater liberality their present funds." Knowing his audience and the regard in which they held the forebears of the community, Gilman named a few whose largesse had benefitted all: George Calvert, Charles Carroll, John Eager Howard, John McDonogh, George Peabody, Moses Sheppard, William Henry Rinehart, and of course Johns Hopkins. It was time for a new generation of donors to support the emerging endeavor.

Gilman had always been known as an advocate for students, whether the Yale undergraduates he mentored or the those he taught at the University of California. It was fitting, then, that the penultimate portion of Gilman's remarks was addressed squarely to the "youth of Baltimore." Gilman recounted what had been accomplished by men with far fewer resources and under much more challenging circumstances, such as Michael Faraday, Georges Cuvier, Louis Agassiz, Alexander Hamilton, and Carl Frederich Gauss. He reminded the prospective Hopkins students what this day and this ceremony were all about. With a rhetorical flourish reminiscent of Henry V and his famed St. Crispin's Day speech, Gilman finished with a bang: "I say it is for you, bright youths, that these doors are opened. Enter the armory and equip yourselves."[36]

Gilman closed his address with a pledge to the trustees that his approach to governance would be collaborative and to the public that the institution he was charged with leading would be free of any sectarian or political control, but "pervaded by the spirit of an enlightened Christianity." The new president avowed, "In both these propositions I now as then express my cordial and entire concurrence." Buoyed by the significance of the day and the goodwill messages extended by universities throughout the country, Gilman conveyed special thanks to his friend Charles Eliot: "Most welcome among their utterances are the words with which the oldest college in the land extends its fellowship to the youngest of the band."[37]

Gilman concluded: "Our work now begins."[38]

### Reaction to the Inaugural Address

The *Sun* reported that Gilman's address elicited generous applause, with the president receiving hearty congratulations on stage at the conclusion of his remarks: "The assemblage dispersed well pleased with the inauguration of the Johns Hopkins University and its president, and the incidents attending it."[39] Reviewing the history of the university's first decades of existence, one scholar maintains that the institution's desire was for the long-ignored investigative function of the university to be given a whole new emphasis. This was what would propel the new university to the forefront of American higher education. Notwithstanding, Hugh Hawkins avers, a casual listener "might have sat through Gilman's inaugural and missed this point altogether; his words tended to conceal the radically new position to be given research."[40] This may have been the case, but over time the vision of the "new" type of American university would succeed, according to one observer, because "Gilman boldly nailed the flag of research to the mast by organizing Johns Hopkins as (primarily) a graduate university."[41] Still, one must acknowledge that thanks in part to public pressure, Hopkins ultimately adopted a collegiate element and became more inclusive to undergraduates.

The relationship between undergraduate and postgraduate students would continue to evolve during Gilman's tenure, as would decisions about the allocation of scarce resources. The uncertainty of the university's finances—owing to restrictions on the endowment—was compounded by the absence of a strong college to feed men and money into the graduate ranks. This last factor is discussed at length by the higher education historian John Thelin, who underscores the much different state of affairs at Johns Hopkins in 1910, concluding that the university builders "had certainly underestimated their dependence on a base of primary and secondary education." Thelin asserts that the health of the American university was inextricably tied to the availability of the public high school, "an institution that was not yet universally accessible." President Angell of Michigan had stressed this in his presentation to the board in June 1875, prior to which the University of Michigan had been working for years with state governments and local communities to certify public high schools, thus ensuring a steady and qualified stream of potential students. Alas, "Michigan remained exceptional rather than typical."[42] Gilman and his colleagues, while still aspiring to establish the finest graduate programs available anywhere, would realize soon enough that without undergraduate enrollment and its attendant tuition reve-

nue, they could not accomplish what they envisioned. It is clear that Gilman's thinking had continued to develop before his inaugural speech, resulting in a view of the
university that was more complex than the graduate-specific institution he referenced
in his Cornell address at Sidley Hall in 1871. Gilman's views continued to evolve, and
the Hopkins model that would develop during his presidency was an institution that
offered a range of opportunities to teachers, students, and the public.[43] The years following Gilman's tenure, with all the challenges of managing enrollment and the sig-
nificantly reduced endowment income, would prove trying indeed for the university.

## Gilman's "Flair for Eminence"

Just a few weeks before his inauguration, the new president used his first report to the
board to state categorically that the Hopkins faculty would advance knowledge and
educate youth through the institution's unqualified commitment to research. The
power of the university, Gilman stressed, would depend upon the character demonstrated by permanent professors in their research, in their classroom lectures and tutelage of advanced students, in the example they set as both students and investigators, and in their championing truth wherever it might take them. All this activity
would result in "publications through the journals and the scientific treatises which
will make the University in Baltimore an attraction to the best students, and serviceable to the intellectual growth of the land."[44]

Gilman was evangelical in his advocacy. Because of his unyielding commitment to
the new concept of research and its dissemination, the sociologist Lewis Feuer called
Gilman the "veritable St. Paul of the scientific method," at the head of a university
"newborn with a scientific mission and with no theological heritage to surmount."[45]
Another commentator referred to Gilman as "the patron saint of the American graduate school."[46] Given an opportunity to speak about Hopkins before the American
Philosophical Society, Gilman proclaimed, "In this wonderful epoch of intellectual
activity, when light beams from such unexpected sources, on so many crypts, dis-
pelling the shadows and ghosts with which they had been occupied, Universities and
Academies stand like priests at the altar of truth, keeping bright the coals from which
the torches of research are lighted."[47]

Gilman was indefatigable in his efforts to bring repute to his institution. "No other
American university president," contended Abraham Flexner, "has shown equal zest or
flair for eminence."[48] This was manifest most abundantly in the noteworthy public in-
tellectuals, scholars, scientists, professors, statesmen, and other luminaries Gilman rou-
tinely brought to campus for lectures—all free and open to the public. The salutary
impact on the city was impossible to quantify. One example is the gift of John W.
McCoy, a native Baltimorean who was born in 1821 and spent his entire life in the city,
amassing a considerable fortune through mining and finance. Like Mr. Johns Hopkins a lifelong bachelor, McCoy willed his substantial fortune to the university in
1888. Upon McCoy's death the following year, his bequest was the largest gift the
university had received since its founding; and it was timely, since the university was

facing significant financial challenges. McCoy's unrestricted gift, valued at five hundred thousand dollars, included an impressive art collection—bequeathed to the Peabody Institute—his home, his eight-thousand-volume library, and additional assets.[49] McCoy maintained that the Johns Hopkins University had "been the most important influence that has grown up in Baltimore since I was a boy." When pressed to elaborate on the university's importance, McCoy responded, "It has made all of us here want to seem that we know something, and by and by we will."[50]

Just as at the Sheffield School at Yale and at the University of California, Gilman's fervor for his new university was both contagious and boundless. He often quoted Ralph Waldo Emerson's maxim "Nothing great was ever achieved without enthusiasm." A member of the inaugural class of fellows in 1876 was the renowned Sanskrit scholar Charles Rockwell Lanman. His assessment was that "with Mr. Gilman, enthusiasm was a divine gift, and from his living flame he was able to kindle the sacred torch in the hand of others."[51] Gilman's zeal for Hopkins meant, literally, taking all the advantages of a research university and making them immediately accessible to the broader community. This was a "town-gown" experiment on a scale that Baltimore had never experienced, nor had any urban university been so active in taking its programming into a major city. Gilman was bent on discovering and applying new knowledge, but he was also committed to providing Baltimoreans access to knowledge by introducing them to ideas and experts. He would do it by bringing the experts to them.

## Thomas Henry Huxley Comes to Campus

Just months after the new president's pledge to host the best and brightest, Thomas Huxley, one of the most prominent names in the scientific world, came to campus. The two men had met during Gilman's trip to Europe in 1875, when the president attended one of Huxley's presentations at South Kensington, during which the famed biologist offered "a minute delineation of the differences of vegetable and animal life in the earliest stages." So impressed was Gilman with Huxley's exact way of speaking and the directness of his exposition that he called him "the most felicitous of lecturers on science whom I ever heard."[52] Huxley would lobby Gilman to recruit his assistant, Henry Martin, to join the Hopkins faculty—as has been noted—which Martin did in the fall of 1876.

Huxley had been contemplating an American tour for some time, writing to his friend Charles Darwin in early 1874 that "I have had an *awfully* tempting offer to go to Yankee-land on a lecturing expedition, and I am seriously thinking of making an experiment next spring."[53] Arrangements were made for Huxley to address the twenty-fifth annual convention of the American Association for the Advancement of Science in Buffalo on August 25, 1876. This was to be followed with an address in Nashville on September 7 (Huxley had been wanting to visit his sister, Eliza, who had moved to Alabama years before; the family reunion was planned for Tennessee so as to avoid the stifling heat of the Deep South) and then three public lectures in New York City.

In June 1876, while in Scotland for three months of lectures, Huxley received a formal invitation from Gilman—forwarded to him by his wife, in London—to give "the inaugural discourse at the Johns Hopkins University."[54] Gilman had proposed a date of Huxley's choosing, sandwiched between his Nashville and New York obligations.[55] Huxley responded affirmatively to Gilman just days after receiving the invitation, writing of his eagerness "to accept the proposal with which you and your Trustees honor me."[56] After visiting family—and the campuses of Fisk and Vanderbilt Universities in Nashville—the Huxleys departed for Maryland, via Cincinnati, and arrived in Baltimore, where they were greeted by John Work Garrett (still serving as a Hopkins trustee) and hosted at his home.

Huxley's lecture was on Tuesday, September 12, 1876. As the university had no rooms that could seat more than two hundred, the event was held at the Academy of Music, the site of the February inaugural ceremony. One account asserted that the event attracted "one of the most distinguished audiences ever assembled in Baltimore," with an estimated audience of two thousand.[57] Another exclaimed that the Academy was "crowded at noonday from pit to dome with the beauty, wealth, and intelligence of a great American city."[58]

The invitation to Huxley proved a double-edge sword. Some hailed the famed scientist's visit as an academic imprimatur of the embryonic university; at the same time, ever since his debate over Darwinism with England's Bishop Samuel Wilberforce sixteen years earlier, Huxley's name had been synonymous with infidelity and agnosticism.[59] One editor called Huxley "that blatant infidel" and believed his dangerous writings were subversive to religious faith. When he arrived in town, the *Baltimore Bulletin* assailed Huxley for being an adherent of the doctrine of evolution, other than which, according to the *Bulletin*, there was "no more frightful heresy extant."[60]

Despite what some maintained and the newspapers reported, Huxley's lecture was not the official opening of the Hopkins academic term, as that event was marked with a gathering of trustees, faculty, staff, and students on the evening of October 3, 1876. Some incorrectly viewed the Huxley oration as the "official launching" of instruction at Hopkins. Nor was it intended to mark the inauguration of the university, as Gilman's ceremony had been held the previous winter. It did not help that the university and the Baltimore press continually publicized the event as the "opening," the "formal opening," and the "inauguration" of Hopkins. In its special edition on Huxley's speaking tour, the *New York Tribune* wrote of his Maryland oration, "The formal opening of the Johns Hopkins University at Baltimore took place Sept. 12, at 11 a.m., in the Academy of Music. Prof. Huxley delivered the opening address."[61] Huxley himself added to the confusion in his concluding remarks with the wish and hope "that the university, the career of which begins today" would prosper and thrive from that moment forward.[62]

The fact is that instruction would not commence for another three weeks. Professor Huxley's presentation was the first of the public lectures planned to give Baltimore citizens an opportunity to hear some of the leading scholars of the day. As a consequence, there were no formalities except the presentation of the speaker—no music, no prayer, no remarks from a trustee, and no benediction. Writing years later, Gilman recalled that he had proposed to two of the most religious trustees that there be an introductory prayer and that they had said no, "preferring that the discourse should be given as popular lectures are given at the Peabody Institute and elsewhere, without note or comment."[63]

Gilman remembered that "many people, who thought that a university, like a college, could not succeed unless it was under some denominational control, were sure that this opening discourse was but an overture to the play of irreligious and anti-religious actors." The new president recounted the position of those critical of the university's hosting the speaker: "Huxley was bad enough; Huxley without a prayer was intolerable."[64]

The program began with Gilman graciously introducing Huxley, reminding the audience of the role English scholars had played in the development of American colleges and asserting, "We are glad of such an educational alliance and heritage." The president then exhorted Huxley to tell his countrymen upon his return to England that the words of John Greenleaf Whittier (in his poem "To Englishmen") had never been more true:

"Thicker than water," in one rill
Through centuries of story
Our Saxon blood has flowed, and still
We share with you its good and ill,
The shadow and the glory.[65]

Huxley's speech, lasting seventy-five minutes, was benign and hardly incendiary, focusing on medical education, examinations, and the future of higher education in America. His remarks were published in full the next day in the *Sun* and the *New York Times*. Huxley summarized his own educational philosophy, stating that more room should be made for scientific studies and modern languages, and he urged the use of laboratories and museums—pedagogical innovations at the time—in conducting research. His speech was widely printed in the East but also disseminated to the West; it struck a chord with William Watts Folwell, president of the University of Minnesota, who wrote Gilman asking for an introduction to Huxley. Folwell, who was in the process of organizing colleges and departments, told Gilman that "soon after planning our Secondary Department here, I had the satisfaction to learn that we had included in it just those elements of Sciences proposed by Professor Huxley."[66]

Among the more quotable Huxley statements interspersed throughout his speech were "A man's worst difficulties begin when he is able to do what he likes," and "There is but one right, and the possibilities of wrong are infinite."[67] However, if some statements were easily recalled, for some listeners there was no missing the fact that God was never mentioned, nor was there mention of the role of religion in the education process. For committed believers, Huxley's greatest sin was that of omission.[68]

Gilman recorded years later that the speech "was appropriate and well received, but it had no glow, and the orator did not equal his reputation for charm and persuasiveness."[69] The *New York World* seemed to concur, stating bluntly that "the first part of his address is rather dull to people who do not lie awake at nights determining what a university ought to teach."[70] Sounding a similar refrain to Johns Hopkins' and Daniel Coit Gilman's commitment to building men and not buildings, Huxley exhorted the Hopkins trustees not to construct "by any hands higher than those of a bricklayer, who will do for them exactly as they want and nothing else." When B&O Railroad shares "have gone up to $1,000 premium, and when every professor is as fully endowed as he wishes to be, and every library is as large and well furnished as it ought to be," that would be the time for the university to "send for an architect and let him put a façade on the edifice." In Huxley's view, nothing could be better than making provisions from the endowment for "those who are competent to make research and to investigate."[71] In spite of what some viewed as Huxley's laconic British delivery, the scientist would close his remarks, to rapturous approval, with this final comment:

> It is my most earnest wish and hope that the university, the career of which begins today, may fulfill this high mission to its fullest extent [applause]; that its outgrowths may become centers of intelligence, foci of intellectual life in the United States; and on the next centenary of your Republic let me hope that you will attain such a position that the students of all nations will flock here as in former days they flocked to Oxford, to Paris, and to Bologna. [Applause.] Permit me to fancy that among the English part of that population there may linger a dim tradition at that time that at the commencement of your work, an Englishman was permitted to address you as he has done today, to look upon your hopes as his hopes, and to consider your success as his joy. [Great applause.][72]

News coverage of the event was overwhelmingly positive, with the *Tribune* noting that "the audience signified their approbation vehemently."[73]

## "Reap the Whirlwind"

While Huxley's address was received favorably by some, no one was prepared for the reaction in other quarters. "Professor Huxley was invited; he accepted, he came to Baltimore, he addressed a crowded assembly—and then came the storm," wrote Gilman. The reaction from religious publications was much more pointed and critical. Gilman reflected years later, "We had sowed the wind and were to reap the whirlwind."[74] A correspondent for the *New York Observer*, a Presbyterian weekly, lamented that Huxley's speech was not attended by even the simplest of religions exercises: "If the neglect was due to the unchristian or materialistic sentiments of the authorities, then we can only say, God help them, and keep students away from the precincts of the young institution. . . . We await with much anxiety the future action of the authorities of the Johns Hopkins University."[75]

Gilman was in receipt of a letter to a local Presbyterian minister, John Leyburn, sent by a New York colleague, S. S. Prince, of the *New York Observer*. Decades after the episode, Gilman was still smarting and added, parenthetically, that both the writer and the recipient had "now gone where such trifles have no importance." Nevertheless, he still felt strongly enough to include portions of the letter in his *Launching* memoir, with emphasis added by him: "*It was bad enough to invite Huxley. It were better to have asked God to be present. It would have been absurd to ask them both.* I am sorry Gilman began with Huxley. But it is possible yet to redeem the University from the stain of such a beginning. No one will be more ready than I to herald a better sign."[76]

Reverend Leyburn, who also served as a trustee of Princeton University, proved a staunch defender of Gilman. In a letter to yet another offended publication, the *Presbyterian*, Leyburn assured the readers "that there was prayer at the inauguration & a full & very evangelical one & that there was no more reason for prayer before Huxley's than before any other College or Lyceum lecture."[77] The *Sun* tried to put the issue to bed by publishing articles in defense of the proceedings and lambasting those who chose to chastise Gilman and Hopkins: "Seeing that when the president of the institution was inaugurated last February the offering of prayer by a clergyman on the platform was a part of the exercises, all this affected indignation and pharisaical cant are wasted."[78] The paper opined a few days later that had Huxley "remained in the country until the 3rd of October his lecture would have been but the first of a series intended to continue throughout the year, and we do not see why religious exercises should be called for before such an opening."[79]

Gilman could only hope that the flare-up over the episode had been extinguished. Those looking for offense or for signs of overt antagonism toward religion would find additional fodder in 1877 when the second-year fellow William Keith Brooks, who had earned a PhD at Harvard under the tutelage of Louis and Alexander Agassiz, delivered sixteen public lectures on biology with a heavy concentration on the ideas of Charles Darwin.[80] Even though the Huxley speech was long past, Gilman recalled decades later, it would take "several years before the black eye gained its natural color."[81]

For all the barbs directed at Gilman for his invitation to Huxley, the presence of someone of such preeminent stature in the scientific world gave Hopkins instant cachet and immediate visibility. Huxley himself noted the university's commitment to blending the well-established models of Germany and England into a uniquely American setting, and his remarks would give a boost to scientists and science educators as they continued their quest to emerge from the shadows of the traditional higher education structure.[82] The kerfuffle caused by Huxley's speech would linger for some time, as Gilman observed, but the university had to focus on formally opening the campus to its incoming students and to a crop of remarkable young men, the inaugural Hopkins fellows.

# CHAPTER SIX

# *Advancing Knowledge Far and Wide*

The year 1876 was truly momentous for Baltimore and the Johns Hopkins University. In February, Daniel Coit Gilman delivered his inaugural speech. In September, Thomas Huxley made his world-famous address at the same podium and in the same venue. And then in October, America's newest university opened its doors. No other institution had tried from scratch what Hopkins planned to do: award graduate fellowships; launch learned societies, publish scholarly journals, and found a university press; focus heavily on original research; and establish a hospital connected to a school of medicine.

At the heart of the new Hopkins enterprise were graduate fellowships. Andrew White had counseled the trustees the previous year to provide funding for advanced study through fellowships, to budget for their allotment, and then to watch what happened. Spurred by the board's willingness to follow this advice, Gilman began the selection process enthusiastically. After reviewing the original class of Hopkins fellows, the historian Edwin Slosson asked rhetorically in 1910 what university president would be willing to place a list of his own fellows next to those at Hopkins "with the assurance that they will prove to be, on the whole, men of as much distinction as these."[1] No university could meet such a challenge, as no other had created this type of system, certainly not on the scale attempted at Hopkins.

By the deadline at the end of June, 152 fellowship applications had been received.

Just over one hundred applicants were deemed eligible for the ten available slots. Overwhelmed by the interest that spring, the trustees doubled the number of fellowships.[2]

## The Hopkins Fellows

With the announcement of the Hopkins fellowships, Gilman and the trustees had uncovered a demand for graduate training in America. All students needed was to be enticed to avail themselves of the opportunity for free schooling. The historian Richard Storr observed that it was one thing for a few to sense a need for highly trained men in America but "another thing for immature B.A.'s to give up the opportunity for quick fortunes in order to become specially trained for anything."[3] In his third annual report to the trustees, Gilman reviewed the numbers that illustrated his prescience in advocating for graduate fellowships. With a core group of twenty fellows in the first three years, the number of graduate students remained steady: fifty-four in 1876–77, fifty-eight in 1877–78, and fifty-five in 1878–79.[4] "Thus," wrote Abraham Flexner, "compared with other institutions of learning, the Johns Hopkins in a single bound outstripped them all in the number of advanced students and in the emphasis on research."[5] Nicholas Murray Butler believed the genius of Gilman's approach was that by opening the fellowship opportunity to the general population (provided the applicant was male and white), Hopkins "attracted to it at once the most promising of younger scholars."[6] This tranche of talent would descend on Baltimore and set a standard for every other graduate school to emulate.

With a generous stipend, the fellows were free from monetary concerns and thus able to focus on their areas of specialty. Of the original twenty fellows, thirteen would go on to hold professorships in American colleges and universities, two became scientists in government service, three were well-respected private scholars and consultants, and two triaged into the practice of law.[7] Yet another novel approach was that Gilman showed no reservation about offering fellowships to scholars in fields in which he had no faculty members—political science, engineering, and philosophy. By doing so, Gilman demonstrated several things: first, hope for expansion of the faculty; second, faith in these advanced students to discipline themselves and complete independent work; and third, commitment to address these voids among his faculty by appointing visiting lecturers.[8] This last strategy attracted subject-matter experts to Hopkins and augmented the faculty ranks in areas where permanent professors had yet to be hired.[9]

No American university had ever provided such an opportunity—and afforded such freedom—to graduate students. The first official historian of Gilman's alma mater was George Wilson Pierson. During his forty-seven-year career at Yale, Pierson was a keen observer of American higher education, noting that Gilman succeeded at Hopkins for myriad reasons: the eminence of the people he imported to Baltimore, the spectacular salaries he was able to pay (especially in relation to other institutions), the visiting lectureships he established, and "the royal fellowships" he was able to offer America's brightest men. "In a word," said Pierson, "Gilman closed the gap between need and demand for advanced studies by first 'hiring' his students." While the concept was not new, the challenge was a financial one. Up until 1876, no other university had had resources enough to cover "beyond the barest church-mouse necessities."[10]

Clearly, those who arrived in Baltimore to be part of Hopkins were there for one reason: to study. Students found lodging with local families, many of whom were still feeling the economic effects of both the Civil War and the depression of 1873 and were glad to host paying boarders.[11] The neighborhood surrounding the campus created a unique environment, compelling one student—Woodrow Wilson—to tell his fiancée that he was "surrounded by picked specimens of the university men, fellows of various character but equal enthusiasm in intellectual pursuits."[12]

## "Millions for Genuine Research, but Not One Cent for Show"

The downtown structures housing America's newest university were modest to say the least, especially in contrast with what would be planned and erected at the University of Chicago and Stanford University in the coming decades. Chances were, the Hopkins campus was inferior to what these postgraduates had experienced in bucolic college towns around the country as undergraduates. Of much more importance to Gilman was what transpired within the walls of these ordinary buildings. An 1891 report to the board of trustees included a long discussion about the need for new buildings. Gilman advised the board, "A very simple structure will be more convenient than any other. *Quietness* and an abundance of *space, air*, and *light* are the essentials."[13] Fifteen years into his tenure, Gilman provided an even clearer view of this philosophy while revealing his hopes for the future campus in his annual report to the trustees:

> Every stranger is surprised that the Johns Hopkins University is so unworthily housed. I am no advocate of extravagance in any department of the University. I think that professors, instruments, and books are of more importance than splendid buildings. With our present resources, I should be sorry to see the trustees begin the construction of such beautiful quadrangles and such halls of knowledge as adorn and ennoble other seats of learning. These, I hope, will come in the future, as the University proves itself worthy of the gifts of great benefactors.[14]

Upon his arrival in Baltimore in the late 1880s, Eugene T. Allen, one of Ira Remsen's PhD chemistry students, recalled the marked contrast to Amherst, the quiet New England college from which he had just graduated. One day on Little Ross Street, the site of Hopkins' Dalton Hall and its chemical laboratory, a man with a strong Irish accent approached Allen and asked, "Is this the Johns Hopkins University the papers are braggin' so much about? Why, Trinity College, Dublin, would turn this into an academy."[15] Richard Ely, head of the Hopkins Department of Political Economy from 1881 to 1892, recalled a conversation his wife had overheard in a trolley car as it passed the university building: One of the passengers had asked, "What is this we are passing?" The other had replied, "I don't know. I think it must be a piano factory." And

Looking east down Little Ross Street at the original Johns Hopkins University campus, 1895. *Left to right:* Levering Hall and McCoy Hall (*left side of street*); Administration Building, Hopkins Hall, Chemical Laboratory, and Biological Laboratory (*right side of street*). (Photo courtesy of University Archives, Sheridan Libraries, Johns Hopkins University)

another passenger had observed that Hopkins had "millions for genuine research, but not one cent for show."[16]

Gilman's position on buildings versus men was praised by President Angell. On the commemoration of the university's twenty-fifth anniversary, Angell noted that "what makes a great university, is not bricks and mortar, but men. I could not conceal my joy, in the early days of the institution, at the self-restraint which led the President and Trustees to content themselves with these modest homes in which this University was housed, scarcely to be distinguished from the business houses upon the streets around them, while they went scouring the world for the best men that could be found on the two continents to bring here."[17] In this one sentence, Angell summarized Gilman's philosophy of investment in human capital as the paramount priority.

Whatever the physical infrastructure lacked, the people inside more than made up for it, as the quantity of the stipends offered was matched by the quality of the awardees. Four of the original class—Herbert Adams (Heidelberg), William Brooks (Harvard), Charles Lanman (Yale), and Harmon Morse (Göttingen)—had already earned doctorates before their arrival Baltimore. They came to an environment that was devoid of administrative tradition and red tape but expected high achievement

Interior of history seminar room, History and Politics Seminary, Hopkins Hall on the old campus, 1895. Herbert Baxter Adams is at the lectern addressing students. Note the lettering on the far wall: "History is past Politics and Politics present History." (Photo courtesy of University Archives, Sheridan Libraries, Johns Hopkins University)

and significant contribution. With language befitting his discipline of philosophy, Josiah Royce described what it was like to be among the first class of fellows:

> Here at last, so we felt, the American University had been founded. The academic life was now to exist for its own sake. The "conflict" between "classical " and "scientific" education was henceforth to be without significance for the graduate student. And the graduate student was to be, so we told ourselves, the real student. The undergraduate was not yet quite clear of the shell; but the graduate could imagine himself to have grown at least his pin-feathers. The beginning of the Johns Hopkins University was a dawn wherein " 'twas bliss to be alive." Freedom and wise counsel one enjoyed together. The air was full of rumors of noteworthy work done by the older men of the place, and of hopes that one might find a way to get a little working-power one's self. There was no longer the dread upon one lest a certain exercise should not be well written, or a certain set examination not passed. No, the academic business was something much more noble and serious than such "discipline" had been in its time. The University wanted its children to be, if possible, not merely well-informed, but productive. She preached to them the gospel of learning for wisdom's sake, and of acquisition for the sake of fruitfulness. One longed to be a doer of the word, and not a hearer only, a creator of his own infinitesimal fraction of a product, bound in God's name to produce it when the time came.[18]

## Hits and Misses

Gilman and his colleagues paid very close attention to the fellows selected, as the stipends were renewable and some continued their association with Hopkins as full-time faculty long after their fellowships ended. For example, among the inaugural class of fellows, two, Brooks and Morse, were made associates (equivalent to an assistant professor) before entering into their fellowships. Morse has been discussed previously in terms of his relationship with Ira Remsen. On Remsen's recommendation, Morse's salary was increased to one thousand dollars, and he would remain at Hopkins until his retirement from active teaching in 1916. Brooks, was brought to the attention of Gilman by Alexander Agassiz, son of Louis Agassiz and president of the National Academy of Sciences. Agassiz's assessment of Brooks included this observation in a letter to Gilman: "He has had a little practice in teaching, he is not a very cultivated man but is good at heart and extremely anxious to devote himself to Natural History."[19] Brooks would make Hopkins his "mental home," according to a profile by Stanford University president David Starr Jordan, serving the university from 1876 until his death in 1908.[20]

Gilman personally responded to those who applied, and his letterpress books from 1876 to 1880 illustrate the level of detail in each response. To one candidate he said that no definitive word could be communicated until after June 1, 1876, "but certainly your papers are such that I think you may be encouraged to expect the appointment."[21] This letter was to Herbert Baxter Adams, founder of one of Hopkins' original seminars and the first secretary of the American Historical Association.

Admittedly, there were some notable "misses" in the awarding of the Hopkins fellowship, and Gilman transmitted the bad news in handwritten notes. The most significant omission among the inaugural class had to be the economist John Bates Clark. Not only did Clark author the influential 1899 text *The Distribution of Wealth* but a medal named for him was awarded annually "to that American economist under the age of forty who is judged to have made the most significant contribution to economic thought and knowledge."[22] When Clark submitted his application for the Hopkins fellowship, it was apparent to the selection committee that his own ideas and philosophies around economic theory and politics were still coalescing. In conveying the trustees' decision, Gilman wrote Clark that "we must judge of you by what we have before us, not by any theoretical estimate of your attainments, and though we have been interested in your views, yet they are hardly sufficient to warrant an appointment, when we have so many complete and thoughtful theses from other applicants."[23] Upon learning of his refusal, Clark wrote Gilman asking what this meant for his future prospects of employment at Johns Hopkins. He asked Gilman whether another opportunity might present itself "provided my proposed little work were so fortunate as to prove some value to the science."[24] Gilman tried his best to be encouraging and responded to the forlorn Clark: "The doors here are certainly 'not closed forever.' Try again. Why not come here and reside as a graduate for a year. We want such men as you."[25] Even in communicating rejection, Gilman always remained encouraging and consistently fulfilled his role as mentor to an entire generation of striving academics and administrators.

Clark decided to remain in Minnesota and continue teaching at Carleton, where one of his favorite students was Thorstein Veblen. Enrolling at Hopkins to study philosophy, Veblen too would be denied a scholarship and transferred to Yale, where he earned his PhD in 1884.[26]

Clark's work resulted in substantial contributions to his discipline during the course of his career. In 1892 he left Carleton for a professorship in political economy at Amherst. At the same time, Clark accepted a lectureship in economics at Johns Hopkins. When he sought a more permanent position at Hopkins, this time as chair of political economy after Richard Ely left for the University of Wisconsin, there was a very public airing of details pertaining to Clark and his potential employment in Baltimore. Writing to Gilman in early 1895, Clark bluntly expressed his feelings after reading a story in the *Springfield Republican* "stating that I have received and declined a call to the Johns Hopkins University. I am very much annoyed at seeing it. I have been very careful myself about making the facts known."[27]

Factoring into the calculus of the situation was a delay on the part of the Hopkins trustees as they weighed Clark's request to be released early in his first year at Hopkins in order to lecture back at Amherst. Gilman responded that he saw "no reason why the Trustees should not grant your request." However, some members of the board questioned Clark's commitment to Hopkins. Gilman informed Clark that the board "would not approve of divided allegiance. When you come here, it is to be one of us spending all your force here." In a very pointed conclusion, Gilman exhorted the emerging economist: "Now is your opportunity. Do not fail to seize it, for you may be sure of a hearty welcome to a field of great influence."[28] Unpersuaded, Clark accepted a position at Columbia and remained on the faculty there until 1923. Gilman had lost out on one of the greatest economists of his generation. Nonetheless, when he learned of Clark's decision, Gilman wrote, in his typical gracious manner: "The matter is settled, and you will carry to Columbia my very best wishes for happiness and success. . . . I am sorry that the delay of our Trustees—to which I assented as I supposed in your interest—gave an opportunity for our friends in New York to press their claims."[29] Gilman may have been on the short end of the Clark lottery in the first round of fellowship selection, but the subsequent classes (1877 and 1878) were equal to the first.[30]

In his personal correspondence, Gilman kept his friends and colleagues apprised of the fellowship application and selection process, revealing that several subjective factors played into the trustees' decision to award the coveted stipends. To Andrew White, Gilman wrote, "A diploma is not essential; a liberal education is. . . . I agree with you that it would be amiss not to include as 'candidates' this year's graduates."[31] To Charles Eliot, Gilman wrote that the applications of 11 "Harvardians" were among the 102 applications considered. Among those selected, Gilman singled out John Henry Wheeler, in philology, and Ernest Sihler, in classics, for their "exceptionalism." Gilman went into much more personal detail about a third applicant, Ernest Fenollosa, the famed American Orientalist. Gilman acknowledged that he was "in intellectual capacity, very conspicuous among the philosophers." However, the suspicious view of Fenollosa and his reputation, as expressed to Gilman by some of the trustees, prevailed in weighing his application: it was decided "that it would not be right to honor him here, if at home his record is not clean."[32] Hopkins was small enough that Gilman could pay attention to every single detail about the prospective candidates.

## Emergence of the Hopkins PhD

By 1878, two years into the fellowship program, four participants were deemed worthy to receive the first PhDs: Henry Carter Adams (political economy), Thomas Craig (mathematics), Josiah Royce (philosophy), and Ernest Sihler (classics). Regulations for the Hopkins doctorate would appear in the *Registers* throughout the 1870s and "were never quite so grueling as for those first groups of Ph.D.'s," according to Hugh Hawkins.[33] For one observer, the most stimulating influence that higher education in America has ever known came from the Johns Hopkins in its early days, "an influence out of all relation to the size of the institution and due solely to the impact of a small, homogeneous group, operating uncompromisingly at the highest possible level."[34] Ten years after the initiation of the graduate stipends, Gilman reported to the trustees that "much of the success of the institution is due to the system of fellowships," with 134 recipients in Hopkins' first decade alone.[35] In his last annual report to the trustees, the twenty-sixth, Gilman provided a full accounting of PhDs awarded in the university's first quarter century. From the initial 4 degrees awarded in 1878 until 1901 the total number conferred was 579.[36] By comparison, Harvard University—with its 240-year head start on Hopkins—produced 320 PhDs from 1876 to 1902. The roster of students and fellows in Hopkins' first years would go on to populate distinguished faculties of American universities for the next fifty years. No other institution even came close in terms of productivity. But as with the fellows selected for graduate awards, the university had always been fixed on the *quality* of the Hopkins doctorate as much as they were on the *number* of PhDs produced.

During Gilman's long tenure, the requirements for the PhD at Johns Hopkins became the standard for American graduate schools.[37] That standard was codified, in large part, thanks to the American Association of Universities and its original five members (Harvard, Columbia, the University of Chicago, the University of California, and Johns Hopkins). A letter signed by the presidents of these founding institutions was sent to nine of their colleagues inviting them to attend the first annual meeting in Chicago in February 1900. All nine institutions accepted the offer to join the association.[38] At its second annual meeting, in February 1901, the association accepted a resolution from the Federation of Graduate Clubs outlining the minimum requirements for the American PhD, which were based largely on what had been developed twenty-five years earlier at Johns Hopkins.[39] In his examination of American higher education institutions, the British historian and diplomat James Bryce singled out the graduate school at Johns Hopkins for "the honour of having led the way . . . a notable instance in which the educational spirit and enterprise of Americans have out-stripped the conservatism or the poverty of English and Scottish seats of learning."[40]

In addition to the degree requirements for the doctorate, the means of delivering content—the seminar, sometimes referred to as the seminary—and other methods of instruction were first developed in Baltimore before being implemented elsewhere. Many of these pedagogies are still common today. Initiated at the university's opening in 1876, the Seminary of Historical and Political Science, open only to graduate students and faculty, met each Saturday morning at the Maryland Historical Society, first under the direction of Austin Scott and then under Herbert Baxter Adams. The weekly sessions included a brief lecture by the seminary director followed by a discussion of various subjects assigned beforehand to the students.[41] A famous photo of Herbert Baxter Adams and his seminary from 1895 shows the professor at the head of a large table inside Hopkins Hall, his students all around, with this axiom on the wall above them: "History is past Politics and Politics present History." Papers prepared for the seminary were sometimes presented on other occasions, as was the case with "Disturbances in Barbados in 1876," written by John Franklin Jameson and presented on a Friday evening in November 1880 at a meeting of the Historical and Political Science Association in Hopkins Hall.[42]

Given the small initial staff Gilman employed, necessity was the mother of invention, as Hopkins developed another novel approach for doctoral candidates: the use of external examiners. Through this practice, the president adroitly introduced both the university and its graduates to the entire American education landscape, resulting in immediate academic respectability for the inchoate institution.[43]

Revisions to the degree requirements in the first decade included a lapse of three years (originally it had been two years) from the bachelor's to the doctorate and pursuit of two subordinate subjects.[44] Another significant modification to the Hopkins PhD came in 1887, when the university mandated the publication of theses. Further, 150 copies had to be provided for use by the library for exchange purposes.[45] Some scholars have concluded that this requirement was in response to superb work completed by early graduate students that had been neither published nor preserved. One casualty of the early years was the thesis work of John Dewey, who successfully completed his doctorate in philosophy in 1884 under the tutelage of Professor George Sylvester Morris. A professor at the University of Michigan, Morris had been coming to Hopkins to lecture on the history of philosophy since 1878; Dewey took three courses from him in his first year of graduate study and two more during his second year.[46] Dewey's thesis, "The Psychology of Kant," was not published and no longer exists.[47] Upon the successful defense of his thesis, Dewey took a teaching position at the University of Michigan, where he remained until joining the faculty of the newly formed University of Chicago in 1894.[48]

As a former librarian, Gilman was attuned to trends in the area of holdings and shared resources. An affinity for libraries was evident throughout Gilman's life, and the university's desire to preserve the work of graduate students—and to make it available to other institutions—is yet another manifestation of his abiding belief in the benefit of such practices. One interesting connection to modern library services is Gilman's mentoring of Joseph Cummings Rowell, the father of the interlibrary loan program.

In 1870, two years before Gilman's tenure as president commenced in Oakland, Rowell entered the University of California as a freshman. Library holdings at the time totaled a scant one thousand volumes. In July 1874 Rowell graduated with twenty-two classmates at a ceremony presided over by President Gilman. This was only the second graduating class in the history of the university and the first to have received instruction on the Berkeley campus. Upon receiving his degree, Rowell was appointed recorder of the faculties, secretary to President Gilman, and lecturer in English. The following year, he received an unexpected appointment: university librarian. This was the beginning of his forty-four-year tenure in the position, as he took the modest collection of thirteen thousand volumes (Gilman had been responsible for its substantial increase since 1870) and made it one of the largest libraries in the nation.[49]

Back in 1875, a few days into his new role as librarian, however, Rowell had been at a complete loss as to how to begin cataloguing the university's collection. Up to that point, the library had been overseen by faculty on a part-time basis. Rowell's appointment signaled a belief that the library needed to be administered by someone devoted full time to its organization and development. "I needed information as to how libraries were conducted," Rowell recalled in informal presentations throughout his life.[50] Determined to learn how libraries were run at other places institutions, Rowell took out a life insurance policy, borrowed funds against it from a trusting friend, and set off on a ten-week trip to the East. Commencing in Madison, Wisconsin, Rowell then headed to the Eastern Seaboard, making multiple stops between Bowdoin College to the north and Washington, DC, to the south.

Rowell sent Gilman a letter in October 1875 detailing his experience: "I am glad for many reasons that I took the trip East, although it has left me sadly burdened with debt." Rowell estimated that he had visited between "thirty and forty libraries," among them Cornell, the Astor Library in New York City, the Boston Public Library, Yale, Harvard, Brown, Princeton, and the Library of Congress, before heading west and spending time at the Chicago Public Library. Gilman had provided Rowell a "letter of introduction" just like the one provided to Gilman by Johann Gottfried Flugel for his European trip in 1855. The letter, Rowell related to Gilman, "procured a welcome for me wherever I went." The former Gilman protégé ended his report with thanks "for the kindness you have so invariably shown me and which will not, trust me, be forgotten to my last day. Everything I am and have I owe to you."[51]

## Family Happenings—and Crises

Since the passing of his first wife, Mary Ketcham, in 1869, Gilman had attended to all his duties at Yale, California, and Hopkins as a widower. Shortly after Mary's passing, Gilman's sister Louisa had come to live with the family and assist with his two daughters.[52] On June 13, 1877, Gilman married Elizabeth Dwight Woolsey (from a prominent Cleveland, Ohio, family and niece of Yale president Timothy Dwight Woolsey) in Newport, Rhode Island. In Lilly—as friends and family called her—Gilman had "found one who during more than thirty years was a devoted and sympathetic companion, the sharer of his interests in great affairs and of his home affections."[53] Even the hypercritical John Franklin Jameson (awarded the first history PhD at Hopkins) called the new Mrs. Gilman a charming hostess, and although she appeared not to be at all learned in his estimation, he found her "very bright."[54] Daniel and Lilly spent the summer of 1877 in Europe, returning to Baltimore in early September.

With Lilly's arrival in the Gilman home, "Aunty Lou" returned to the family home in Norwich. A fixture in the Gilman girls' lives for many years, Louisa had brought much by way of education and training. On the occasion of Elisabeth's 1880 confirmation in St. Paul's Church, Gilman wrote to Louisa, "You would be pleased if you could see the seed which you planted. . . . She has had gentle teaching these last three winters from her most devoted mother—teaching quite in accord with what you used to give."[55] The significance of the day spurred young Elisabeth to write: "I am going to try, with God's help, to be less selfish, not trying to have my own way in everything. And to be sweeter to Alice and not be rude or saucy to Mama and Papa. Lizzie Gilman."[56]

Upon their return from Europe, Daniel, Lilly, and the two girls settled into Mr. Johns Hopkins' former home on West Saratoga Street, which had been among the many properties gifted to the hospital by Hopkins himself. Gilman's daughter Elisabeth would recall of Lilly: "To my sister and me the stepmother became in a very beautiful way, a real mother. Her charm, intelligence and her graciousness as hostess won her friends on every side."[57] Life was good for the Gilmans as they grew accustomed to their new surroundings and routine. All this would be dramatically disrupted just a few weeks later, however, by an unexpected—and extremely public—family crisis.

Daniel's younger brother, William (known to family and close friends as Willie), was a successful businessman on Pine Street, the insurance industry's hub in lower Manhattan. William was well educated and had followed his two older brothers at Yale, undoubtedly trying his best to maintain the family's image and reputation. Edward was tapped for Scroll and Key in 1843, and Daniel, as has been noted, was active in Skull and Bones his entire life.[58] However, no similar record of achievement exists for William Jr.'s time at Yale. He left New Haven before completing his degree, heading to New York to work in insurance and plying his father's connections. William enjoyed an Icarus-like climb and achieved significant financial success at a very early age. He and his family grew accustomed to a certain lifestyle while giving generously of their time and means to various charities. However, during various ebbs in the economy, William could not make good on his pledges and concocted a forgery scheme. He forged scrip from an insurance company and then used the forgeries as collateral for loans. According to some chroniclers, William pursued the graft undetected for years but grew increasingly sloppy with his crimes. One clumsy alteration of a stock certificate to read $30,000 instead of $3,000 was made during the financial panic of 1877. Things began to unravel for him shortly thereafter.

The 32-year-old absconded in early October 1877 after discovery was made of his forgeries, first estimated to be in excess of $200,000. The final accounting would not be far off and was the equivalent of nearly $5 million in today's dollars. William's misdeeds dominated the front page of the *New York Times* for ten days, with headlines such as this one from October 3: "Vast Forgeries Exposed: A Wealthy and Trusted Criminal." After an outline of the alleged wrongdoing—"Downtown was electrified yesterday morning by whispers of the discovery of a very large forgery involving the good name of one of the most highly respectable business men of that region"—each article then provided William's genealogy and affiliations: "He comes from one of the oldest and most respected New York families. . . . He was one of the most prominent members of Rev. Dr. Houghton's Church and Superintendent of its Sunday-school, and was otherwise among the foremost in deeds of piety."[59] Readers were constantly reminded of the Gilman family lineage. Daniel's position as president of Johns Hopkins, as well as that of their older brother, the Reverend Edward Gilman, of the American Bible Society, were noted in nearly every account.

William hid away in the city while reports speculated about when the swindling had begun, one article concluding that the Sun Mutual Insurance Company failure of 1871 had set the scheme in motion.[60] Efforts by friends to effect a compromise with his victims—"the forger's available assets were found to be of themselves too insignificant to be an object"—ultimately failed, and William agreed to turn himself in.[61] The *Times* then reported: "There was no need of trial; sentence was forthwith pronounced, and before the sun had set the miserable man was on his way to Sing Sing. It was a terrible conclusion to a career of falsehood and hypocrisy. . . . There is not much pity mingled with the satisfaction we feel when the rascal is locked up at last, and is out of mischief for a while." The paper continued: " 'Bristol Bill,' flung into a felon's cell, after being caught in a burglarious exploit, suffers no pang of disgrace. The man who has a virtuous, high-minded wife, innocent children, and honorable brothers and sisters to lament his fall, is of all men most miserable."[62] William's October 12 confession was printed in full in the *New York Times*.[63]

Originally sentenced to five years of hard labor at Sing Sing, Gilman was transferred to Auburn State Prison shortly after his conviction. The *New York Times* covered the prison relocation on page 1. William was accompanied by both his pastor, Dr. George H. Houghton, and his brother-in-law, George Lane, with the reporter noting, "They joined the prisoner in the Auburn car, and handed him a lunch from Delmonico's, consisting of cold soup, cold meats, fruit, &c." Details continued: "Dr. Houghton and Mr. Lane engaged in low conversation with the convict, and at times he shed tears freely. At Garrison both gentlemen bade him goodbye, getting off the train at that station. Before parting the three kissed each other, and all wept."[64] The family had never endured anything quite so public nor so damaging. A month after he was sent to prison, an accounting of William's debts (to the penny)—totaling $187,201.38—and the roster of those whom he had swindled was published in the *New York Times*.[65]

William had married Catherine Beecher Perkins, of the prominent New England Beecher family, in 1859 and had seven children, only three of whom lived past childhood.[66] When William was sent to prison, Catherine suffered a mental breakdown and was committed to the Retreat for the Insane, in Hartford, Connecticut, for a time. She partially regained her faculties and returned to live with her daughter, Bessie, and her two young sons, Francis and George Houghton (the latter of whom would later marry his cousin, the prominent humanist and feminist Charlotte Perkins). An extremely vivacious and active girl of 14, Bessie took mysteriously ill and died suddenly in 1879.

Shortly after the funeral, Catherine insisted on going to Auburn to visit William, although she was hardly in any condition, physically or mentally, to undertake such a venture. On her way home, she called on Governor Lucius Robinson in Albany to importune him to release her husband. Robinson denied the entreaty. This was in keeping with Robinson's position to refuse all pardon requests for the crime of forgery. His rationale was explained in a letter to former governor Horatio Seymour that also appeared in the *Times*: "Forgery seems to have become the usual and fashionable crime of intelligent and educated men of previous good reputation. Indeed, it is a crime which cannot well be committed except by persons of considerable education."[67] The trauma of Bessie's death, combined with Governor Robinson's refusal to pardon William, proved too much for Catherine. Shortly after returning home she passed away. According to Charlotte Perkins Gilman, Catherine was "out of her mind when she died."[68] Members of Catherine's family and William's sister Maria then traveled to Albany to plead with Robinson a second time. According to the *New York Sun*, "The Governor was unable to resist the pathetic appeal, and this afternoon Miss [Maria] Gilman telegraphed friends in Norwich: 'William is pardoned. Postpone the funeral.' "[69] When Maria took the governor's pardon to William at Auburn Prison, he refused to accept it, insisting that he serve the full sentence. After much pleading, Gilman acquiesced and left Auburn with his family members.

As one might expect from a stoic and upright New England family, there was little mention among the Gilman siblings during this time about Willie or his circumstances. William did, however, resurface in a significant manner after Daniel stepped aside at Hopkins and began the process of organizing his papers and recording his remembrances. As noted earlier, Fabian Franklin's biographical work on Gilman had portions written by other authors. The first chapter, on Gilman's boyhood, was written entirely by William, with substantial input from Daniel. A flurry of letters back and forth between the two began in 1902, after Gilman's retirement from Hopkins.[70] William was energetic and earnest in his efforts to compile the materials, and on more than one occasion Daniel found it impossible to keep up. He wrote to his younger brother, "Your frequent bulletins are very acceptable, but I cannot respond with equal vivacity."[71] William remained in Norwich for the rest of his life, living with his sisters in the family home on Washington Street. His eyesight got progressively worse as he grew older, and he passed away on March 30, 1922, just five months before his younger sister Louisa.[72]

## Learned Societies, Learned Journals, and the Hopkins Press

In the midst of establishing a home with his new wife and dealing with his brother's crimes, Gilman was only one year into leading a fledgling university. In his 1876 inaugural address he had outlined the five institutions of modern society responsible for promoting higher education, among them learned societies. Such organizations had flourished in England but had never taken hold in America. Gilman viewed their establishment at Hopkins as an antidote to the extreme specialization of self-centered departments. "Rarely was intra-university associationalism so consciously nurtured by an administration," opined Hugh Hawkins, "or nurtured to so serious an academic purpose, as at Johns Hopkins."[73] In the university's first year, Gilman organized social gatherings in either Hopkins Hall or the library to which were invited trustees, professors, instructors, and advanced scholars. The initial gatherings included lectures on a range of varied topics, including excavations at Olympia by an eyewitness; the Bayreuth festival, by an auditor; the US Fish Commission, by a collaborator; the Biological Laboratory, by the biologists; and the Peabody Institute, by the provost.[74] Learned societies would follow the next year.

The first to be organized, in early 1877, was the Philological Association; Basil Gildersleeve would be its only president, serving in that capacity until his retirement in 1915. At the inaugural meeting, Gildersleeve expressed the desire that the meetings provide participants with "a healthy stimulus to research," while keeping all abreast of advances in science. Thus the maiden meeting had no agenda and comprised a formal paper, minor communications, and reports on the contents of various philological journals. Professor Lanman then read the first formal paper, titled "The Two Original Ka-Sounds in Indo-European."[75] The next society to be founded was the Scientific Association, organized in October of that same year and chaired by Ira Remsen. James Sylvester was elected president; Remsen, vice president; and William Story, associate in mathematics, secretary.[76] This broad association certainly contained mathematicians among its number, but a subgroup within it decided to form their own society, the Mathematical Conference. Its appellation changed to Mathematical Society, and, after Sylvester's departure for England in 1883 the group was helmed by Simon Newcomb.

Then came the Historical Association, whose name was changed in December 1877 to the Historical and Political Science Club. Gilman was asked to be its permanent chair, with Austin Scott, associate in history, as vice president. A full accounting of the activities of each of these societies, in addition to the research conducted and articles submitted for publication by faculty, was relayed to the board by Gilman in his third annual report. He would continue this practice throughout his tenure.[77] Membership in the latter group was extended to some lawyers and clergymen of Baltimore, and its meetings were very popular and well attended, so much so that other faculty—Lanman, Sihler, and Royce—participated regularly in the programs. These groups were not clubs; they were formally sanctioned university entities. But for Gilman, the purpose of these associations was to promote interdisciplinary commu- nication, foster faculty-student interaction, and provide a forum for visitors to ad- dress various topics. Over time, other functions would be added, such as holding memorials for colleague who died and presenting graduate theses, with a critique and defense.

The Metaphysical Club was founded in October 1879, when the eccentric and brilliant Charles Sanders Peirce was appointed lecturer in logic. Peirce was a member of a club by the same name that met in Cambridge in 1872 (founded in January 1872, it dissolved the following December) and counted among its members Oliver Wen- dell Holmes Jr. and William James. His five years at Hopkins constituted Peirce's only academic appointment in his career. It culminated in the 1883 publication of *Studies in Logic by Members of the Johns Hopkins University*, a landmark work focused on the field of symbolic logic.[78] Peirce would leave Hopkins in 1884 after Simon Newcomb brought to Gilman's attention aspects of the philosopher's personal life and marital status that the president felt compelled to report to the executive committee of the board.[79] The trustees did not renew Peirce's lectureship, and Stanley Hall (professor of psychology and first president of Clark University) joined the faculty at Hopkins. Hall tried to reorganize the club, but it was officially disbanded in 1885.

Other societies had offshoots and splinter associations. For example, when some found the meetings of Gildersleeve's Philological Association too formal and classical for their purposes, a Modern Language Club formed. Likewise, an Archaeological Society emerged in 1884. Only the remnants of the original Philological Association remain to this day, in the form of the Society for Classical Studies, which publishes its research scholarship in the *Transactions of the American Philological Association*. There are currently other associations and societies, formed more recently, at Hop- kins. But the foundation associations were a worthy complement to the seminaries, allowing more interaction between faculty, students, and the broader community. "The master-pupil demarcation of the classroom and seminar was a proper function of the university," according to Hugh Hawkins, "but the societies symbolized a livelier comradeship of searching."[80] Still, Gilman admitted in his twelfth report to the trust- ees that his vision of the role of these societies was not complete; he acknowledged merely that they continued "to be important auxiliaries in the work of the University." While participation in the associations may have ebbed and flowed based on leader- ship and faculty involvement, Gilman saw to it that abstracts of some of the principal papers submitted were printed in the university *Circulars*.[81]

## Promoting Original Research "Far and Wide"

Another emphasis at the outset aligned with Gilman's belief in publishing the activ- ities and discoveries of the faculty to a broad audience: the founding of scholarly journals and a university press. Professor James Sylvester's replacement at Hopkins, Simon Newcomb, wrote a lengthy article for the *North American Review* shortly before Hopkins' founding in which he bemoaned the fact that in the United States' first one hundred years a lack of support of scientific research had resulted in a "paucity of scientific publications." In Europe—or as Newcomb called them, the "intellectual nations"—one found that science had a "fostering mother" in Germany's universities, in France's government, and in England's scientific societies. "And if science could find one here," Newcomb concluded, "it would speedily flourish." Newcomb suggested as a remedy "the support of two or three first-class journals of exact science. We say exact science, because this is the department which is worst supplied in this respect; taking mathematics at one extreme and medicine at the other, we can pretty accurately gauge the exactness of each science by the difficulty its cultivators find in supporting journals devoted to it." Newcomb maintained that the future prospects of mathematical sciences in America could very well depend on those committed to the field securing "five or six thousand dollars per annum."[82] As the Hopkins historian French observed, "It was one thing to recognize the need thus clearly and quite another thing to attempt to supply it."[83]

The genesis of the first Hopkins journal came just weeks after the official opening of the university.[84] A prospectus written in longhand by W. E. Story, a University of Leipzig PhD who spent a year at Harvard before joining the Hopkins faculty as the math department's first associate, and signed by Sylvester, Newcomb, Rowland, and Story was distributed broadly to American mathematicians. In it the authors expressed the desired outcomes of the journal, including a wish for "a periodical of a high class published in America, in which Mathematicians might interchange ideas and impart their investigations and discoveries." The solicitors further requested that "any suggestions that you may deem likely to be conducive to the success of the undertaking" be submitted "by letter directed to the Johns Hopkins University to the address of any of the undersigned."[85]

The publication, the *American Journal of Mathematics*, despite emanating from an infant institution, was an unqualified success and remains to this day the oldest continuously published journal in the United States. The first ten volumes printed articles from eighty-nine authors, and the world's leading mathematicians were among the regular contributors.[86] A motto for the new journal, borrowed from the New Testament by Basil Gildersleeve, was "The evidence of things not seen." Sylvester offered a paraphrase: "The clinching of the Invisible," which he claimed was the leading idea of mathematics.[87] This journal and the others the university would soon take on were published "under the auspices" of the university, with the production and budget of each presumably being the responsibility of its editor. However, the Hopkins trustees were on the hook as a financial backstop for subscriptions (each copy cost five dollars) and extended a private assurance that additional funds would be forthcoming should a deficit be incurred. In sum, the trustees made the difference between solvency and failure.[88]

Group photograph of early faculty, 1900. *Left to right:* Basil Lanneau Gildersleeve, Henry Augustus Rowland, Daniel Coit Gilman, William Henry Welch, and Ira Remsen. (Photo courtesy of University Archives, Sheridan Libraries, Johns Hopkins University)

Gilman had persuaded the board to support this first Hopkins-based journal; Ira Remsen would advocate for a chemistry-oriented publication a few months later. Remsen's approach, however, was slightly different, as he proposed publication of "Notes from the Chemical Laboratory," which would run fifty to sixty pages per year. Originally, overtures were made to the editors of the *American Journal of Science* to include the notes in their pages or even in a supplement. These overtures were rejected, but Gilman and Remsen remained undeterred and decided to become even more ambitious in their proposals. Remsen suggested that the board of trustees back a standalone journal of national scope open to other chemists across the country. In April 1879 the *American Chemical Journal* was launched with an original publication goal of six issues per annum. This was increased to eight, then ten, then monthly issues by 1899. Remsen served as editor for thirty-five years. Upon his retirement—and the publication's fiftieth volume—the journal was taken over by the American Chemical Society. Other journals would follow: the *American Journal of Philology* in 1880, *Johns Hopkins University Studies in Historical and Political Science* in 1882, and *Modern Language Notes* in 1886.

The publication of the first two journals fell within the bailiwick of yet another Gilman innovation, the Johns Hopkins Press. While his friend Andrew White, had formed the first university press in America at Cornell in 1869, it fell on hard times and was subsequently shuttered in 1884. (Today's Cornell University Press began operations in 1930.) Presses at other institutions experienced fits and starts as well. However, the distinction as America's oldest continuously operating university press belongs to the Johns Hopkins Press, founded by Gilman in 1878.[89] Gilman's thinking was simple: Commercial publishing in the late nineteenth century was extremely competitive. Further, costs would be prohibitively high, with markets far too small to attract commercial presses looking for profits. Recruiting the faculty had shown Gilman just how specialized their research and writing would be—but this was just what he wanted. As he said unequivocally in his inaugural, his job was to recruit the fittest teachers and then constantly encourage them "to do their very best work." Their best, however, might also be so esoteric as to have a limited readership. Charles Scribner, of the famed Scribner publishing house, was instrumental in forming a university press at his alma mater, Princeton. He sounded a similar refrain: "What is accomplished if the work of a lifetime grows mouldy in the drawer of a desk?"[90]

The manager of the Hopkins Press was Nicholas Murray, librarian of the university and uncle to Nicholas Murray Butler. President of Columbia University from 1902 to 1945, Nicholas Murray Butler first founded his own journal, the *Educational Review*, in 1890 and served as editor for thirty years. Gilman and Butler collaborated on various projects for many years, including Butler's presentation of several lectures at Hopkins on educational issues.[91] In soliciting a contribution from Gilman for the journal's first issue (which Gilman submitted), Butler told Gilman, "It is hoped and expected that the *Review* will from the outset, make good its title to place among the really scientific publications of this country."[92] A common refrain throughout Gilman's educational life was his unrelenting commitment to publishing results of research whether by means of academic presses or scientific journals, and he even contributed his own scholarship from time to time. It was one thing to have faculty, staff, and students committed to the discovery and development of new knowledge on campus, but the responsibility of disseminating and applying these discoveries on behalf of society was something Gilman took on with a zestful exuberance that forever transformed American higher education. The university officially published its first book in 1887. Three years later, the press changed its name from Publication Agency of the University to Johns Hopkins Press.[93]

In addition to the scholarly journals produced by the press, three publications reflected the total work of the university: the *Register* was the catalog; the *Annual Report* was akin to the presidential reports issued at Harvard and Columbia; and the *Circulars*. The last, "peculiarly a product of the Hopkins environment," began as slender octavo announcements of dates and courses.[94] This began to change, however, shortly after the university's founding, as the *Circulars* resembled more the *University Reporter* issued in Cambridge, England, with course lists (and the students enrolled in them), proceedings from the university's various societies (with abstracts of the papers read before them), and occasionally a full-length article (they later printed monograph series, facsimile editions of biblical manuscripts, and Professor Rowland's maps of the solar spectrum).[95] In December 1879 the trustees granted permission for the publication of *Official Circulars of the University*, in a quarto form, under the direction of the president of the university.[96] Originally intended for local consumption, the *Circulars* morphed into what might be called a widely recognized scientific journal with semi-annual distribution.[97] Gilman would call the *Circulars* "photographs of the horse in motion" and explained the need for such a publication "as a convenient channel for acquainting the public at large with the condition of progress."[98] A review of the *Circulars* suggests that probably no other institution in America recorded its own events and contributions in more detail.[99]

Perhaps the most fitting tribute to Gilman's prescience in funding the learned journals, publishing the *Circulars*, and founding the press—albeit wholly unintended, one might surmise—is found in *Johns Hopkins University Circular* 210. Thirty-two years after the institution's founding, its university press listed the scholarly journals and other publications for the year 1908. In reviewing this list of materials and the information disseminated in each, one must bear in mind a statement made by Gilman: "It is one of the noblest duties of a university to advance knowledge, and to diffuse it not merely among those who can attend the daily lecture—but far and wide."

— *American Journal of Mathematics*, Frank Morley, Editor
— *American Chemical Journal*, Ira Remsen, Editor
— *American Journal of Philology*, Basil Gildersleeve, Editor
— *Studies in Historical and Political Science*, Under the direction of the Departments of History, Political Economy, and Political Science
— Johns Hopkins University Circular
— Johns Hopkins Hospital Bulletin
— Johns Hopkins Hospital Reports
— *Contributions to Assyriology and Semitic Philology*, Paul Haupt and Friedrich Delitzsch, Editors
— *Memoirs from the Biological Laboratory*, William K. Brooks, Editor
— *Modern Language Notes*, A. Marshall Elliott, Editor
— *American Journal of Insanity*, Henry M. Hurd, Editor
— *Terrestrial Magnetism and Atmospheric Electricity*, L. A. Bauer, Editor
— *Reprint of Economic Tracts*, J. H. Hollander, Editor
— Report of the Maryland Geological Survey
— *Report of the Johns Hopkins University*, presented by the President to the Board of Trustees
— *Register of the Johns Hopkins University*[100]

Rarely can one look back over the arc of a career and witness the fulfillment of nearly every stated objective. But that is exactly what one finds in both the list of Hopkins Press publications in *Circular* 210 and the tribute to President Gilman in *Circular* 211. Gilman knew precisely what was needed and what he intended to do in circulating "far and wide" the work of his faculty. He may not have been the scholar some critics desired in a university president, but no one better promoted the work of his fellow faculty. Consider the words Gilman used to express his desires for the Hopkins faculty in his first report to the board, in January 1876, seven weeks before his official inauguration:

> It is their researches in the library and the laboratory; their utterances in the class room and in private; their example as students and investigators, and as champions of the truth; their publications through the journals and the scientific treatises which will make the University in Baltimore an attraction to the best students, and serviceable to the intellectual growth of the land. In selecting a staff of teachers, the Trustees have determined to consider especially the devotion of the candidate to some particular line of study and the certainty of his eminence in that specialty; the power to pursue independent and original investigation, and to inspire the young with enthusiasm for study and research; the willingness to co-operate in building up a new institution; and the freedom from tendencies toward ecclesiastical or sectional controversies.[101]

The Hopkins fellowships, the PhD, the learned societies and journals, and the Hopkins Press were all elements of the university conceived of, implemented by, and effected through Daniel Coit Gilman.

One immediate proof of the university's emphasis on primary research was discovered in the nascent laboratories of Professor Ira Remsen. Long an opponent of "practicalism," Remsen repeatedly refused all offers of consultant positions from private industry as long as he remained affiliated with the university. As Hawkins notes, one of Remsen's students suggested that private industries might support the institution and cited German examples to buttress his argument. Remsen responded "that he could think of no worse fate for the university than such an invasion."[102] In 1879, one of Remsen's students, Constantin Fahlberg, a European chemist studying with Remsen as a postdoctoral fellow, was assisting with experiments on the oxidation of toluene, a coal tar derivative. Various accounts of events exist, but Fahlberg apparently discovered an unusual sweetness after unintentionally licking his finger during lunch in the lab. Remsen moved on to other projects, but Fahlberg recognized the enormous commercial potential of his serendipitous finding. Fahlberg began secretly working to refine the substance that he would subsequently call—because of its intense sweetness—saccharin.[103] The discovery made Fahlberg extremely wealthy, but neither Remsen nor the university ever received, or even claimed, a royalty. What Remsen sought was recognition for his work, not remuneration.[104] A perpetual debate in Hopkins' early years centered on the application of research for practical purposes. The institution's stance evolved over time as research and discoveries led to real-world applications and could be monetized, thus increasing the university's bottom line. But offices of technology transfer and sponsored research did not exist at universities in the nineteenth century. The first two decades of the institution's existence revealed just how precarious its financial standing was.

### Financial Challenges Arise

The Johns Hopkins University was off and running, with all its novel elements in place, but it needed money to sustain the vision Gilman had outlined and the trustees had supported. At the center of the institution's fiscal model was the share price of the B&O Railroad. Both Johns Hopkins and John Work Garrett had been unfailingly bullish about the B&O's stock, for all its ebbs and flows. But Hopkins was no longer around to rescue the railroad from ruin as he had done in the past, and the reality was settling in that whatever the university was able—or unable—to do was inescapably tied to the railroad's stock price. If there was no dividend paid to shareholders, there would be no income for the university.

Garrett, who had built his career through opinionated and autocratic leadership, had a seat on both the university and hospital boards and forcefully expressed his views about the direction both entities should take. Following the Great Railroad Strike of 1877, also known as the Great Upheaval, Garrett told shareholders that dividends were to be paid in the form of additional stock and not cash. Notwithstanding, he remained sanguine and announced to shareholders that the 7 percent dividend paid in 1878 would increase to 8 percent in 1879 and 1880 and 10 percent in the years 1881–84.[105] This news was encouraging for investors, especially coming on the heels of the labor unrest. The strike had been precipitated by news that the railroad was reducing salaries for workers, the second such pay cut in eight months, with July 16, 1877, designated as the day Garrett would cut employees' wages by 10 percent.[106] The strike had eventually been put down by unofficial militias, the National Guard, and federal troops after sixty-nine days, but not before the rioting, which stretched from Maryland to Missouri, caused millions of dollars in damage and an estimated one hundred deaths.

Stock instead of cash was not what the university trustees wanted. The campus had been open for less than eighteen months, and they needed cash for operations, not more stock in a struggling railroad. Deprived of funds, the trustees voted to sell the stocks they had received as dividends. Garrett promised his fellow trustees on October 6, 1879, that the B&O would pay a 4 percent cash dividend the next day; he further pledged that the university's income from the B&O would double in the next decade. While Garrett could keep the first promise, the second was much more troublesome.[107]

Given that the university was now the third-largest shareholder in the B&O— behind the city of Baltimore and Garrett himself—the sale of their shares flooded the market and devalued the stock. Most concerning to Garrett, however, was that the sale allowed outside parties to purchase the stock and jeopardize the city's and his control of the railroad. This episode, together with disagreements about Garrett's vision for the university—including his insistence that it stay on a path of "immediate practical benefit to the community"—and its eventual physical location, led him to resign from the board in 1883.[108] Garrett would die a year later at the age of 64.[109]

Garrett's role in the larger Baltimore community and his commitment to Johns Hopkins in the early years were unequaled. Gilman wrote of him years later:

> His country seat, at Montebello, was adjacent to that of Johns Hopkins. They were close friends, and must have had many confidential talks with respect to the proposed foundations. In the early days of the University Mr. Garrett was most cooperative. He opened his house to the professors and lecturers, as they came on from time to time, and in other ways showed his strong desire for the success of the institution. Unfortunately, he differed in opinion from most of the trustees regarding the policy which should be pursued in the construction of buildings in the heart of Baltimore. This alienated him from active service, and before the controversy was closed his health became seriously impaired, and his death soon followed.[110]

Despite Garrett's break with the trustees and the university, his family's intimate connection with, and support of, the Johns Hopkins legacy would continue for generations. John and Rachel Garrett's only daughter, Mary Elizabeth Garrett, would play an extremely vital role relative to the health sciences components of the university.[111]

## More Specifics of the Hopkins Will: Caring for the Indigent Sick and the Children's Orphanage

Long before coming to Baltimore, Daniel Gilman had been well prepared to run a university. He had spent years as an academic administrator of one type or another. But Johns Hopkins' will had called not only for the creation of the university but for the establishment of a hospital and a medical school as well. These were new and complicated arenas. Gilman's only experience with health sciences had been during his brief tenure in California, when the university took on both a small medical college and a pharmacy school in early 1873. What was proposed in Baltimore would be on a considerably larger scale and prove much more challenging—and impactful.

The hospital, at the explicit directive of Johns Hopkins, had its own board, and the founding documents included much more detail concerning its purpose and even its construction and design. Hopkins went so far as to specify that he wished "the large grounds surrounding the hospital buildings to be properly closed by iron railings, and to be so laid out and planted with trees and flowers as to afford solace to the sick and be an ornament to the section of the city in which the grounds are located."[112] The university and the hospital were both incorporated in 1867, and the board of trustees of the hospital met for the first time in 1870 for the purposes of organization. Elected as chair was a close friend of Johns Hopkins and a fellow Quaker, Francis T. King (also a university trustee, nominated for the position by fellow university trustee and board president, Galloway Cheston), with Lewis N. Hopkins as vice chair. King had been in the first graduating class of Haverford College in 1835, had served as the first chairman of the board of trustees at Bryn Mawr College, and like Mr. Hopkins had vowed at an early age to retire from business after achieving significant financial success and focus on charitable causes and benevolent service.[113]

As noted earlier, Dr. John Fonerden's passing in 1869 left a seat to be filled on the boards of trustees of the university and the hospital. Dr. James Carey Thomas would take his place among the university's trustees, while the vacancy on the hospital's board was filled by Joseph Merrefield, a successful merchant who had married Johns Hopkins' favorite cousin, Rebecca Janney.[114] Merrefield would serve on the board until 1902, when he was struck and killed by a train in downtown Baltimore.[115] In addition to King and Lewis Hopkins, other hospital trustees included seven from the university's board of trustees: John Garrett, George Dobbin, Galloway Cheston, Thomas Smith, William Hopkins, Francis White, and Charles Gwinn. The other "unique" hospital trustees were Richard M. Janney and Dr. Alan P. Smith, a surgeon who would also be appointed a university trustee in 1881.

Following their 1870 inaugural meeting, the hospital trustees would not gather again until March 1, 1873, when they would meet to receive from Johns Hopkins the deed for the property upon which the proposed hospital was to be built. Six years prior, the Maryland Hospital for the Insane at Baltimore had occupied the site purchased by Hopkins. Its board of visitors had included King, Dobbin, and Fonerden, along with Hopkins himself. When the state of Maryland decided to relocate the hospital, progress was slow and construction was not completed until 1872, at which time patients were relocated. Questions then arose about the future of the old facility, given that the hospital was $150,000 in debt and the legislature refused to appropriate any funds to pay off the obligation. An appeal was made to Mr. Hopkins to buy the old hospital in anticipation of the new one he had expressed a desire to found. He agreed, but only if the city roads across the property were closed. This was done when the Baltimore City Council passed an ordinance closing all the roads that crisscrossed the site, and the action was subsequently confirmed by the Maryland General Assembly.[116]

The hospital trustees would continue to purchase additional property, and the tract would be further expanded after Hopkins' death, with the additions paid for with the first year's income from the initial endowment. The total parcel would amount to fourteen and a half acres.[117] In his letter of transmittal dated March 10, 1873, Hopkins described the parcel and his desires for the institution to be built on that site in great detail. Hopkins' specificity in his communications to the hospital trustees stands in stark contrast to the paucity of detail he offered his university trustees.

Hopkins left little question as to who should be treated and the purpose of the hospital that would bear his name: "The indigent sick of this city and its environs, without regard to sex, age, or color who require surgical or medical treatment . . . and the poor of the city and State, of all races, who are stricken down by any casualty, shall be received into the hospital without charge, for such periods of time and under such regulations as you may prescribe."[118] Immediately preceding this directive in Hopkins' letter is this requirement of the trustees: "It will be your duty hereafter to provide for the erection upon other ground, of suitable buildings for the reception, maintenance and education of Orphaned colored children. I direct you to provide accommodations for three or four hundred children of this class . . . to the maintenance of the Orphans' Home intended for such children."[119]

Hopkins wanted the hospital construction to begin in the spring of 1874. No deadline was set, however, for the orphanage. The acreage for the hospital had been secured and was being conveyed to his trustees. Hopkins estimated that additional property he was leaving the trustees—a stock of warehouses in downtown Baltimore that at the time produced a healthy revenue stream, as the storefronts were leased to businesses—could be valued at $2 million. This property produced a yearly income of $120,000, which Hopkins projected would be sufficient for the operations of the hospital and the orphanage. He left the trustees with this charge: "If the Hospital and Orphans' Home are not built at my death, it will be your duty to apply the income arising from this property to their completion. When they are built, the income from the property will suffice for the maintenance."[120] This was an optimistic projection, to be sure. Economic vicissitudes and a terrible disaster would dramatically impact the revenue.

The Great Baltimore Fire of 1904 destroyed 1,545 buildings over 140 acres of the city, including the entire town laid out in 1730.[121] The leveled structures included scores of Hopkins' income-producing warehouses. This loss left the hospital and the medical school in acute financial straits, which no one could have anticipated thirty years earlier. But a surprising savior stepped forward: the Rockefeller Foundation. By the turn of the century the Rockefellers were well on their way to displacing John Garrett and Johns Hopkins in railroad and banking control by acquiring the Western Maryland Railroad, among many other interests. In the wake of the devastating fire, the Rockefeller Foundation created the Johns Hopkins School of Hygiene and Public Health, endowed the medical school, and compensated the university for its losses in the calamity.[122]

For the time being, however, the trustees had to grapple with Hopkins' explicit instruction to begin construction on the hospital posthaste. For myriad reasons, work on the multistructure complex was delayed, and the hospital would not officially open until 1889. The Orphans' Home—at least the facility of three hundred to four hundred beds that Hopkins described in his will—never materialized. Nonetheless, President King did obtain authority from the state legislature early on to construct the facility "in any part of the State that may be deemed best by the Board," and this action was reported to the trustees at an April 1874 meeting.[123] The trustees hired John Niernsee, the head architect of the Baltimore & Ohio Railroad, whose projects included the Clifton Estate and the South Carolina State House, to design the facility. His plans and renderings for the building are housed in the Legislative Reference Library, in Baltimore City Hall. They were never used.[124] Nonetheless, the trustees remained committed to fulfilling Hopkins' stated wishes. At an April 1875 meeting the hospital board established four standing committees, one of which was for the "colored orphan asylum"; the member of that committee were trustees Joseph Elliott, Thomas Smith, William Hopkins, Francis White, and Francis King as an ex-officio member.[125]

But before these trustees were empaneled to begin their committee work, a parcel of twenty-three acres—Font Hill Heights on the Frederick Road, just north of the Mt. Olivet Cemetery—was proposed for the orphanage and subsequently purchased. At a board meeting in January 1875, the land was reported as having been surveyed and secured. At the same meeting, a letter from "the Managers of the Shelter for Colored Orphans" was read and recorded in the minutes. The letter detailed events following the death of Johns Hopkins that had materially impacted the orphanage and its operations. First, the public now believed "that the Asylum to be founded under his bequest, has already, or will very soon, take the place of ours." Second, monetary support had plummeted; Mr. Hopkins himself had been an ardent financial backer of the shelter. And third, the managers feared that "we shall soon be under the painful necessity of closing the only asylum for colored children now in the city." To remedy the acute situation, the managers proposed a one-year lease for their facility, with a two-year renewable option at three thousand dollars per year, or eighty dollars per child, while the Hopkins-funded facility was being constructed.[126] The matter was forwarded to a committee of four trustees to consider the proposal and report back to the full board at the next meeting.

In February 1875, the hospital trustees took up the proposal and approved the arrangement outlined in the letter from the managers of the existing orphanage. President King was authorized to lease the Font Hill property.[127] A board of visitors for the orphanage made up of twenty-nine women was then appointed by the hospital board, with Julia Valentine serving as president. Valentine subsequently presented a lengthy report to the board detailing the asylum's opening at 206 East Biddle Street, its operation, and the state of the twenty-six children under care.[128] In 1876 the trustees approved the purchase of the Biddle Street property and increased the annual budget.[129] Three years later, the number of children at the asylum had grown to sixty-five, and a request was made to increase the facility's budget again.[130]

The asylum would remain at the Biddle Street location for nearly two decades, but it was persistently pressed for space as the population grew. Finally, at an April 1891 meeting, the board considered the issue of moving the asylum and "enlarging the work." A written report was requested for the next meeting, in October, when the following resolution was approved by the entire board: "That it is inexpedient at present to change the location of the Colored Orphan Asylum now supported by the Johns Hopkins Hospital, or to enlarge its accommodations, in view of the fact that we are looking forward to the building at as early a day as is practicable, of an Asylum, in accordance with the directions of Mr. Hopkins' will."[131] This, of course, never happened, as the trustees were contending with how to open a school of medicine and other matters that in their view were more pressing. It should also be noted that two of the founding trustees of both the university and hospital—Judge George Dobbin and President Francis King—died within six months of each other during this same time period.

In 1895 the board authorized the standing committee to expand the asylum on property purchased along Remington Avenue (adjacent to the future Homewood campus site) to accommodate fifty additional children, with a charge to develop a reorganization and management plan. This original acquisition of property was augmented by a contiguous parcel the following year.[132] Perhaps portending what the future of the facility might hold, in 1896 the trustees approved putting the medical care of the children at the asylum "under the charge of the physicians of the Hospital."[133] This arrangement continued until 1913, when the trustees of the hospital converted the asylum into a convalescent home and school for crippled colored children who had received orthopedic treatment at the Johns Hopkins Hospital. However, the home was closed in 1917, never to reopen.[134]

These were very challenging times for the hospital trustees as they struggled to adhere to the restriction in Hopkins' bequest that only endowment earnings were to be used for capital construction for both the hospital and the orphanage. Time had to pass for the funds to accrue income before any capital improvements could be made. It appears that the trustees earnestly strove to follow the spirit of Hopkins' will in fulfilling his desire to see the orphanage established and thrive; following the *letter* of the bequest proved much more difficult. With limited resources, the trustees continued in their intention to focus on the hospital and, subsequently, on the medical school.

Leaving a legacy among the Black community in the form of a four-hundred-bed orphanage was important to the founder. However, it appears to have become a secondary concern of the trustees, whose overarching concern was the design, construction, and opening of the hospital. Unable to construct a new orphanage with the resources at their disposal, the board decided to use what then existed, expanding and increasing the scope of the endeavor as it moved along its evolutionary arc until its closure in 1917. The Font Hill property acquired by the hospital trustees in 1875 is now the site of a public, four-hundred-student college-preparatory boarding school for at-risk students.[135] Founded in 2008, in many ways the SEED school is fulfilling the charge Johns Hopkins conveyed to the hospital trustees in 1873 "to provide for the erection upon other ground, of suitable buildings for the reception, maintenance and education" of children.[136]

## Hospital Programming and Dr. John Shaw Billings

The building committee had originally suggested George Frederick, designer of the Baltimore City Hall, as the architect of the hospital. But "after mature deliberation," the committee reversed course and unanimously recommended that John Niernsee receive the commission.[137] However, before design of the hospital could commence, the trustees wanted advice about how the facility should connect with the medical school. Their search for the nation's leading expert in this area would lead to a decades-long relationship with a distinguished doctor.

John Shaw Billings and Daniel Coit Gilman first met just after the latter had been appointed president of the Johns Hopkins University. Gilman called on Billings at the Office of the Surgeon General, in Washington, DC, in the spring of 1875. Billings' relationship with the Hopkins Hospital Board of Trustees had begun more than a year earlier, however, in the early stages of the trustees' work. Niernsee would be given the responsibility of design, but there was little consensus among the trustees regarding the layout, form, and function of the multibuilding complex.[138] In search of expert counsel, President King contacted the Office of the Surgeon General and requested a meeting with Billings.[139] While the details of their conversation are unknown, the official hospital record does indicate that in March 1875 the board of trustees authorized King to issue a letter to five physicians, including Billings, requesting their assistance in planning and organizing the hospital.[140] Billings obliged with an exhaustive report. In a display of magnanimity and cooperation, the trustees published all the proposals, believing that the materials presented by the five doctors would benefit the entire medical community.[141]

A native of Indiana, Billings filled many roles during his distinguished career, including modernizing the entire Library of the Surgeon General's Office. Billings was well respected by his fellow physicians for his skill as a surgeon, but it was clear that his true genius lay in his organizational abilities. Years later, William Welch—recruited to Hopkins by Gilman at the urging of Billings after the two medical doctors first met in Germany in November 1876—was asked what the United States had contributed to medicine. Welch responded: first, the discovery of anesthesia; second, the discovery of insect transmission of disease; and third, the development of the modern public health laboratory. The fourth contribution, asserted the famed Hopkins pathologist, was the "Army Medical Library and its Index Catalogue, and this library and catalogue are the most important of the four."[142] The index catalog was entirely Billings' doing.

Before becoming known for his organizational skills, Billings had distinguished himself in the Civil War, leading a unit in combat as medical director of the Army of the Potomac in April 1863 and serving as a field surgeon at the battles of Chancellorsville, Gettysburg, the Wilderness, Cold Harbor, and Petersburg. He was known as "one of the ablest American surgeons of his time."[143] A partial paralysis of his left leg in July 1864 had led to his assignment to the Office of the Surgeon General, where he remained until his retirement thirty-one years later.[144]

Billings was hired by the hospital board of trustees in June 1876 at an annual salary of three thousand dollars plus traveling expenses for shuttling back and forth between his home in Washington and the hospital site.[145] Immediately, Billings departed on a three-month tour of medical facilities throughout England and Europe. This was in keeping with Johns Hopkins' charge in the original letter of instructions to the hospital trustees: "It will therefore be your duty to obtain the advice and assistance of those at home or abroad who have achieved the greatest success in the construction and management of hospitals."[146] It also aligned with Billings' view that the main site of medical science had migrated from France to Germany since 1850: "As regards scientific medicine, we are at present going to school in Germany."[147]

Toward the end of his travels in Europe, Billings sent a letter from Dresden to Gilman—now just a few months into his tenure as president—and reported, "I have been very successful in meeting the men that I wanted to meet, and in getting at the methods and appliances relating to the medical teaching that I most wanted to see."[148] One opinion he sought while overseas was that of Florence Nightingale, the Lady with the Lamp, to whom he had sent the earliest sketch plans for the hospital, the training school for nurses, and the children's orphanage. Nightingale responded with twelve pages of notes, for which Billings offered his "sincere personal thanks," saying that he did not "think it probable that I should do otherwise than agree with them."[149]

Billings returned to America and revised his original design, emphasizing the need for a close partnership between the hospital and the medical school and full-time clinical positions.[150] In a December 1876 issue of *American Architect and Building News*, the block plan and the sketch plans by Niernsee and Billings were published, but no elevations were included. After Niernsee completed his drawings and was paid for his work, he resigned in 1877 to return to a project he had initiated before the Civil War: the South Carolina Statehouse in Columbia. While Niernsee would remain a consultant on the project until his death in 1885, the trustees hired the Boston firm of Cabot & Chandler to take up the work. Misperceptions emerged early on about who did what on the hospital project. A February 1877 *Baltimore Sun* story reported, "It is known that the plans of the Johns Hopkins Hospital, prepared by Dr. Billings, with some modifications by the trustees, will be carried out." Niernsee submitted his version of the events to the editor: "Mr. Niernsee writes that it would be more correct to say 'That the plans of the hospital designed by John R. Niernsee, have been accepted as being in accordance with the views of the building committee, with some modifications by their medical advisor, Dr. J. S. Billings.' "[151]

Regardless of who got the public credit, the board was busy trying to digest Billings' forty-six-page report on recommended hospital designs and essential elements. His proposal launched yet another Hopkins advancement, this time in the proposed layout of the multistructure complex and the interface between the new facility and a medical school:

> In attempting to prepare a plan for the organization and construction of a Hospital at Baltimore, under the provisions of the Johns Hopkins' Trust, it is necessary first to consider the probable organization of the Johns Hopkins' University, for the reason that the plan of the Hospital must depend upon the extent to and the manner in which it is to be used as an instrument of medical education, and upon the more or less intimate connection which it is to have with the Medical School. If the course of medical education proposed is to be that usually given in this country, and

to the class of students which form the majority of those now attending our medical colleges, it will be extremely difficult, if not impossible, to devise a Hospital which shall equally subserve the best interests of the patients and the convenience and wishes of the students and professors. I am decidedly of the opinion, however, that we have at present in the United States not only enough, but too many of the ordinary sort of medical colleges, and that the opportunity which is now presented of forming an institution for medical instruction which, being entirely independent of students, can therefore afford to consult their welfare instead of their wishes, is one of which an attempt should be made to take the fullest advantage, and such, I have reason to believe, is the intention of the trustees. It seems to me that this school should aim to produce quality, and not quantity; and that the seal of its diploma should be a guarantee that its possessor is not only a well-educated physician, in the fullest sense of the word, but that he has learned to think and investigate for himself, and is therefore prepared to undertake, without danger of failure from not knowing how to begin, the study of some of the many problems still awaiting solution.[152]

This initial report was followed with additional information from Billings, culminating in a January 11, 1877, meeting of the hospital trustees, in which the board heard in great detail what Billings had learned during his European tour.[153] Based on what he had observed and the requisite elements that would separate this facility from all others, Billings put forward the sketch plans and requested that the trustees authorize him to begin working with the architect to prepare construction drawings. He was particularly focused on ventilation and insisted that patients in the various wards have access to "light, pure air, warmth, etc."[154]

In asking whether the money could "be better employed in building a cheaper Hospital, which shall also be more compact and cheaper to manage," Billings played devil's advocate. Certainly, this was an option the trustees might entertain, he said. The question before the board was a financial one, he acknowledged, but he believed that what was proposed complied with what the founder had envisioned in expressing his desire that the facility bearing his name might "compare favorably with any other institution of like character in this country or in Europe." By nature, the trustees were an accomplished, competitive group of successful entrepreneurs, attorneys, executives, doctors, and public servants. Billings was convinced that to be the best, the trustees had to spend money, not cut corners, and not make excuses. Billings closed with this compelling argument: "Certainly I have seen nothing which I think superior, or in some respects equal to it, and if it has a medical, surgical and nursing staff, and a superintendence of corresponding quality, I am quite sure that the results of treatment obtained in it will not be surpassed elsewhere."[155]

With Billings' guiding documents in hand and his recommendation before them, "the trustees acted as they were advised," noted Abraham Flexner, author of *Medical Education in the United States and Canada*, the groundbreaking study of American medical education in 1910. "The Hospital started a new era in hospital construction and management as well as in medical education."[156] Not only would the result be the most modern hospital of its time but it was the first facility in which doctors and nurses could be taught at the same time that patients were being treated.[157] This would be America's first teaching hospital.[158]

While the hospital trustees would adopt all of Billings' recommendations, they were startled both by the projected cost (over $1 million) and the proposed construction time for the seventeen-building complex (three years).[159] Billings pulled no punches, telling them that the project represented "a solid and substantial group of buildings, and a comparatively costly one."[160] Billings did not want the university to scrimp on the hospital nor rush the time to construct it; this commitment to doing it right was shared by President King. Gilman would note that King "could not be hurried" and was severely limited by the restriction that only the income of the endowment could be used for capital construction.[161] For this and many other reasons, the Hopkins Hospital would not be ready until May 1889, more than a decade after the adoption of Billings' plan.[162]

## Why a Hospital and a Medical School?

For years, many have speculated about what exactly motivated Johns Hopkins to found a hospital. Some attribute his desire to various conversations with friends, fellow philanthropists, and medical doctors. Others maintain that it stemmed from his own brush with death while in his thirties. Clearly Hopkins' life experience had a profound impact on what he chose to do with his wealth and helped direct his desires to improve lives through access to better facilities and the best available health care. When the cholera epidemic swept the East Coast in 1832, Horatio Jameson, the nation's expert on the disease, recorded that "in the city of Baltimore there died of cholera, during the summer of 1832, eight hundred and fifty three persons, a very great majority of whom were the most worthless; but a few of our best citizens were its victims. Here then is a mortality of about one in 96; and, of persons of respectability, one, we believe, in a thousand."[163] Among those infected with the disease was 37-year-old Johns Hopkins.

Given the absence of any journals or correspondence, the only account of Hopkins' illness is recorded by his grandniece Helen Hopkins Thom: "His health had never been the same since an attack of cholera, contracted in 1832, had resulted in a very severe illness."[164] Cholera remained a significant challenge in Baltimore for decades, and the hospital Hopkins founded would play a substantial role in public health from its outset. Recognizing the university's ability to deploy experts in addressing yet another outbreak, the trustees requested that Professors Remsen and Martin, along with Billings, "determine the preventative methods, which are, in their judgment, best adapted to avert or lessen, the danger of Cholera in this community in the year 1885."[165]

Hopkins would lose an older brother to another horrid disease: in 1840 Mahlon died of yellow fever. The grip such epidemics had on the city revealed the dearth of competent nurses and the tremendous lack of facilities, with makeshift hospitals for the indigent sick hastily set up in private homes and on a campus outside the city. Hopkins recognized the need for a first-rate, modern hospital in Baltimore. But he also wanted a medical school to accompany it.

Nine of the original twelve university trustees also served on the hospital board, and they applied the same relentless energy and attention to crafting the university as they would to the health sciences operation. The interlocking nature of the boards was an indication that Johns Hopkins wished the two foundations to work closely together—and they did.[166] In his directions to the hospital trustees, Hopkins made explicit his desire to see the hospital inexorably aligned with the medical school, which opened its doors in 1893: "In all your arrangements in relation to this hospital, you will bear constantly in mind that it is my wish and purpose that the institution should ultimately form a part of the medical school of that university for which I have made ample provision by my will."[167] This relationship between the medical school the hospital would have a profound ripple effect as early graduates spread across the country, bringing with them the Hopkins model of "clinician-scientists."[168] The proposed medical school would also transform medical education and practice, but getting it funded and running would take every ounce of Gilman's skill and diplomatic ability.

If Hopkins believed his adopted city needed a hospital, how, asks John French, did he arrive at the idea of linking this facility and the university through a school of medicine? Hopkins was "curiously insistent on it," and so were his hospital trustees.[169] One must recall the emphasis placed on the medical school by Harvard's Charles Eliot when he met with the board in June 1874. The uniqueness of the opportunity Hopkins had was clear in light of President Eliot's assessment of medical education in America at the time: "medical schools everywhere in this country are exceedingly poor." Eliot asserted that the trustees' opportunity to found "a proper medical school in this community is a very precious one."[170] Just as graduate fellowships had brought the brightest advanced students in America to Hopkins in 1876, when the medical school opened in 1893 a similar phenomenon occurred. The Hopkins innovation of "bedside teaching" brought the nation's best medical students to Baltimore. As these students graduated, they in turn carried Hopkins' educational methods to other schools.[171]

Uncertainty about when the hospital or the medical school might open did not prevent Gilman from proposing a preparatory course for those wishing to study medicine. Gilman had promised as much in his inaugural address when he said that "in the meantime we have an excellent opportunity to provide instruction antecedent to the professional study of medicine."[172] A detailed list of prerequisites, courses, degree requirements, and even stipulations for language proficiency (in either French or German) was included in the university *Circulars*. With an emphasis on the core courses in physics, chemistry, and biology, the BA degree was "so planned as to give

Johns Hopkins University Hospital at the time of its opening, 1889. (The Alan Mason Chesney Medical Archives of the Johns Hopkins Medical Institutions)

those students who follow it a liberal education equivalent to that afforded by the other courses leading to the same degree." Among the minor course offerings were drawing, English, and logic and psychology.[173] This all fit within Gilman's view of how the medical ecosystem operated: "Medicine and surgery are based on pathology; pathology rests on physiology, physiology upon chemistry, chemistry upon physics, and physics upon mathematics." Further, the best candidate "should have a good command of English, French, German and Latin. Logic will teach him how to reason; history and literature will refresh his weary hours."[174] The outline Gilman delivered to the trustees was built upon a speech he had delivered to the Medical Society of California in 1873, in which he outlined five prerequisites to ensure that the university's medical school would "have no superior on this continent": "to adopt the best methods of American and foreign schools, to keep our schools open throughout the year, to institute a judicious subdivision of specialties, to establish a suitable standard of admission, and a high standard of graduation."[175]

The medical historian Gert Brieger notes that Gilman's thoughts contained principles upon which the Hopkins School of Medicine would be founded, twenty years

before the school opened. "His ideas," Brieger contends, "while not fully to take hold in the 1870s, were in the air, so to say." The medical professionals Gilman hired—Billings, Welch, and others—focused much more on the details of these reforms and helped put them into practice. Nonetheless, Gilman's commitment to outlining the curriculum long before the university welcomed its inaugural class in 1893 qualifies him as an early and important figure in late nineteenth-century medical education.[176]

Part of Gilman's genius in launching the university's lecture series was to showcase both his own faculty and visiting subject-matter experts. During Billings' series of lectures on the history of medicine, he delivered an especially noteworthy presentation in December 1877, in which he asked, "In view of the present condition of Medical Education in this country, how should the Johns Hopkins University organize its Medical Department?"[177] Billings then provided his answers. First, medical students needed the opportunity to observe disease in the patient at the bedside. Sir William Osler, one of the original four doctors recruited to Hopkins, initiated the practice of grand rounds upon the opening of the Hopkins Hospital in 1889. This teaching technique was precisely what Billings envisioned. Given that the hospital would have a limited capacity to offer bedside instruction, Billings recommended that class size be capped at twenty-five. Second, Billings advocated "the promotion of original research and discovery in Medicine, including the making known of these discoveries."[178] This aligned with Gilman's priorities for the university.

Billings' greatest contribution to the revolution in medical education, however, was not in the design of the facility but in his ideas about the purposes of the medical school and its relationship to the hospital.[179] When the university welcomed its first students in 1876, Billings was appointed lecturer in the history of medicine. Gilman had sent Billings a note outlining the lecture series program and inviting him to present: "I have put you down for ten, but should be glad to say twenty, if your own views change."[180] Billings responded that ten lectures would "not permit of anything like a complete survey of the history of medicine"[181] and requested that he present during the 1877–78 academic year. He did so, delivering a series of twenty lectures on medical history, legislation, and education.[182] Held in the old Hopkins Hall on Howard Street, they were well received and well attended, and excerpts were published by the university.[183] There were, on average, some fifty attendees at each session.[184]

Adding to his myriad responsibilities, Billings advised Gilman about whom to hire as the first medical faculty. Just as he had done with the original six Hopkins faculty, Gilman set about to hire the best professionals of the time. The first was William H. Welch, possibly the world's leading pathologist. William Osler would say of his fellow physician, "In addition to a three-story intellect, Welch has an attic on top."[185] A member of a distinguished New England family of physicians and community leaders, Welch completed his medical training at Columbia before spending time in laboratories in Germany and then opening his own at Bellevue Medical College (now New York University Medical School). Welch's first meeting with Billings was in 1876 in Germany; Billings formally interviewed Welch in New York in 1884 for a position at Hopkins. Writing to Gilman, Billings reported, "I saw Dr. Welch and had a long talk with him—heard him lecture—and saw him directing work in his laboratory. . . . He is a good lecturer—and excellent laboratory teacher, and has a keen desire for an opportunity to make original investigations being activated, I think, by the true scientific spirit. . . . Upon the whole I think he is the best man in this country for the Hopkins."[186]

Gilman then met with Welch in Baltimore, showed him the university, and introduced him to several trustees—and after lunch he offered him a professorship in pathology. Just as his predecessors had done before him, Welch was to spend the next year in Europe, "where he will make such purchases and pursue such inquiries as will enable him to be the most useful when he returns to Baltimore."[187] Thus began the Welch era at the Hopkins School of Medicine. Welch wasted no time in getting to work. Months after his arrival, the trustees approved space within the hospital (not yet opened) for Welch to perform autopsies.[188]

Hyperbole from a subject-matter expert may be excused in this description of Welch by Abraham Flexner: "From his appointment in 1884 to the day of his death in

*Four Doctors*, by John Singer Sargent, 1906, paid for by Mary Elizabeth Garrett. *Left to right:* William Henry Welch, William Stewart Halsted, William Osler, and Howard Atwood Kelly. (Photo courtesy of University Archives, Sheridan Libraries, Johns Hopkins University)

1934, Welch was the undisputed and unquestioned leader in the veritable revolution that took place in American medicine and public health. He had, as we shall see, able coadjutors—most of them of his own choosing; but he was the general in chief."[189] These able coadjutors included the first three colleagues Welch would personally recruit to Hopkins, all in 1889: William Osler (professor of medicine and chief physician to the hospital), William Halsted (professor of surgery), and Howard Kelly (professor of gynecology). Added to the original four in 1893 were Franklin Mall (professor of pathology),[190] William Henry Howell (professor of physiology), and John Jacob Abel (professor of pharmacology). This roster of young faculty demonstrates Welch's ability to attract to the Hopkins School of Medicine some of the most gifted young professionals ever amassed at one institution—all of whom believed that they could change the way medicine was taught and practiced. One writer maintained that Welch's legacy "lay in his ability to stir other men's souls."[191] Welch's service knew no bounds: in 1917 he joined the army, serving as staff assistant to the Surgeon General of the Army. In recognition of his contributions during World War I, Welch was promoted to brigadier general in the Medical Reserve Corps in 1921, at the age of 70.[192]

## Yet Another Responsibility for Gilman

With hospital construction nearing completion, a medical staff and a support staff needed to be hired and put into place. The trustees recognized that someone had to oversee the entire operation, and quickly. Billings had been offered the position of hospital director but respectfully declined. President King sent for Gilman (then in his thirteenth year as president) in December 1888 and told him, in confidence, that his health would prevent him from getting the hospital staffed and opened. Without consulting any of his fellow hospital trustees or even asking the university trustees (the majority of whom served on both boards), King asked Gilman to step in and serve as interim hospital director. Gilman recorded in his diary that he had to speak about it with Lilly first. "She encouraged me," he wrote on December 11. King then conferred with Judge Dobbin, Francis White, and Galloway Cheston, who, Gilman recorded, "were taken by surprise but concurred. The first two came to see me and hoped I would accept,—but I should *not* lodge there."[193] Half of Gilman's salary would be covered by the hospital and half by the university. Gilman agreed to the terms. He could now add another responsibility to his list of Hopkins duties: from January to August 1889 he served as interim director of the hospital.

In typical Gilman fashion, he dove headlong into the assignment. The day after his appointment was made official, Gilman traveled to New York with William Welch ("Long talk all the way about candidates and organization," reads his journal entry for January 26, 1889) to see firsthand how the city's best hotels and finest hospitals handled linens and towels, since he believed clean linens were essential for patient comfort. He also instituted Sunday visiting hours so that working people need not lose a day's wages during the week. No detail escaped his attention, and he read the current literature and solicited the perspectives of experts in America and Europe on best practices at the world's most reputable facilities.[194] Correspondence during this seven-month tenure fills an entire letterpress book and illustrates the attention Gilman devoted to finding the right personnel for each position.[195] Gilman was involved in every detail of hiring the first employees: the superintendent of buildings and grounds, the housekeeper, and the superintendent of nurses. With the various search committees launched at once, Gilman also employed the assistance of the hospital's doctors, writing to Osler that three candidates for head nurse were coming to interview "on Saturday morning, March 16, and I look for you at the same time to aid in the selection."[196]

Although he had declined the position of hospital director, Billings remained involved, and Gilman acknowledged his role: "I noted what you say with respect to a title, and I think we can agree upon something at once distinctive and honorable."[197] After consulting with the executive committee of the hospital trustees, Billings was given the title of medical adviser to the president. Gilman would lean on the distinguished doctor for input on personnel and other issues during the interim period.[198] Gilman, however, was clearly in charge, and he tackled the task of staffing the hospital with the same zeal with which he had recruited the original faculty members to Baltimore nearly fifteen years earlier.

For the hospital and its administration, there was no more important position than that of director, and Gilman immediately took up the search. The name of Henry Mills Hurd—widely recognized as one of the world's experts in psychiatry, who would later become editor of the monumental four-volume 1916 work *Institutional Care of the Insane in the United States and Canada*—emerged from various communications. Gilman contacted the president of Hurd's alma mater, James Angell of the University of Michigan, telling his old friend that "we cannot afford to make a mistake" and soliciting his opinion of Hurd.[199] A few days later, Angell responded with an unqualified endorsement of Hurd: "We have tried more than once to persuade him to take a medical chair here. He is refined, scholarly, gentlemanly, conciliatory in manner, capable of managing men pleasantly. He is a man of noble and elevated character."[200]

Gilman extended the offer to Hurd, and he accepted, assuming the superintendent's position nearly three months after the hospital's opening.[201] Upon his arrival at Hopkins, Hurd knew that he was stepping into a place unlike any other in America. He made this observation about Billings and his hospital design: "These plans influenced hospitals in a way unparalleled in the history of hospital construction, and gave a tremendous impetus to better hospitals by directing the attention of medical men, sanitarians, and others to the absolute necessity of certain great essentials, *viz.* more perfect ventilation and heating, and the prevention of contagion."[202]

Billings' formal association with the university came to an end when the hospital opened, but he stayed active in medical education, serving as professor of hygiene at the University of Pennsylvania while maintaining his connection to the Office of the Surgeon General in Washington until his official retirement in 1895. But before he left Baltimore, Billings offered remarks at the official opening of the Hopkins Hospital on a spectacular spring day in May 1889, before an enormous crowd. "It is the old lesson so often expounded, apparently so simple and yet so hard to learn," Billings said at the end of his remarks, "that true happiness lies in helping others; that it is more blessed to give than to receive." It was almost a farewell address from Colonel Billings, the former Union field surgeon who had seen so much human suffering firsthand and then devoted his life to helping address it. The hospital, for him, in many ways represented a physical embodiment of this unyielding commitment. Billings continued,

> In some respects we today have a much wider outlook than the men of a thousand years ago. This hospital is designed, as I have told you, to advance medical science as well as to give relief to the sick poor, but the fundamental motive is the same—to help others.
>
> We have here the beginning of an institution which shall endure long after the speakers and the audience of today shall have finished their life-work and have passed away. Founded in the interests of suffering humanity, intimately connected with a great university, amply provided with what is at present known to be essential to its work, we have every reason to predict for it a long and prosperous career, with steadily progressing improvement in organization and methods, and enlargement of its activity and influence.
>
> Let us hope that before the last sands have run out from beneath the feet of the years of the nineteenth century it will have become a model of its kind, and that upon the centennial of its anniversary it will be a hospital which shall still compare favorably, not only in structure and arrangement, but also in results achieved, with any other institution of like character in existence.[203]

## "Movers in the Scheme"

The school of medicine did not open according to the projected timeline, which would have had it open at the same time as the hospital. This was a source of great disappointment to all those affiliated with Johns Hopkins, and it also created a tremendous sense of urgency. In an 1892 report to the hospital board of trustees, Hurd was direct in his assessment and blunt in his recommendation. While upwards of sixty students had subscribed to the medical-related courses prescribed by Gilman and an equal number were expected the next year, this fell far short of the number required to field a class of qualified, prospective students for a medical school. Hurd concluded:

> Every year renders it more and more evident that this Hospital must continue to be hampered in its work until the medical school of the University is established. . . . It is evident also that the post graduate courses now given do not meet the expectations of the country and that the wonderful opportunity which is open to the University to initiate medical teaching of the highest character is being allowed to slip away. The Hospital has now waited three years for the University to complete arrangements for the medical school, but the enterprise is still unfinished. New departments and new buildings claim the energies and funds of the University, and little thought seems given to the Department which was definitely mentioned by the Founder of the University and Hospital and for whose organization so much money has already been expended by both these institutions. Under the circumstances it seems imperative that the Hospital should cooperate with the University in completing the Endowment required. There is a universal demand for better

medical education, and when the school opens its facilities will be immediately uti-
lized by the picked men of the country. From present appearances such a department will be a source of definite income to the University rather than an expense.[204]

Lack of effort or desire on the part of the trustees was not the source of the medical
school delay. President King's assertion "that the Medical School would be opened as
soon as sufficient revenue could be got from the investments that are now unremu-
nerative to enable the Trustees to start its work" made the front page of the *New York
Times* in May 1890. King's report further asserted that "the proposed standard of the
school would be equal to any in Germany, and the courses of study just as thorough.
The professors already secured stand at the head of the profession." King's comments
ended with a summary of the "movers in the scheme," who had determined to raise
two hundred thousand dollars on the condition that female students would be admitted to the school: "The ladies now have several good colleges devoted to liberal education. The Johns Hopkins will outrank them all, and the women propose if possible
to effect an entrance into our school so as to pursue a higher course of study."[205]

The "scheme" to which King referred had first been broached with Gilman on
January 1, 1889, by the trustee Dr. James Carey Thomas and the eldest of his ten children, M. Carey Thomas (then professor of English and dean at Bryn Mawr College).
As Gilman noted in his journal on January 1, 1889, during an "hours long" talk they
had asked whether the university would "accept a gift of $100,000 from several persons
on condition that women might be rec'd to med school *on same terms as men*." Gilman
was circumspect. "I said be careful how you quote me." The president "promised to
consider carefully any written proposal, and to return either a personal or official answer as might be required but at present I am non-committal."[206]

M. Carey Thomas was one of the original four Baltimoreans (all daughters of
university trustees) who formed the Women's Fund Committee, which was unyielding in its commitment to "the most advanced medical education for women."[207] In
addition to Thomas, the group included Mary Elizabeth Garrett (daughter of John
Work Garrett); Mary Gwinn (daughter of Charles J. M. Gwinn, Johns Hopkins' attorney); and Elizabeth King (daughter of Francis T. King, president of the hospital
trustees and member of the university board).[208] This committee represented four-
fifths of the famed Friday Evening, a self-named group of friends so designated for
their bimonthly dinner, social, and discussion gatherings. By this time, Julia Rebecca
Rogers had withdrawn from the group and did not have anything to do with the Hopkins School of Medicine.[209] Efforts to recruit others to their cause for equal access to
medical education for women culminated in an organizational meeting at Bessie King's
home on May 2, 1890. The Women's Fund Committee's goal was simple enough: to
raise sufficient funds to establish the Hopkins School of Medicine and then to offer the
gift on the condition that women be admitted to the school on the exact same basis
as men. A circular explaining their plans concluded: "There is every reason to think
that the gift with the proposed condition will be accepted if offered at the present time,

The Friday Evening Group. Mary Elizabeth Garrett (*center*); *clockwise from lower left:* M. Carey Thomas, Mamie Gwinn, Elizabeth (Bessie) King, and Julia Rogers. (Photo courtesy of Bryn Mawr College Libraries, Special Collections Department, College Archives)

but that, should the medical school open without women among its students, it would be difficult to secure their admission later."[210] In their efforts the committee resembled a modern-day political campaign, with a national organization, a media strategy, prominent women in charge of each local committee, and female physicians, leading cultural and literary figures, and the best-known feminists of the day listed among the supporters.[211] Nancy McCall, of the Chesney Medical Archives at Hopkins, adds that this remarkable effort also employed the strategies of "intermeshing with the male political structure, enlarging upon Quaker heritage, and aligning support of powerful, high-placed fathers."[212]

Since his initial meeting with the Thomases in early 1889, Gilman had been pre-occupied with serving as interim director of the hospital. Once a permanent director arrived, he departed for a nine-month sabbatical in Europe and the Middle East with his family. The Women's Fund was now prepared to offer one hundred thousand dollars to the trustees, provided that the university "shall agree, that, by resolution, when its Medical School shall be opened, women whose previous training has been equivalent to the preliminary medical course prescribed for men, shall be admitted to such school upon the same terms as prescribed for men." Of the money raised, Mary Garrett had contributed nearly half; seven hundred other donors had made up the balance.[213] On October 28, 1890, the university trustees approved a resolution accepting the gift, pledging to invest it, and referring to the fund as The Women's Medical School Fund. But they added a substantial new condition to the resolution: a general fund of five hundred thousand dollars. "Then, and not until then," the resolution stipulated, "will a Medical School be opened by this University; and then, and not until then, will the terms attached thereto be operative."[214]

That all of this had transpired in Gilman's absence from campus led the Women's Fund Committee chairwoman to ask for the president's reaction. Gilman responded in a letter of November 1, 1890, which was published in the Baltimore newspapers:

> Dear Madame,
>
> Since I came home from Europe many persons have asked me for an expression of opinion with respect to the undertaking in which the ladies of Baltimore and their friends in other parts of this country have been engaged, but as no communication had been received by our trustees, and as no official action had been taken by them I have not been willing to say anything which could be regarded as an official utterance. But now the proposition of the committee of ladies has been formally presented to the trustees and unanimously accepted by them I get leave to say to you, and through you to the committee of which you are the chairman, that I am sure that your efforts will result in great good. . . . Without doubt the university and the hospital here founded are to be a great power in the advancement of medical education, and it is but right that those women who wish to study and practice the healing arts should have, if properly prepared, the highest opportunities that can be offered. I hope it is not presuming too much if I add one more remark. It would be a noble act, a memorable event in the history of higher education, if the women of this country should complete the endowment which they have so successfully initiated.[215]

With this public statement, Gilman was doing two things. First, he was stating the university's position on admitting women into professional programs. Until that time, the admission policies for female students had been ad hoc, to say the least, based on an 1877 board resolution. At that time, the trustees had expressed "their willingness to confer with the managers of any institution which may be organized on a plan akin to that of Girton College, as to the extent to which the instructions of this institution can be made available." The resolution closed with the stipulation "that for the present, the Board declines to receive young ladies as students in the usual classes, and as attendants upon lectures not specially excepted."[216]

Over the next decade, certain trustees argued that the university should modify its position. President King, while serving as head of the hospital trustees, was also the chair of the board planning for the launch of Bryn Mawr College, labeled by some as the "Miss Johns Hopkins University." Judge George Brown, another trustee, wrote to Gilman after reading a report on coeducation: "We have not heard the last on that question and I am prepared for a serious fight on the subject. In almost every respect, there is no place so well adapted to try the experiment as the Johns Hopkins."[217] "But Brown," notes Hugh Hawkins, "was in advance of most of the trustees. There was not major reversal of policy."[218] Nonetheless, Garrett and her gift would force a significant change, at least for professional school admissions, in subsequent years. Brown believed the committee had done immeasurable good: "The movement has had a wide and powerful effect in calling attention to the importance of giving the best medical education to women."[219]

Second, Gilman was expressing in his letter to the committee his unqualified hope that Garrett and her associates would complete the endowment on their own. The university was in financial straits. Two years earlier, Gilman and the institution had weathered yet another hardship, and as he had stated in his 1889 annual report to the trustees, "The year that is now closed has been one of the most interesting in the history of the University. . . . A series of appropriate remedies have averted the threatened danger, and have given us renewed confidence in the future of the University."[220] Prospects for the B&O had once again collaterally impacted the university's operations, and Gilman was forced to leave important positions unfilled, increase tuition, cut scholarship stipends, and reduce library and laboratory funding. Further alarm ensued when Judge Dobbin, the university's last connection to the B&O, was dropped from the railroad board in November 1888.[221]

The president persuaded the trustees to launch an emergency campaign in hopes that other drastic measures could be avoided. William Wallace Spence, a friend of Johns Hopkins and a prominent Baltimore financier, agreed to lead the effort.[222] The response was overwhelming and led to an oversubscription, announced in May 1889. On the occasion of the university's twentieth-anniversary celebration in 1896, a publication was released highlighting the institution's first two decades. Among the notable fundraising efforts reported was the emergency fund that amassed $105,367—mostly from Baltimore residents, including several board members and Gilman himself, who donated $5,000—thus helping the university stave off further cuts and salary reductions.[223] In the commemorative report, immediately preceding the list of donors to the emergency fund, is an entry headed "The Mary Elizabeth Garrett Fund": "In

December, 1892, Miss Mary E. Garrett presented to the Trustees the sum of $306,977, the amount needed to complete the proposed endowment of $500,000 for the Medical School." Gilman had persuaded the Women's Fund Committee to accept his charge to come up with the balance of the required five hundred thousand dollars, and Mary Garrett had personally made up the difference.[224]

Garrett transmitted the funds to the university in a letter dated December 22, 1892. In addition, she outlined her conditions and established a "committee for life" made up of the following: Mrs. Henry Hurd, Mrs. Ira Remsen, Mrs. William Osler, Miss M. Carey Thomas, Miss Mary M. Gwinn, and Miss Mary Garrett. Other of Garrett's conditions included the opening of the medical school in the autumn of 1893, "devoted to the education of both men and women," their admission based on the same criteria of rigorous preliminary medical preparation. These criteria were much more demanding than anything else that existed in America at the time. Among the prerequisites proposed for the mandatory four-year doctor of medicine degree included a bachelor's degree from Hopkins or from an approved college or Scientific school or passage of an entrance examination that demonstrated a satisfactory knowledge of "French, German, physics, chemistry and biology."[225]

Both Welch and Osler would note years later that some of their concerns had been unfounded. "As it turned out, the embarrassments and difficulties which we feared in the novel venture of co-education in medicine never materialized," wrote Welch. He continued that they were, however, "alarmed, and wondered if any students would come or could meet the conditions for we knew that we could not."[226] Osler famously wrote his medical colleague, "Welch, it is lucky that we get in as professors; we never could enter as students."[227]

Garrett further stipulated that the funds would revert to her, or others she appointed, should the conditions outlined not be met. At the end of the document was a schedule of payments beginning in 1894 and ending in 1899, at 5 percent interest. Two days later, the trustees accepted the gift and agreed to the conditions with this conclusion: "The School, when opened, will, we believe, because of its connection with the Johns Hopkins Hospital, and because of the gifts which it has already received, and especially this last munificent gift, afford to the women and men of this country, whose requirements and training may enable them to enter upon its course of instruction, unsurpassed opportunities for the scientific study of medicine."[228]

At the April 3, 1893, meeting of the university's board of trustees, a memorandum of understanding between the university and the hospital outlining details of organization and operation of the new medical school was proposed and referred to the executive committees of the boards of the two entities.[229] The president and the then professors (Welch, Remsen, Martin, Hurd, Osler, Halsted, and Kelley) constituted the advisory board of the school and were required to report to the trustees from "time to time." Everything was now in place, and instruction was ready to begin. Eighteen students entered the Johns Hopkins University School of Medicine when it opened in October 1893. Five of the eighteen had completed degrees in arts at Hopkins. Three

The Johns Hopkins School of Medicine graduating class of 1897. The inaugural group included three women, one of whom—Mary Packard—graduated but was omitted from the class photograph. William Welch, the school's first medical professor and dean, is seated in the middle. (The Alan Mason Chesney Medical Archives of The Johns Hopkins Medical Institutions)

members of the inaugural class were women: Cornelia Church (Smith College), Mabel Glover (Wellesley College), and Mary Packard (Vassar College). Packard would be the only woman among the seventeen graduates in 1897, although she was excluded from the class graduation photograph.[230]

Thus began an entirely new epoch of medical education in the United States. In his assessment of medical education in North America, Abraham Flexner offered this perspective sixteen years after the doors to the Hopkins School of Medicine opened: "This was the first medical school in America of genuine university type, with something approaching adequate endowment, well equipped laboratories conducted by modern teachers, devoting themselves unreservedly to medical investigation and instruction, and with its own hospital, in which the training of physicians and the healing of the sick harmoniously combine to the infinite advantage of both. The influence of this new foundation can hardly be overstated. It has finally cleared up the problem of standards and ideals; and its graduates have gone forth in small bands to found new establishments or to reconstruct old ones."[231]

Mary S. Packard, an alumna of Vassar College, was the first female to graduate from the Hopkins Medical School, in 1897. (Photo courtesy of Archives and Special Collections, Vassar College Library, Photo File 11.34)

## The Hopkins Experiment

As recorded in his will, Johns Hopkins most desired that his estate be used for the creation of a hospital, a university, and an orphanage. Now, a century and a half after his death, a world-class hospital and university bear his name and carry on his legacy. His third wish—the orphanage—did not die with him, but it did not come into existence as he had envisioned. Many conjectures might be offered as to why this did not materialize—financial pressures, turnover among the membership on both the university and hospital boards, the desire to see the hospital constructed and the medical school established overriding other considerations. According to the terms of Hopkins' will, nothing could be done until the founder's death. Johns Hopkins would never see what came of his bequest, but he left it to others, all carefully chosen for their assignments, to carry out his wishes.

Gilman often referred to Hopkins in speeches and reports as that "large-minded citizen of Maryland, who by noble gifts for the advancement of learning and the relief of suffering, has won the gratitude of his city and his country."[232] With the opening of the university, the hospital, and the medical school, Hopkins' Baltimore experiment was fully operational except for the orphanage. Some contend that "no single event contributed more to the reformation of American medical education than the opening in 1893 of the Johns Hopkins School of Medicine under the leadership of Welch."[233]

Elements of this new model—commonplace on campuses throughout the world today—were instituted by the president and the board of trustees: awarding graduate fellowships, emphasizing investigations and discovery, building the best laboratories, establishing scholarly journals and a university press, and joining a teaching hospital with a school of medicine. Roger Geiger would note that "if any single development had shifted values in American higher education, it was the remarkable success of Johns Hopkins. . . . Gilman's radical experiment represented the leading edge of graduate education and the academic revolution."[234] Trials and uncertainties lay ahead, to be sure, for those who would take these Hopkins-named institutions into the future. But what the first president and his cohort of faculty, staff, and students had done was birth the modern American research university.

# CHAPTER SEVEN

# The Slater Fund and Attempts to Integrate Hopkins

In addition to being the president of two of America's newest universities, Gilman was repeatedly called upon to serve as a board member and an adviser. He rarely said no. Gilman made reference to some of these activities at the 1897 inauguration of William Lyne Wilson, president of Washington and Lee University in Lexington, Virginia. Quoting Plato—"Let those who have lamps pass them on to others"—Gilman averred, "For more than twenty years, Mr. President, I have carried in my hand a lamp thus lighted in Baltimore."[1] Apart from his significant achievements within the academy, Gilman's volunteer service is truly remarkable as well.

Maryland is a southern state, and in multiple roles as a trustee and adviser Gilman gained extensive knowledge of southern colleges and universities. One in particular, the College of William and Mary in Williamsburg, Virginia, attracted his attention. The second-oldest college in America, William and Mary predated Gilman's own university by 183 years and was the site of the founding of Phi Beta Kappa in 1776. The college had closed its doors at the outset of the Civil War, reopened briefly—thanks to personal funds put forward by its sixteenth president, Benjamin Stoddert Ewell—but had been forced to shutter again in 1882. Despite two interruptions when the college was closed, Ewell's tenure as president would span the years 1854 to 1888.

Ewell, an 1832 graduate of West Point, second lieutenant in the US Army, and later a colonel in the Confederate army, was the older brother of General Richard Ewell, a senior commander under Stonewall Jackson and Robert E. Lee. President Ewell served as adjutant to his younger brother and returned to Williamsburg after the war to find the college in ruins. Ewell mortgaged the family farm in order to reopen the college in 1869, only to have his own property foreclosed upon and the college closed a second time. In the midst of his efforts to reopen William and Mary, President Ewell received a visit from the Gilman family in May 1887. Daniel, his wife Lilly, and their daughter Alice spent several days walking about the campus with Ewell, stunned at how decrepit it had become. Lilly thought the college "a most pathetic place, full of the past with no present but one of dreary decay."[2] Notwithstanding, in keeping with the theme of the lamp and spark that he would reference ten years later at Washington and Lee, Gilman wrote to Ewell upon their return to Baltimore:

> Our visit to William and Mary has been the daily theme of conversation ever since our return. For years I have looked forward to such an opportunity as we enjoyed, under your guidance, to see the old town, the historic College, the portraits, the books, the monuments and the other relics, which indicate what lofty purposes and high hopes were brought to Virginia by the early settlers. The familiar history has been made real by our visit. I esteem it a very great privilege that we could see what we saw under your guidance. You seem to me the embodiment of the *genius loci*— the watchful and faithful guardian of a grand idea. As long as you live we may be sure that the spark of fire will not disappear from the sacred altar. I share your hope and faith that some liberal hand will bring fresh offerings to the shrine, and that the flames will again burn brightly for the enlightenment of the youth of Virginia. My love of historical continuity is so strong that I hope we may see a new and stronger college rise on the old foundations. May you live to see the new era. Yours sincerely, D. C. Gilman[3]

A few months later, the college's fortunes did a final about-face when the Virginia General Assembly approved an annual subsidy of $10,000 and the doors to William and Mary opened to students in October 1888. On the occasion of the college's two-hundredth anniversary, Congress approved a $64,000 bequest to rebuild the Wren Building, which Union troops had burned in 1862. The Hopkins professor and founder of the famed Seminary of Historical and Political Science, Herbert Baxter Adams, had written a pamphlet in support of the college in 1887, and in addition to Gilman's advocacy of the college, several other faculty at Hopkins played significant roles in its revival. In 1905, just three years before his death, Gilman was awarded an honorary doctorate by William and Mary, the last such honor he received.

Throughout Gilman's presidency at Hopkins, people would write to his office requesting information and documents—university circulars detailing course offerings, copies of lectures by visiting faculty, reference books on medical education, chartering documentation for the university itself. On one occasion, Joseph Rowell, librarian of the University of California, relayed to Gilman that the alumni association of the university wanted a larger representation on the state's board of regents and inquired about "the method of appointment or election of the governing body of the institution over which you preside."[4] One can only speculate as to what was going through Gilman's mind when he read this request, given how different his experience with the board of trustees at Hopkins was from his experience with the board of regents at the University of California.

In addition to the individual mentoring Gilman did throughout his career, he was approached by institutions and their governing boards for his expertise and advice. His mark can be discerned even on universities rarely associated with him. In Cleveland, for instance, a Yale alumnus named Leonard Case Jr. donated $1 million in 1877 for the creation of the Case School of Applied Science. Case had studied the Hopkins model, emulating the board appointments and governing structure on what was being done in Baltimore. But the institution he envisioned was unique in a significant respect: in the heart of a major city would be founded a technically oriented private institution whose curriculum focused on enhancing economic development.[5] Two of Case's trustees, R. P. Ranney and the Reverend Thomas B. Wells, began a correspondence with Gilman in June 1880. Wells wrote in his first letter to Gilman, "I hope that your well known zeal in the cause of higher education may lead you to give me a moment of your time."[6] Wells' request was not unusual, nor was the president's response as he provided the Case trustees with direction on how best to establish their new venture in Ohio.

The Case Institute would merge with Western Reserve University in 1967 and gain entry into the Association of American Universities in 1969, becoming the top-ranked academic institution in Ohio. Nearly a century earlier, in his letter of instruction to board members, Case himself had included Huxley's address at Hopkins from September 1876.[7] Of particular note were comments Huxley made at the American Association for the Advancement of Science in Buffalo shortly after his arrival in the United States, in which he related his observation that wealthy men in America contributed to scientific institutions "in a way to which we are totally unaccustomed in England." Huxley noted that when an Englishman became rich, he would buy an estate and found a family. Not so in the United States: "The general notion of an American who becomes rich is to do something for the benefit of all people, and to found an institution whose benefits shall flow to all."[8]

In addition to volunteering in various capacities at both the national and international levels, Gilman also focused on local issues, answering the call of the Baltimore mayor William T. Malster to serve on a bipartisan commission charged with drafting a new city charter. Seeking to overcome the disjointedness of ward-based government (Baltimore comprises more than three hundred neighborhoods), the commission submitted a draft to the Maryland General Assembly that was subsequently approved in 1898.[9] But before his service on this commission, Gilman helped address other endemic challenges. The longtime *Baltimore Sun* writer Antero Pietila notes that biographers have dutifully recorded Gilman's multiple successes as president of Johns Hopkins, "yet they overlook his civic engagement in Baltimore. It was astonishing."[10] When the journalist H. L. Mencken was a young reporter for the *Baltimore Morning*

*Herald*, he was assigned to cover the Baltimore School Board. Mencken later recalled the first board meeting he witnessed at which Gilman was in attendance:

> My contacts with Mr. Gilman were those of a young newspaper reporter and an older and very distinguished man. Thus I can't say that I knew him well, but I certainly had many chances to see him in action. The general belief was that he was too busy to give the public schools any serious attention and that his appointment was hardly more than an effort to augment the dignity of the administration. But Gilman fooled everyone. At the very first meeting he attended he "horned" into the minutest details of the Board's work and within a couple of weeks he was the real boss of the whole school system. I remember very well sitting at a School Board meeting at which he devoted himself for an hour to drawing up blank forms for various interdepartmental reports and to instructing the superintendents in the details of a filing system that he had apparently invented. He was the sort of man who simply couldn't leave things to chance. Everything that came under his purview had to be arranged precisely and he never forgot a single detail.[11]

Interested in public improvement and committed to a host of social causes, Gilman founded the Baltimore branch of a growing international movement called the Charity Organization Society in 1881 and became its first president. When invited to address the New York chapter of the society, Gilman concluded with his own personal philosophy, which undergirded everything he did: "Science and faith, allies and not foes, will reach their highest achievement when they can point to the disappearance of urban poverty and to the prevalence throughout our cities of health, comfort, virtue, cleanliness, knowledge, temperance and godliness."[12]

Gilman even relied on his training as a geographer when he was recruited by President Grover Cleveland in 1896 to serve on a commission to study the border dispute between Great Britain and Venezuela over the latter's boundary with British Guiana. At the first meeting of the group, Gilman was given the task of seeking and making maps, in effect deciding exactly which records the commission would utilize for its deliberations.[13] A treaty between the parties was concluded in early 1897, referring the issue to arbitration, and the commission was disbanded.[14] Additional board participation included serving as a trustee for the Peabody Fund and the Russell Sage Foundation. Gilman succeeded Carl Schurz as president of the National Civil Service Reform League, serving from 1901 to 1907. Other roles—again, all voluntary—included serving as president of the American Oriental Society, president of the American Social Science Association, vice president of the Archaeological Institute of America, member of the US Naval Academy's board of visitors, and executive officer of the Maryland Geological Survey.

### The Education of the Freedmen

Gilman's work in government, education, philanthropy, and even foreign affairs was as broad as it was notable. However, outside of Hopkins there was no entity that re-

*John Fox Slater*, by Herbert von Herkomer, oil on canvas, 1883. The industrialist John Fox Slater founded the Slater Fund for the Education of Freedmen. Gilman would serve as a fund trustee for twenty-six years, including twelve as president. (Photo courtesy of John Fox Slater Memorial Museum)

quired more attention or to which he gave more time than the John Fox Slater Fund. Gilman would assume leadership positions as a trustee of the Slater Fund until his passing in 1908, first as secretary from 1882 to 1891 and then as president following the death of President Rutherford B. Hayes in 1893. Gilman remained in the latter role until his own death fifteen years later.[15] It is somewhat puzzling, therefore, that neither of Gilman's previous biographies address his work with the Slater Fund, nor did Gilman write in any detail about his experience as a longtime board member in either of his books on university governance and higher education policy. There is, however, a substantial record of correspondence between Gilman and others about the work of the fund, especially with John F. Slater himself and subsequently with Slater's only son, William. William maintained a close relationship with Gilman for many years following John's death in 1884. Gilman's association with the Slater Fund also reveals a national issue that is still the subject of contentious debate: the role of white philanthropy in the education of African Americans in the post-Reconstruction South.

During his days at Yale, Gilman first met Justin Morrill when he hosted the Vermont senator at the Sheffield Scientific School. In subsequent years the two men exchanged letters about Morrill's efforts to secure added "endowments," as he called them, for the original legislation of 1862. Morrill hoped to get supplementary federal funds to benefit more citizens, particularly African Americans. Morrill wrote to Gilman in January 1876: "I have since made two speeches when trying for an additional endowment, and hope to make one more—having introduced another bill. I think the South needs our aid."[16] The southern states certainly did need assistance; nonetheless, that help didn't arrive quickly. The second Morrill Act, known as the Agricultural Act of 1890—helping to establish HBCUs throughout the South—passed fourteen years *after* Morrill wrote Gilman.

Much has been written about efforts during Reconstruction to provide educational opportunities for freed enslaved people, but most especially about the Freedmen's Bureau and why it ultimately failed. President Abraham Lincoln's successor, Andrew Johnson, of Tennessee, vetoed the extension of the Freedmen's Bureau in 1866; however, the House and the Senate mustered the votes to override Johnson's veto, thus extending and expanding the bureau for two more years.

But the deficiencies of the Freedmen's Bureau went well beyond a lack of government resources. Eric Foner, arguably the nation's leading expert on Reconstruction, asserted that the greatest failing of the bureau was "that it never quite comprehended the depths of racial antagonism and class conflict in the postwar South."[17] Likewise, William McFeely contended that the federal efforts failed newly emancipated Black people by "substituting paternal supervision for man to man respect."[18] The bureau would die "its second and final death" when its legal mandate expired in mid-1868, even though its agents still clung "to the vision of a just and equal society."[19] It seemed as if everything conspired to make the bureau an irritant to the wounds it sought to heal, and its failure did nothing but highlight the inability of the North to effect reconciliation.[20] Despite its failures, W. E. B. Du Bois would write of the Freedman's Bureau that it represented "one of the most singular and interesting of the attempts made by a great nation to grapple with vast problems of race and social condition"[21] and was "the most extraordinary and far reaching institution of social uplift that American has ever attempted."[22]

Private funds, foundations, and endowments tried to fill the vacuum created by the failure of government intervention. Modern American charitable foundations trace their roots to the years immediately following the Civil War, during which enormous fortunes were amassed and trusts established with education as a primary focus. Private philanthropists attempted to achieve what the government could not. Two foundations in particular—the Peabody Education Fund, founded in 1867, and the John Fox Slater Fund, established in 1882—are considered the precursors to later and larger efforts, such as those endowed by the industrialists Andrew Carnegie and John D. Rockefeller.[23] As the first of its kind, the Peabody Education Fund served as the model and inspiration for modern foundations.[24]

Three older Black universities—Fisk, Hampton, and the University of Atlanta (now Clark Atlanta University)—received private support from the Peabody Education Fund in the form of tuition grants for several years before the original HBCUs were founded.[25] Efforts by the government to establish the HBCUs were not without their critics, however. As noted by Du Bois, a graduate of Fisk and Harvard, the "Negro colleges, hurriedly founded, were inadequately equipped, illogically distributed, and of a varying efficiency and grade."[26] In response to Du Bois' seminal work, *The Souls of Black Folk*, the *New York Times* wrote that a "review of [the work of the Freedmen's Bureau] from the negro point of view, even the Northern negro's point of view, must have its value to any unprejudiced student—still more, perhaps, for the prejudiced who is yet willing to be a student."[27]

## The John Fox Slater Fund

Gilman would be recruited by a prominent citizen of his hometown in Connecticut, John Fox Slater, to the board charged with overseeing a new educational fund. The Slater Fund, established in 1882, was unlike any other in American history. Born into a family of Rhode Island manufacturers, young John F. Slater showed rare business aptitude and was made chief of one of his father's mills at the age of 17. He was described by his pastor, the Reverend S. H. Howe, as possessing "profound insight and exhaustive knowledge of affairs and men, with mental grasp and business training, some have believed, sufficient to have wisely controlled the financial interests of a nation." In a short period of time, Slater accumulated significant wealth and began setting his sights on how to distribute it for the greatest good. Reverend Howe maintained that the Civil War provided just the vehicle for Slater: "The issues of the great civil war which unloosed the fetters of the slave, but which did not qualify him for responsible duties of citizenship, gave Mr. Slater his great opportunity."[28] What distinguished the Slater Fund from the Peabody and other education foundations that would follow was Slater's stipulation that funds be used exclusively for African Americans.[29]

Slater decided to focus his efforts on Black education for several reasons, including his friendship with Moses Pierce.[30] A native of Rhode Island and Slater's neighbor in Norwich, Pierce would spend evenings with Slater discussing a whole host of issues, including Pierce's service as a trustee of the Hampton Institute in Virginia and his various philanthropic interests. An original incorporator and trustee of the Norwich Free Academy, Pierce contributed four thousand dollars in 1882 to construct a two-story brick workshop at Hampton.[31] When Pierce died in 1900, his will designated an endowment—the Edwin Milman Pierce Fund—"specifically for training industrial arts teachers for the common schools serving the African American population in the South."[32] The two men shared an interest in the education of Black citizens and were willing to spend large sums of their own money to achieve this end.

### Leonard Bacon and Atticus Haygood

Another influence on Slater was his pastor in Norwich, Leonard Woolsey Bacon. As described by Louis D. Rubin Jr., a cofounder of the *Southern Literary Journal,* "Bacon was controversial, polemical, something of a gadfly to Congregationalists and a scandal to the more evangelical sects."[33] Bacon would later become pastor of the Independent Presbyterian Church in Savannah. The *New York Times* reported that during Bacon's tenure in Georgia a prominent citizen, Thomas H. Harden, leveled these charges against the minister: "It is stated on reliable authority that you [Dr. Bacon] have said to some of the citizens of Savannah, first, that you favor mixed schools, black and white, in Savannah; second, that you would not object to your daughter walking in the street leaning on the arm of a negro man; third, that you would not object to the marriage of your daughter to a negro man if she were willing to marry him. Will you please answer through the public press and say whether any or all these reports represent you correctly or are slanders?" According to the *Times,* "The queries have created a great sensation. Dr. Bacon is advising with his friends as to what course to pursue."[34]

While serving in Norwich, Bacon delivered a sermon one Sunday about the "opportunity of advancing human welfare by the proper use of wealth." When the service ended, John Slater, who had been in the congregation that day, told Bacon that he had decided to contribute a million dollars for Black education.[35] Originally, there was talk of Bacon himself serving on the Slater Fund board, but the idea was ultimately abandoned given the potentially controversial nature of the fund. Considering that some in the South might view the activities of the fund as combustible, Bacon's presence on the board could prove to be a liability, "so having played a primary role in bringing the Slater Fund into being, Bacon bowed out of the picture once the work had begun."[36] Nonetheless, Bacon did help the board select the fund's general agent, who would be charged with visiting Black schools throughout the South and recommending the best allocation of resources. Bacon heartily endorsed Atticus G. Haygood (whom Slater referred to as a "capital gentleman") in a letter to President Rutherford B. Hayes, the chair of the Slater board, just weeks before the fund was incorporated.[37] Haygood had been elected president of Emory College in December 1875 and was charged by the board of trustees with "raising money with which to endow the college."[38]

John Slater asked Gilman for his perspective on how the board should be constituted as early as 1880. Gilman wrote that "the body should be large enough to admit of some diversity in the qualification of the members, small enough to secure efficiency," or more specifically, it should number between five and fifteen, with the optimal number being nine. (Slater settled on ten.) Further, Gilman advised that part of the board should be made up of men "capable of managing a large financial responsibility and a part should be capable of judging of the standing of education institutions and the value of different methods of instruction." Gilman's belief that the board should be populated with men of "broad Christian views, wise, patriotic and humane" aligned with Slater's vision. With a view toward the future, Gilman concluded that board members "should have power to fill vacancies in their own number. It would seem to me desirable that they should live in different parts of the country and belong to different religious denominations, so that trust may not be administered in any narrow, sectarian, or provincial way."[39] Gilman ended his memorandum with this final suggestion, some of which was incorporated in the letter of direction to the first board of trustees: "The object which I have in view is primarily to provide for the instruction of the colored population of this country, and especially to fit them to be good citizens and for this end I desire and direct that the income, after paying the necessary expenditures for its management, shall be given to states for the education of teachers, white or colored, who intend to devote themselves to the instruction of the blacks."[40] With Atticus Haygood as the agent of choice, invitations to join the board were conveyed and incorporation documents were prepared.

For a southerner of his time, Haygood had written a most uncommon book—*Our Brother in Black*—especially given his role as a Methodist clergyman, erstwhile Confederate chaplain, and president of Emory. His progressive views caught the attention of George I. Seney, a New York banker who, when introduced to Haygood's statements, helped address Emory's impecunious state more than anyone else in its history. One of Haygood's speeches, "A Thanksgiving Sermon," delivered to the students of Emory College and the citizens of Oxford, Georgia, on November 25, 1880, was especially impactful. Addressing the gathering, Haygood began, "I come now to mention some reasons why we of 'the South' should both 'thank God and take courage.' "[41] Haygood noted among the blessings "the restoration of our relations to the general Government. . . . Possibly some do not go with me here. Then I must go without them, but I shall not lack for company; and as the years pass, it will be an ever-increasing throng." Slavery no longer existing, Haygood exclaimed: "For this fact, I devoutly thank God this day!"[42] Haygood posited that the freedmen's future was inextricably linked to education:

> How soon they shall realize the possibilities of their new relations depends largely, perhaps most on themselves. Much depends on those who, under God, set them free. By every token this whole nation should undertake the problem of their education. That problem will have to be worked out on the basis of co-operation; that is, they must be helped to help themselves. . . . Much also depends upon the South-

ern white people, their sympathy, their justice, their wise and helpful co-operation. This we should give them, not reluctantly, but gladly, for their good and for the safety of all, for their elevation and for the glory of God.[43]

President Haygood concluded with this final charge:

> We are to do the work of today, looking forward and not backward. We have no divine call to stand eternal guard by the grave of dead issues. Here certainly we may say, "Let the dead bury their dead."
>
> My friends, my neighbors, and my pupils, I declare to you today my hope is, that in twenty years from now, the words "the South" shall have only a geographical significance. . . . There is nothing weaker or more foolish than repining over an irrevocable past, except it be despairing of a future to which God invites us. Good friends, this is not 1860, it is 1880. Let us press forward, following the pillar of cloud and of fire always.[44]

A copy of the sermon found its way to New York and into the hands of George Seney, a devout Methodist and graduate of Wesleyan University. So moved was Seney that he requested a meeting with Haygood in his New York office. After their first encounter, the East Coast banker made his first gift to Emory, sight unseen. By the end of 1881 Seney's total giving to the fledgling Atlanta college amounted to $130,000: $5,000 to repay its debts, $50,000 for construction, and $75,000 to establish a new endowment.[45] Haygood's work at Emory and with the Slater Fund was both evangelical and educational. "For myself," Haygood attested, "I have reached a conclusion about this educational work among the Negroes of the South: *it is God's work.* . . . It is high time that those who are trying to do good should have knowledge of each other."[46]

Haygood retained his position at Emory but also became the Slater Fund's agent in November 1882, doing both jobs until 1884. The first faculty member in the history of Emory to be elected to the American Academy of Arts and Sciences, Haygood devoted all his time to the Slater Fund for the next seven years.[47] Of the partnership between Haygood and Rutherford B. Hayes, Louis D. Rubin Jr. wrote, "Thus began a working relationship between a Methodist minister from Georgia and a former United States President from Ohio, which in the decade that followed would provide a chapter of no little color and interest in the history of Negro education."[48]

Not to be outdone by the Peabody Education Fund, whose board members were of the highest stature, reputation, and accomplishments, Slater assembled his own A-list of luminaries representing politics, the judiciary, industry, finance, the clergy, and education. In addition to the founder's son, William A. Slater, the original nine trustees included Rutherford B. Hayes (nineteenth president of the United States), Morrison R. Waite (chief justice of the United States), William E. Dodge (cofounder of the Phelps-Dodge Corporation), Phillips Brooks (rector of Boston's Trinity Church and lyricist of "O Little Town of Bethlehem"), Daniel C. Gilman (president of Johns

Hopkins University since 1875), John A. Stewart (banker and acting president of Princeton University), Alfred H. Colquitt (governor of Georgia), Morris K. Jesup (banker, philanthropist, and president of the American Museum of Natural History), and James P. Boyce (pastor, founder, and first president of the Southern Baptist Theological Seminary). The incorporation documents from 1882 include biographical sketches of the members.[49] In his instructions to the trustees, John Slater made his intentions very clear:

> GENTLEMEN: It has pleased God to grant me prosperity in my business, and to put it into my power to apply to charitable uses a sum of money so considerable as to require the counsel of wise men for the administration of it. It is my desire at this time to appropriate to such uses the sum of one million of dollars ($1,000,000); and I hereby invite you to procure a charter of incorporation under which a charitable fund may be held exempt from taxation, and under which you shall organize; and I intend that the corporation, as soon as formed, shall receive this sum in trust to apply the income of it according to the instructions contained in this letter. The general object which I desire to have exclusively pursued, is the uplifting of the lately emancipated population of the Southern States, and their posterity, by conferring on them the blessings of Christian education. The disabilities formerly suffered by these people, and their singular patience and fidelity in the great crisis of the nation, establish a just claim on the sympathy and good will of humane and patriotic men. I cannot but feel the compassion that is due in view of their prevailing ignorance, which exists by no fault of their own. But it is not only for their own sake, but also for the safety of our common country, in which they have been invested with equal political rights, that I am desirous to aid in providing them with the means of such education as shall tend to make them good men and good citizens— education in which the instruction of the mind in the common branches of secular learning shall be associated with training in just notions of duty.[50]

Slater stated that he had been "encouraged to the execution in this charitable foundation of a long-cherished purpose, by the eminent wisdom and success that has marked the conduct of the Peabody Education Fund in a field of operation not remote from that contemplated by this trust."[51] Slater's gift would propel him into the forefront of philanthropists a full decade before titans like Carnegie, Rockefeller, and Vanderbilt began establishing foundations of their own. For his efforts on behalf of African American education, Slater was presented the Medal of Honor in 1883.[52]

The trustees themselves would look to the paragon of private giving during this time period in American education, George Peabody, in their response to Slater's charge: "If this trust is successfully managed, it may, like the gift of George Peabody, lead to many other benefactions. As it tends to remove the ignorance of large numbers of those who have a vote in public affairs, it will promote the welfare of every part of the country, and your generous action will receive, as it deserves, the thanks of good men and women in this and other lands."[53] Like Mr. Johns Hopkins years earlier, the peripatetic Peabody and his largesse cast a long shadow on all those who endeavored to follow his lead and endow funds for the education of the freedmen.

## The Slater Fund and Black Industrial Education

The Slater Fund played a significant role in the expansion of industrial education in Black normal schools and colleges by offering financial aid exclusively for the development of Black industrial education. In a speech to the Norwich Academy in 1886, Gilman noted, "I wish there were time to give you an account of the good which that fund is doing; of the encouragement it affords to a noble and self-sacrificing band of teachers in all the Southern States; and especially of the influence it has had in the promotion of a respect for labor, because the trustees have insisted that manual training or handicraft shall be promoted simultaneously with mental and moral education."[54] A decade later, Gilman recalled the weight of responsibility that he and his fellow trustees had felt as they attempted to provide educational opportunities across a broad spectrum for millions of Black citizens: "It is no wonder that the statesmen, the philanthropists and the scientific men of the world are looking with profound interest upon the solution of a problem which is unprecedented in the history of mankind."[55] While the goal of improved education for Black Americans was broadly shared by these northern advocates, the means to that end would be the subject of debate for years to come.

Agent Haygood supported what was known as the Hampton model, developed by Samuel Chapman Armstrong and Booker T. Washington at the Hampton Institute in Virginia. Haygood noted that the Hampton faculty viewed industrial training as the best intellectual and moral discipline for "those who are to be teachers and guides of their people."[56] Haygood maintained the importance of industrial education for Black people so that they could build better homes: "The right thing is not to despise the cabin, but to get ready to build and furnish the cottage. If the cottage is not only to be built, but to be furnished and made a home of, then both men and women must have industrial training as well as book-learning. Book-learning alone will make the people whose good we seek today unhappy in the cabin; it will not of itself give them the ability to get into cottages, or to make homes of them when they get them. . . . God's law of labor is a great and saving mercy to the race."[57]

The bitter debate over the purposes of Black education persisted well into the twentieth century. Many northern industrial philanthropists (Slater, Peabody, William H. Baldwin Jr., John D. Rockefeller, George Eastman, Andrew Carnegie, and others), together with some Black educators and most white southern school officials, aligned with the Hampton model and its emphasis on the industrial education of emancipated enslaved people, only to find that their support of this view ran headlong into the aspirations of many former enslaved people and their progeny. Under the Hampton model, some argued, their children were pushed into a system of industrial education that presupposed Black political and economic subordination. James Anderson, dean of the University of Illinois College of Education, asserts that the actions of these foundations "made it abundantly clear that white industrialists and landowners were to be the main beneficiaries of black industrial training."[58] The historian John Hope Franklin was even more pointed: "The advocates of Jim Crow in education found vigorous and enthusiastic support in the Peabody Fund."[59] After the soldiers, agents, and missionaries had left, the Peabody Fund "remained an influence upon Southern education for nearly fifty years."[60] In addition to his service on the Slater Fund board, Gilman would be a Peabody Fund trustee from 1891 until his death.

That there were inequities in funding for schools based on curricula, location, and demographics is incontestable. Further, the Slater Fund is credited with causing several Black schools to give more weight to vocational programs during the 1880s than to other educational emphases.[61] For the first three decades of the twentieth century, white elites sought to control Black elementary, secondary, normal, and college education. Dominant white groups may have suspected that former enslaved people were a docile and tractable people; however, "the actions of the freedmen during the Civil War and Reconstruction periods convinced all parties that the blacks had their own ideas about learning and self-improvement."[62]

## W. E. B. Du Bois and the Slater Fund

Among the most vocal opponents of the Hampton model was W. E. B. Du Bois, who in March 1892 requested a scholarship from the Slater Fund to study at the University of Berlin. He sent a letter of application and a thorough biographical sketch to the board. President Rutherford B. Hayes then penned this two-line note in forwarding the request to Gilman: "My Dear Sir, I return you the paper of Du Bois—his autobiography. I hope he will turn out well."[63] Gilman's assessment of Du Bois, after meeting with him in person, was communicated in a note to the Slater Fund treasurer, Morris Jesup: "He expects to earn a good salary when his studies are more advanced and so no reason why he may not do so. He appears to be strong, sensible, intelligent, upright, and promising."[64]

The executive committee approved a scholarship in the amount of $375, together with a loan for the same amount, and Du Bois set sail for Germany on June 25, 1892. As required by the board, Du Bois sent reports to the trustees on his studies and progress. Two years later, he requested a renewal of his scholarship, and Gilman had to relay the disappointing news that the trustees had met to consider "the question of giving aid to advanced students, and reached the conclusion that it was not best to renew your appointment, or to make any other at present." Instead, Gilman advised Du Bois that he should return to Harvard and present himself for further studies in pursuit of a PhD, asserting that "the Harvard degree would be, in all respects, as advantageous to you as that of Berlin." Gilman ended his letter to Du Bois with the following: "The Slater Trustees inquired particularly in respect to your course of study, and some of them expressed, with great earnestness, the hope that, on returning to this country, you will devote your talent and your learning to the good of the colored race."[65]

Du Bois became the first African American to earn a PhD from Harvard and was the first to be invited to present a paper at the annual conference of the American Historical Association. He advocated for countless worthy causes and had a scholarship record unmatched by any public intellectual of his time.[66]

Upon learning of President Rutherford B. Hayes' death in January 1893, Du Bois wrote to the Slater Fund trustees: "I desire to express to you hereby, my sincerest gratitude for the scholarship which at your last annual meeting you were pleased to grant me. I am especially grateful to the memory of him, your late head, through whose initiative my case was brought before you, and whose tireless energy and singleheartedness for the interests of my Race, God has at last crowned. I shall, believe me, ever strive that these efforts shall not be wholly without results."[67] Of his time at Harvard, Du Bois would write in 1933 that although the university was not "a perfect expression of the American soul, or the place where the average American could have found adequate training for his life work," it perhaps "came nearer that high eminence than any other American institution had before or has since."[68]

At least one other African American graduate student (and fellow Fisk University alumnus) petitioned the Slater Fund for support during this period: Lewis B. Moore. Moore was enrolled in a PhD program at the University of Pennsylvania when he addressed a letter to President Hayes in July 1892, arguing that the "great need of our race is LEADERS: men who are able to go to the root of matters, men who can do original work—make original plans for the welfare of the race." Moore's request was not to go to Europe, as he preferred to remain at Penn: "I have excellent opportunities there and hope to help prove that the Negro race is able to produce men of thought, as well as 'orators.' . . . All we ask, I repeat, is a chance—the same chance given to others."[69] Moore completed his doctorate at Penn and subsequently taught several subjects at Howard University, including mathematics, history, English, Latin, and literature, eventually serving as dean of the Teachers College from 1899 to 1919.[70]

The agent in charge of administering the Slater Fund since its inception in 1882, Haygood resigned from his position in 1891 and was replaced by Jabez Lamar Monroe Curry, who also became chairman of the Slater Fund's Educational Committee. At the time, Curry was serving as the agent for the Peabody Education Fund, and he would continue in that role while assuming the same role with the Slater Fund—further evidence of the increasing cooperation and consolidation of northern philanthropies. At one point, Jesup wrote to Gilman (then a trustee of both the Slater and Peabody Funds) urging him to consider "whether any arrangement cannot be made between the two Funds to act together, with reference to the future."[71] Such trends continued well into the twentieth century. As Professor William Watkins noted, "Their interlocking directorates guaranteed united and coordinated activity."[72]

Curry and Haygood may have shared educational and racial views, but their approaches to spending the funds were quite different. During Haygood's tenure (and his training as a clergyman), his belief that religious ministers could be trained to help spread the fund's educational philosophy was manifested in these disbursement proportions: 62.4 percent to assorted colleges and universities; 9 percent exclusively to Hampton and Tuskegee; and 21.4 percent to private secondary schools. When Curry succeeded Haygood in the 1890s, the disbursements were more reflective of his belief that the training of teachers was the most effective strategy: 51.5 percent to colleges; 36.7 percent to Hampton and Tuskegee; and only 1 percent to private secondary schools.[73] Curry's observations in a 1901 Slater Fund report illustrate his position in the perpetual debate over the best approach for Black education: "The accepted methods of education in their general scope are of doubtful application to Negroes. Some need the best intellectual training that they may become leaders of the industrial, social, intellectual, and religious life of the race, but, as things now are, the great mass need to be fitted for domestic and mechanical and agricultural occupations which will produce the means of living and ensure self-respect and comfortable self-support."[74]

Cognizant of ongoing national discussion and disagreement around the freedmen's education and in an effort to contribute to the public discourse, in 1894 the trustees began circulating a series of occasional papers.[75] The first paper stated their intention "to publish from time to time papers that relate to the education of the colored race."[76] Successive papers carried an announcement that ended with the following: "The Trustees believe that the experimental period in the education of the blacks is drawing to a close. Certain principles that were doubted thirty years ago now appear to be generally recognized as sound. In the next thirty years better systems will undoubtedly prevail, and the aid of the separate States is likely to be more and more freely bestowed. There will also be abundant room for continued generosity on the part of individuals and associations. It is to encourage and assist the workers and the thinkers that these papers will be published."[77]

Perhaps the trustees sensed that the federal government might not be as generous with its support, thereby leaving "abundant room for continued generosity on the part of individuals and associations," as they would describe it. Publishing the occasional papers was meant to encourage and assist the "workers and thinkers" involved in the ongoing efforts.[78] A total of twenty-nine were issued between the years 1894 and 1935, each with a distinct author and covering a range of subjects. A few examples include *Statistics of the Negroes in the United States* (no. 4, 1894) and *Occupations of the Negroes* (no. 6, 1895), both by Henry Gannett of the US Geological Survey; *A Study in Black and White: An Address at the Opening of the Armstrong-Slater Trade School Building, November 18, 1896* (no. 10, 1897), by Gilman; *Negro Universities in the South* (no. 13, 1913) and *Duplication of Schools for Negro Youth* (no. 15, 1914), both by William T. B. Williams, field agent of the Slater Fund and later dean of the Tuskegee Institute; and *Southern Women and Racial Adjustment* (no. 19, 1917), by L. H. Hammond, president of Paine College in Augusta, Georgia.[79]

Over the course of the Slater Fund's life, the trustees' own views evolved, as did the demographic of those receiving the endowment's support. For example, the minutes of the board's twentieth meeting, on April 10, 1895, included a debate on the question of "furthering the education of the colored woman in morality," with evidence that

Mrs. E. C. Hobson had offered to investigate this question, whereupon the trustees authorized the treasurer "to pay all necessary expenses for such an inquiry."[80] The fund's treasurer, Jesup, was a good friend of Elizabeth Hobson's. Hobson embarked on a tour of Black schools and homes in five southern states. Her subsequent recommendation to the Slater Fund was that the trustees should sponsor the teaching of sewing, cooking, and first aid. They agreed, creating the Southern Industrial Classes, a pilot program in Norfolk, Virginia, "for introducing practical and 'industrial' education for both sexes into colored public schools."[81] With Mrs. Hobson as president, the program continued until 1912, when the Norfolk school board took over the work.

By that time the Slater Fund had expanded funding across the South to increase the number of public county "schools for Negroes" providing instruction on the eighth-grade level and higher. In 1914 the Peabody Education Fund merged with the Slater Fund, and the two operated together for more than twenty years. While John Fox Slater had included a provision that his fund be dissolved after thirty-three years (following its establishment in 1882), it continued its work until 1937, when the Randolph Fund (founded in 1936 to honor Virginia Randolph, the first Jeanes Supervising Industrial Teacher) and the Jeanes Fund (whose formal name was the Negro Rural School Fund of the Anna T. Jeanes Foundation, founded in 1907 by the Philadelphia philanthropist) both merged with the Peabody and Slater Funds. The final result was the institution known today as the Southern Education Foundation (SEF), the first foundation formed to unite southerners and northerners in an effort to provide a quality education for all people in the South.[82] With an investment of $1 million in 1882, the Slater Fund, together with other foundations, had ultimately contributed more than $4 million to schools in eighteen states.[83]

In addition, Gilman was named one of the original trustees of the John D. Rockefeller General Education Board in 1902. A review of the board's membership reveals the intersection of prominent private philanthropies of the age: William H. Baldwin Jr., Jabez L. M. Curry, Frederick T. Gates, Daniel Coit Gilman, Morris K. Jesup, Robert C. Ogden, Walter Hines Page, George Foster Peabody, and Albert Shaw.[84] Originally endowed by Rockefeller with $1 million, the board would disburse more than $324.6 million over the span of its existence, from 1902 to 1964.[85]

Debates continue over the ultimate impact of endowments such as the Peabody and Slater Funds on the educational infrastructure put in place in the South after Reconstruction. The Slater Fund played a significant role both in the funding and and in the perpetuation of skills training in the trades for African Americans, a fact that Gilman underlined in his 1896 speech "A Study in Black and White," which he gave at the opening of the Armstrong-Slater Trade School Building at Hampton University. However, he also acknowledged that "those who are interested in the uplifting of blacks, believe that, next to freedom and religion, the greatest boon that the more favored can bestow upon the less favored, is to give them opportunities for becoming skilled 'workmen.'" Nonetheless, he concluded, "May I urge you, my hearers, a like recognition of the pleasure of work—not merely animal exertion, although that may have its pleasures, but the combination of intelligence and labor." Quoting President Hayes ("Add to labor intelligence and to scholarship handcraft"), Gilman then cited the Hampton graduate Booker T. Washington: "Right here comes the value of industrial education combined with first-class literary training; it has a modifying, sobering influence, resulting in teaching the colored youth that the road to the highest permanent success and development is by slow graduations, and nature permits of no reversal in the process."[86]

## Gilman's Slater Fund Experience and the Temporary Integration of Hopkins

Gilman, then, stood front and center in the important national debates focused on Black education, the post-Reconstruction era, and the end of the Freedmen's Bureau. His service with the Slater Fund certainly aligned with Mr. Johns Hopkins' commitment to providing access to education "for all most deserving of choice, because of their character and intellectual promise; and to educate the young men so chosen free of charge."[87] What is noticeably absent, however, is any discussion by Gilman regarding his own views on the subject, nor did he record in any detail his views on race, integration, or the education of African Americans at Johns Hopkins.

Nonetheless, Gilman would be presented with a unique case—and a golden opportunity—when an African American student named Kelly Miller wrote twice to Hopkins for information about graduate studies in the mid-1880s. A native of South Carolina, Miller had been born in 1863, five years before W. E. B. Du Bois and seven years after Booker T. Washington, placing him chronologically between the two most important figures of the transitional period. Miller, in turn, identified with both the "radical" and the "conservative" Black leadership in America at the time.[88] Washington advocated industrial training for artisans, Du Bois stressed a broader education for the elite, and Miller simply noted that the system was working in the right direction whether it "pushes up from the bottom or pulls up from the top."[89]

Miller graduated from Howard University with a stellar academic record in just three years, working at the US Pension Office to support himself. Upon earning his degree in 1886, Miller gave his parents a farm he had purchased with funds saved during his studies.[90]

Upon his graduation Miller was offered a full-time position in the Pension Office. There he met Simon Newcomb, a Naval Observatory astronomer in charge of the Nautical Almanac and a mathematics professor at Johns Hopkins.[91] Newcomb was one of the first faculty appointments at Hopkins and served as editor of the *American Journal of Mathematics*, published by the Johns Hopkins Press.[92] Newcomb's tutelage would prove invaluable as Miller weighed higher education opportunities.

As early as July 1885, while still an undergraduate at Howard, Miller had written to inquire about admission to the PhD program in mathematics at Hopkins. Unable to find the information he desired in the university's *Register*, Miller wrote again in December 1885. If he were admitted at Hopkins, he asked, "would I be allowed to

Members of the Howard College graduating class of 1886 included Kelly Miller (*left*), Josephine Turpine (*center*), and William Palmer (*right*). Miller was the first African American to attend the Johns Hopkins University, admitted to the graduate program in mathematics in 1887. After two years, he withdrew from the university but ultimately earned a PhD in mathematics from Howard University. A prolific writer and essayist, Miller was called the "Bard of the Potomac." (Photo courtesy of University Archives, Sheridan Libraries, Johns Hopkins University)

enter as a candidate for the degree Ph.D. and spend any portion of the time here in Washington? If so, under what conditions?"[93] There is no evidence of any response from Johns Hopkins University to Miller's inquiries. Undeterred, Miller asked Newcomb to help him prepare for his postgraduate plans. Newcomb obliged and secured the services of Captain Edgar Frisby to help tutor Miller in geometry and calculus. Additional tutors were hired to help Miller in French and German, given that Hopkins required fluency in both languages for admission to the doctoral program.[94]

With a year of study and preparation under his belt, Miller then asked Newcomb to inquire directly of President Gilman about his admission to Hopkins. Miller later recorded that a trustee and prominent railroad official—Robert Garrett, son of Robert Work Garrett[95]—"advanced the opinion that the founder of the university, being a Quaker, stipulated that neither race nor color should form a bar against admission to either hospital or university. Other members of the Board seemed to have accepted his views as correct, so my name was placed upon the roll, and I entered upon a two years Post-Graduate course in Mathematics, physics, and astronomy."[96]

The record of Miller's time at Hopkins is scant, absent any documentation of trustee discussion about him or his academic performance. Miller did, however, recollect being treated with "cool, calculated civility" during his time on campus, and he recorded his impressions of his first meeting with Gilman as a new graduate student. Ushered into the president's office, Miller found Gilman to be "a dignified, courteous gentleman, who received me graciously. He stated that I was the only colored student that the University had ever admitted, and being one among many I would naturally be the subject of observation. He stated that the opportunities and facilities of the University would be open to me, and all the rest depended upon myself. He also advised me that if they had a number of colored students the way might be easier and smoother."[97]

Like some other Hopkins students in the early days, Miller was unable to cover expenses—a predicament at odds with the founder's original intent to educate young men "free of charge."[98] The fortunes of the university had waned considerably, in part because of the founder's prohibition against selling any B&O Railroad shares. Hopkins' intent had been to keep the railroad and its affairs free of political influence, but in practice, the sinking stock of the B&O resulted in the university realizing no income. As a consequence, the trustees were forced to raise tuition from $100 to $125 in 1888. Miller could only afford to stay on for one more year before entering the workforce, when he would be employed first as a teacher of mathematics at M Street High School in Washington, DC, and then, six months later, as a mathematics instructor at Howard University.[99] Before hiring Miller, the president of Howard University, Jeremiah Rankin, wrote to Gilman: "I want to know about his fitness morally and intellectually and practically, to give instruction in this University."[100] Gilman did not respond directly to the inquiry but asked Professor Newcomb to do so. Two days later, Newcomb responded to Gilman: "Dr. Rankin's letter is herewith returned. I have written him all I can say about Mr. Miller."[101] There is no copy of Newcomb's recommendation, but his endorsement must have helped, as Miller began his employment at Howard in 1890, remaining there for more than forty years as a distinguished administrator and faculty member. At the first Hampton Conference in 1897, Miller said he believed in industrial education but insisted that Black citizens also needed a college education. From that moment forward, Miller was consistent in his message: both industrial and higher education were required. "Each is efficient," he maintained, "neither is sufficient."[102]

Miller reached out to Gilman in 1900 with a letter that began, "You will probably remember me as the colored student who attended upon the graduate course of the Johns Hopkins University," and he followed with a petition for Gilman's support of Miller's application to be superintendent of the colored public schools of the District of Columbia. Miller included with his letter several copies of speeches he had given, including one at the Hampton Institute entitled "The Primary Needs of the Negro Race."[103] With a nod to the Hampton model (Miller obviously knew his audience), Miller encouraged members of his race to focus on natural resources, production, commerce, and ownership:

> The distinguished men of the race so far have risen upon the dead necessities of the masses. The sick must be healed, the ignorant must be enlightened, the vicious must be restrained, the poor must have the gospel preached to them. While these pursuits are necessary, they do not touch the bed-rock of our economic structure. Those who reach distinction on such conditions stand as marble statues on pedestals of clay. The primary sources of wealth are agriculture, mining, manufacturing, and commerce. These are the lines along which the intelligent energy of the race must be directed in the future. They must take the industrial initiative. The earth will yield up her increase as willingly to the skillful persuasion of a swarthy as of a fair businessman; the markets of the world know no article by its color; steam and electricity, wind and wave, heat and cold, are blind forces and therefore can see no race distinctions.[104]

Decades after Miller left Baltimore, a Hopkins professor, Broadus Mitchell, contacted the Office of the Registrar to inquire about the circumstances surrounding the admission of Hopkins' first African American graduate student in 1887. Mitchell had been alerted to the case of another Black student, Edward S. Lewis, whose application for admission to Hopkins' Department of Political Economy in 1937 had been denied. His application had been held for nearly eighteen months, and at one point in the process Lewis had written to then president Isaiah Bowman about the status of his application. Bowman's elusive response included this: "I have to say that the question of your admission to the graduate school of this university was discussed by the Academic Council, and up to the present time, the council has not submitted a recommendation on the question. . . . No member of the faculty with whom I have talked has expressed any unwillingness whatsoever to teach negroes."[105]

Why, then, the university's inaction on Lewis's application for admission? This was the question Mitchell wanted answered. Mitchell had developed a reputation for activism on campus and throughout the state, earning a spot on the socialist ticket for governor of Maryland in 1934. That same year, Gilman's youngest daughter, Elisabeth, would be a socialist candidate for the US Senate. The two candidates used their respective campaigns to respond to the explosion of labor activism, to raise the issue of class and race, and to address the rash of lynchings on Maryland's Eastern Shore.[106] Gilman had run for governor in 1930 and throughout her life would seek other political offices, including those of US senator (1934, 1938), mayor of Baltimore (1935), and sheriff of Baltimore (1942). She did not succeed in any of these races.

There is no doubt that Lewis was eminently qualified to study at Hopkins. He had earned a bachelor's degree from the University of Chicago, and at the time of his application to Hopkins he was pursuing a graduate degree in economics at the University of Pennsylvania.[107] Mitchell called the Hopkins Office of the Registrar in January 1939 to ask for additional information on the Miller admission case. The university's registrar at the time, Irene M. Davis, reported to President Bowman: "Mr. Miller's admission here is a matter of record and his name appears in the Half Century Directory. . . . [Mitchell] asked me whether or not I had any knowledge of the University's policy at that time and I said that I had not because no statement concerning the admission of students of the colored race appeared in the circular." Davis confessed to President Bowman that there was "some information in Mr. Miller's application which I did not see fit to give to Dr. Mitchell," and she admitted that she had "known for many years that Mr. Miller was a student here." Her next statement strains all credulity: "I had always understood that those who admitted him were unaware of the fact that he was colored." After reviewing Miller's correspondence and his application documents, Registrar Davis concluded, "I am inclined to doubt that, because his connection with Howard University, a negro institution, is clearly stated in the application and in the supportive letters." The cover page to Miller's application—"the blank" as Davis denoted it—had one word, underscored twice, in the middle of the page: "colored." Davis recognized the handwriting as that of Thomas R. Ball, registrar at Hopkins from 1889 to 1923 and at one time personal secretary to President Gilman. Davis surmised, "Of course, we do not know when Mr. Ball made that note—it may have been at the time when the application was submitted or at some later time."[108]

President Isaiah Bowman, well known for his hostility toward Jewish faculty and students, displayed bigotry "even more virulent regarding black applicants to Hopkins."[109] As the Miller episode came to a close, it was apparent that Bowman's heavy-handed tactics were wearing thin throughout the community. And while the local press was concerned about the persistent reports of faculty desertions stemming from the internal disorder at Hopkins, it also appeared to have fewer qualms about "exposing the institutional racism that Hopkins shared with many universities, largely embracing their class elitism."[110] The university, it seems, was content with admissions practices until after World War II, when the signing into law, for example, of the GI Bill by President Franklin D. Roosevelt in June 1944 forever changed the composition of entering classes of students, including those at Johns Hopkins.

Mitchell would write of the handling of Lewis' case in the journal *Frontiers of Democracy*: "Johns Hopkins offers no reason for excluding this Negro. The explanation is a disgraceful one; that despite every qualification of training and competence, he is excluded because of his color."[111] In the end, Mitchell's advocacy for the Baltimore native Lewis to be admitted to Hopkins would lead to his own resignation from the university in April 1939 to take a teaching position at Occidental College in Los Angeles. Lewis eventually earned a PhD at New York University and became head of the New York Urban League.[112]

More than forty years earlier, in his 1896 speech at the Hampton Institute, and just a few years removed from Kelly Miller's tenure as a graduate student at his own university, Gilman—who occupied a seat on a board fundamentally committed to industrial education for Black people—had acknowledged that "opportunities are also provided for the exceptional cases that require professional instruction."[113] Holding the paternalistic view of the white-controlled philanthropic organizations of the time, Gilman—along with his fellow Slater trustees and whites of the time period—"believed that blacks were not capable of dealing with the rigors of a classical academic curriculum."[114]

But it appears that Gilman viewed Kelly Miller as the exception to the rule. Such a perspective certainly aligns with views expressed in 1901 by the Slater Fund's agent, J. L. M. Curry, cited above. Given the paucity of records and the lack of Gilman's discussion, either in correspondence or in speeches, of issues relative to access to universities for minority students, we are left to come to our own conclusions about Hopkins and its admission practices during his tenure and in the decades following. Perhaps, indeed, they were policies rooted in the social attitudes toward minority populations that were prevalent in Maryland at the time.[115] But that would leave us with the question, What might have happened had Miller been admitted and completed his studies at Hopkins, decades before *Brown v. Board of Education* in 1954 and the Civil Rights Act of 1964?

Not until 1945, when Frederick I. Scott applied and eventually matriculated, would Hopkins welcome its first African American undergraduate. Given Hopkins' history of innovation in so many other areas, one might expect it to be among the leaders in affording opportunities for African American students in an integrated environment, but it was not. There is no telling what "might have been" should such a thing have occurred, especially in a southern state like Maryland.

# CHAPTER EIGHT

# *Allies, Not Rivals*

In the wake of all the successful firsts launched by Gilman at Hopkins during his tenure, in May 1896 there was an attempt to recruit Gilman away from the university to the superintendency of New York City's public schools. Gilman had had some experience with the New Haven public school system in the 1860s, but much had changed in public education over the three decades since then. That such lobbying efforts were undertaken to lure a 65-year-old from his career in higher education to a completely new arena speaks to Gilman's prodigious skills, among them his unsurpassed organizational ability. Learning of the recruitment campaign, the Hopkins faculty banded together and signed a letter imploring their president to stay: "We most earnestly hope that you may see it to be your duty to remain in the place which you have filled with such distinction. We need not tell you what confidence and enthusiasm in respect to the future such a determination on your part would inspire in us all."[1] Gilman would remain in Baltimore another five years, responding to the faculty's message: "I could receive no greater reward than the assurance that those with whom I have lived and worked day by day for twenty years still wish me to remain with them."[2]

Gilman was persuaded to stay, and he maintained his primary residence in Baltimore for the rest of his life. The first signature on the 1896 faculty letter to Gilman was that of Ira Remsen, recruited to Hopkins by the president twenty years earlier as the chair of chemistry. Upon Gilman's official resignation from the university in 1901,

Daniel Coit Gilman, aged 70, portrait photograph in academic robes, seated in the President's Chair, 1900. (Photo courtesy of University Archives, Sheridan Libraries, Johns Hopkins University)

Remsen was installed as the second president in 1902. Gilman could reflect with enormous satisfaction on what had been accomplished in the previous twenty-five years. While he was certainly healthy, Gilman was also stretched very thin. Together, his presidencies at Berkeley and Hopkins had extended nearly three decades. At age 70 he was ready to focus on other matters, such as his philanthropic board service and compiling his experiences and observations into memoirs and histories.

Still, many were taken aback by the news of Gilman's resignation. His friend and fellow Yale classmate Reverend Jacob Cooper wrote Gilman from his office at Rutgers about the "painful surprise" the news of his retirement had caused: "You have, in a preeminent degree, executive ability, which is as rare a gift as that of a great poet or Military Commander. In addition to this, you have Intimate *Clairvoyance* in the work of Education. . . . I greatly regret the step you propose to take. But your life has shown a wise and Divinely-ordered course; and the same Light in which you have walked will shine upon you to the end."[3] Gilman's response to Cooper was characteristically direct: "We have come to a new epoch, and the man who inaugurates new measures should have before him a reasonable prospect of twenty years' service. Altho I am well, I am not young and I am involved in many educational and philanthropic cares and duties. To these I can give much more time if I am free from the daily duties of administration."[4] Gilman put it even more succinctly in his *Launching of a University*, published in 1906, when he described his decision to give up the presidency at Hopkins "not because I was tired of it, not because I was conscious of bodily infirmity, but out of deference to the widespread uses of this country, which suggests that, at a certain age, seniors should make way for juniors."[5]

The news of his leaving Hopkins caught his best friend, Andrew White, then serving as ambassador to Germany, especially off guard. White learned of the resignation through "the newspaper cutting," telling his friend of his shock given the "evidences of vigor, both physical and intellectual" Gilman had displayed at their most recent encounter. "But," White told Gilman, "you have done a most noble work: Indeed, if Johns Hopkins University were to close its doors tomorrow, your work upon the higher education of the country would be a most marked feature of American Educational History during the second half of the nineteenth century. There is no University worthy of the name in the United States which has not felt the influences of that which you have done at Baltimore."[6]

Gilman's official last day in office was Commemoration Day, February 22, 1901. No ceremonial function or valedictory address marked the date. All the recognition of the first president's tenure—and the formal investiture of Remsen as the second— would take place a year later. Some suggested that Gilman might have stepped down to take on a new challenge, one led by one of the nation's richest men, Andrew Carnegie, a notion Fabian Franklin described as "wholly without foundation."[7] But while Carnegie may not have prompted his resignation, he would certainly shape Gilman's final years. And the key to pairing Gilman with Carnegie was White.

## The Idea of a National University

Andrew White and Andrew Carnegie both maintained homes in New York City and had become acquainted through various literary circles in the early 1880s.[8] White had retired from the Cornell presidency in 1885 but persuaded Carnegie to join the university's board of trustees in 1890. Carnegie served on Cornell's board for twenty-nine years, giving generously to a variety of projects over that span. In 1903, for instance, Carnegie paid the bills—more than $150,000—incurred by students who suffered from typhoid fever during the epidemic in 1902–3.[9] The relationship White had cultivated with Carnegie would lead to Gilman's involvement in a scheme of such magnitude and potential as to eclipse any other philanthropic undertaking in American history.

For years White had been developing a bold idea for a national university in Washington, DC. He envisioned an institution staffed by a faculty "who lead the country in power to investigate and teach" and having a student body who would gain entry through competitive examinations and would not be required to pay tuition.[10] Washington offered abundant advantages: the national museums and their extensive collections, the National Patent Office, the Library of Congress and its unmatched holdings, and the concentration of talent. No other city in America could offer such resources.

White outlined these advantages and more, adding that "within an hour's distance northward are the chemical, physical, and biological laboratories of Johns Hopkins University. . . . A little more distant southward is the University of Virginia, which could easily be brought into relations with the proposed institution in a manner profitable to both." Finally, White opined that supplementary facilities might be offered by other institutions at "various points more or less remote," such as the Naval Academy at Annapolis.[11] White would later assert that this new Washington-based teaching institution would be one of the "noblest institutions in the world. It would have as its right wing the grand old University of Virginia, as its left wing the Johns Hopkins University in Maryland, each of these preserving its identity, but all strengthening one another."[12]

White was hardly the first to advocate for a national university in America; the idea had been discussed by the delegates of the Constitutional Convention in 1787, and such an undertaking had been called for explicitly by George Washington in his First Inaugural Address. Washington stated his belief that there was nothing "which can better deserve your patronage than the promotion of Science and Literature" and that the acquisition of knowledge was "the surest basis of public happiness" and essential to the "security of a free Constitution."[13] For America to be a great nation, cultivation of the arts, sciences, and literature was essential.[14] Washington returned to the idea in his Eighth Annual Address to Congress: "I have heretofore proposed to the consideration of Congress, the expediency of establishing a National University; and also a Military Academy." As he saw it, the former was important not only for "national prosperity and reputation" but also to prepare the "future guardians of the liberties" in the "science of Government." Meanwhile, the military academy would secure freedom by creating "an adequate stock of Military knowledge for emergencies."[15]

Congress would help Washington with the second part of his proposal by establishing a national military academy at West Point, New York, in 1802, but funds for building a national university were never appropriated. Washington continued to promote his plan well into retirement. He felt so strongly that he gave from his own personal wealth, bequeathing "fifty shares which I hold in the Potomac Company . . . towards the endowment of a UNIVERSITY to be established within the limits of the District of Columbia."[16]

Knowing of Carnegie's interest in endowing some type of new institution, White hoped that the national university he desired might be that institution. The two men had visited several educational institutions along the West Coast in 1892, and White used the experience to plant the seed of the idea with Carnegie. Nearly a decade after their trip, White continued to lobby for such an institution in the nation's capital.[17] The impervious Scot had no interest. He told White: "Gov. Stanford made a useless rival as you and I saw when in San Francisco to the State University. I could be no party to such a thing."[18] Carnegie may have been slow to form an opinion, but once he had, he rarely deviated from it.

Although he was not interested in creating a national university, Carnegie did plan to give away vast sums of money to still undetermined recipients. Even hints at what the steel magnate might do with his prodigious fortune precipitated wild speculation. Carnegie had set off a feeding frenzy among university presidents with his publication of "Wealth" in the *North American Review* in June 1889, which included his famous axiom "The man who dies thus rich, dies disgraced."[19] Six months later, Carnegie followed up with "The Best Fields for Philanthropy," also in the *Review*, in which he cited Cornell, Hopkins, and Stanford as examples of what private support could make possible. "It is reserved for very few to found universities, and, indeed, the use for many, or perhaps any, new universities does not exist," Carnegie wrote. "More good is henceforth to be accomplished by adding to and extending those in existence."[20] This observation resulted in solicitations from campuses across America for music halls, dormitories, teaching salaries, even unrestricted endowments. The then president of Pennsylvania State College, George W. Atherton, went so far as to offer the naming rights to his institution: "I cannot give up the hope that you will think favorably of making this institution *Carnegie University*," he wrote to Carnegie.[21] But for the moment, Carnegie knew what he wanted to do with his fortune. As he wrote to a friend, "I am clearly of the opinion that I can do most good by selecting one field and sticking to it, and that field, as you know, is Free Libraries for the people."[22]

That Carnegie chose the steps of the Carnegie Library in Braddock, Pennsylvania— the first to open of the nearly seventeen hundred public libraries Carnegie would fund in the United States alone—to explicate his view of the uselessness of traditional college education is telling. The self-made industrialist used the occasion in 1889 to distinguish between book learning and the practical education he felt was much more worthwhile in the industrial age. Before the assembled steelworkers and influential Pittsburghers, Carnegie let loose: "Men have sent their sons to colleges to waste their energies upon obtaining a knowledge of such languages as Greek and Latin, which are of no more practical use to them than Choctaw." These students had been educated, Carnegie continued, "as if they were destined for life upon some other planet than this.

They have in no sense received instruction. On the contrary, what they have obtained has served to imbue them with false ideas and to give them a distaste for practical life."[23]

Carnegie's opinions on the existing higher education system in America were not unique. In many ways, they resembled the arguments made against Gilman's efforts at the University of California to establish a college of letters on par with what other leaders wanted to see, namely, a college of agricultural and mechanical arts. Ten years earlier, William Parsons Atkinson, professor of English and history at the Massachusetts Institute of Technology, had written that the "popular idea of a young scholar is that he should be a pale and spectacled young man, very thin, and with a slight and interesting tendency to sentimentality and consumption." After all, Atkinson concluded, the accepted view among many was that "parents send their weakly children to college."[24] Nevertheless, it was not the disdain of magnates and businesspeople like Carnegie that most seriously undermined the teaching of the classics in tradition-laden American institutions. On the contrary, it was the rapid advancement of scientific knowledge and the demand for more practical education brought on by the Industrial Revolution and the Morrill Act of 1862, the inflexibility of the old curriculum vested in the hands of those determined to maintain the "classical education" as they viewed it, and the dismal pedagogy prevalent on college campuses across the country.[25] To place it in a Hopkins context, Carnegie's ever-evolving views on higher education were more aligned with what John Work Garrett advocated (practical programs of study for the local population) than with what Judge George Brown envisioned (a university much broader in scope and international in its impact).

Still, Carnegie chose to express his initial philanthropic support of higher education in America by donating to institutions that were innovative in their approach and unique in their practices. In 1899 he contributed $50,000 to the Stevens Institute of Technology and $100,000 to the Cooper Union. Two years later, Carnegie would serve on the boards of trustees at both schools. Other recipients of Carnegie's munificence were Booker T. Washington's Tuskegee Institute in Alabama and the Hampton Institute in Virginia. In 1903 Carnegie gave $600,000 worth of US Steel bonds to the Tuskegee endowment, with a provision that a portion of the revenue from the bonds be used by Washington "for his wants and those of his family during his life or the life of his widow." Carnegie admired Washington greatly: "To me he seems one of the foremost of living men because his work is unique. The modern Moses, who leads his race and lifts it through Education to even better and higher things than a land overflowing with milk and honey."[26]

In New York City, Carnegie donated funds to establish programs directed at nontraditional students: "I know of no work more important than to give the young people who work during the day a chance to learn at night."[27] But his largest donation to higher education did not go to American institutions. In his home country of Scotland, the Carnegie Trust for the Universities of Scotland (St. Andrews, Glasgow, Aberdeen, and Edinburgh) was incorporated by royal charter in 1902, the year following his initial gift of $5 million. At the suggestion of Prime Minister Arthur James Balfour, Carnegie increased his endowment by another $5 million.[28] But this was just the beginning.

When Carnegie wrote his *North American Review* articles in 1889, he was wealthy. By March 11, 1901—the day after he sold his steel company to J. P. Morgan—Carnegie was *very* wealthy. The Morgan deal made Carnegie the richest man in America, unseating John D. Rockefeller. Sixty-five years old, in good health, and with no business to attend to, Carnegie turned his attention to what could be accomplished in his adopted country, giving more than $350 million to various causes over the remainder of his life.[29] But in 1901 Carnegie's attention was focused on the proposed institution in Washington, and he reached out to White, then in Berlin, to ask for help. Carnegie invited White to come to Skibo, his recently constructed castle in Scotland, to discuss his plans—and he asked that White bring Gilman along.

## White, Gilman, and Carnegie

White wrote to Gilman in May 1901 about his advocacy efforts "in a certain quarter," including his unqualified support of Washington, DC, as "the site for a great American university." White had lent his support, he emphasized to Gilman, in a "platonic and rather self-sacrificing spirit, for first of all in my affections is, of course, Cornell." Fearing that such an opportunity might never occur again, White informed Gilman that should such an institution be created, "you would, in my opinion, have more to say regarding the organization, selection of its faculty, etc. than any other person. In fact I have already, in correspondence on the subject, stated as my conviction that you are the man from whom most is to be expected in the matter." Without mentioning the source of the potential funding in the body of his letter, White wrote this first paragraph in the postscript: "You have doubtless divined the person above mentioned. I have felt quite sure that you would, but under strict injunctions not to say anything about such a project being under discussion, I did not feel at liberty to mention the name." Admitting that he had heard from the person that very morning, White quoted the injunction relayed to him: "Please write Gilman and arrange meeting at Skibo. Middle of July will suit us."[30]

Later on in his note, White finally offered "Mr. C" as a clue, as if Gilman had not deduced the donor by then. White had unbridled enthusiasm for what this could mean for both Cornell and Hopkins, but he exhorted Gilman with an even longer view of what their collaboration could potentially produce: "It is a chance for us to render to education and to our country the culminating service of our lives; and I am ready to throw down everything in order to do my part in presenting the matter."[31] White was relentless in his lobbying for a national university with Carnegie, even appealing to the Scot's vanity by stressing the "immortality of the Founder." Carnegie pushed back, saying that such an institution was not needed, reiterating the importance, again, of a meeting in Scotland. His retort to White was characteristically direct: "Don't care two cents about future 'glory.' I must be satisfied that I am doing good wise beneficial work in my day. Better come to Skibo and confer."[32]

Gilman would consider White's letter and the invitation from Carnegie from his summer home, Over Edge, in Northeast Harbor, Maine. Citing his workload and his desire to write, in addition to the hope that the clearer conditions of the coast would improve his daughter's health, Gilman declined the offer to travel to Scotland and meet with Carnegie in person. One can only conjecture what might have come from such a meeting.[33] While he understood Gilman's commitment to relieving Elisabeth's suffering by staying in Maine, White was disappointed that his friend could not join him, and he wrote Gilman in mid-August: "For if the matter which takes me to Scotland and which we both have so much at heart shall come to anything, you are the person who must do most to give the enterprise the required organization."[34] Not nearly as wedded to the idea of a national university as White, Gilman had written an open letter in *The Century* in 1897 advocating for a "learned society" built around the Smithsonian Institution, which would result in "less friction, less expense, less peril" and would have "the prospect of more permanent and wide-spread advantages to the country than by a dozen denominational seminaries or one colossal University of the United States."[35]

Although he missed the meeting in Scotland, Gilman continued to share White's enthusiasm for what Carnegie's gift might mean for American higher education, and he agreed to a meeting with Carnegie in the fall. Gilman's plan for his post-Hopkins life was completely disrupted by this introduction to Carnegie. Gilman had recorded that he was "looking forward to a period of comparative leisure" when the "evangelist of beneficence (as I venture to call him), who has preached and practices 'the gospel of wealth,' completely altered the outlook."[36] Also in attendance at the meeting with Carnegie—at the donor's request—was someone whom Gilman knew very well, dating back to their first encounter in Washington, DC, in 1875: Dr. John Shaw Billings.

After retiring from the Office of the Surgeon General, Billings had been recruited to the directorship of the New York Public Library by Andrew Carnegie in 1896, a position he held until his death in 1913.[37] When the library opened in 1911, the public hailed Billings as its new director: "SOUL OF THE NEW LIBRARY IS BILLINGS, ITS CHIEF," exclaimed the *Evening Mail*. "One gasps at the many lives he has led, the many appointments he has filled, and his gigantic work among libraries and hospitals. . . . This is the man who has charge of the vast literary material at the disposal of the reading public, the genius of the new library."[38]

Long before the library's grand opening, however, Carnegie had needed someone to oversee the combination of the Tilden Trust and the Astor and Lenox Libraries; Billings had succeeded in accomplishing this, earning Carnegie's unreserved trust. Billings' biographer described his relationship with Carnegie as "a remarkable one, based beyond doubt on mutual respect and on something approaching affection."[39] It was no surprise, then, that Billings joined the meeting at Carnegie's Manhattan home on November 16, 1901, between the philanthropist and Gilman.

## The Institution Is Established

Carnegie knew of Gilman by reputation and through his relationship with Andrew White. At the November 16 meeting, America's wealthiest man got right to the point. "You must be president," Carnegie told Gilman.[40] Carnegie pressed Gilman and Billings for their visions regarding the $10 million endowment and the ultimate nature of the institution. Gilman recalled,

> Mr. Carnegie raised many hard questions: How is it that knowledge is increased? How can rare intellects be discovered in the undeveloped stages? Where is the exceptional man to be found? Would a new institution be regarded as an injury to Johns Hopkins, or to Harvard, Yale, Columbia, or any other university? What should the term "knowledge" comprise? Who should be the managers of the institution? How broad or how restricted should be the terms of the gift?
>
> These are only examples of the perplexing problems which presented themselves to one who was not anxious for fame; not devoted to a hobby; not inclined to impose limitations, but who had an eye single to the good of his adopted country, and through our country to the good of the world.[41]

In Gilman and Billings, Carnegie had recruited two men combining ability with unusual capacity, as was his practice. Known for pithy sayings and oft-quoted truisms, Carnegie is reported to have suggested these lines for his epitaph: "Here lies the man who was able to surround himself with men far cleverer than himself."[42]

Gilman's reports of the inaugural meeting and Billings' various memoranda, however, reveal a chasm between the two men over the fundamental nature of Carnegie's endeavor.[43] On the one hand, Gilman and White shared a commitment to the German research university model and envisioned the creation of something akin to a university. On the other hand, Billings maintained that this new venture should promote original research, offer some advanced instruction, and use scholarships and stipends to support the work going on inside of *existing* laboratories and institutions. Years of government service had taught Billings about the capriciousness of congressional funding; as a result, he conceived of an entity that could support research, that was inoculated from the vicissitudes of the government, and that had, at its core, a commitment "to expand known forces and to discover and utilize unknown forces for the benefit of mankind."[44] As events unfolded, Billings' view apparently aligned more closely with Carnegie's vision.[45]

In subsequent weeks, Billings played the most influential role in outlining the structure of the institution. Many of the ideas in his memoranda addressed to Carnegie in late November made their way into the institution's creation documents.[46] Gilman was encouraged and kept White apprised of developments, writing from Baltimore in early December that matters had "moved with extreme rapidity, and I have not kept up with all the proceedings. . . . *The result is grand* and its effect, if I am not mistaken, will be to inspire and strengthen every institution in the land."[47]

This view matched what Carnegie had written to President Theodore Roosevelt in late November 1901, confessing that he had considered "the propriety of fulfilling one of Washington's strongest wishes, the founding of a University at Washington." However, as Carnegie told Roosevelt, he believed that if Washington were "with us today, he would decide that under present conditions greater good would ensue from cooperation with, and strengthening of, existing universities throughout the country, than by adding to their number."[48] The means to this end would be an institution headquartered in Washington, DC, and Carnegie sought to enlist President Roosevelt's help. Nevertheless, from Carnegie's letter to Roosevelt the press mistakenly extrapolated that a national university was in the offing. The *New York Times* ran a headline on its front page that read "Carnegie Millions for a University." The article contended that Carnegie would not ask for an appropriation; rather, "the government is simply to be the trustee of the magnificent endowment, just as it administers the fund bequeathed by Smithson [namesake of the Smithsonian Institution]." "Even yet all these details have not been arranged," the article admitted, 'so that little more than the outline of his gift can be published."[49]

Carnegie initially intended to finance the institution with bonds, not cash. His hope was that Roosevelt might prevail upon Congress to pass a joint resolution bestowing official approval on the new enterprise, effectively making the government the holder of these private bonds. However, such an arrangement could suggest a conflict of interest, which was something the Republican Party did not want with an election (Theodore Roosevelt's first as a presidential candidate) approaching. The press began reporting details of the late December 1901 meeting between the two men, along with specifics of Carnegie's proposal. The blowback caused Carnegie to entirely abandon the idea of involving the federal government. Gilman met with Carnegie after his meeting with Roosevelt and wrote White shortly thereafter: "I saw our munificent friend on Monday in Washington, where he went for a conference with the President. Much opposition has developed on one point, the acceptance by Congress of U.S. Steel Corp. bonds, and the donor withdraws the original form of his proposition." Noting that Carnegie was "both deliberate and prompt; slow to form an opinion,—quick to give his opinions form," Gilman told White that the philanthropist had returned immediately to New York with the intention of instituting a private corporation.[50]

Carnegie summoned a select group of men to his home on December 27, 1901. In attendance were the proposed officers of the Carnegie Institution: Gilman as president; Abram S. Hewitt (former US congressman and mayor of New York City) as chairman of the board of trustees; Dr. John Billings as vice chair of the board; and Charles D. Walcott (director of the US Geological Survey) as secretary. The group helped Carnegie draw up a list of prospective trustees and draft a letter inviting them to join.[51] In speaking to the men, Carnegie quoted a letter from President Roosevelt: "I congratulate you especially upon the character, the extraordinarily high character, of the trustees."[52]

The first meeting of the board of trustees of the Carnegie Institution of Washington, on January 29, 1902. *Standing, left to right:* Carroll D. Wright, S. Weir Mitchell, S. P. Langley, D. O. Mills, John S. Billings, Abram S. Hewitt, William W. Morrow, Wayne MacVeagh, Charles L. Hutchinson, William N. Frew, Daniel C. Gilman, Henry L. Higginson, Henry Hitchcock, Charles D. Walcott, and William Lindsay. *Seated, left to right:* D. B. Henderson, William P. Frye, Lyman J. Gage, Elihu Root, John Hay, and Andrew Carnegie. (Photo courtesy of Carnegie Institution of Washington)

The Carnegie Institution of Washington was officially incorporated on January 4, 1902, in Washington, DC. Three weeks later, the invited trustees and Carnegie assembled in one of the State Department's diplomatic state rooms, at the behest of Secretary of State John Hay, for their inaugural meeting. The significance of the location was not lost on Gilman, who observed that above the chair of the presiding officer hung the portraits of Daniel Webster and Lord Ashburton, "as if the old country and the new were alike cognizant of the proceeding."[53] The formal articles were read, the temporary officers chosen, and then Carnegie offered brief remarks: "Gentlemen, your work now begins. Your aims are high; you seek to expand known forces—to discover and utilize unknown forces for the benefit of man. Than this, there can scarcely be greater work."[54] Carnegie concluded by quoting the deed of trust, which spelled out the Institution's objectives:

> 1) To promote original research, paying great attention thereto as one of the most important of all departments; 2) To discover the exceptional man in every department of study whenever and wherever found, inside or outside of schools, and enable him to make the work for which he seems specially designed his life work; 3) To increase facilities for higher education; 4) To increase the efficiency of the universities and other institutions of learning throughout the country, by utilizing

and adding to their existing facilities and aiding teachers in the various institutions for experimental and other work, in these institutions as far as advisable; 5) To enable such students as may find Washington the best point for their special studies, to enjoy the advantages of the museums, libraries, laboratories, observatory, meteorological, piscicultural, and forestry schools, and kindred institutions of the several departments of the government; 6) To ensure the prompt publication and distribution of the results of scientific investigation, a field considered highly important.[55]

In recounting the events of the day, the *New York Times* cited portions of the deed and Carnegie's desire not to interfere with existing institutions but "to aid rather than hinder them," with the overarching goal of promoting original research.[56]

Still stirred by the prospect of what had just been launched, Gilman wrote to his family in Connecticut two days later: "As you told me that you were watching the papers, you have doubtless learned all that there is to be told of the plans of the C.I. of Washington—and of my connection with it." Gilman revealed an excitement that belied his age: "This is the best opportunity for usefulness that has ever come to me, and it makes me feel as if I were forty once more. I see so much to do, and I am so happy to be a part in the doing."[57] His abundant enthusiasm would be tempered, however, as the institution took shape. And unlike in his previous experiences as a chief executive, much would happen, in terms of both policy development and organization, without his direct involvement.

The last item of business in the inaugural board meeting was approval of the bylaws. While the members of the executive committee were yet to be named (they would be ratified the next day), their rights, duties, and responsibilities were enumerated: "The Executive Committee shall, when the Board is not in session and has not given specific directions, have charge of all arrangements for administration, research and instruction." The bylaws also explicitly stated that the executive committee "shall make arrangements for the custody of the funds of the Institution; keep an accurate account of all receipts and disbursements, and submit annually to the Trustees a full statement of the finances of the Institution, and a detailed estimate for the expenditures of the year."[58]

Although merely pro forma, the board had to officially ratify Carnegie's selection of the institution's officers as well. While Gilman would be elected chair of the executive committee the next day, as president he was now subordinate to the executive committee. This arrangement—one he had never experienced before—would prove to be a source of perpetual friction in the coming months.[59]

## Divergent Opinions Emerge

The purpose of the Carnegie Institution had been stated in the deed of trust: to help scholars avail themselves of all that Washington, DC, had to offer; to assist universities in becoming more efficient by using existing facilities and adding new ones; and to cooperate with universities in the dissemination of the results of scholars' work. These objectives aligned with both Gilman's and White's visions for the institution and their decades-long advocacy at Hopkins and Cornell. Gilman's successor at Hopkins, Ira Remsen, told Billings that the academic world was made up of men who understood the meaning of research. Remsen believed, therefore, that it made good sense for the new funding entity to support those who had already established reputations and whose projects were in line with the scope of the Carnegie Institution.[60]

Although he harbored a deep-seated antipathy toward the traditional university and its curricula, Carnegie had populated his inaugural board with "college men": Abram Hewitt, in addition to his service in elected office, known for contributions to the founding of the Cooper Union and his work with both Columbia University and Barnard College; Seth Low, president of Columbia; Carroll Wright, US commissioner of labor and future president of Clark University; and William Frew, future president of Carnegie Tech in Pittsburgh.[61] Even so, "there was an aloofness from, or a coolness to, the university world on the part of Carnegie and the trustees," according to the historian Nathan Reingold. The institution's leadership (particularly Billings as vice chair of the board and Walcott as secretary) was determined that the new entity should separate teaching from research. Their governing model was neither the German university nor any other form of university but rather the Royal Institution of Great Britain. Known as the home of such laudable scientists as the chemist Humphry Davy and the physicist and chemist Michael Faraday, the Royal Institution was founded in 1799 and granted its royal charter a year later. Institutions such as the Royal Institution informed Billings' opinion that America needed laboratories analogous to those found in England, where "they do no teaching," as he would state in a February 1902 memorandum.[62] Billings and Walcott believed that the principal purpose of supporting original research could best be accomplished by full-time scientists unencumbered by teaching.[63]

The trustees held their first meeting on January 29 in Washington, DC. The next day, they reconvened for a mere ninety minutes—long enough to hear from President Gilman and attend to some organizational matters. Speaking extemporaneously, Gilman summarized the areas into which the new institution could move: first, the encouragement of investigation in cooperation with existing institutions; second, the encouragement of unusual talent (e.g., the discovery of "the exceptional man," as outlined in point 2 of the deed of trust); and third, the publication of papers and books that might be passed over by the traditional presses and publishing houses because of their esoteric nature. Given the potential pitfalls in codifying the institution's course, Gilman advised moving slowly: "I do not think we can do much to start the work during the next six months, and before the annual meeting occurs next fall."[64] This lack of urgency proved to be a serious misstep. In the face of Gilman's deliberative pace, Billings and Walcott seized the opportunity to shape both the governance structure and policy.[65]

At the conclusion of Gilman's remarks, the trustees selected seven of their membership to function as an executive committee: Elihu Root, Abram Hewitt (80 years old at the time of the institution's founding, he would pass away a year later), Carroll D. Wright, John Billings, S. Weir Mitchell, Charles Walcott, and Gilman as chair. The minutes state that the Committee on Plan and Scope reported that it had held a "hasty meeting" just before the full board meeting and proposed a few changes to the bylaws approved the day prior. All the changes pertained to the responsibilities and rights of the executive committee, including the selection of an appropriate site for an administrative building and reporting to the full board both its plan "upon the work which should be undertaken" and the "estimates for expenditures required."[66]

The full board of trustees was not scheduled to meet again until November 25, 1902. In the interim, the executive committee convened eight times and made decisions that had long-term consequences for the institution. Gilman spent the better part of the spring and the entire summer in Europe, missing some of the committee's most important discussions. In organizing the Johns Hopkins University, Gilman had struck out boldly and sought counsel from established authorities in America and abroad, but in the end he had made up his own mind. He did not follow the same pattern in organizing the Carnegie Institution of Washington.[67]

In *The Launching of a University*, Gilman makes opaque references to what happened during his initial tenure at the institution, asserting, again, that careful deliberation was needed: "The opportunity is one that requires the most careful consideration, for everyone knows that institutions which are plastic in their incipiency soon harden like cement."[68] Perhaps his lack of initiative was owing to fatigue or age. What is known is that the self-trained paleontologist Walcott (aged 52 and one of the youngest trustees) and the ever-persistent Billings (he would miss only one full board meeting and only thirteen of the ninety-nine executive committee meetings during his tenure) did not squander the chance to exert their influence.[69] Carnegie was explicit in his overarching objective of promoting research; the specifics, however, were murky. Not dissimilar to Johns Hopkins' instructions to his original university trustees, the formal founding papers for the institution were both sweeping in their scope and obscure in their particulars.[70] The lack of specificity permitted Billings and Walcott to effect their considerable control.

Between the inaugural board meeting and Gilman's departure for Europe in April, the pace of activity at the institution was dizzying. Nearly a thousand circular letters—addressed to the "Heads of American Institutions and to Others Interested in the Work of Investigation"—had been sent out to scholars across America requesting suggestions, opinions, and advice as to what fields the institution should occupy and the best methods of carrying out its work. Eighteen advisory committees were appointed, each made up of prominent scholars.[71] On the recommendation of these subcommittees, research was initiated in seventy-two different fields of inquiry.[72]

After the inaugural board meeting in January, Gilman visited Harvard, Yale, and MIT to confer with colleagues and solicit input.[73] Billings and Gilman were both busy, but Walcott was perhaps most inundated with work. In addition to populating the committees, responding to the deluge of inquiries, and considering possible sites for the institution's headquarters, he put together a statement of "purposes, principles, organization and policy" on behalf of the executive committee.[74] This statement, revised by Walcott at the behest of Billings and fellow committee member S. Weir Mitchell, eliminated all mention of "advanced instruction" and would serve as one of the most important statements of policy in the early years of the Carnegie Institution.[75]

Gilman met with Carnegie in early April to apprise him of recent developments and then left shortly thereafter for Europe. He planned to meet with the foremost scientists across the Continent and familiarize himself with practices applicable to the institution. After thirty years as a university president, Gilman was accustomed to having the latitude to coordinate all the various activities and areas of focus. But given his absence from the day-to-day activities of the institution (from mid-April to the end of August) and the frenetic pace of Billings and Walcott, the best he could do was bring back "abundant material for consideration in the autumn." In a note to Walcott from Europe, Gilman added that he was growing "impatient for the period of reflection and formulation."[76]

Gilman made one last stop to visit Carnegie at his castle in Scotland before setting sail for the United States aboard the White Star Line's *Majestic* on September 17, 1902.[77] No record exists of what the two men discussed at Skibo. Carnegie wrote Gilman shortly afterward, reporting on Andrew White's reception of an honorary doctorate from the University of St. Andrews and expressing his disappointment at not being able to make the November meeting: "Pray explain my absence to your distinguished colleagues. I hope they can all attend."[78]

The executive committee met in October with Gilman in attendance, just a few weeks before the full board was slated to gather in Washington. As the second meeting drew closer, it was clear that the trustees' agenda and the report of the executive committee were the work of Billings and Walcott. Gilman had planned to present his own report to the trustees with an appendix titled "Suggestions in Respect to the Methods by which the Founder's Requirements may be carried out." However, when Gilman sent a draft copy of his report to Walcott, the board secretary advised him to eliminate the appendix, as "every point has been covered in the Report of the Executive Committee, of which you are a member."[79]

Always inclined to avoid controversy, Gilman decided not to present a separate appendix. In the minutes of the meeting, Gilman's written submission is very brief, with two direct references to the institution's duty to "carry out the Founder's instructions" and his observation that "the methods of administration of the Carnegie Institution thus far developed are general rather than specific."[80] Gilman did, however, advocate for an annual allocation of ten thousand dollars to bring students to Washington for research, and this amount was included in the executive committee's report.[81]

## Gilman Resigns as President

Gilman's feelings about his work at the Carnegie Institution during the ensuing months are difficult to determine, as his correspondence with Billings and Walcott during this period is sparse. His primary account, *The Launching of a University*, provides little insight, and journal entries are terse. In recording the events leading up to his resignation, Gilman simply wrote: "Before doing this, I informed Mr. Carnegie."[82]

Gilman would later gather together notes and letters from the period, writing on the cover page: "Papers pertaining to my resignation & to the amended by laws, etc. If the laws had been adopted in their present form, it is not likely that I would have resigned."[83] Would matters have gone differently if Andrew White had been in closer proximity during this period and not stationed in Berlin? White did not attend any of the meetings during Gilman's tenure as president of the Carnegie Institution.[84] His first in-person meeting was the meeting at which the trustees received Gilman's resignation.[85]

This was, arguably, one of the most interesting periods of Gilman's career. In typical fashion, Gilman was demure in describing his two-year tenure and commended the institution's trustees for "seeking, before the full initiation of the work intrusted [*sic*] to them, to secure the light that many men of many minds will throw upon the problem. They will endeavor to follow the wise example of the founder, and seek only to promote the progress of knowledge and the good of the mind."[86] What is abundantly clear, however, is that Gilman was not happy with the relationship between the president and the executive committee. Seeing no way to either alter the codified governance structure or define his role as president more clearly, Gilman, aged 73, decided to step down.

At the December 8, 1903, meeting of the board, Gilman informed the trustees of his intention to leave the presidency the following year, "and this early notice is given in order that the Trustees may be prepared to take such action as may seem to them wise." At the end of his resignation letter Gilman stated forthrightly that "as the title of the chief executive may perhaps be changed, I will add that I am not a candidate for reappointment under any other designation."[87] Gilman was not being obtuse, as others had serious misgivings about the governance structure. Henry Higginson, the chair of the committee charged with finding Gilman's replacement, wrote to Henry Pritchett, then president of MIT, to gauge his interest in the position. One of the first iterations of the revisions to the governance structure included a provision that classified the institution's top position as director instead of president. Upon learning of this arrangement, Pritchett responded to Higginson, "I look upon the Carnegie Institution as the most interesting effort the world has known for the development of a national interest in research. . . . I have therefore all the more regret in saying that the administrative plan you outline is one under which I do not think I would be useful."[88]

Recognizing the shortfalls of the evolving governance structure, Gilman secured a change to the bylaws that placed the direction of the institution squarely in the hands of the president, subject to confirmation by the trustees. Specific language in article 4 of the bylaws (approved at Gilman's final meeting, in December 1904) stipulated, among many other things, that all proposals and requests for grants be referred to the president, that he was "to devote his entire time to the affairs of the Institution," and that he was to serve as an ex-officio member of the executive committee.[89] Most important in these revisions was to make explicit at least some of the responsibilities of the chief executive officer and to clarify the relationship between the president and the executive committee.[90]

Gilman remained a trustee and a member of the executive committee for the rest of his life. His successor as president, Robert Simpson Woodward, came to the Carnegie Institution from Columbia University, where he had been dean of pure science, and according to one account, he "achieved the strong executive leadership Gilman sought but could not obtain."[91] His first report to the full board as president runs eighteen pages and underscores the preeminent role of the president in the day-to-day leadership of the institution.[92]

The prolific historian Charles Andrews remembered Gilman as "no lover of controversy. He saw in it only a grievous intellectual waste. His kindly and sympathetic nature was opposed to warfare of any kind and his faith in the value of cooperation led him to regret the expenditure of time and energy in acrimonious debate."[93] Upon learning of the president's resignation, Carnegie wrote Gilman the following:

> It was a surprise to me that you felt it necessary to give up your labors. Two things I cannot deny. It is your duty to harbor your strength, and, second, that you will retire knowing that you have given the Institution a splendid start. You promised to remain Trustee—for so much, thanks.
>
> All great men have their special feature. If I were asked what yours was, I should say, that which draws all men after him, pleasing everybody and offending nobody, doing the absolutely necessary ungentle things in a gentle way. You illustrate the supreme force of gentleness, and among all that have benefitted thereby, none more than your humble servant, with whom you have been uniformly gentle, even in your admonitions.
>
> *I like you.*[94]

## The Final Years

Since his appointment as president of the University of California in 1872 Gilman had shouldered the responsibilities of chief executive for more than thirty years, from Berkeley to Baltimore and finally Washington, DC. He was now ready to focus on writing, continuing his other board service, traveling, and spending more time with his family at Over Edge in Maine. From the time he returned to the East Coast in 1875 until 1908, Gilman spent seven summers in Europe, one in Alaska and California, and a long winter holiday (1889–90) in the Mediterranean. But his preferred place of respite was in Maine.

Daniel Coit Gilman and daughter Elisabeth playing chess at Over Edge, Maine, 1900. (Photo courtesy of University Archives, Sheridan Libraries, Johns Hopkins University)

Gilman and his wife had been invited to Northeast Harbor in 1885 as guests of Charles and Grace Eliot. The Gilmans were struck by the beauty of the place and the pleasantness of the neighbors, so much so that Eliot began looking for suitable plots of land on which Gilman could build his own cottage. A few weeks after their departure, Eliot wrote Gilman of his scouting: "If Sutton's Island would suit you, an estate of 40 acres can be had there for a moderate sum—say $3,000. I have just been bargaining on behalf of a friend for a small lot there."[95] After a few seasons in a Northeast Harbor hotel, the Gilmans determined to buy a parcel and construct their own place.

It was at Over Edge (appropriately named for its location on a rocky cliff overlooking the harbor) that Gilman spent the majority of the summer months, attending to his correspondence and completing his various writing projects. In 1898 he wrote the introduction to a new edition of Alexis de Tocqueville's *Democracy in America* and compiled a series of essays and speeches titled *University Problems in the United States*.[96] The next year, Gilman completed the biography of his friend and mentor James Dwight Dana. Gilman's final work was a series of original essays on the formative years of the Johns Hopkins University that appeared in *Scribner's Magazine* and were later included in his 1906 book, *The Launching of a University*. When not at Over Edge with his family, Gilman commuted from his Baltimore home on Park Avenue to Washington, DC, for Carnegie Institution board meetings and to New York for Peabody and Slater Fund meetings.

Gilman was a man of faith, and his speeches and communications are replete with expressions of his beliefs and references to scripture. He would continue his association with the American Bible Society, of which he was elected president in 1903. Edward Whiting Gilman, Gilman's older brother, was an ordained Congregational minister and had been employed by the society as a corresponding secretary in 1871, serving in that capacity until his death in 1900.[97] On the occasion of the British and Foreign Bible Society centennial, the younger Gilman wrote that "the Bible by its influence on character, public as well as private, claims a leading place not only in religious and intellectual life, but in political history."[98] His frequent use of biblical phrases throughout his life reveals a more than superficial familiarity with the Bible.

Gilman's speech at the opening of the Hopkins Hospital in 1889 could have been delivered over the pulpit at any Baltimore place of worship. Gilman closed that day by invoking the words of the apostle Paul in 1 Corinthians in speaking about his adopted city: "Upon one hill of Baltimore rises a temple, 'whose guardian crest, the silent cross' is an emblem of the Christian faith [Holy Cross Church on Federal Hill]; upon another, a lofty column reminds us of the patriots' hope [George Washington Monument in Mount Vernon Place]; upon a third, the Hôtel-Dieu is placed—the house of charity [Hopkins Hospital atop the then named Loudenslager's Hill]. Significant triad! 'Here abideth Faith, Hope and Charity, but the greatest of these is Charity.' "[99]

Further, Gilman's life demonstrated a commitment to a theology that could be applied to urban industrial society, while revealing, perhaps, that the New England religion of his youth was ill equipped to address America's postbellum challenges. Thus, Gilman saw his work within higher education—in addition to all his volunteer activities—as an application of "true" religion as described in the Epistle of St. James: "Pure and undefiled Religion is to visit the fatherless and widows in their affliction and to keep himself unspotted from the world."[100]

The apple did not fall far from the tree in the case of Gilman's younger daughter, Elisabeth. According to her biographer, Ross Jones, the papers of both Gilman and his daughter reveal a persistent effort by Gilman "to share his liberal social campus, his energy, and his commitment to social services" more with Elisabeth than with his other daughter, Alice.[101] As the avowed socialist and perennial candidate for various political offices approached her seventy-fourth birthday in 1941, she got together with friends in Baltimore who recalled her decades of commitment to worthy causes and service to society's most vulnerable citizens. "I have never met anybody with a more direct institutional faculty for discovering a need," stated Elisabeth's Episcopal clergyman, Reverend Arthur B. Kinsolving, of Old St. Paul's Church. "She inherited her genius in this respect from her father. The daughter is equal to the father. She is one of the truest Christians I have known in a ministry of nearly sixty years."[102] The Johns Hopkins economics professor Sidney Hollander called her "one of America's grandest institutions. She stirred Baltimore as Einstein stirred the universe."[103] Hailed as one of the truly great social activists of her generation, Elisabeth would play a key role in collecting and maintaining her father's voluminous papers and worked for years to ensure his educational legacy.

After resigning from the Carnegie Institution presidency in 1904 and freed from day-to-day management responsibilities, Gilman stayed busy. His prodigious letter writing did not let up, and he continued to keep a daily record in his appointment book. On the first page of his 1907 booklet, Gilman recorded this quote from Horace Walpole, the fourth Earl of Oxford: "I now fancy that Old Age was invented by the Lazy."[104] Gilman was never idle, and his schedule is replete with trips all along the East Coast for various appointments, speaking engagements, and board meetings.

## One Last Trip to Europe

Well into his late seventies, Gilman's love of travel remained undiminished. Some retired executives golf, others learn to paint, some buy up acreage and work the land—but Gilman traveled. Throughout his life he found rest and rejuvenation in extended travel. After Gilman's tenure as director of the Hopkins Hospital in 1889, he had requested a long sabbatical, from October 16, 1889, to July 7, 1890. During his time away from campus, Ira Remsen served as acting president. The family traveled to Europe, and Gilman kept an entire journal of their extensive travels, including a cruise up the Nile River and Easter Sunday in Jerusalem.[105] On their way home through Europe, the Gilmans were hosted in Oxford by Professor James Sylvester, who was keen on showing his friend and family "a real poet's May," when the English gardens were "looking their loveliest."[106] Gilman, Lilly, Alice, and Elisabeth would cross the Atlantic again in 1900 and 1902; the latter trip marked the last transatlantic journey for the entire family.

Daniel and Lilly, however, would enjoy another extended European vacation from the end of March until early October 1908, this time joined by Daniel's younger brother, William.[107] Before their trip, Gilman's journal entries were scant, with the first three weeks of 1908 including simple entries relative to his own health or the situation of others: "cold persists; indoors!" (January 14), "ear troublesome" (January 19), "death of MK Jessup" (January 22). The first bit of good news for 1908 was recorded on Valentine's Day with this modest entry: "Elected member of Academy of Arts and Letters."[108]

While Gilman remained active throughout his life and was in relatively good health, he had complained to his physician in 1907 of feeling weaker and tiring much more easily. The diagnosis was heart disease. His doctor thought that an extended trip overseas would allow him to relax and recuperate from the burden of his incessant writing and board service. The Gilmans set sail for Europe in late March and spent several weeks in Italy. From Villa d'Este at Lake Como, Gilman recorded on June 19 that he had cabled his friend and fellow Yale alumnus William Howard Taft "rejoicings" on news of his presidential nomination at the Republican National Convention in Chicago. A few weeks later, on his birthday, Gilman simply recorded, "Seventy Seven! Laus Deo [praise God]."[109] The entirety of the trip was spent in Italy and Switzerland.

Feeling rested and ready to get back to his various projects and volunteer service,

Lilly Woolsey Gilman and Elisabeth Gilman, 1909. (Photo courtesy of University Archives, Sheridan Libraries, Johns Hopkins University)

Gilman set sail for New York in late September with his wife and brother, arriving home on October 7. A dutiful journal writer throughout his life, Gilman's very last entry was the next day: "Annual Meeting of Trustees of Peabody Ed. Fund at the Waldorf Astoria." Upon concluding his business in New York, Gilman took the train to visit family in Norwich, never imagining that it would be his final journey to the place of his birth.

Sixty years earlier, Gilman had left this same small town first for New York, then for Yale, then for Europe. He would lead new universities in Berkeley and Baltimore, return to Europe numerous times, and spend summers along the coast of Maine. Now, at the end of yet another Atlantic crossing, he had returned to Norwich. It was there—on October 13, 1908, shortly after dinner, and back among the siblings who loved him fiercely and the townspeople who admired him greatly—that he peacefully passed away while preparing to take an evening drive through town. Ninety-nine days after celebrating his seventy-seventh birthday in Europe, Gilman was gone.

Daniel Coit Gilman was buried in the the Yantic Cemetery, just over a half mile from the place of his birth. Less than two years later, his wife of more than thirty years and closest confidante, Elizabeth Dwight Woolsey, passed away. She is buried next to her husband in Norwich.

### "An Almost Irreparable Loss"

The business of the Peabody Education Fund was the last board duty Gilman attended to in life, and now the service he rendered to so many organizations over the span of his career would be recalled by countless others. In learning the news of Gilman's passing, the Peabody Education Fund recorded, "In the death of Dr. Gilman the Board has met with an almost irreparable loss. . . . There were few men in the country who had the knowledge and experience that Dr. Gilman enjoyed in all matters relating to education. . . . They part with him with extreme regret, and will cherish the memory of his services in this Board as among the most important in its history."[110]

Gilman had lived in Baltimore since the age of 44. He had dedicated the best years of his personal and professional life to building the Johns Hopkins University and improving the surrounding community. Just days after his death, the Peabody Institute of Baltimore convened a special meeting to approve a resolution honoring Gilman:

> Wisely chosen and called, he came to Baltimore in 1875. It was a period of transition in Maryland, where, as a consequence of the great upheavals resulting from the Civil War "old things had passed away." The time was propitious for the beginning of a new order and, seeing a unique opportunity, for his constructive genius to build upon the broad foundation which Mr. Johns Hopkins had laid, Mr. Gilman promptly availed himself of it. Now, after the lapse of little more than thirty years, a university is his monument and every institution of learning honors his name.[111]

The successful trajectories of Gilman's own career and the university he led for twenty-five years ran parallel. As a consequence, he was regularly sought out for his wisdom and expertise on a host of higher education issues. As the reputation of the Johns Hopkins University continued its rise, others requested the institution's founding documents to serve as a road map. One example demonstrates the university's international reach less than a decade into its formal existence.

The peripatetic Thomas Davidson, a Scottish philosopher and lecturer who was once considered for a teaching post in Latin at Hopkins, wrote Gilman from Rome in 1884 on behalf of an Italian colleague. Professor Sebastiano Turbiglio, a philosopher

and university reformer, had asked which American universities were the most successful, and Davidson had named three, with Hopkins at the head of the queue. Turbiglio
requested a copy of the "statutes" of the university's establishment, and of course
Gilman obliged. In turn, Davidson responded that the founding documents had been
"delivered to Prof. Turbiglio, who derived much information and instruction from
them, and who desires me to return you his best thanks."[112]

Throughout a lifetime of service to education, Gilman was truly liberal in what he
shared and with whom. His catholicity in sharing his views with all those who asked
on countless subjects knew no bounds. In today's vernacular, Gilman stayed in his
lane; he did not waste time on things beyond his control, and he refused to fret over
recruiting competitions or engage in inter-institutional squabbles. He reported to the
trustees on the sixteenth anniversary of the university's founding:

> There should be no "rivalry" among those who are endeavoring to advance knowl-
> edge, promote good government, and provide for the education of youth. All wisely
> managed institutions should be allies, not rivals. But there may be emulation. The
> sacrifices that are made and the gifts that are bestowed elsewhere should excite our
> zeal, and lead us all,—the trustees, the professors, the benefactors, the neighbors,
> and the friends of this university, to endeavor, with more earnestness than ever, to
> build up in Baltimore a home for science, literature, philosophy, and all the liberal
> arts.[113]

These were not just platitudes. Gilman believed what he said, and he repeatedly
showed it. The generosity Gilman demonstrated was valued, and these institutions
reciprocated by conferring honorary degrees upon Gilman during his tenure at Hopkins and after: Harvard University (1876), St. John's College, Maryland (1876), Columbia University (1887), Yale University (1889), the University of North Carolina
(1889), Princeton University (1896), the University of Toronto (1903), the University
of Wisconsin (1904), Clark University (1905), and the College of William and Mary
(1905).[114]

Columbia's Nicholas Murray Butler best expressed the dismay over the loss of so
eminent a friend, colleague, and visionary. Butler noted how an "obscure Baltimore
merchant" who had left his fortune to found a university and hospital was now known
the world over thanks to Daniel Coit Gilman, "by the men whom he invited to his
side, by the forces which they together set in motion, and by the scientific and literary
achievements of themselves and their students."[115]

# Conclusion

Gilman lived in an age in which the pace was slower—even as the Industrial Revolution made its relentless advance—and letters, notes, and other communications were often a person's most treasured possessions. To read the correspondence between Gilman and the thousands of people to whom he sent and from whom he received letters is to be transported back to a time when letters were composed with a dip pen, copies were carefully preserved in letterpress books, and memory boxes were filled with letters on personalized stationery with intricately designed monograms and elaborate salutations. Gilman and his contemporaries would often devote entire days to thoughtful correspondence with meticulous penmanship.

So the gift he received at the celebration of his retirement from the Johns Hopkins University was both fitting and priceless. Hundreds of guests attended this three-day event in February 1902, which marked the official torch passing to the new president, Ira Remsen, as well as the ceremonial send-off for Gilman after a quarter century of service. There were all the commemorative speeches one might expect. On the afternoon of the first day alone, speakers included Principal William Peterson of McGill University, President Arthur Hadley of Yale, President Charles Dabney of the University of Tennessee, and President William Rainey Harper of the University of Chicago. Harper, who would die in office four years later at age 49, extolled Gilman with these words:

During this first period the Johns Hopkins University has been the most conspicuous figure in the American university world, and to its achievements we are largely
indebted for the fact that we may now enter upon a higher mission. I desire to
present upon this occasion the greetings and the congratulations of the scores of
institutions in the West and Far West which have been strengthened by the presence
of their faculties of Johns Hopkins men, and have been encouraged and stimulated
to higher work by the influence of Johns Hopkins Ideals.[1]

Serving as US ambassador to Germany, Gilman's best friend, Andrew White, was
unable to attend the ceremonies but referred to his colleague's work as "peculiarly
original and valuable. He rendered a great service by it to every other institution of
advanced learning throughout the whole country."[2]

At the conclusion of Gilman's farewell address, Woodrow Wilson—whom the
Hopkins alumni had selected to speak at the Friday assembly and whom the Princeton trustees would promote to the university presidency in June 1902—directed his
remarks to the retiring president: "And in token of our confidence in the validity and
permanence of the ideals which you have set before us and in grateful acknowledgment of all that you have done for us and for the world, we have hereunto subscribed
our names." Wilson then presented Gilman with a magnificent leatherbound, gold-
leafed book. Hopkins graduates from 1878 to 1902—1,012 men in total—had signed
their names on individual cards that included their degree and year of completion, as
well as the institution where they were employed.[3] To review these names is to see how
Hopkins graduates populated the ranks of higher education at the beginning of the
twentieth century more quickly and more forcefully than did the graduates of America's other distinguished institutions, all of which had a head start by decades, if not
centuries, on the country's first modern research university.

"Hopkins men" filled the rosters of the most reputable departments on the nation's
most celebrated campuses: Cornell, Yale, Harvard, Clark, Columbia, City University
of New York, the University of Texas, the State University of Iowa, the University of
Nebraska, Worcester Polytechnic Institute, the University of Michigan, Northwestern, Cornell, Princeton, the University of California, Tulane, Brown, and Rutgers,
to name just a few. Their impact extended beyond higher education, with graduates
including the editors of the *Baltimore American* and the *Baltimore News*; the rector of
Christ Church, Norfolk; the assistant secretary and librarian of the Maryland Historical Society; and a geologist at the United States Geological Survey.

Upon seeing all these names in the book of alumni—the thousand-plus Hopkins
men—and experiencing a flood of emotions, Gilman rose to accept the gift from
alumni who had known only one president during their time as students and offered
these words:

The deepest streams are those most silent. I do not know what to say in return for
this magnificent evidence of your affection. Least of all do I know what to say in

return for these kind words, except that I could not receive them were I not sure that they belong as well to those gentlemen on the left [the Hopkins faculty were all seated on the left side of the stage] with whom I have been associated. It is their work, let me tell you, and not mine; it is their work which has made possible the occasion which we are celebrating, and which has been the occasion of your getting this beautiful volume,—those that are here and those that are gone. I wish I had a thousand hands, and I wish I could shake hands with every one who is here, and with all those whom you represent. Go on, my brothers; bear the banner wherever you go, the banner of our University. God's blessing be with you.[4]

In hiring the faculty, establishing the university's curriculum, and holding the institution to a standard previously considered impossible to maintain, Gilman was not seeking out, as the inimitable H. L. Mencken described, "students eager only to grab their degrees and escape into the bond business." Rather, Hopkins attracted a different kind of learner and opened its doors to those "who desired to devote their whole lives to augmenting the sum of human knowledge."[5] The influence of Johns Hopkins on American higher education was completely out of proportion to its size, wealth, or age. Gilman had placed the institution in a position to extend its influence for decades to come. One example illustrates this point: a quarter century after Gilman's departure, the famed psychologist J. McKeen Cattell found that of 1,000 distinguished American scientists, 243 were Hopkins graduates.[6]

In his 1876 inaugural address, Gilman had spoken of launching "our bark upon the Patapsco." As a geographer and orator, Gilman often used the topography of a place to illustrate a point, and Baltimore is a port city. Likewise, a biblical phrase Gilman liked to use from time to time came from Ecclesiastes: "Cast thy bread upon the waters: for thou shalt find it after many days." The faith it took for Gilman to launch his metaphorical boat and cast his bread upon the waters in and around Baltimore had led to an educational transformation. It was an experiment whose success no one could guarantee; but succeed it did, and today's world stands as the beneficiary.

Every member of our society is advantaged when the maximum number of citizens obtain as much education as possible, rendering even truer the axiom that higher education in America must be viewed as a public good rather than a private benefit. Likewise, it can be argued that an institution like the Johns Hopkins University—with all the collateral advances accruing to the world from its discoveries, research, and innovations—should be applauded when it chooses to focus its resources on the intellectual pursuits of its faculty, staff, and students. The university Gilman helped to establish was committed, as he explicitly stated, to the "acquisition, conservation, refinement, and distribution of knowledge."[7]

Gilman might be lesser known than others of his generation, as his own work earned him little fame or lasting notoriety. He was not distinguished for his original research nor for any singular contributions to his discipline. Rather, the beneficiaries of his indefatigable efforts were men and institutions whose work and contributions

Gilman Hall on the Homewood Campus, 1920. (Photo courtesy of University Archives, Sheridan Libraries, Johns Hopkins University)

he facilitated, supported, and promulgated. A former student of Gilman's at Hopkins, Abraham Flexner, called him "the most effective educational advocate our country has produced."[8]

Today's modern research university is a multibillion-dollar enterprise, impacting each of us in ways that would have been impossible for Gilman and his colleagues in the late nineteenth century to envision. And many of the elements that make up these complicated institutions—graduate fellowships, the emphasis on primary investigations and discovery, the funding of the best laboratory and research spaces, scholarly journals, university presses, the sprawling health sciences complexes with teaching hospitals—were put in place by a Yale-trained geographer, immediately recognizable by his muttonchop beard.

Daniel Coit Gilman was known for many things during his remarkable life. But his enduring legacy will always be that of father of the modern research university, a uniquely American invention that remains the envy of the world.

NOTES

## Preface

1. Johns Hopkins' paternal great-grandmother was Margaret Johns, daughter of Richard Johns of Calvert County, Maryland. In 1700 Margaret Johns married Gerard (sometimes spelled "Gerrard") Hopkins, a "man of some note" and a member of the committee assigned to welcome Charles Calvert, the fifth baron of Baltimore, to Maryland in 1732. Gerard Hopkins and Margaret Johns had ten children, the youngest of whom they named Johns. The second Johns Hopkins, grandson of the first, was born in 1795 to Samuel and Hannah Janney Hopkins on his family's tobacco plantation in southern Maryland. Thom, *Johns Hopkins: A Silhouette*, 3; see also Stimpert, "Johns Hopkins University," 125. The *s* at the end of *Johns* has often been left off. On one occasion, former Hopkins president Milton Eisenhower, invited to address a convention of ophthalmologists in Pittsburgh, was introduced by the chair of the event as the president of "John" Hopkins University. As he began his remarks, Eisenhower acknowledged how delighted he was to be in "Pittburgh." Vozella, "Cheesecake on the tart side."

2. Fabian Franklin, a student of the famed English mathematician James Joseph Sylvester, earned his PhD in mathematics at Hopkins in 1880 but left the field in 1895 to pursue writing and journalism. Utilizing a trove of primary source materials, he published *The Life of Daniel Coit Gilman* in 1910, two years after Gilman's death. Abraham Flexner, who graduated from Hopkins with a bachelor's degree in classics at age 19 but was best known for his 1910 work, *Medical Education in the United States and Canada*, authored *Daniel Coit Gilman: Creator of the American Type of University* in 1946. Flexner had been approached by Gilman's younger daughter, Elisabeth, in 1935 to write a proper biography of her father, but at the time he was in the midst of authoring a university-initiated volume on Dr. William Welch. Flexner's work on Gilman was finally released in 1946. Fourteen years later, Professor Hugh Hawkins wrote *Pioneer: A History of the Johns Hopkins University, 1874–1889*, which is considered the definitive work on the early years of the Johns Hopkins University. Hawkins' beginning chapters focus on the recruitment of Gilman as president and his building of the faculty and are exceptionally well done. And finally, Francesco Cordasco followed Flexner and Hawkins with a short work called *The Shaping of American Graduate Education: Daniel Coit Gilman and the Protean Ph.D.*, published in 1973.

In crafting his monumental work on the early years of Hopkins, Hawkins noted that Franklin's 1910 book includes "long quotations from letters and other documents, some of which are now lost." Franklin also included sections written by others: the first chapter, about Gilman's boyhood and youth, was written by Daniel's younger brother, William; the second, detailing his work at Yale as a librarian and professor, was written by Emily H. Whitney and Margaret Whitney, daughters of the late Yale professor and celebrated philologist William Dwight Whitney; the third was contributed by William Carey Jones, a law professor at the University of California. The remaining five chapters were written by Franklin. Writing in 1960, Hawkins made this observation about Franklin's work: "The fact that each section is written by someone near Gilman during the period covered gives this book considerable value as a primary source; at the same time, however, it prevents the unity and critical approach which a new Gilman biography could provide." Hawkins, *Pioneer*, 341.

3. John K. Wright, "Daniel Coit Gilman"; see also Arthur P. Young, "Gilman in the Formative Period."

4. The reference to the "new" education, as opposed to the more classical curriculum, comes from an article in which Gilman discussed European universities' emphasis on "original inquires and investigations." See Gilman, "Scientific Schools in Europe," 328. Further, Hugh Hawkins details the Hopkins trustees' 1874 discussion with President Charles Eliot about his connection to the "new education" at Harvard, which entailed the introduction of science and modern languages as equals to the classics, as well as an elective system. Hawkins, *Pioneer*, 7–8.

5. Woodrow Wilson, quoted in Flexner, *Daniel Coit Gilman*, 105–6, my emphasis.

6. World University Rankings.

7. Cole, *Great American University*, 4.

8. Current Hopkins faculty who are Nobel laureates are the molecular biologists Peter Agre and Carol Greider, the geneticist Gregg Semenza, and the astrophysicist Adam Riess. Other Hopkins laureates include recipients in medicine, physics, chemistry, economics, and physiology, and two Nobel Peace Prize awardees, Woodrow Wilson in 1919 and Jody Williams in 1997. See Johns Hopkins University, "Nobel Prize Winners."

9. National Science Foundation, "Rankings by total R&D expenditures."

10. National Science Foundation, "Higher Education Research and Development Survey, Fiscal Year 2018."

11. Gilman, *University Problems in the United States*, 4.

12. Geiger, *American College in the Nineteenth Century*, 27.

13. Leslie, "Dreaming Spires in New Jersey," 116.

14. Hawkins, *Pioneer*, 32–33.

15. See Hawkins, "University Identity."

16. Pierson, "American Universities in the Nineteenth Century," 89–90.

17. *Addresses at the Inauguration of Daniel C. Gilman*, 37.

18. Daniel Coit Gilman (hereinafter DCG), quoted in Hawes, *To Advance Knowledge*, 2; see also Clement, "Library and University Press Integration."

19. Geiger, *To Advance Knowledge*, 8. The original six departments were the Departments of Ancient Languages (Greek, Latin, comparative philology); Modern Languages (English, French, German, Spanish, Italian); Mathematics (pure and applied); Physical Sciences (chemistry and physics); Natural Sciences (geology, mineralogy, zoology, botany); and Moral and Historical Sciences (ethics, political economy, history, international and public law). See Johns Hopkins University, *Second Annual Report*, 27; see also French, *History of the University*, 50–56.

20. Rudolph, *American College and University*, 271.

21. Geiger, *History of American Higher Education*, 324.

22. Slosson, *Great American Universities*, 373.

23. Huxley, "University Education," 8. Huxley's other speeches included one to the American Association for the Advancement of Science in Buffalo, New York; one at the University of Tennessee in Knoxville; and a series of three lectures at Chickering Hall in New York. All Huxley's speeches are archived in the Thomas H. Huxley file, Daniel Coit Gilman Papers, MS 1,

series 1, box 24, folder 22, Johns Hopkins University Special Collections, https://jscholarship
.library.jhu.edu/handle/1774.2/42387 (hereinafter Gilman Papers, JHU).

24. Veysey, *Emergence of the American University*, 164.

25. Cordasco, *Shaping of American Graduate Education*, 111–12; see also Johns Hopkins University, *Twenty-Sixth Annual Report*, 6–7.

26. Gilman, "The Johns Hopkins University," 464.

27. Greene, "The Johns Hopkins University," 68.

28. Cordasco, *Shaping of American Graduate Education*, 131.

29. *Johns Hopkins University Celebration of the Twenty-Fifth Anniversary*, 105–6.

30. Cole, *Great American University*, 20–21.

31. Greene, "The Johns Hopkins University," 68.

32. Barry, *Great Influenza*, 58.

33. Veysey, *Emergence of the American University*, 163–64.

34. Jameson diary, quoted in Hawkins, *Pioneer*, 102.

35. Gilman, "Inaugural Address," 30.

36. Minor, "Gilman's Legacy."

37. Shils, "Order of Learning in the United States," 28. Roger Geiger summarized Shils' description of the Hopkins founding as extravagant but not unreasonable. See Geiger, *To Advance Knowledge*, 7.

38. Gilman, "Inaugural Address," 63.

### Introduction

1. Boorstin, *Americans*, 171. Half the size of New York City by 1820, Baltimore had grown into America's third-largest city, with a population of more than 62,000.

2. Thom, *Johns Hopkins: A Silhouette*, 14. No full-dress biography of Johns Hopkins has ever been undertaken; one reason might be that there are no personal papers in existence. As a consequence, Helen Hopkins Thom, who was not a historian but Hopkins' grandniece, compiled a book (first published by the Hopkins Press in 1929) filled with anecdotes and oral family history. For decades, this book has served as the primary source of information on Johns Hopkins' early years.

3. Very few letters penned by Johns Hopkins have been found. This one, dated 25 April 1840, was addressed to his mother, Hannah, and is part of the Alan Mason Chesney Medical Archives at the Johns Hopkins University. Among many other things in the letter, Johns confessed to this mother that he had "led a life of great devotion to worldly pursuits but in the death of my friend and brother Mahlon, a total change has been brought about in my feelings." Johns Hopkins to Hannah Hopkins, 25 April 1840, Alan Mason Chesney Medical Archives, Johns Hopkins Hospital (hereinafter Chesney Medical Archives), https://medicalarchivescatalog.jhmi.edu/jhmi_permalink.html?key=276434.

4. Jacob, "Mr. Johns Hopkins," 14.

5. Stimpert, "Johns Hopkins University," 126.

6. Jacob, "Mr. Johns Hopkins," 15.

7. Holloway, *Famous American Fortunes*, 337.

8. Gary Lawson Browne, *Baltimore in the Nation*, 142.

9. Bond, *When the Hopkins Came to Baltimore*, 23.

10. Bond, *When the Hopkins Came to Baltimore*, 23.

11. Stimpert, "Johns Hopkins University," 126.

12. Jacob, "Mr. Johns Hopkins," 15.

13. Thom, *Johns Hopkins: A Silhouette*, 31.

14. Stimpert, "Johns Hopkins University," 127. Gerard died in 1835 at age 26; Mahlon, in 1840 at 35; and Philip, in 1844 at 37. Johns would outlive Philip by thirty-nine years, passing away at the age of 78.

15. Matthew Page Andrews, "History of Baltimore from 1850," 231.

16. Pietila, *Ghosts of Johns Hopkins*, 17.

17. Charles Carroll, quoted in Daniel Walker Howe, *What Hath God Wrought*, 563.

18. Ryan, *Studies in Early Graduate Education*, 16.

19. Sander, *John W. Garrett*, 76–77.

20. Sander, *John W. Garrett*, 76–77.

21. Andrew Anderson, "In Memory of John W. Garrett, October 21, 1884," Gilman Papers, JHU, MS 1, series 1, box 16, folder 19, "John Work Garrett," https://jscholarship.library.jhu.edu /handle/1774.2/42099.

22. Stover, *History of the Baltimore and Ohio Railroad*, 161.

23. Sander, *John W. Garrett*, 102.

24. Sander, *John W. Garrett*, 102–3.

25. "Presidential Election."

26. Denton, *Southern Star for Maryland*, 30.

27. Summers, *Baltimore and Ohio*, 46.

28. Summers, *Baltimore and Ohio*, 49.

29. Bond, *When the Hopkins Came to Baltimore*, 24.

30. Brown, *Baltimore, the 19th of April 1861*, 60.

31. Browne, *Baltimore in the Nation*, 214–15. See also Catton, "Baltimore Business Community and the Secession Crisis," 70–77.

32. *New York Times*, 15 April 1861, and *Chicago Tribune*, 16 April 1861, both quoted in Sander, *John W. Garrett*, 123.

33. Radcliffe, *Governor Thomas H. Hicks of Maryland*, 74–75.

34. "Important from Maryland."

35. With federal troops occupying the city, "outside forces now directed Baltimore realities." Browne, *Baltimore in the Nation*, 215.

36. Sander, *John W. Garrett*, 126.

37. Jacob, "Mr. Johns Hopkins," 15; see also Stimpert, "Johns Hopkins University," 127.

38. Summers, *Baltimore and Ohio*, 65–67.

39. Weber, *Northern Railroads in the Civil War*, 76–77.

40. Pietila, *Ghosts of Johns Hopkins*, 31.

41. Donald, *Lincoln*, 558–60.

42. *The Crutch* (Annapolis, MD), 4 February 1865, quoted in Toews, *Lincoln in Annapolis*, 21.

43. Chernow, *Grant*, 525.

44. John Russell Young, *Around the World with General Grant*, 332.

45. "George Peabody: The Funeral at Westminster Abbey."

46. Dilts, *Great Road*, 246n432.

47. Address on George Peabody, 1893, Daniel Coit Gilman Papers, MS 582, series 2, box 5, folder 33, Yale University Special Collections (hereinafter Gilman Papers, Yale).

48. Thom, *Johns Hopkins: A Silhouette*, 41.

49. French, *History of the University*, 18.

50. Peabody would also influence another wealthy Baltimorean toward philanthropy. Enoch Pratt served as a trustee for the Peabody Institute. In the 1880s Pratt introduced an interesting

model for library construction and operation: he would help fund the completion of a main library and four branch libraries in Baltimore if the city would agree to fund their ongoing operation and maintenance. Pratt's model helped to inspire Andrew Carnegie and the unprecedented scale on which he expanded libraries throughout North America. See "Public Libraries in the U.S."

51. Address on George Peabody, 1893, Gilman Papers, Yale.

52. Hawkins, *Pioneer*, 4.

53. Parker, *George Peabody: A Biography*, 158.

54. Abbott et al., *Evergreen*, ix; see also Sander, *Mary Elizabeth Garrett*, 55–56.

55. Allen Bond maintained that the Maryland Academy of Sciences cherishes a tradition "that at a noon-day lunch in its old building on Mulberry Street, Mr. Hopkins finally decided upon the use of his wealth for the great endowment. I have been fortunate enough to find a little sketch of Mr. Hopkins' plans published in 1871, two years before his death and evidently issued under his authority or that of his trustees." Bond, *When the Hopkins Came to Baltimore*, 26.

56. Sander, *John W. Garrett*, 238–39.

57. Gilman, *Launching of a University*, 11–12.

58. Parker, "George Peabody's Influence," 113.

59. The entirety of Hopkins' last will and testament and the recording documents can be found in the appendix to Thom, *Johns Hopkins: A Silhouette*.

60. Olson, *Baltimore*, 192.

61. Thom, *Johns Hopkins: A Silhouette*, 60.

62. In 2013, the Johns Hopkins University launched the Hopkins Retrospective, a multidisciplinary project geared toward rediscovering the university's history: https://retrospective .jhu.edu/our-initiatives/reexamining-hopkins-history. In December 2020, university administrators announced a new finding based on this contemporary scholarship and asserted that Mr. Hopkins, long believed to be a lifelong and staunch abolitionist, had at one time been an enslaver. In the recently discovered 1850 census record, four enslaved individuals are listed in the Hopkins household, but these individuals were not included in the census of 1860. In an official statement dated 9 December 2020, "Reexamining the history of our founder," university administrators wrote that "considerable additional research will be needed before we have a full picture of his life"; historians like Martha S. Jones and other university faculty are actively pursuing such work. The title of this new initiative is Hard Histories at Hopkins. On the project's website (https://hardhistory.jhu.edu/about/) the Hopkins Retrospective and the SNF Agora Institute are listed as a collaborators. For the full statement, see https://president.jhu .edu/meet-president-daniels/speeches-articles-and-media/reexamining-the-history-of-our -founder/. "Going forward, my work will involve investigating our founder's relationship to slaveholding and, as much as possible, understanding the lives of those he held enslaved," wrote Dr. Jones in a *Washington Post* op-ed titled "The founder of Johns Hopkins owned enslaved people. Our university must face a reckoning," which also appeared on 9 December 2020. Recent panel discussions sponsored by the Hopkins Retrospective have focused on additional research and emerging details. See "Conversations on Slavery, Racism, and the University, Panel 1, Methodologies," https://www.youtube.com/watch?v=2kxjObicuww&t=424s; "Conversations on Slavery, Racism, and the University, Panel 2, Legacies," https://www.youtube.com /watch?v=5Ghgf_ceDWo&t=4554s; and "Conversations on Slavery, Racism, and the University, Panel 3, The Future," https://www.youtube.com/watch?v=AqiTtFaQxjk&t=61s.

63. Jacob, "Mr. Johns Hopkins," 17.

64. Hopkins Register of Wills, in Maryland State Archives, Baltimore County Register Of Wills (Inventories), 1666–1969, CM155, 1873–74, Book name OPM 11, Film Reels CR 9093-1.

65. Charles Piece, quoted in Sander, *John W. Garrett*, 289.

66. "Obituary Record: Charles J. M. Gwinn," 4; see also also "Obituary of Charles J. M. Gwinn."

67. Thom, *Johns Hopkins: A Silhouette*, 103.

68. Thom, *Johns Hopkins: A Silhouette*, 102.

69. Hawkins, *Pioneer*, 102–3.

70. Thom, *Johns Hopkins: A Silhouette*, 103.

71. Hofstadter and Smith, "Gilman Recalls the Early Days."

72. Certificate of Incorporation, 1876, RG 01.001, Records of the Board of Trustees, JHU, series 1.

73. Lanier, *Poems of Sidney Lanier*. Lanier would die a year later, at 39, of tuberculosis.

74. Certificate of Incorporation, 1876. See also French, *History of the University*, 17–21.

75. Hawkins, *Pioneer*, 4. Hawkins further notes that certain of the trustees had been active participants "in the remarkable educational achievements of the Friends; three were trustees of Haverford and one of Guilford in North Carolina" (5).

76. In French's *History of the University Founded by Johns Hopkins*, John Fonerden is listed as a trustee of both the university and the hospital on the basis of the 1867 incorporation documents for both entities, although he is not included in Mr. Hopkins' original letter of instruction, dated 10 March 1873. Dr. Fonerden passed away in 1869, and his replacement on the university board, Dr. James Carey Thomas, was elected to fill this vacant seat at the board's first official meeting in 1870. Fonerden's replacement on the hospital board was Joseph Merrefield.

77. Gilman, *Launching of a University*, 36.

78. Gilman, *Launching of a University*, 27–38. Gilman devotes an entire chapter, "Johns Hopkins and the Trustees of His Choice," to Hopkins and the selection of his inaugural board.

79. "Death of Johns Hopkins," *Baltimore Sun*, 25 December 1873, https://www.newspapers.com/image/372398315/.

80. "Death of Johns Hopkins," *Baltimore American and Commercial Advertiser*, 25 December 1873.

81. Hopkins destroyed all his papers before his death. Hugh Hawkins notes that the "only biography of the founder, Helen Hopkins Thom's *Johns Hopkins: A Silhouette*, is valuable for family tradition and personal reminiscence, but undependable in matters relating to the university." Hawkins, *Pioneer*, 341.

82. Gilman, *Launching of a University*, 36.

83. Hawkins, *Pioneer*, 5–6.

84. Brown, *Old World and the New*, 25.

85. Brown, *Need of a Higher Standard*, 9.

86. Brown, *Need of a Higher Standard*, 14.

87. Hawkins, "George William Brown and His Influence," 183.

88. Brown, *Need of a Higher Standard*, 11.

89. Hawkins, "George William Brown and His Influence," 174.

90. Brown, *Need of a Higher Standard*, 10.

### Chapter 1 · Yale and the Life-Giving Springs of New Haven

1. Gillman, *History of the Gillman Or Gilman Family*, 234–40.

2. Franklin, *Life*, 5. A summation of the Gilman family genealogy was first outlined in this biography by Franklin.

3. Dwight, "Eighth Paper," 82. Other contributors to the collection include Frederick Au-

gustus Porter Barnard (former chancellor of the University of Mississippi and president of Columbia College), E. G. Robinson (president of Brown University), James Angell (president of the University of Michigan), and Andrew White (president of Cornell University).

4. Franklin, *Life*, 6.

5. Franklin, *Life*, 6.

6. Journal entry, 14 September 1848, Gilman Papers, JHU, MS 1, series 10, box 2, folder 1. Gilman's entry two weeks later, on 27 September 1848, details his train departure from New York City at 7:00 a.m. for New Haven "to enter college" by 11:30 a.m., with a recitation of an algebra lesson that same day at 4:00 p.m.

7. White, "Eleventh Paper."

8. Kelley, *Yale: A History*, 180.

9. Altschuler, *Andrew D. White*, 28.

10. Bishop and Kingsbury, *History of Cornell*, 33.

11. Rogers, *Andrew D. White*, 16.

12. DCG to Elizabeth Coit Gilman, 5 October 1848, Gilman Papers, Yale, MS 582, series 1, box 3, folder 169.

13. DCG to Elizabeth Coit Gilman, 28 June 1849, Gilman Papers, Yale, MS 582, series 1, box 3, folder 169.

14. DCG to William Charles Gilman, 18 June 1849, Gilman Papers, Yale, MS 582, series 1, box 3, folder 178.

15. DCG to William Charles Gilman, 18 June 1849, Gilman Papers, Yale.

16. DCG to Elizabeth Gilman, 30 November 1849, Gilman Papers, Yale, MS 582, series 1, box 3, folder 183.

17. Franklin, *Life*, 405.

18. Franklin, *Life*, 9–10.

19. Journal entry, 16 December 1848, Gilman Papers, JHU, MS 1, series 10, box 2, folder 1.

20. Richards, *Skulls and Keys*, 153–54.

21. William Welch, quoted in Richards, *Skulls and Keys*, 188.

22. Jarrett, "Yale, Skull and Bones," 30.

23. Richards, *Skulls and Keys*, 137–38.

24. Arnold, *Shiloh 1862*, 88.

25. Richards, *Skulls and Keys*, 99.

26. Cooper, *William Preston Johnston*, 9–10.

27. DCG to Elizabeth Coit Gilman, 17 May 1851, Gilman Papers, Yale, MS 582, series 1, box 3, folder 169.

28. DCG to Elizabeth Coit Gilman, 17 May 1851, Gilman Papers, Yale.

29. Gilman Papers, JHU, MS 1, series 1, box 55, folder 22, "Theodore Dwight Woolsey," https://jscholarship.library.jhu.edu/handle/1774.2/43709.

30. William C. Gilman, "Daniel Coit Gilman, 1831–1908," 211.

31. Gilman used this phrase in an address at Yale titled *The Sheffield Scientific School of Yale University: A Semi-centennial Historical Discourse, October 28, 1897*, 37. The complete statement reads: "For one such institution, now celebrating its majority, permit me to acknowledge with filial gratitude, the impulses, lessons, warnings and encouragements derived from the Sheffield Scientific School, and publicly admit that much of the health and strength of the Johns Hopkins University is due to early and repeated draughts upon the life-giving springs of New Haven."

32. Franklin, *Life*, 15.

33. "Scholars Without Money."

34. Mayer, *Young Man in a Hurry*.

35. Gilman, *Launching of a University*, 8.

36. Andrew White to Elizabeth Dwight Woolsey Gilman, 3 May 1909, quoted in Franklin, *Life*, 322.

37. Hawkins, *Pioneer*, 17.

38. DCG to William Charles Gilman, 7 February 1854, Gilman Papers, JHU, MS 1, series 10, box 3, folder 7.

39. Richard Cobden to DCG, 3 January 1853, Gilman Papers, JHU, MS 1, series 1, box 9, folder 30, https://jscholarship.library.jhu.edu/handle/1774.2/41806.

40. Cobden to DCG, 13 January 1853, Gilman Papers, JHU, MS 1, series 1, box 9, folder 30, https://jscholarship.library.jhu.edu/handle/1774.2/41806.

41. White to Elizabeth Dwight Woolsey Gilman, quoted in Franklin, *Life*, 323–24. Gilman must have delivered exactly what Cobden requested, as a later message to Gilman from his host stated how gratified the association had been with his remarks: "You could not have said anything more useful and appropriate. Believe me." Cobden to DCG, 26 January 1853, Gilman Papers, JHU, MS 1, series 1, box 9, folder 30, https://jscholarship.library.jhu.edu/handle/1774.2/41806. There is no further record of correspondence between the two men except for a letter from Cobden to Gilman dated 29 September 1854, in which Cobden thanked Gilman for his "kind remembrances of me after so great a variety of interesting adventures on the Continent. It would indeed be a gratification to me to hear your accounts of all you saw, especially in Russia." Cobden to DCG, 29 September 1854, Gilman Papers, JHU, MS 1, series 1, box 9, folder 30, https://jscholarship.library.jhu.edu/handle/1774.2/41806. Cobden would continue association with various American thinkers and policymakers and hosted another of Gilman's mentors, the celebrated common-school reformer Henry Barnard, during the latter's trip to Europe in 1854. See MacMullen, *In the Cause of True Education*, 198–201.

42. DCG to Dear Friends at Home, 3 February 1854, Gilman Papers, Yale, MS 582, series 1, box 3, folder 178.

43. Franklin, *Life*, 14.

44. DCG to William Charles Gilman, 3 February 1854, Gilman Papers, Yale, MS 582, series 1, box 3, folder 178.

45. DCG to William Charles Gilman, 3 February 1854, Gilman Papers, Yale.

46. Peirce, *Trials of an inventor*, 167–69.

47. DCG to William Charles Gilman, 7 February 1854, Gilman Papers, Yale, MS 582, series 1, box 3, folder 178.

48. In a letter to his father from Berlin in early 1855, Daniel recounted in great detail the difficulty he had had in receiving payment for his services from Goodyear after multiple attempts. "Finally I wrote him," Daniel recalled, "respectfully but decidedly that it is my last request, 'before taking other steps,' I did not say what 'to vindicate my claim.'" Goodyear acknowledged the debt owed Gilman, but his failure to pay forced Daniel to "decide the question as to whether or not I had better set my face homewards toward the close of next summer." DCG to William Charles Gilman, 5 January 1855, Gilman Papers, Yale, MS 582, series 1, box 3, folder 178.

49. DCG to William Charles Gilman, 6 March 1854, Gilman Papers, Yale, MS 582, series 1, box 3, folder 178.

50. While Gilman was still uncertain about which career path he should choose, others within his Yale circle felt a strong pull toward the ministry. Jacob Cooper was one of these and closed an October 1853 letter to Gilman from his home in Somerville, Ohio, with news that he

had passed the theology examinations and was now licensed to preach. Cooper, reared in poverty on a farm in southern Ohio, wrote in the same letter about his plans to study "Philosophy, Dogmatic Theology, Hebrew, and Civil Law" in either Berlin or Göttingen, but at the time of his letter he had not decided which would be best. Jacob Cooper to DCG, 21 October 1853, Gilman Papers, JHU, MS 1, series 1, box 10, folder 11. Cooper would ultimately choose Berlin, earning his PhD in 1854 and then completing a master's degree in law at Yale before taking up a teaching post at Centre College in Danville, Kentucky. He spent the rest of his career as a professor of Greek and philosophy at Rutgers College. But before both men left for Europe, Cooper tried to persuade Gilman to join him in Germany: "Nothing could be more agreeable than to have you for a companion throughout the entire expedition. Indeed there are few if any of all my acquaintances in whose society absence from home could be borne as pleasantly."

51. DCG to Maria Gilman, April 1854, quoted in Franklin, *Life*, 29.

52. Hart, "Protestant Enlightenment Revisited," 689.

53. DCG to Henry Barnard, 20 July 1854, quoted in Cordasco, *Shaping of American Graduate Education*, 12.

54. DCG to William Charles Gilman, 6 March 1854, Gilman Papers, Yale, MS 582, series 1, box 3, folder 178.

55. Franklin, *Life*, 27.

56. Arthur P. Young, "Gilman in the Formative Period," 121.

57. Journal entry, 30 January 1855, Gilman Papers, JHU, MS 1, series 10, box 2, folder 2.

58. Martin, *American Geography and Geographers*, 14.

59. Gilman, "Humboldt, Ritter, and the New Geography," 285.

60. Gilman Papers, JHU, MS 1, series 10, box 2, folder 2. Ritter was indeed old at the time: 76. He would die in 1859.

61. Young, "Gilman in the Formative Period," 121.

62. J. G. Flugel to DCG, 21 March 1855, Gilman Papers, Yale, MS 582, series 1, box 1, folder 50.

63. "1855 Europe," Gilman Papers, JHU, MS 1, series 10, box 2, folder 2.

64. DCG to family, 19 June 1854, quoted in Franklin, *Life*, 24.

65. Young, "Gilman in the Formative Period," 123.

66. "Notes on Universities-Colleges Teaching," Gilman Papers, JHU, MS 1, series 2, box 3.

67. "Notes on Universities-Colleges Teaching," Gilman Papers, JHU.

68. "1855 Europe," Gilman Papers, JHU

69. "Notes on Universities-Colleges Teaching," Gilman Papers, JHU.

70. See Veysey, *Emergence of the American University*, 10.

71. Dorn, *For the Common Good*, 96.

72. Barnard to DCG, 22 November 1853, Gilman Papers, JHU, MS 1, series 1, box 3, folder 25, https://jscholarship.library.jhu.edu/handle/1774.2/41547.

73. MacMullen, *In the Cause of True Education*, 196–97, 308.

74. Thursfield, *Henry Barnard's American Journal of Education*, 223–24. See also Gilman Papers, JHU, MS 1, series 1, box 3, folder 25, "Henry Barnard," https://jscholarship.library.jhu.edu/handle/1774.2/41547.

75. DCG to William Charles Gilman, 31 July 1854, Gilman Papers, JHU, MS 1, series 10, box 2, folder 8.

76. Thursfield, *Henry Barnard's American Journal of Education*, 223.

77. Thursfield, *Henry Barnard's American Journal of Education*, 338.

78. Gilman, "Scientific Schools in Europe," 315.

79. Gilman, "Scientific Schools in Europe," 315.

80. Gilman, "Scientific Schools in Europe," 316.

81. Gilman, "Scientific Schools in Europe," 316–17.

82. Royal Commission for the Exhibition of 1851.

83. Council of the Society of Arts, *Report of the Committee*, 14.

84. Council of the Society of Arts, *Report of the Committee*, 14.

85. Gilman, "Scientific Schools in Europe," 318.

86. Gilman, "Scientific Schools in Europe," 321.

87. Gilman, "Scientific Schools in Europe," 327.

88. Gilman, "Scientific Schools in Europe," 328.

89. DCG to the Honorable Green Kendrick, 30 May 1856, Gilman Papers, Yale, MS 582, series 1, box 1, folder 82a.

90. DCG, quoted in Flexner, *Daniel Coit Gilman*, 9.

91. Gilman, *Launching of a University*, 195–96.

92. Bishop and Kingsbury, *History of Cornell*, 35.

93. DCG to William Charles Gilman and Elizabeth Coit Gilman, 9 March 1857, Gilman Papers, Yale, MS 582, series 1, box 3, folder 169.

94. DCG to William Charles Gilman and Elizabeth Coit Gilman, 9 March 1857, Gilman Papers, Yale.

95. Franklin, *Life*, 45–52.

96. Franklin, *Life*, 70.

97. Records of Norton's Cadets, Gilman Papers, Yale, MS 582, series 2, box 4, folder 4a.

98. Young, "Gilman in the Formative Period," 123.

99. Woolsey to DCG, quoted in Franklin, *Life*, 78–79.

100. "1865–6," Gilman Papers, JHU, MS 1, series 10, box 2, folder 5.

101. "1865–6," Gilman Papers, JHU.

102. DCG to Edward Gilman, 2 August 1865, quoted in Franklin, *Life*, 81.

103. *Connecticut Common School Journal* 21 (1866): 17–22.

104. John K. Wright, "Daniel Coit Gilman," 381.

105. Wright, "Daniel Coit Gilman," 384.

106. Gilman, *On the structure of the earth*.

107. See Geiger, "Rise and Fall of Useful Knowledge."

108. Thomas Lounsbury, quoted in Gilman, *University Problems in the United States*, 126–27.

109. Flexner, *Daniel Coit Gilman*, 9.

110. Reynolds, "Education of Engineers."

111. Storr, *Beginnings of Graduate Education in America*, 9–14.

112. Brubacher and Rudy, *Higher Education in Transition*, 61.

113. Ricketts, *History of the Rensselaer Institute*, 29. The institution officially changed its name from the Rensselaer School to the Rensselaer Institute in 1832 and then finally to the Rensselaer Polytechnic Institute upon the New York State Legislature's ratification in 1861. Ricketts, *History of the Rensselaer Institute*, 66, 104.

114. Thursfield, *Henry Barnard's American Journal of Education*, 224.

115. Reynolds, "Education of Engineers," 470.

116. Reynolds, "Education of Engineers," 471–72.

117. Brubacher and Rudy, *Higher Education in Transition*, 61–62.

118. Woolsey, quoted in Franklin, *Life*, 82–83.

119. Ross, *Democracy's College*, 56. Morrill would be elected to the US Senate in 1866. He died in office in 1898, having served in Congress for nearly forty-four years.

120. Ferrier, *Origin and Development*, 43.

121. Gilman Papers, Yale, General Correspondence, MS 582, series 1, box 1, folder 101, "Justin Smith Morrill, 1858, 1868."

122. Morrill, *Speech of Hon. Justin S. Morrill*, 15.

123. Sorber, *Land-Grant Colleges and Popular Revolt*, 54; see also Cummins, *Bethany College*, 88–89.

124. Croft, "U.S. Land-Grant University System."

125. Thelin, *History of American Higher Education*, 76.

126. Cummins, *Bethany College*, 88.

127. Justin Morrill to Ira Davis, 8 December 1948, quoted in Ross, *Democracy's College*, 48.

128. Wayland, *Report to the Corporation*, 57.

129. Geiger, "Rise and Fall of Useful Knowledge," 154.

130. White, quoted in Ferrier, *Origin and Development*, 44–45.

131. Key, "Economics or Education," 198.

132. Stemmons and Schenker, *Connecticut Agricultural College*, 58.

133. Stemmons and Schenker, *Connecticut Agricultural College*, 61–62.

134. Thelin, *History of American Higher Education*, 77.

135. Ross, *Democracy's College*, 54–55.

136. Gilman, *Our National Schools of Science*, 12.

137. Stemmons and Schenker, *Connecticut Agricultural College*, 63.

138. Stave, *Red Brick in the Land of Steady Habits*, 5–6.

139. Hawkins, *Banding Together*, 5.

140. Franklin, *Life*, 104–5.

141. Sorber, "Creating Colleges," 48.

142. Sorber, "Creating Colleges," 48.

143. *Sheffield Scientific School Semi-Centennial Historical Discourse*, 28 October 1897, Gilman Papers, Yale, MS 582, series 2, box 5, folder 36.

144. DCG to N. B. Van Slyke, Esquire, 9 February 1867, Gilman Papers, Yale, MS 582, series 1, box 2, folder 151.

145. DCG to Cooper, quoted in Franklin, *Life*, 88.

### Chapter 2 · *The House of Our Expectations in California*

1. Ferrier, *Henry Durant*, 34–35.

2. Marsden, *Soul of the American University*, 135.

3. Wollenberg, *Berkeley*, 23.

4. Sherman Day migrated to California in 1849 and remained there until his death in Berkeley in 1884. In a letter dated 25 December 1874, Day presented Gilman with a first-edition copy of his father's landmark work, *Day's An Introduction to Algebra*, published in 1814. Day's Christmas letter included this line: "I presume the memory of Daniel C. Gilman runneth not back near so far as the date of its imprint. But to me it is redolent of the memories of my youthful days; of my father, then in his prime; of his younger associates Silliman and Kingsley; and of that clear headed old engraver Nathaniel Jocelyn who engraved the diagrams, and who put up the Old Clock at the Lyceum which used to strike solar time." Gilman Papers, JHU, MS 1, series 1, box 12, folder 2.

5. Ferrier, *Origin and Development*, 138.

6. Gilman, *Launching of a University*, 176.

7. Tewksbury, *Founding of American Colleges and Universities*, 204–5.

8. Ferrier, *Henry Durant*, 9.

9. Stadtman, *University of California*, 27.

10. State of California, *Statutes of California*, 504–5.

11. State of California, *Statutes of California*, 507.

12. State of California, *Statutes of California*, 509.

13. State of California, *Statutes of California*, 509.

14. Marsden, *Soul of the American University*, 137.

15. Ferrier, *Origin and Development*, 235–36.

16. Geiger, *History of American Higher Education*, 187.

17. Silliman, *Truly Practical Man*, 3.

18. Silliman, *Truly Practical Man*, 5.

19. Silliman, *Truly Practical Man*, 12.

20. Barnard, "California Educational Society," 790.

21. National Educational Association, *Journals of Proceedings*, 58. At this same meeting in California, Swett was called upon to make remarks. He stated, "I am willing to be taken as an example of the early days in California. We worked hard, but we were ambitious. We had a good time. A good many of us came out here expecting to make our fortune in the mines. We didn't. And then we turned in and did some pretty good work in the public schools" (63).

22. Silliman, *Truly Practical Man*, 15–16, 17.

23. Stadtman, *University of California*, 29.

24. Silliman, *Truly Practical Man*, 17.

25. Silliman, *Truly Practical Man*, 18.

26. Silliman, *Truly Practical Man*, 19.

27. Silliman, *Truly Practical Man*, 22.

28. Robert Semple, quoted in John Ross Browne, *Report of the Debates In the Convention of California*, 18.

29. Saunders, "California Legal History," 456.

30. Douglass, *California Idea*, 21–22.

31. Browne, *Report of the Debates in the Convention of California*, x.

32. Browne, *Report of the Debates in the Convention of California*, x.

33. Browne, *Report of the Debates in the Convention of California*, 204; see also Ferrier, *Origin and Development*, 8.

34. Ferrier, *Origin and Development*, 219. Reverend Bushnell was originally offered the presidency in 1856. "The call was neither accepted nor declined—decision being held in abeyance. The College was so desirous of securing him that the call was left open for three years after his return to his work at Harford in January 1857." Ferrier, *Henry Durant*, 35. In *Origin and Development* Ferrier offered this further clarification: "For several years it was thought that Dr. Bushnell would return to California and take the presidency of the College to which he had been called in 1856. Formal declination having been made finally the College in 1863 sought Professor W. T. Shedd of Union Theological Seminary, New York, for the position. Dr. Shedd declining, Professor R. D. Hitchcock was called. He declined also. No further effort was made and Dr. Willey, the vice-president, continued to act as president until the College became part of the University. Before Dr. Shedd was called, an endowment of $25,000 was subscribed, contingent on his acceptance and coming. There were fourteen $1,000 subscriptions, among the persons subscribing that amount being Governor Low, Thomas Starr King and Henry Durant. Many of these subscriptions were re-made when effort was made to secure Dr. Hitchcock" (219).

35. Stadtman, *University of California*, 18–19.
36. Gilman, "Bishop Berkeley's Gifts to Yale College," 148.
37. Storr, *Beginnings of Graduate Education in America*, 2.
38. See Arthur P. Young, "Gilman in the Formative Period," 126. In his last year as librarian at Yale, Gilman wrote two articles on Berkeley and his contributions. See Gilman, "Bishop Berkeley's Gifts to Yale College"; and Gilman, "Bishop Berkeley in America."
39. Berkeley, *Works of George Berkeley, D.D.*, 365–66; see also Stadtman, *University of California*, 14.
40. Wollenberg, *Berkeley*, 26.
41. Durant, quoted in Stadtman, *University of California*, 30.
42. Stadtman, *University of California*, 30.
43. Ferrier, *Henry Durant*, 79.
44. Wollenberg, *Berkeley*, 27.
45. Stadtman, *University of California*, 32–33.
46. Stadtman, *University of California*, 33.
47. Stadtman, *University of California*, 34.
48. Stadtman, *University of California*, 34. Before a president and faculty could be hired, buildings constructed, courses organized, and instruction launched, the board of regents had to be selected and seated. Provisions in the Organic Act stipulated a first group of six ex-officio members, including the governor. A second set of regents was then to be appointed by the governor with the consent of the Senate. Rounding out the board, the third component—called "honorary" members, a moniker that created a fair bit of confusion—would be elected by the fourteen regents: eight gubernatorial appointees and six ex-officio members. That the entire process was somewhat cumbersome was a view shared by many, and the "honorary" classification was eliminated by the revision of the Political Code in 1872. When finally complete, the inaugural university board was made up of the following: four state officials, eight attorneys, two doctors, a railroad vice president, a Unitarian minister, a nurseryman, two farmers, a gas company president, a manufacturer, and former state superintendent of public instruction. All were white and male. Stadtman, *University of California*, 515n3.
49. Stadtman, *University of California*, 37; see also Ferrier, *Origin and Development*, 288–96.
50. State of California, *Statutes of California*, 256.
51. State of California, *Statutes of California*, 253.
52. Ferrier, *Origin and Development*, 302–3.
53. Ferrier, *Origin and Development*, 305.
54. *San Francisco Examiner*, 16 October 1868; see also Pelfrey and Cheney, *Brief History of the University of California*, 9–10.
55. Stadtman, *University of California*, 48.
56. Stadtman, *University of California*, 48–49.
57. Stadtman, *University of California*, 51.
58. Franklin, *Life*, 111; Stadtman, *University of California*, 52.
59. Donnelly, "Scientists of the Confederate Nitre and Mining Bureau," 71. Before arriving in San Francisco in April 1869, LeConte had been on the faculty of the South Carolina College, which became the University of South Carolina in 1865. The professor's home in Columbia was in the path of General William Tecumseh Sherman's "march to the sea"; among the articles destroyed by fire in the Union Army's swath was the manuscript for a volume on general physics, the product of LeConte's life's work. See Stevens, "Sketch of Professor John LeConte," 116. John and Joseph attempted to protect these papers and valuables from Sherman's troops, leaving

Columbia on 16 February 1865. John was captured along with the wagons of possessions and personal effects on 19 February and taken by the Federal forces to the border of North Carolina. He was then released and returned to Columbia. An 1841 graduate of the College of Physicians and Surgeons in New York City, John LeConte practiced medicine for a time in Savannah, Georgia, before being named chair of the Department of Natural Philosophy and Chemistry at Franklin College in Athens (Franklin College, named for Benjamin Franklin, was the founding college of the University of Georgia). Disagreements with the aging university president, Alonzo Church, led LeConte to resign his post and teach for a short time at his medical alma mater in New York City. Dyer, *University of Georgia*, 90–92. An accomplished scholar and noted physicist, LeConte is best known for his 1857 discovery of the sensitivity of flame to musical vibrations. This breakthrough led to the use of flames for the detection of sounds too delicate for the human ear to perceive and for the optical analysis of compound tones. Joseph LeConte, five years younger than John, was a graduate of the Lawrence Scientific School at Harvard and worked with the famed Louis Agassiz, America's foremost scientist of the day. In 1905 LeConte Hall at the University of Georgia was named in honor of Joseph LeConte and his academic contributions. It originally housed the Department of Biology but is now home to the Department of History. LeConte wrote a controversial book in 1982 titled *The Race Problem in the South*, and recent debates have ensued on the Athens campus as to whether LeConte's portrait and name should be removed from the structure. Osakwe, "UGA professors and students discuss." Finding academic positions hard to come by after the Civil War, the two men considered going to Mexico but were encouraged to head west to California. Among those endorsing them for faculty appointments were prominent scientists such as James Mill Pierce and Agassiz of Harvard, Henry of the Smithsonian Institution, and Silliman of Yale. Stadtman, *University of California*, 50–55. Before the war, Joseph had left Athens to follow John to South Carolina College in 1857, and this pattern would repeat itself more than a decade later. John arrived in Berkeley in April 1869, and Joseph arrived the following September, to remain on the faculty until his death in 1901.

60. Stadtman, *University of California*, 49.

61. Stadtman, *University of California*, 49.

62. Thompson's first wife, Lucy Olivia Bartlett, died in 1852. Thompson then married Daniel C. Gilman's sister Elizabeth in 1853. Their son, Dr. William Gilman Thompson, was a graduate of the Sheffield Scientific School, earned his medical degree from Columbia, and studied overseas in Germany. He founded the New York Clinic for the Functional Re-education of Disabled Soldiers, Sailors, and Civilians (later named Reconstruction Hospital and then merged with NYU Bellevue). See "Medicine and Surgery in the Army and Navy," 687.

63. Ferrier, *Origin and Development*, 325.

64. Edward Tompkins to Reverend Henry Whitney Bellows, quoted in Franklin, *Life*, 113–14.

65. Tompkins to DCG, quoted in Franklin, *Life*, 114–15; Ferrier, *Origin and Development*, 325–26.

66. Martin Kellogg to DCG, quoted in Ferrier, *Origin and Development*, 327.

67. Ferrier, *Henry Durant*, 83.

68. Stadtman, *University of California*, 49.

69. Ferrier, *Henry Durant*, 83.

70. DCG to Tompkins, quoted in Franklin, *Life*, 117. About Gilman's candidacy at Yale, his biographer Abraham Flexner noted, "Forward-looking Yale men had hoped that he might

succeed President Woolsey; but the Corporation was still too conservative to take a step as radical as was the election of Charles W. Eliot to the presidency of Harvard in 1869. Yale did not wholly stagnate, but progress was little accelerated by the election of Noah Porter." Flexner, *Daniel Coit Gilman*, 16.

71. Mary Ketcham Gilman death notice, Gilman Papers, JHU, MS 1, series 12, box 1.

72. DCG to Tompkins, quoted in Franklin, *Life*, 116.

73. "Sheffield Scientific School, 1868–1871," Gilman Papers, Yale, MS 582, series 3, box 7, folder 16.

74. President Woolsey would later say of Professor Silliman: "He, in his prime, was our standing orator, the principal medium between those who dwelt in the academic shade and the great public." Quoted in Kelley, *Yale: A History*, 171. Silliman Sr. would remain on the faculty until 1853, having arrived at Yale in 1799.

75. Kelley, *Yale: A History*, 172.

76. Hawkins, *Pioneer*, 18.

77. New Charter—New President Yale newspaper clippings, 1870–1871, Gilman Papers, Yale, MS 582, series 3, box 7, folder 12.

78. Kelley, *Yale: A History*, 238.

79. Franklin, *Life*, 106.

80. Franklin, *Life*, 117–18; Stadtman, *University of California*, 63.

81. DCG to White, 18 May 1872, letterpress book 7 (November 1865–March 1891), Gilman Papers, JHU, MS 1, series 4, box 4.2.

82. Ross Jones, *Elisabeth Gilman*, 12.

83. De Pasquale, "Elisabeth Gilman Was a Fierce Advocate for Social Justice."

84. Ferrier, *Origin and Development*, 331; Franklin, *Life*, 118.

85. Governor Newton Booth to DCG, quoted in Ferrier, *Origin and Development*, 331.

86. Regents to DCG, and DCG to Andrew J. Moulder, 2 August 1872, quoted in Ferrier, *Origin and Development*, 331.

87. University of Illinois Alumni Association, *Fortnightly Notes*, 17–18.

88. Franklin, *Life*, 119.

89. DCG to White, 17 September 1872, quoted in Franklin, *Life*, 107.

90. DCG to Noah Porter, 12 September 1872, Gilman Papers, Yale, General Correspondence, MS 582, series 1, box 1, folder 114.

91. Porter to DCG, 13 September 1872, Gilman Papers, Yale, General Correspondence, MS 582, series I, box 1, folder 114.

92. Douglass, *Conditions for Admission*, 4.

93. Stadtman, *University of California*, 63.

94. Gilman, *Building of the University*, 3.

95. Gilman, *Building of a University*, 4.

96. Gilman, *Building of a University*, 4.

97. Gilman, *Building of a University*, 5–6, 7.

98. Gilman, *Building of a University*, 7.

99. Gilman, *Building of a University*, 8.

100. Brechin, *Imperial San Francisco*, 282.

101. Brechin, *Imperial San Francisco*, 282. Reverend Bushnell's hometown newspaper, the *Hartford Courant*, made special mention of Gilman's speech and references to the pioneering work of Bushnell: "The services of that enthusiastic scholar, whom California would gladly

have kept if Connecticut would have spared him, are honorably recorded in your early college annals, and are not forgotten by those who labored with him; but I cannot forbear to utter at this time the name of one to whose counsels and whose benedictions my presence here is due—the name of Horace Bushnell." "Recognition of Dr. Bushnell's Services in California," *Hartford Courant*, 19 November 1872, 2, in Gilman Papers, JHU, Gilman Scrapbooks (Europe, California), MS 1, series 7, box 1. See also Gilman, *Building of a University*, 8–9.

102. Gilman, *Building of a University*, 304.
103. Gilman, *Building of a University*, 9.
104. Gilman, *Building of a University*, 10.
105. Gilman, *Building of a University*, 10–11.
106. Gilman, *Building of a University*, 11.
107. Gilman, *Building of a University*, 11–12.
108. Gilman, *Building of a University*, 13.
109. Gilman, *Building of a University*, 15–24.
110. Gilman, *Building of a University*, 26–27.
111. *New York Daily Tribune*, 22 November 1872, in Gilman Papers, JHU, Gilman Scrapbooks (Europe, California), MS 1, series 7, box 1.
112. Stadtman, *University of California*, 64.
113. *University Echo* (San Francisco), March 1873, quoted in Ferrier, *Origin and Development*, 342.
114. Stadtman, *University of California*, 65.
115. Stadtman, *University of California*, 65.
116. See Stadtman, *University of California*, 41–44.
117. Steven Finacom, "Long on the move." The portrait now hangs in the Heyns Room of the Doe Library.
118. Ferrier, *Origin and Development*, 349.
119. Stadtman, *University of California*, 66.
120. DCG, quoted in Ferrier, *Origin and Development*, 343.
121. DCG, quoted in Ferrier, *Origin and Development*, 343.
122. Ferrier, *Origin and Development*, 344.
123. DCG, quoted in Franklin, *Life*, 130.
124. Booth, quoted in Ferrier, *Origin and Development*, 345–46.
125. Stadtman, *University of California*, 66.
126. "Gain of a Man."
127. Ferrier, *Origin and Development*, 355.
128. Barker, *Henry George*, 219. It is interesting to note that Barker, a three-time Yale graduate, served as chair of the Johns Hopkins University Department of History from 1967 to 1972. His mother, Alice Albro, was the first woman to be awarded a PhD from Yale in 1898. See Rasmussen, "Charles A. Barker."
129. Henry George, quoted in Franklin, *Life*, 146.
130. George, quoted in Ferrier, *Henry Durant*, 87.
131. DCG to Board of Regents, quoted in Franklin, *Life*, 142.
132. Douglass, *California Idea*, 50.
133. Barker, *Henry George*, 220.
134. Barker, *Henry George*, 219.
135. Douglass, *California Idea*, 49.
136. George, quoted in Franklin, *Life*, 146. The San Francisco's Mechanics' Institute was

founded in 1854 and actively participated in the university's early development, hosting technical classes and presenting lectures on a variety of topics.

137. Stadtman, *University of California*, 70.

138. Samuel F. Butterworth, quoted in "Investigation of the Alleged Frauds," 464.

139. See "Investigation of the Alleged Frauds."

140. "Report of Assembly Committee," 8.

141. "Report of Assembly Committee," 9.

142. Stadtman, *University of California*, 70–71.

143. The memorial, in its entirety, can be found in Pinney, Swinton, and Carr, *University of California and its relations to industrial education*, 109–12.

144. Pinney, Swinton, and Carr, *University of California and its relations to industrial education*, 110–11; see also Swett, *Public Education in California*, 264–67.

145. "Report of the Joint Committee," 45.

146. "Report of the Joint Committee," 46–87.

147. "Report of the Joint Committee," 46.

148. Stadtman, *University of California*, 74.

149. Stadtman, *University of California*, 74.

150. The relationship between Gilman and Carr was even more complex. See Stadtman, *University of California*, 71–78. When the board of regents asked Carr to resign his position at the university in 1874 over "imposing evidence of his incompetence," he refused and was subsequently dismissed on 11 August 1874. The next year, Carr was elected California superintendent of public instruction, a position he held until January 1880.

151. Douglass, *California Idea*, 50.

152. Stadtman, *University of California*, 77.

153. Daniel Coit Gilman, "Agricultural Schools at the University of California," Gilman Papers, Yale, MS 582, series 2, box 4, folder 9.

154. Swinton testimony, "Report of the Joint Committee," 26–27.

155. Swinton's entire testimony can be found in "Report of the Joint Committee," 23–32. The book authored by Pinney, Swinton, and Carr, *The University of California and its relations to industrial education*, published in late 1874, includes only a portion of the sworn testimony from Swinton, a lengthy article by Carr in response to the Grangers and Mechanics, and Pinney's "New Education."

156. Swinton, "Professor Swinton's Testimony," 55.

157. Swinton, "Professor Swinton's Testimony," 56.

158. Stadtman, *University of California*, 75.

159. Swinton, "Professor Swinton's Testimony," 55–74.

160. "University and Its Management." George concluded his editorial with this final flourish: "It was a great misfortune that the Agricultural College was grafted upon the old private literary College of California, only, as it has proved, to be swallowed up by it; and it was a great misfortune that a Board of Regents, composed exclusively of rich professional men, was put in charge of it. Better a frame shanty where such a man as Professor Carr would show young farmers how far science can aid in making two blades of grass grow instead of one, than fine buildings, a pompous Board of Regents, a big staff of professionals and lots of donations from millionaires, without any attempt to supply the great want."

161. Pinney, "New Education," 96.

162. "Report of the Joint Committee," 4.

163. "Report of the Joint Committee," 5.

164. Douglass, "Creating a Fourth Branch of State Government."

165. DCG to Louisa Lane, 2 June 1874, quoted in Franklin, *Life*, 162–63.

166. DCG to White, 12 May 1874, quoted in Franklin, *Life*, 162.

167. Gilman, *Building of a University*, 16.

168. Cordasco, *Shaping of American Graduate Education*, 47.

169. Gilman, "Plea for the Training of the Hand," 14–15.

170. Cordasco, *Shaping of American Graduate Education*, 45–46.

171. Franklin, *Life*, 161.

172. Governor Henry Haight to DCG, quoted in Franklin, *Life*, 161; see also Ferrier, *Origin and Development*, 360.

173. Franklin, *Life*, 159–60.

174. Franklin, *Life*, 160–61.

175. White to DCG, 10 July 1874, Gilman Papers, JHU, MS 1, series 1, box 52, folder 21, https://jscholarship.library.jhu.edu/handle/1774.2/43619.

176. DCG to White, 12 May 1874, quoted in Franklin, *Life*, 162.

177. DCG to White, 21 June 1874, quoted in Franklin, *Life*, 163.

178. Reverdy Johnson Jr. to DCG, 23 October 1874, quoted in Franklin, *Life*, 184.

179. DCG to Johnson, 10 November 1874, Gilman Papers, JHU, MS 1, series 1, box 25, folder 40, https://jscholarship.library.jhu.edu/handle/1774.2/42441.

180. DCG to White, 4 November 1874, quoted in Franklin, *Life*, 171.

181. White to DCG, 8 December 1874, Gilman Papers, JHU, MS 1, series 1, box 52, folder 21, https://jscholarship.library.jhu.edu/handle/1774.2/43619.

182. DCG to Booth, 9 December 1874, quoted in Franklin, *Life*, 171–72.

183. "Loss of a Man."

184. John Dwinelle to DCG, 18 December 1874, https://jscholarship.library.jhu.edu/bitstream/handle/1774.2/41961/01_13_21.pdf?sequence=1&isAllowed=y.

185. Dwinelle to DCG, 12 February 1875, quoted in Franklin, *Life*, 172.

186. Stadtman, *University of California*, 88–89.

187. "Resolution of the University of California Board of Regents, March 10, 1875," RG 01.001, Records of the Board of Trustees, JHU, series 2.

188. DCG to Johnson, 3 March 1875, Gilman Papers, JHU, MS 1, series 1, box 25, folder 40.

189. Gilman, *Statement of the progress*, 22–23. Agriculture, Mechanics, Mining, Engineering, and Chemistry constituted the College of Science; Classics and Literature made up the College of Letters.

190. Gilman, *Statement of the progress*, 38.

191. Gilman, *Statement of the progress*, 12.

192. Gilman, *Statement of the progress*, 41–42.

193. Gilman, *Statement of the progress*, 47. The number of female students had steadily increased from eight in 1870–71 to thirty-nine in 1874–75.

194. Douglass, *Conditions for Admission*, 22.

195. "Resolution of the University of California Faculty, April 29, 1875," RG 01.001, Records of the Board of Trustees, JHU, series 2.

196. Franklin, *Life*, 174.

197. DCG, notes, quoted in Franklin, *Life*, 174–75.

198. See Stadtman, *University of California*, 88. Verne Stadtman was named the University of California centennial editor in 1964. During the next four years, he wrote the 100-year history, *The University of California, 1868–1968*, and edited and oversaw the production of the

other special volumes being published as part of the celebration of the University's hundredth birthday. See SFGATE, "Verne A. Stadtman."

199. Ferrier, *Origin and Development*, 367.

200. Stadtman, *University of California*, 85.

201. Barker, *Henry George*, 220.

202. Geiger, *History of American Higher Education*, 323.

### Chapter 3 · The Three Great Advisers

1. Hawkins, "Three University Presidents Testify," 101; see also Hawkins, *Pioneer*, 8.

2. Gilman, *Launching of a University*, 37.

3. James Carey Coale to William Gilman, 20 November 1874, Gilman Papers, JHU, MS 1, series 1, box 9, folder 28. Coale was a local banker, merchant, and codirector of the Baltimore & Ohio Railroad along with Johns Hopkins. A graduate of Haverford College, he was also a devout Quaker.

4. Coale to William Gilman, 20 November 1874, Gilman Papers, JHU.

5. Agassiz, "Opinions of Professor Agassiz," xliii; "Are American Colleges of an Inferior Character?"

6. French, *History of the University*, 24.

7. Hawkins lists all the titles ordered by the Trustees. It is impossible to know how many of them the board actually read, but the list represents a broad sample of authors, perspectives, and subject matters: university histories by Josiah Quincy and Noah Porter, scholarly reflections by Herbert Spencer and James Orton, and educational-reform treatises by Horace Mann and Goldwin Smith. Hawkins, *Pioneer*, 329–31; see also Cordasco, *Shaping of American Graduate Education*, 56–58.

8. Finch, *Carey Thomas of Bryn Mawr*, 45. In 1870, Dr. Thomas was the first person elected by the board to take his position as a trustee. At the time of his death in 1897, Thomas was one of only three original trustees who had helped with the organization of the university, and his activity throughout this entire period is amply evidenced. "He believed that Baltimore had then an opportunity such as had never before occurred in this country to establish a university of the highest character, which would be of service to the State, the country, and the world. Whatever tended toward the attainment of this ideal received from him unfailing encouragement." "Death of Dr. James Carey Thomas."

9. Executive committee minutes, 7 May 1874, RG 01.001, Records of the Board of Trustees, JHU, series 2, 2.

10. James McCosh to DCG, 24 January 1876, Gilman Papers, JHU, MS 1, series 1, box 31, folder 6, http://jhir.library.jhu.edu/handle/1774.2/42654.

11. Gilman had traveled extensively throughout Europe with then Professor Porter, and the letters between the two men were prolific. However, upon Gilman's departure from Yale in 1872 there was a marked drop-off in their correspondence. While it is impossible to know what transpired between them, Hawkins wrote that the drop-off might have been caused by "some letter of inquiry" in 1881. *Pioneer*, 9. The time period referenced by Hawkins, May 1881, includes a letter from Porter to Gilman with the following closing paragraph: "I almost feel convinced of many sins of omission in passing through Baltimore so many times without calling upon you. It would give me no small pleasure to do so and have resolved, but am always driven for time." Porter to DCG, 10 May 1881, Gilman Papers, JHU, MS 1, series 1, box 38, folder 26, http://jhir.library.jhu.edu/handle/1774.2/42921. Porter finally made good on his promise to stop in Baltimore, but not until April 1883. Porter thanked Gilman and his wife for their "cordial

and careful hospitality," signing the letter, "With cordial greetings to the household." Porter to DCG, 22 April 1883, Gilman Papers, JHU, MS 1, series 1, box 38, folder 26, http://jhir.library .jhu.edu/handle/1774.2/42921.

12. For their time and efforts, both Angell and Eliot merely sent notes with details of the expenses they had incurred. For Eliot, the cost of train transport was $37.53 round-trip from Boston. When the presidents received stipends of $500 each for their contributions, they were incredulous, but appreciative. Eliot wrote back to the board: "I was perfectly sincere in what I said to you about compensation for the little service which I could render to your Board, as my note informing you of the amount of my travelling expenses will testify." He continued, "Nevertheless, I accept with many thanks the very liberal fee which the Committee has sent me, partly being influenced in my own mind by the unanimous opinion of your committee, partly by a sense of duty to my profession which is notoriously underpaid in general, and partly, I confess, by the very agreeable sense that this $500 will enable me to go yachting this summer with my two boys with an easy mind, which otherwise I could hardly have done, for I happen to be poor this year." Charles Eliot to Johnson, 9 June 1874, JHU Board of Trustees Correspondence, 1874–1876, RG 01.001, series 4, box 2, folder 8. As Andrew White was unable to make the visit to Baltimore (offering instead to host Hopkins trustees in Ithaca, which he did in September 1874), he incurred no expenses and sought no compensation. He did propose, however, that if he incurred any costs, "I am perfectly willing to throw them in as a contribution of my mite toward your enterprise." White to Johnson, 1 May 1874, JHU Board of Trustees Correspondence, 1874–1876, RG 01.001, series 4, box 2 folder 8.

13. Hawkins, "Three University Presidents Testify," 102.

14. Rudolph, *American College and University*, 245.

15. Hawkins, *Pioneer*, 9.

16. Parshall and Rowe, *Emergence of the American Mathematical Research Community*, 54.

17. Gilman, *Launching of a University*. The rest of the page reads, "And of the long continued cooperation of Basil L. Gildersleeve and Ira Remsen."

18. White to James Carey Thomas, 13 March 1874, Gilman Papers, JHU, MS 1, series 1, box 52, folder 21, https://jscholarship.library.jhu.edu/handle/1774.2/43619.

19. Eliot to DCG, 20 May 1875, Gilman Papers, JHU, MS 1, series 1, box 13, folder 44, https://jscholarship.library.jhu.edu/handle/1774.2/41983.

20. Eliot to Johnson, 9 June 1874, JHU Board of Trustees Correspondence, 1874–1876, RG 01.001, series 4, box 2, folder 8.

21. *Johns Hopkins University Celebration of the Twenty-Fifth Anniversary*, 133.

22. Hawkins, "Three University Presidents Testify."

23. White, *Autobiography*, 1:255.

24. White, *Autobiography*, 1:255.

25. Becker, *Cornell University*, 123.

26. White, *Autobiography*, 1:257.

27. White, *Autobiography*, 1:257.

28. White, *Autobiography*, 1:261.

29. White, *Autobiography*, 1:275–76.

30. White maintained a lectureship at Michigan for some time afterward, "But at last my duties at Cornell absolutely forbade this, and so ended a connection which was to me one of the most fruitful in useful experiences and pregnant thoughts that I have ever known." White, *Autobiography*, 1:283.

31. Rogers, *Andrew D. White*, 50.

32. Becker, *Cornell University*, 81.

33. Hawkins, "Three University Presidents Testify," 100.

34. Becker, *Cornell University*, 111.

35. Dorn, *For the Common Good*, 116; see also Hawkins, *Pioneer*, 7.

36. Geiger, *History of American Higher Education*, 288; see also Williams, *Origins of Federal Support*, 46–49.

37. The trustees entered into the administration of their trust on 6 February 1874 and would receive the principal part of the university bequest from the executors of Mr. Hopkins' estate on 18 March 1875. "Thereafter their meetings and conferences were frequent. Thus eight years has passed since Mr. Hopkins' purposes were made known to the Trustees before they were in a position to go forward." Franklin, *Life*, 38.

38. White to Dr. James Carey Thomas, 13 March 1874, Gilman Papers, JHU, 1.

39. White to Thomas, 13 March 1874, Gilman Papers, JHU, 3.

40. White to Thomas, 13 March 1874, Gilman Papers, JHU, 4. On the basis of his experiences traveling through Europe, White also contended, "A theory that the dormitory system protects the morals of students is utterly unfounded. The dormitory system, bound with all the safeguards of the colleges of Oxford and Cambridge in England when it has been carried to its perfection has proved a far worse school of morals than any other system ever devised. This is a simple fact of which proofs can be easily obtained" (4–5).

41. White to Thomas, 13 March 1874, Gilman Papers, JHU, 5.

42. White to Thomas, 13 March 1874, Gilman Papers, JHU, 7.

43. White to Thomas, 13 March 1874, Gilman Papers, JHU, 10–11.

44. White to Thomas, 13 March 1874, Gilman Papers, JHU, 17–18.

45. Rogers, *Andrew D. White*, 136. Rogers outlines the topics White covered and noted that "White's lectures and manner of delivery were unusually popular with the undergraduates in that day when the usual history class was conducted by the prosaic question and answer method" (136–40).

46. White, quoted in Rogers, *Andrew D. White*, 199.

47. Rogers, *Andrew D. White*, 200.

48. White to Thomas, 13 March 1874, Gilman Papers, JHU, 15.

49. White to Thomas, 13 March 1874, Gilman Papers, JHU, 20–21.

50. White to Thomas, 13 March 1874, Gilman Papers, JHU, 22–23.

51. White to Thomas, 13 March 1874, Gilman Papers, JHU, 24.

52. White to Thomas, 13 March 1874, Gilman Papers, JHU, 31.

53. White to Thomas, 13 March 1874, Gilman Papers, JHU, 27, 28.

54. Minutes of the Trustees, 1 March 1875, RG 01.001, Records of the Board of Trustees, JHU, series 2, 1:20.

55. Minutes of the Trustees, 1 March 1875.

56. Henry James, *Charles W. Eliot*, 1:135.

57. James, *Charles W. Eliot*, 1:135–36.

58. Johnson to Eliot, quoted in Hawkins, "Three University Presidents Testify," 103. The members present for Eliot's testimony included trustees Galloway Cheston, George Dobbin, George Brown, Charles Gwinn, Reverdy Johnson, Lewis Hopkins, William Hopkins, James Carey Thomas, Francis White, and Thomas Smith. Absent trustees were Francis King and John Work Garrett. See President Eliot's remarks, 4 June 1874, RG 01.001, Records of the Board of Trustees, JHU, series 4.

59. President Eliot's remarks, 2.

60. Eliot, "New Education." Eliot framed his article by stating the desire to "review the recent experience of this country in the attempt to organize a system of education based chiefly upon the pure and applied sciences, the living European languages, and mathematics, instead of upon Greek, Latin, and mathematics, as in the established college system" (204).

61. President Eliot's remarks, 3.

62. Eliot, "New Education," 205.

63. President Eliot's remarks, 4–5.

64. President Eliot's remarks, 6.

65. President Eliot's remarks, 6–7.

66. President Eliot's remarks, 8, 9.

67. President Eliot's remarks, 10.

68. Hawkins, *Pioneer*, 10.

69. President Eliot's remarks, 10.

70. President Eliot's remarks, 12–13.

71. President Eliot's remarks, 17.

72. President Eliot's remarks, 14–15.

73. President Eliot's remarks, 17.

74. President Eliot's remarks, 17–18.

75. President Eliot's remarks. The rules run from p. 17 to p. 20.

76. President Eliot's remarks, 28–29.

77. President Eliot's remarks, 29–30. Eliot does not identify the doctor in question as a Harvard Medical School graduate. However, John Barry does in *Great Influenza*, 33.

78. Ludmerer, *Learning to Heal*, 37.

79. Bledstein, *Culture of Professionalism*, 275–76.

80. Hawkins, *Pioneer*, 11.

81. President Eliot's remarks, 41.

82. President Eliot's remarks, 33–34.

83. President Eliot's remarks, 35.

84. President Eliot's remarks, 35.

85. Storr, *Beginnings of Graduate Education in America*, 130–32.

86. President Eliot's remarks, 44.

87. President Eliot's remarks, 45.

88. President Eliot's remarks, 48.

89. President Eliot's remarks, 47.

90. President Eliot's remarks, 49.

91. President Eliot's remarks, 49–50.

92. President Eliot's remarks, 50.

93. President Eliot's remarks, 50–51.

94. Duderstadt, "Diversity," 201.

95. President Angell to Johnson, 12 May 1874, JHU Board of Trustees Correspondence, 1874–1876, RG 01.001, series 4, box 2, folder 8.

96. Angell to Johnson, 16 July 1874, JHU Board of Trustees Correspondence, 1874–1876, RG 01.001, series 4, box 2, folder 8.

97. Angell to Johnson, 16 July 1874, JHU Board of Trustees Correspondence.

98. The trustees present were Galloway Cheston, Francis King, Francis White, Reverdy Johnson, Thomas Smith, James Carey Thomas, and Judges George Dobbin and George Brown. The four absent trustees were Charles Gwinn, Lewis Hopkins, William Hopkins, and John

Work Garrett. Garrett was the only trustee who did not attend either in-person meeting. President Angell's remarks, 3 July 1874, RG 01.001, Records of the Board of Trustees, JHU, series 4.

99. President Angell's remarks, 1.

100. Judge George Dobbin, quoted in President Angell's remarks, 2. Dobbin was referring to City College, a public preparatory school that after 1875 included the first year of college work. Hawkins, "Three University Presidents Testify," 108.

101. Hawkins, *Pioneer*, 10.

102. President Angell's remarks, 2.

103. President Angell's remarks, 4.

104. President Angell's remarks, 5.

105. President Eliot's remarks, 7.

106. President Angell's remarks, 8.

107. President Angell's remarks, 9.

108. Hawkins, "Three University Presidents Testify," 106.

109. President Angell's remarks, 10.

110. President Angell's remarks, 11.

111. President Angell's remarks, 12.

112. Shaw, *University of Michigan*, 8:1773–74.

113. President Angell's remarks, 14.

114. President Angell's remarks, 14–15.

115. President Angell's remarks, 15.

116. White to DCG, 30 September 1874, Gilman Papers, JHU, MS 1, series 1, box 52, folder 21, https://jscholarship.library.jhu.edu/handle/1774.2/43619. The trustees did indeed visit the University of Michigan after spending time with White at Cornell. Angell would record, nearly thirty years later, that he and Professor Henry Frieze had had dinner with the group, trying to impress upon them that "the thing to do was not to go and erect another college like the four hundred already existing in this land, but to strike out boldly at once, and make a great graduate university. Whether we made any impression upon them, or not, I do not know." Angell, *President Angell's remarks*, 134.

117. White to DCG, 30 September 1874, Gilman Papers, JHU. Gilman responded: "I am of course deeply interested in what you say of the Hopkins Trustees. Their reception at New Haven amused me more than it surprises me. There is no doubt among our old friends a latent indifference if not an open distrust of what is doing at the upper end of College street [i.e., at the Sheffield Scientific School]. I feel grateful to you for the good word you said for me to these gentlemen, and confess that I should consider their proposition if it were made." DCG to White, 18 October 1874, quoted in Franklin, *Life*, 170.

118. White to DCG, 30 September 1874, Gilman Papers, JHU.

119. Gilman, *On the Growth of American Colleges*.

120. White to DCG, 30 September 1874, Gilman Papers, JHU.

### Chapter 4 · *Gilman the Recruiter*

1. White to DCG, 10 July 1874, Gilman Papers, JHU. At the request of President U. S. Grant, White would serve as a commissioner to Santo Domingo to study the feasibility of the United States annexing the Dominican Republic. White would also serve as ambassador to both Russia and Germany, and he was offered the presidency of Stanford University, which he declined, instead recommending his former student David Starr Jordan for the post.

2. Eliot to DCG, 1 July 1874, Gilman Papers, JHU, MS 1, series 1, box 13, folder 44, https://jscholarship.library.jhu.edu/handle/1774.2/41983.

3. All the trustees except Charles Gwinn (who was ill) were present for the meeting. Gilman, *Launching of a University*, 37.

4. Gilman, *Launching of a University*, 37–38.

5. DCG to Louise Gilman, 31 December 1874, quoted in Franklin, *Life*, 191.

6. Communications between Johnson and Gilman reveal that the Hopkins trustees wished Gilman to "offer my views in respect to salary." Gilman was demure and responded, "I should prefer to say nothing more than this, that my decision will not turn upon any such point. You would wish to have me live in a becoming manner, and to exercise toward the students and friends of the institution, a quiet but generous hospitality. This I should endeavor to do in a spirit which you will approve and for which I am sure you will in some way provide." DCG to Johnson, 10 November 1874, Gilman Papers, JHU.

7. Johnson to DCG, 4 January 1875, Minutes of the Trustees, RG 01.001, Records of the Board of Trustees, JHU, series 2, 1:16.

8. Johnson to DCG, 4 January 1875, Gilman Papers, JHU, MS 1, series 1, box 25, folder 44, https://jscholarship.library.jhu.edu/bitstream/handle/1774.2/42441/01_25_44.pdf?sequence=5&isAllowed=y.

9. Parker, "George Peabody," 245.

10. "George Peabody Assailed."

11. Johnson to DCG, 4 January 1875, Minutes of the Trustees, 1:17.

12. DCG to Trustees, 30 January 1875, Minutes of the Trustees, RG 01.001, Records of the Board of Trustees, JHU, series 2, 1:18.

13. DCG to Johnson, 30 January 1875, Minutes of the Trustees, RG 01.001, Records of the Board of Trustees, JHU, series 2, 1:21.

14. DCG to Johnson, 30 January 1875, Minutes of the Trustees, 1:22.

15. DCG to Johnson, 27 February 1875, Gilman Papers, JHU, MS 1, series 1, box 25, folder 40.

16. DCG to Johnson, 27 February 1875, Gilman Papers, JHU.

17. DCG to Johnson, 27 February 1875, Gilman Papers, JHU; see also Franklin, *Life*, 176–77.

18. Sander, *Mary Elizabeth Garrett*, 96.

19. Brown, *Need of a Higher Standard*, 12.

20. Hawkins, "George William Brown and His Influence," 184.

21. See M. Dwight Collier to DCG, 6 April 1875, Gilman Papers, JHU, MS 1, series 1, box 9, folder 43, https://jscholarship.library.jhu.edu/handle/1774.2/41819.

22. George J. Brush to DCG, 14 May 1875, Gilman Papers, JHU, MS 1, series 1, box 7, folder 6, https://jscholarship.library.jhu.edu/handle/1774.2/41690.

23. William W. Folwell to DCG, 26 May 1875, Gilman Papers, JHU, MS 1, series 1, box 15, folder 25, https://jscholarship.library.jhu.edu/handle/1774.2/42054.

24. Gilman, *Launching of a University*, 49.

25. The entire "Plan of Procedure" is outlined in Johns Hopkins University, *Second Annual Report*, 25–29.

26. Gilman, *Launching of a University*, 13–14.

27. Gilman, *Building of the University*, 10.

28. Gilman, *Launching of a University*, 42.

29. Hawkins, *Pioneer*, 41.

30. Executive committee minutes, 1 April 1876, RG 01.001, Records of the Board of Trustees, JHU, series 2.

31. Gilman, *Launching of a University*, 50. This is not to suggest that the trustees did not insert themselves from time to time into hiring decisions in the early days. While he was grateful for the support he received from the board for the emerging chemistry department, Ira Remsen bristled at "a pathetic letter" from an R. D. Williams of Baltimore who was interested in the assistantship in chemistry. Remsen protested to Gilman: "I would not be doing right to recommend him when there are certainly better men at hand. I am sorry for him, but I do not see that I should be influenced in the least by personal considerations. I am sorry that he should have been encouraged by members of the Board of Trustees, as he says he has been, as I am thus placed in a slightly awkward position." Remsen to DCG, 1 June 1876, Gilman Papers, JHU, MS 1, series 1, box 39, folder 37, https://jscholarship.library.jhu.edu/handle/1774.2/42980.

32. Gilman, *On the Growth of American Colleges*, 11.

33. Franklin, *Life*, 196.

34. Hawkins, *Pioneer*, 27.

35. Gilman, "Idea of the University," 361–62.

36. See Grauer, "Six Who Built Hopkins."

37. Gilman, *Launching of a University*, 14.

38. Gilman Papers, JHU, MS 1, series 10, box 2, folder 9.

39. "West Point Graduates."

40. Eliot to DCG, 20 May 1875, Gilman Papers, JHU.

41. James, *Charles W. Eliot*, 2:13.

42. Eliot to DCG, 23 March 1876, Gilman Papers, JHU, MS 1, series 1, box 13, folder 44, https://jscholarship.library.jhu.edu/handle/1774.2/41983.

43. Gilman, *Launching of a University*, 15.

44. Hawkins, *Pioneer*, 30.

45. Gilman Papers, JHU, MS 1, series 10, box 2.

46. Gilman, *Launching of a University*, 15. The board's executive committee authorized Gilman to enter into negotiations with Rowland and make him an "at will" employee "at a salary not exceeding $1,000 per annum." Executive committee minutes, 21 June 1875, RG 01.001, Records of the Board of Trustees, JHU, series 2.

47. DCG to Professor Peter Michie, 21 June 1876, Gilman Papers, JHU, MS 1, series 4, box 1, folder 1.

48. Hawkins, *Pioneer*, 46.

49. Johns Hopkins University, *First Annual Report*, 22. For details of Rowland's appointment, see Minutes of the Trustees, 3 April 1876, RG 01.001, Records of the Board of Trustees, JHU, series 2, 1:20.

As with all faculty appointments, the trustees required a fourteen-day waiting period before the position was officially ratified and certified. The trustees' minutes note two weeks later: "On motion of Dr. Thomas the nomination of Henry A. Rowland to be Professor of Physics was also finally approved" (53). Although he was engaged by the university just a week after meeting Gilman at West Point in June 1875, Rowland's appointment as professor of physics was not officially ratified by the board until 17 April 1876, the same day that Ira Remsen's appointment in chemistry was approved. French, *History of the University*, 346.

50. DCG to JHU Trustees, Minutes of the Trustees, 23 July 1875, RG 01.001, Records of the Board of Trustees, JHU, series 4, box 2.

51. DCG to JHU Board of Trustees, 23 August 1875, quoted in Franklin, *Life*, 202.

52. DCG to JHU Board of Trustees, 30 August 1875, quoted in Franklin, *Life*, 204.

53. DCG to Galloway Cheston, 3 October 1875, cited in Franklin, *Life*, 209.

54. DCG to Cheston, 3 October 1875, quoted in Franklin, *Life*, 210.

55. DCG to Cheston, 3 October 1875, quoted in Franklin, *Life*, 211.

56. Henry A. Rowland to DCG, 14 August 1875, Gilman Papers, JHU, MS 1, series 1, box 40, folder 33, https://jscholarship.library.jhu.edu/handle/1774.2/43028.

57. Rowland to DCG, 25 August 1875, Gilman Papers, JHU, MS 1, series 1, box 40, folder 33, https://jscholarship.library.jhu.edu/handle/1774.2/43028.

58. Gilman, *Launching of a University*, 71.

59. Sweetnam, *Command of Light*, 7.

60. Sweetnam, *Command of Light*, 7.

61. Mendenhall, *Biographical Memoir of Henry Augustus Rowland*, 120.

62. Mendenhall, *Biographical Memoir of Henry Augustus Rowland*, 134. Mendenhall was an accomplished scientist and educator in his own right, being the first appointed professor at the Ohio State University. He later served as superintendent of the US Coast and Geodetic Survey and president of the Worcester Polytechnic Institute.

63. "Death of Professor Henry A. Rowland," 65.

64. Rhodes, "Founding America's First Research University," 24.

65. I. M. James, "James Joseph Sylvester," 248. See also Roth, "Jews in the English Universities."

66. University of Cambridge: A Cambridge Alumni Database, "Sylvester, James Joseph (SLVR831JJ)."

67. Osler, *Aequanimitas*, 180.

68. James, "James Joseph Sylvester," 250.

69. Yates, "Sylvester at the University of Virginia," 198–99. For an even more detailed account of Sylvester's brief time at the University of Virginia, see Feuer, "America's First Jewish Professor."

70. Parshall, *James Joseph Sylvester: Life and Work*, 2.

71. A.L., "Late Professor Sylvester," 348.

72. Parshall, *James Joseph Sylvester: Life and Work*, 137.

73. Gilman, *Launching of a University*, 69.

74. Cheston to DCG, 7 September 1875, Gilman Papers, JHU, MS 1, series 1, box 8, folder 52, https://jscholarship.library.jhu.edu/bitstream/handle/1774.2/41775/01_08_52.pdf?sequence=1&isAllowed=y.

75. Gilman, *Launching of a University*, 66.

76. Incoming correspondence re Joseph Sylvester, Gilman Papers, JHU, MS 1, series 1, box 46, folder 26, https://jscholarship.library.jhu.edu/handle/1774.2/43414.

77. Benjamin Peirce to DCG, 19 September 1875, Gilman Papers, JHU, MS 1, series 1, box 36, folder 42, https://jscholarship.library.jhu.edu/handle/1774.2/42851.

78. Silver, "Secret History of Mathematicians," 556.

79. As Professor Sylvester's letters pose a distinct challenge in terms of legibility, the Gilman Papers contain copies of transcriptions from both telegrams and letters between Gilman and Sylvester in 1875–76. Gilman Papers, JHU, MS 1, series 1, box 46, folder 28, https://jscholarship.library.jhu.edu/bitstream/handle/1774.2/43416/01_46_28.pdf?sequence=1&isAllowed=y.

80. Joseph Sylvester to DCG, 17 December 1875, Gilman Papers, JHU, MS 1, series 1, box 46, folder 34, https://jscholarship.library.jhu.edu/handle/1774.2/43422.

81. Yates, "Sylvester at the University of Virginia," 195.

82. Sylvester to DCG, 17 December 1875, Gilman Papers, JHU.

83. Sylvester to DCG, cable, 4 January 1876, Gilman Papers, JHU, MS 1, series 1, box 46, folder 34, https://jscholarship.library.jhu.edu/handle/1774.2/43422.

84. DCG to G. W. Brown, 8 January 1876, Gilman Papers, JHU, MS 1, series 4, box 1.

85. DCG to Sylvester, 8 January 1876, Gilman Papers, JHU, series 4, box 1.

86. Sylvester to DCG, cable, 10 January 1876, Gilman Papers, JHU, MS 1, series 1, box 46, folder 34, https://jscholarship.library.jhu.edu/handle/1774.2/43422.

87. Sylvester to DCG, cable, 26 January 1876, Gilman Papers, JHU, MS 1, series 1, box 46, folder 34, https://jscholarship.library.jhu.edu/handle/1774.2/43422.

88. DCG to C. F. P. Bancroft, 10 February 1876, Gilman Papers, JHU, MS 1, Ban (various), series 1, box 3, folder 19. Gilman would recall this exchange with Bancroft in his 1876 inauguration at Hopkins. According to Gilman, Bancroft had responded: "Your difficulty applies only to old men who are great; these you can rarely move; but the young men of genius, talent, learning and promise, you can draw. They should be your strength." Gilman, "Inaugural Address," 48.

89. DCG to Bancroft, 10 February 1876, Gilman Papers, JHU, series 4, box 1.

90. Sylvester to DCG, cable, 10 February 1876, Gilman Papers, JHU, MS 1, series 1, box 46, folder 26.

91. Spencer, *Principles of Biology*, 444–45. The exact statement reads: "This survival of the fittest, which I have here sought to express in mechanical terms, is that which Mr. Darwin has called 'natural selection, or the preservation of favoured races in the struggle for life.'" See also Howerth, "Natural Selection."

92. Joseph Hooker to DCG, 31 January 1876, Gilman Papers, JHU, MS 1, series 1, box 46, folder 26, https://jscholarship.library.jhu.edu/handle/1774.2/43414.

93. DCG to Hooker, telegram, 15 February 1876, Gilman Papers, JHU, MS 1, series 4, box 1.

94. Sylvester to DCG, cable, 17 February 1876, Gilman Papers, JHU, MS 1, series 1, box 46, folder 34, https://jscholarship.library.jhu.edu/handle/1774.2/43422.

95. Minutes of the Trustees, 19 February 1876, RG 01.001, Records of the Board of Trustees, JHU, series 2, 1:42. Sylvester's appointment was officially "ratified and confirmed" at the 5 March 1876 board meeting (1:46). Gilman wrote Sylvester with the news of the trustees' action on 14 March 1876. DCG to Sylvester, 14 March 1876, Gilman Papers, JHU, MS 1, series 4, box 1.

96. Gilman even wrote Joseph Henry, first secretary of the Smithsonian Institution, asking him to contact Sylvester and urge him to take the Hopkins offer: "I think he would be glad to know from you that the salary proposed is larger than is commonly paid to literary and scientific men in this country—for I think he had some exaggerated notions on this point." DCG to Henry, 20 November 1875, Gilman Papers, JHU, MS 1, series 4, box 1.

97. A.L., "Late Professor Sylvester."

98. Parshall, "America's First School," 189.

99. Parshall, "America's First School," 189.

100. James, "James Joseph Sylvester," 254.

101. Parshall, *James Joseph Sylvester: Life and Work*, 232.

102. DCG to Thomas Craig, 24 March 1876, Gilman Papers, JHU, MS 1, series 4, box 1.

103. DCG to Sylvester, 30 March 1876, Gilman Papers, JHU, MS 1, series 4, box 1.

104. DCG to Sylvester, 10 April 1876, Gilman Papers, JHU, MS 1, series 4, box 1.

105. Sylvester, *Address Delivered by J. J. Sylvester, F.R.S.*, 6–7.

106. Executive committee minutes, 19 October 1877, RG 01.001, Records of the Board of Trustees, JHU, series 2.

107. Horowitz, *Power and Passion of M. Carey Thomas*, 74.

108. M. Carey Thomas to Trustees, 7 October 1878, Minutes of the Trustees, RG 01.001, Records of the Board of Trustees, JHU, series 2, 1:93–94.

109. Feuer, "America's First Jewish Professor," 190.

110. Executive committee minutes, 25 April 1878, RG 01.001, Records of the Board of Trustees, JHU, series 2.

111. DCG to Christine Ladd, 26 April 1878, Gilman Papers, JHU, MS 1, series 4, box 3.

112. See Ladd, "On the Algebra of Logic."

113. Lamb, "That Time It Took a Student 44 Years."

114. James, "James Joseph Sylvester," 255.

115. Parshall, *James Joseph Sylvester: Life and Work*, 231.

116. Sylvester to Arthur Cayley, n.d., quoted in Silver, "Secret History of Mathematicians," 559.

117. James, "James Joseph Sylvester," 255.

118. Parshall, "America's First School," 189.

119. Parshall, "America's First School," 191.

120. Sylvester to DCG, 24 August 1885, Gilman Papers, JHU, MS 1, series 1, box 46, folder 31, https://jscholarship.library.jhu.edu/handle/1774.2/43419.

121. Henry James, *Charles W. Eliot*, 2:14–15.

122. William Watson Goodwin to DCG, 3 July 1875, Gilman Papers, JHU, MS 1, folder 18.2, https://jscholarship.library.jhu.edu/handle/1774.2/42140.

123. Basil L. Gildersleeve, quoted in Briggs, *Soldier and Scholar*, 2.

124. French, *History of the University*, 35. See also Hamer, "Fate of the Exiled Acadians."

125. Gildersleeve, quoted in Rogers, *Andrew D. White*, 196; see also Briggs, *Soldier and Scholar*, 67–74.

126. This initial influx of American students all completed graduate studies at the University of Göttingen in the 1820s. They were Harvard graduates Edward Everett, George Bancroft, and Joseph Green Cogswell and Dartmouth graduate George Ticknor.

127. Thwing, *American and the German University*, 18. Bancroft would return as the US minister to Prussia, living in Berlin for seven years. Writing to George Ripley in January 1868, Bancroft observed, "We have here more American students at the University than from Italy, Switzerland, Sweden, Denmark, France, Great Britain and Ireland, Spain and Portugal put together, which of course places Americans in high esteem among the professors." Bancroft to Ripley, 17 January 1868, quoted in Howe and Strippel, *Life and Letters of George Bancroft*, 191.

128. Cox, *Civil War Maryland*, 75.

129. Briggs, *Solider and Scholar*, 48–49.

130. Johns Hopkins University, *First Annual Report*, 19–20.

131. *Report of the President of the Johns Hopkins University, 1891*, 29.

132. Gildersleeve to DCG, 11 December 1875, Gilman Papers, JHU, MS 1, series 1, box 17, folder 5, https://jscholarship.library.jhu.edu/handle/1774.2/42118.

133. Minutes of the Trustees, 7 February 1876, RG 01.001, Records of the Board of Trustees, JHU, series 2, 1:40.

134. Gildersleeve to DCG, 10 February 1876, Gilman Papers, JHU, MS 1, series 1, box 17, folder 5, ttps://jscholarship.library.jhu.edu/handle/1774.2/42118.

135. Gildersleeve to DCG, 28 February 1876, Gilman Papers, JHU, MS 1, series 1, box 17, folder, https://jscholarship.library.jhu.edu/handle/1774.2/42118.

136. Briggs, *Soldier and Scholar*, 2.

137. Gildersleeve to Horace Elisha Scudder, 10 August 1891, in Gildersleeve, *Letters of Basil Lanneau Gildersleeve*, 183–84; the quotation from Scudder's letter to Gildersleeve is found in 185n2.

138. Curtis, "Confederate Classical Textbooks"; see also Gildersleeve, *Creed of the Old South*.

139. Gildersleeve, *Creed of the Old South*, 46.

140. Gildersleeve, *Creed of the Old South*, 69.

141. Gildersleeve, *Creed of the Old South*, 51. No matter how many explanations were provided by Gildersleeve or other apologists, for those northerners who witnessed the South's commitment during the war and in its aftermath, there still remained a befuddlement impossible to explain relative to their "cause." In recording the conflicting emotions he experienced upon the South's surrender at Appomattox Courthouse, General Ulysses S. Grant wrote, "I felt like anything rather than rejoicing at the downfall of a foe who had fought so long and valiantly, and had suffered so much for a cause, though that cause was, I believe, one of the worst for which a people ever fought, and one for which there was the least excuse. I do not question, however, the sincerity of the great mass of those who were opposed to us." Grant, *Personal Memoirs*, 721–22.

142. Grant, *Personal Memoirs*, 756.

143. Briggs, *Soldier and Scholar*, 17, 46; Krumpelmann, "Basil Lanneau Gildersleeve," 105.

144. Briggs, *Soldier and Scholar*, 189–90. Gildersleeve is referring to the system of dots and dashes called nikkud (points). These dots and dashes are written above, below, or inside the letter in ways that do not alter the spacing of the line. Text containing these markings is referred to as "pointed" text.

145. Briggs, *Soldier and Scholar*, 220–21.

146. Gildersleeve, *Creed of the Old South*, 24. The book was first published as "The Creed of the Old South" in the *Atlantic Monthly*, January 1892.

147. Briggs, *Soldier and Scholar*, 282–83.

148. Gilman, *Launching of a University*, 14.

149. Lowell, *Letters*, 193.

150. Sylvester to DCG, 7 September 1878m Gilman Papers, JHU, MS 1, series 1, box 46, folder 29, https://jscholarship.library.jhu.edu/bitstream/handle/1774.2/43417/01_46_29.pdf?sequence=1&isAllowed=y.

151. French, *History of the University*, 36.

152. Hawkins, *Pioneer*, 50. Hawkins cites the rumor in a letter from an H. C. White to William Leroy Broun, later the president of what is today Auburn University, dated 25 October 1875.

153. Hawkins, *Pioneer*, 58.

154. See Gikandi, "Basil Lanneau Gildersleeve."

155. "St. Basil of Baltimore."

156. Lossing and Wilson, *Harper's Encyclopaedia of United States History*, 403–4.

157. Gilman, *Launching of a University*, 53.

158. Johns Hopkins Department of Classics, "Gildersleeve."

159. Getman, *Life of Ira Remsen*, 3.

160. Getman, *Life of Ira Remsen*. Fittig would later be awarded the Davy Medal from the Royal Society "for his investigations in chemistry especially his work on lactones and acids." See The Royal Society, "Davy Medal."

161. Edgar F. Smith, *Chemistry in America*, 264.

162. Henry James, *Charles W. Eliot*, 1:296.

163. DCG to Wolcott Gibbs, 4 January 1876, Gilman Papers, JHU, MS 1, series 4, box 1, folder 1.

164. Gibbs to DCG, 18 January 1876, Gilman Papers, JHU, MS 1, series 1, box 16, folder 32, https://jscholarship.library.jhu.edu/handle/1774.2/42112. Hawkins surmises that of Gilman's many disappointments during the faculty recruitment process, "this was one of the most keenly felt." *Pioneer*, 45. Gilman and Gibbs would remain friends throughout their lives, with Gibbs closing a letter to Gilman toward the end of his career at Harvard with this: "Remsen will tell you that I still work." Gibbs to DCG, 26 February 1885, Gilman Papers, JHU, MS 1, series 1, box 16, folder 32, https://jscholarship.library.jhu.edu/handle/1774.2/42112.

165. John Trowbridge to DCG, 29 March 1876, Gilman Papers JHU, MS 1, series 1, box 47, folder 47, https://jscholarship.library.jhu.edu/handle/1774.2/43475.

166. Mendenhall, *Biographical Memoir of Henry Augustus Rowland*, 117.

167. Noyes and Norris, "Biographical Memoir of Ira Remsen," 214.

168. Paul Chadbourne, quoted in Getman, *Life of Ira Remsen*, 42.

169. Hawkins, *Pioneer*, 47. There is no record in the digitized Gilman correspondence of the 12 December 1875 letter Hawkins references.

170. Remsen to DCG, 24 April 1876, Gilman Papers, JHU, MS 1, series 1, box 39, folder 37, https://jscholarship.library.jhu.edu/handle/1774.2/42980.

171. Getman, *Life of Ira Remsen*, 46.

172. Remsen to DCG, 25 July 1876, Gilman Papers, JHU, MS 1, series 1, box 39, folder 37, https://jscholarship.library.jhu.edu/handle/1774.2/42980.

173. Remsen to DCG, 15 August 1876, Gilman Papers, JHU, MS 1, series 1, box 39, folder 37, https://jscholarship.library.jhu.edu/handle/1774.2/42980.

174. Remsen to DCG, 30 May 1876, Gilman Papers, JHU, MS 1, series 1, box 39, folder 37, https://jscholarship.library.jhu.edu/handle/1774.2/42980.

175. Remsen, "Harmon Northrop Morse," 608.

176. See Remsen to DCG, 29 June 1876, Gilman Papers, JHU, MS 1, series 1, box 39, folder 37, https://jscholarship.library.jhu.edu/handle/1774.2/42980.

177. Remsen, "Harmon Northrop Morse," 608–9.

178. Remsen, quoted in Getman, *Life of Ira Remsen*, 48–49.

179. Thomas H. Huxley to DCG, 20 February 1876, Gilman Papers, JHU, MS 1, series 1, box 24, folder 24, https://jscholarship.library.jhu.edu/bitstream/handle/1774.2/42387/01_24_24.pdf?sequence=3&isAllowed=y.

180. Sidney Irving Smith to DCG, 20 March 1876, Gilman Papers, JHU, MS 1, series 1, box 30, folder 27, https://jscholarship.library.jhu.edu/handle/1774.2/42626.

181. DCG to Henry N. Martin, 14 March 1876, cited in Hawkins, *Pioneer*, 48.

182. Daniel Coit Gilman, "On the Selection of Professors," December 1875, manuscript draft to the Johns Hopkins trustees, Gilman Papers, JHU, MS 1, series 1, box 63, folder 26.

183. Martin to DCG, 5 April 1876, Gilman Papers, JHU, MS 1, series 1, box 30, folder 27, https://jscholarship.library.jhu.edu/handle/1774.2/42626.

184. Martin to Gilman, 5 April 1876, Gilman Papers, JHU.

185. Huxley to DCG, 27 June 1876, Gilman Papers, JHU, MS 1, series 1, box 24, folder 24, https://jscholarship.library.jhu.edu/handle/1774.2/42387.

186. Martin to DCG, 21 June 1876, Gilman Papers, JHU, MS 1, series 1, box 30, folder 27, https://jscholarship.library.jhu.edu/handle/1774.2/42626.

187. Johns Hopkins University, *Johns Hopkins University Circulars* 4 (August 1876): 6–7.

188. Johns Hopkins University, *Fourth Annual Report*, 53.

189. Fye, "Profiles in Cardiology," 631.

190. Martin to DCG, 9 April 1877, Gilman Papers, JHU, MS 1, series 1, box 30, folder 27, https://jscholarship.library.jhu.edu/handle/1774.2/42626.

191. Fye, "H. Newell Martin," 145.

192. Fye, "H. Newell Martin," 152.

193. Fye, "H. Newell Martin," 146.

194. Gilman, *Launching of a University*, 52.

195. Henry Newell Martin, "Regulations with regard to experiments upon animals," in Executive committee minutes, 2 March 1885, RG 01.001, Records of the Board of Trustees, JHU, series 2.

196. Martin to DCG, 11 July 1883, Gilman Papers, JHU, MS 1, series 1, box 30, folder 29, https://jscholarship.library.jhu.edu/handle/1774.2/42626.

197. Fye, "H. Newell Martin," 151.

198. Griffin, *Pictorial History of the Confederacy*, 196.

199. Fye, "H. Newell Martin," 154.

200. Fye, "H. Newell Martin," 163.

201. Gilman, *Launching of a University*, 52.

202. Hawkins, *Pioneer*, 51.

203. DCG to Ralph Waldo Emerson, 21 January 1876, Gilman Papers, JHU, MS 1, series 4, box 1.

204. George Lane to DCG, 6 December 1875, Gilman Papers, JHU, MS 1, series 1, box 27, folder 37, https://jscholarship.library.jhu.edu/handle/1774.2/42519.

205. Lane to DCG, 31 January 1876, Gilman Papers, JHU, MS 1, series 1, box 27, folder 37, https://jscholarship.library.jhu.edu/handle/1774.2/42519.

206. Lane to DCG, 15 February 1876, Gilman Papers, JHU, MS 1, series 1, box 27, folder 37, https://jscholarship.library.jhu.edu/handle/1774.2/42519.

207. DCG to Gildersleeve, 4 November 1876, Gilman Papers, JHU, MS 1, series 4, box 1.

208. Lane to DCG, 15 February 1876, Gilman Papers, JHU, MS 1, series 1, box 27, folder 37, https://jscholarship.library.jhu.edu/handle/1774.2/42519.

209. Briggs, *Soldier and Scholar*, 80.

210. Lane to DCG, 27 March 1876, Gilman Papers, JHU, MS 1, series 1, box 27, folder 37, https://jscholarship.library.jhu.edu/handle/1774.2/42519. Adding yet more layers to the Lane-Gildersleeve relationship, the eldest of the four Gildersleeve children, Raleigh, like his father was a Princeton graduate; a celebrated architect, he designed the summer home—the Chimneys in Manchester by the Sea, Massachusetts—for his sister and brother-in-law, Gardiner Martin Lane.

211. E. L. Godkin file, Gilman Papers, JHU, MS 1, series 1, box 17, folder 21, https://jscholarship.library.jhu.edu/handle/1774.2/42134.

212. Hawkins, *Pioneer*, 22–23; see also *Nation* 20 (28 January 1875): 60. The article in *The Nation* would have a long shelf life, as the *Baltimore Sun*'s chief rival, the *Baltimore American*, reprinted the news of Gilman's intention to launch a strictly graduate university. The *American* bristled and demanded that an undergraduate division needed to be established first, asserting that Johns Hopkins had been interested in "education for the people and not sinecures for the learned." *Baltimore American*, 2 February and 6 March 1875, quoted in Hawkins, *Pioneer*, 23.

213. E. L. Godkin to DCG, 12 April 1876, Gilman Papers, JHU, MS 1, series 1, box 17, folder 21, https://jscholarship.library.jhu.edu/handle/1774.2/42134.

214. DCG to Godkin, 14 April 1876, Gilman Papers, JHU, MS 1, series 4, box 1.

215. Godkin to DCG, 16 April 1876, Gilman Papers, JHU, MS 1, series 1, box 32, folder 33, https://jscholarship.library.jhu.edu/handle/1774.2/42713.

216. Woods, Bloomfield, and Warren, "Charles D'Urban Morris," 128.

217. Charles Morris to DCG, 28 June 1876, Gilman Papers, JHU, MS 1, series 1, box 32, folder 33, https://jscholarship.library.jhu.edu/handle/1774.2/42713.

218. Cordasco, *Shaping of American Graduate Education*, 78.

219. Franklin, *Life*, 217–18.

220. Gildersleeve to DCG, 7 June 1876, Gilman Papers, JHU, MS 1, series 1, box 17, folder 5, https://jscholarship.library.jhu.edu/handle/1774.2/42118.

221. Gildersleeve to DCG, 10 May 1876, Gilman Papers, JHU, MS 1, series 1, box 17, folder 5, https://jscholarship.library.jhu.edu/handle/1774.2/42118.

222. Gildersleeve to DCG, 10 June 1876, Gilman Papers, JHU, MS 1, series 1, box 17, folder 5, https://jscholarship.library.jhu.edu/handle/1774.2/42118.

223. Morris to DCG, 16 September 1876, Gilman Papers, JHU, MS 1, series 1, box 32, folder 33, https://jscholarship.library.jhu.edu/handle/1774.2/42713.

224. Salary table, reproduced in Bishop, "Teaching at Johns Hopkins," 514.

225. Hawkins, *Pioneer*, 52; Bishop, "Teaching at Johns Hopkins," 515.

226. Gilman, *Launching of a University*, 53.

227. Gildersleeve, quoted in Woods, Bloomfield, and Warren, "Charles D'Urban Morris," 128.

228. DCG to Mrs. Child, 18 December 1886, letterpress book 6 (1886–87), Gilman Papers, JHU, MS 1, series 4, box 2.

229. "Death of Mr. Charles T. Child."

230. Hawkins, *Pioneer*, 256.

231. John Henry Wright, *College in the University*, 3.

232. Rudolph, *American College and University*, 445.

233. French, *History of the University*, 354.

234. Rudolph, *American College and University*, 446.

235. Hawkins, *Pioneer*, 62.

236. Shryock, *Unique Influence of The Johns Hopkins University*, 9.

237. Flexner, *Daniel Coit Gilman*, 63–64.

### Chapter 5 · *Launching Our Bark upon the Patapsco*

1. The Academy of Music building was designed by the firm of Niernsee & Neilson. Its main feature was the Grand Opera House, site of the presidential inauguration: "The ceiling boasted elaborate frescoes, a 'Crystal Dome,' and a great crystal chandelier with 240 candle-shaped burners lit by an electric battery." At the time of its opening in 1874, the building was one of the most elegant in the city and an altogether fitting site for such an august occasion. Robert L. Alexander, *Architecture of Baltimore*, 201.

2. "Johns Hopkins University: Plans and Prospects." The *Sun* printed both Eliot's and Gilman's speeches in full on the front page.

3. Senator Justin Morrill to DCG, 1 May 1876, Gilman Papers, JHU, MS 1, series 1, box 32, folder 31.

4. Introduction to *Addresses at the Inauguration of Daniel C. Gilman*, 4.

5. Eliot, "President Eliot's Address," 7, 8.

6. Eliot, "President Eliot's Address," 12.

7. Eliot, "President Eliot's Address," 12–13.

8. Gilman, "Inaugural Address," 63.

9. Warren, *Johns Hopkins: Knowledge for the World*, i.

10. Gilman, "Inaugural Address," 20–21.

11. Gilman, "Inaugural Address," 22; see also Hawkins, *Pioneer*, 66–67.

12. Gilman, "Inaugural Address," 23.

13. Gilman, "Inaugural Address," 27.

14. Gilman, "Inaugural Address," 27.

15. Storr, *Beginnings of Graduate Education in America*, 134.

16. Gilman, "Inaugural Address," 29, 30.

17. Gilman, "Inaugural Address," 30.

18. Gilman, "Inaugural Address," 33, 35.

19. Gilman, "Inaugural Address," 36–38.

20. Gilman, "Inaugural Address," 38.

21. "Johns Hopkins University: Plans and Prospects."

22. Gilman, "Inaugural Address," 40, 42–43.

23. Gilman, "Inaugural Address," 50.

24. Hawkins, *Pioneer*, 73; see also French, *History of the University*, 88–89.

25. Johns Hopkins University, *Fourth Annual Report*, 28–30. For a more detailed account of Von Holst's time at Hopkins, see Goldman, "Importing a Historian."

26. Gilman, "Inaugural Address," 50–51.

27. While the university was dependent on all these entities in its early years, Gilman was committed to building the library's own holdings, and by 1900 Hopkins had become the nation's tenth-largest academic library in the country. See Arthur P. Young, "Gilman in the Formative Period," 131.

28. Gilman, "Inaugural Address," 52–53.

29. Gilman, "Inaugural Address," 53.

30. French, *History of the University*, 72.

31. Gilman, "Inaugural Address," 54. While no college for women was ever established at Hopkins, the Women's College of Baltimore City was founded in 1885 in central Baltimore, not far from Hopkins' original campus. The institution changed its name to Goucher College in 1910 and moved to its current location in Towson, Maryland, in 1954.

32. Gilman, "Inaugural Address," 54.

33. Gilman, "Inaugural Address," 54–56.

34. Gilman, "Inaugural Address," 56.

35. John Franklin Jameson was an ardent and persistent critic of the approach taken by Gilman and the history department's Herbert Baxter Adams toward potential benefactors. Jameson commented in 1883 that Adams was misguided in thinking that "it is going to be necessary to do work which will strike a chord in the popular heart of Baltimore in order to succeed and secure advancement." Jameson lambasted Gilman's 1882 commencement address as "full of the usual taffy, flattered the Baltimoreans and lugged in religion to please them." Quoted in Rothberg and Goggin, *John Franklin Jameson*, 274.

36. Gilman, "Inaugural Address," 61.

37. Gilman, "Inaugural Address," 63.

38. Before taking his seat on the dais, Gilman finished where Reverdy Johnson had begun: with a nod to George Washington. Gilman quoted from a speech by the country's first president to the citizens of Baltimore in 1789: "I know the delicate nature of the duties incident to the part I am called to perform, and I feel my incompetence without the singular assistance of

Providence to discharge them in a satisfactory manner; but having undertaken the task from a sense of duty, no fear of encountering difficulties, no dread of losing popularity shall ever deter me from pursuing what I take to be the true interests of my country." Gilman, "Inaugural Address," 64.

39. "The Johns Hopkins University: Plans and Prospects."

40. Hawkins, *Pioneer*, 64.

41. Pierson, "American Universities in the Nineteenth Century," 75.

42. Thelin, *History of American Higher Education*, 134.

43. Hawkins, *Pioneer*, 66.

44. Johns Hopkins University, *First Annual Report*, 20–21.

45. Feuer, *Scientific Intellectual*, 375.

46. Hollis, *Toward Improving Ph.D. Programs*, 14.

47. Daniel Coit Gilman, "The alliance of Universities and the learned Societies," speech before the American Philosophical Association, Philadelphia, 15 March 1880, Gilman Papers, JHU, index 5.4.1 (1858–82), MS 1, series 1, box 3, folder 23.

48. Flexner, *Daniel Coit Gilman*, 80.

49. Johns Hopkins University, *Fifteenth Annual Report*, 21–22.

50. John McCoy, quoted in French, *History of the University*, 380.

51. Lanman, "Daniel Coit Gilman (1831–1908)," 839.

52. DCG, quoted in Franklin, *Life*, 223.

53. Huxley to Charles Darwin, 31 March 1874, quoted in Jensen, "Thomas Henry Huxley's Lecture Tour," 184.

54. Huxley to his wife, quoted in Jensen, "Thomas Henry Huxley's Lecture Tour," 185.

55. DCG to Huxley, 13 July 1876, Gilman Papers, JHU, MS 1, series 4, box 3.

56. Huxley to DCG, 27 June 1876, Gilman Papers, JHU.

57. Jensen, "Thomas Henry Huxley's Address," 261.

58. Flexner, *Daniel Coit Gilman*, 84. One account noted that the "academy was filled in every part" and attended by "many ladies who were of the Society of Friends," with which Mr. Johns Hopkins was affiliated. "Johns Hopkins University: Opening Lecture."

59. Hart, "Protestant Enlightenment Revisited," 694.

60. Quoted in French, *History of the Johns Hopkins*, 83; see also Jensen, "Thomas Henry Huxley's Address," 263.

61. "Professor Huxley in America," 8.

62. "Professor Huxley in America," 14.

63. DCG, quoted in Franklin, *Life*, 220.

64. Gilman, *Launching of a University*, 22.

65. "Johns Hopkins University: Opening Lecture."

66. Folwell to DCG, 30 September 1875, quoted in Jensen, "Thomas Henry Huxley's Lecture Tour," 190.

67. "Professor Huxley in America," 8.

68. Jensen, "Thomas Henry Huxley's Address," 263.

69. Gilman, *Launching of a University*, 21.

70. *New York World*, 16 September 1876, quoted in Jensen, "Thomas Henry Huxley's Address," 264.

71. "Professor Huxley in America," 12–13.

72. "Professor Huxley in America," 14.

73. "Professor Huxley in America," 8.

74. Gilman, *Launching of a University*, 22.

75. "Johns Hopkins University and Professor Huxley."

76. S. S. Prince to Reverend John Leyburn, 3 October 1876, Gilman Papers, JHU, MS 1, series 1, box 24, folder 23, https://jscholarship.library.jhu.edu/handle/1774.2/42387; see also Gilman, *Launching of a University*, 22–23.

77. See Leyburn to DCG, 2 October 1876, quoted in Hawkins, *Pioneer*, 71.

78. "Huxley and Prayers."

79. "The Johns Hopkins University."

80. Hawkins, *Pioneer*, 71.

81. Gilman, *Launching of a University*, 23.

82. Jensen, "Thomas Henry Huxley's Address," 266.

### Chapter 6 · *Advancing Knowledge Far and Wide*

1. Slosson, *Great American Universities*, 377–78.

2. Minutes of the Trustees, 17 March 1876, RG 01.001, Records of the Board of Trustees, JHU, series 2, 1:55.

3. Richard Storr, quoted in Pierson, "American Universities in the Nineteenth Century," 74–75.

4. Johns Hopkins University, *Third Annual Report*, 42.

5. Flexner, *Daniel Coit Gilman*, 79.

6. Butler, "President Gilman's Administration," 52.

7. Slosson, *Great American Universities*, 377–78. A complete list of fellows from 1876 to 1885 can be found in *Report of the President of the Johns Hopkins University, Baltimore, Maryland 1885*, 29–34. Another accepted fellow, P. Porter Poinier, a graduate of the Stevens Institute of Technology in physics, passed away at age 23 in June 1876. The roster of the inaugural class is impressive indeed: Henry Carter Adams, professor of political economy, University of Michigan; Herbert Baxter Adams, professor of American history, Johns Hopkins; William K. Brooks, professor of morphology and founder of the Chesapeake Zoological Laboratory, Johns Hopkins; Thomas Craig, professor of mathematics, Johns Hopkins; Joshua Walker Gore, professor of natural philosophy, University of North Carolina at Chapel Hill; George B. Halsted, professor of mathematics, University of Texas at Austin and later Kenyon College; Edward Hart, professor of chemistry, Lafayette College; Daniel Webster Hering, professor of physics, New York University; Malvern W. Iles, chemist, Leadville, Colorado; William W. Jacques, instructor of engineering, Massachusetts Institute of Technology, and scientist, Bell Laboratories; Charles Rockwell Lanman, professor of Sanskrit, Harvard; D. McGregor Means, professor of political science, Middleburg College, and later attorney at law, New York City; Harmon N. Morse, professor of chemistry, Johns Hopkins; Walter Hines Page, writer, publisher, and US ambassador to England; E. Darwin Preston, US Coast and Geodetic Survey; Henry J. Rice, member, US Fish Commission, and professor of natural science, Brooklyn (NY) High School; Josiah Royce, professor of the history of philosophy, Harvard; Ernest Gottlieb Sihler, professor of Latin, New York University; Frederick B. Van Worst, attorney at law, New York City; and John Henry Wheeler, professor of Greek, University of Virginia.

8. Hawkins, *Pioneer*, 82.

9. Johns Hopkins University, *Second Annual Report*, 14–15.

10. Pierson, "American Universities in the Nineteenth Century," 75. As noted earlier, Andrew White had pled unsuccessfully with his own trustees to implement a similar program, but it was not until 1884 that Cornell created a fellowship fund.

11. French, *History of the University*, 75.
12. French, *History of the University*, 76.
13. *Report of the President of the Johns Hopkins University, 1891*, 23.
14. *Report of the President of the Johns Hopkins University, 1891*, 26.
15. Noyes and Norris, "Biographical Memoir of Ira Remsen," 241.
16. Ely, *Ground under Our Feet*, 103. Ely left Hopkins in 1892 for the University of Wisconsin, where he taught for thirty-two years, becoming one of America's foremost economists and leader of the Progressive movement. But he never forgot who had given him his start in the academy. The title page to his 1938 autobiography reads, "To the memory of Daniel Coit Gilman: First President of the Johns Hopkins University, creative genius in the field of education; wise, inspiring and courageous chief under whom I had the good fortune to begin my career to whom I owe an inestimable debt of gratitude, I dedicate this book."
17. Angell's remarks in *Johns Hopkins University Celebration of the Twenty-Fifth Anniversary*, 136.
18. Royce, "Present Ideas of American University Life," 383.
19. Alexander Agassiz to DCG, 23 March 1876, quoted in Flexner, *Daniel Coit Gilman*, 78.
20. Jordan, *Leading American Men of Science*, 470.
21. DCG to Herbert Baxter Adams, 3 May 1876, Gilman Papers, JHU, MS 1, series 4, box 1.
22. "John Bates Clark Medal."
23. DCG to J. B. Clark, 1 September 1876, Gilman Papers, JHU, MS 1, series 4, box 3.
24. Clark to DCG, 7 September 1876, Gilman Papers, JHU, MS 1, series 1, box 9, folder 2, https://jscholarship.library.jhu.edu/handle/1774.2/41788.
25. DCG to Clark, 15 September 1876, Gilman Papers, JHU, MS 1, series 4, box 3.
26. Diggins, *Thorstein Veblen*, 34–35.
27. Clark to DCG, 21 February 1895, Gilman Papers, JHU, MS 1, series 1, box 9, folder 2, https://jscholarship.library.jhu.edu/handle/1774.2/41788.
28. DCG to Clark, 16 February 1895, Gilman Papers, JHU, MS 1, series 1, box 9, folder 12, https://jscholarship.library.jhu.edu/handle/1774.2/41788.
29. DCG to Clark, 15 March 1895, Gilman Papers, JHU, MS 1, series 1, box 9, folder 12, https://jscholarship.library.jhu.edu/handle/1774.2/41788.
30. Johns Hopkins University, *Third Annual Report*, 46–47. Among the ranks of the second class of fellows were the following, who used the stipends to launch careers across America: Samuel F. Clarke, professor of biology, Williams College; Lyman Hall, professor of chemistry, Haverford College; A. Duncan Savage, assistant curator of fine arts, Brooklyn Institute of Arts and Science; Fabian Franklin, mathematician, writer, journalist, and editor; Christian Sihler, neurologist and the first chief of staff at Lutheran Hospital in Cleveland; Francis Allinson, professor of classical philology, Brown University; Maurice Bloomfield, professor of Sanskrit and comparative philology, Johns Hopkins; Constantine Fahlberg, chemist, Gray's Ferry Chemical Works, Philadelphia; Edwin H. Hall, professor of physics, Harvard; Edward C. Harding, professor of Greek and English, University of Louisiana; Isaac Ott, professor of physiology, University of Pennsylvania School of Medicine; Henry Sewall, professor of physiology, Universities of Michigan and Denver; Washington Irving Stringham, professor of mathematics, University of California, Berkeley; Abram Van Eps Young, professor of chemistry, Northwestern University; Charles R. Hemphill, president, Louisville Presbyterian Theological Seminary; Allan A. Marquand, professor of art history, Princeton; and Charles A. Van Velzer, professor of mathematics, University of Wisconsin.

31. DCG to White, 10 April 1876, Gilman Papers, JHU, MS 1, series 4, box 1.

32. DCG to Eliot, 3 June 1876, Gilman Papers, JHU, MS 1, series 4, box 1. Fenollosa's personal life would be the source of much public discussion later in his career. Following his very public divorce in 1895 and his immediate remarriage to the writer Mary McNeill Scott, Boston society was so outraged that he was forced from his position as curator of the department of Oriental art at the Boston Museum of Fine Arts. "Fenollosa, Ernest Francisco."

33. Hawkins, *Pioneer*, 123. Until 1969 there was no central office for coordinating university publications. These materials are actually an artificial collection rather than a group of records generated by a single university office. The collection consists of both serial and occasional publications from the university's founding in 1876 to the 1990s. The former include circulars, registers, annual reports of the president, directories, student directories, the *Freshman Record*, and phonebooks; the occasional publications include a wide variety of materials, such as brochures and broadsides. https://aspace.library.jhu.edu/repositories/3/resources/952.

34. Flexner, *Universities: American, English, German*, 73–74.

35. Johns Hopkins University, *Eleventh Annual Report*, 15.

36. Johns Hopkins University, *Twenty-Sixth Annual Report*, 6–7. In the decade 1890–1900, Hopkins awarded 365 PhDs, an average of 36 a year.

37. Hollis, *Toward Improving Ph.D. Programs*, 21.

38. The nine universities invited were the University of Wisconsin, Yale, Princeton, Stanford, Clark, Catholic University, the University of Michigan, Cornell, and the University of Pennsylvania. Association of American Universities, *Journal of Proceedings*, 17.

39. Association of American Universities, *Journal of Proceedings*, 23–24. Ernest Hollis notes that the standardization of the American PhD from the first decade of the twentieth century forward was the work of four professional organizations: the American Association of Universities (AAU), the National Association of State Universities (NASU), the Association of Land-Grant Colleges and Universities (ALGCU), and the American Association of University Professors (AAUP). Hollis, *Toward Improving Ph.D. Programs*, 23.

40. Bryce, *American Commonwealth*, 753.

41. Adams describes the seminary structure, method, and function in great detail in his article "Methods of Historical Study," 97–107.

42. Rothberg and Goggin, *John Franklin Jameson*, 5–12.

43. Cordasco, *Shaping of American Graduate Education*, 89. The practice was continued up through the presidency of Ira Remsen, at which time it was discontinued.

44. French, *History of the University*, 341. French offers more detail on the requirement of subordinate subjects as a way to achieve for graduate students something comparable to the group system then in effect with college work: "For example, if a man desired a degree in one of three subjects Latin, Greek, or Sanskrit, he would be likely to choose the other two as his subordinates; a specialist in history would almost inevitably study also political economy and political science; and physics, chemistry, and mathematics constituted an equally natural triad" (341–42).

45. The Federation of Graduate Clubs recommended that the cost for printing be borne by the institution.

46. Dykhuizen, "John Dewey at Johns Hopkins," 106–7. The courses Dewey took under Morris were, in his first year of graduate study, Science of Knowledge (a seminar), History of Philosophy in Great Britain, and Hegel's Philosophy of History; and in his second year, Spinoza's Ethics (seminar) and History of German Philosophy "with special reference to the movement from Kant to Hegel" (107).

47. Dykhuizen, "John Dewey at Johns Hopkins," 112; see also Cordasco, *Shaping of American Graduate Education*, 90.

48. Johns Hopkins University, *Ninth Annual Report*, 75.

49. Peterson, "Joseph C. Rowell." While at Hopkins, Gilman made it a point to include in his annual report to the trustees an accounting from the university librarian, Thomas C. Murray, of the development of the library's holdings. The first of such accountings, included in his second report to the board, runs nearly twenty pages. See Johns Hopkins University, *Second Annual Report*, 30–49.

50. Kurtz, *Joseph Cummings Rowell*, 20.

51. Joseph C. Rowell to DCG, 1 October 1875, Gilman Papers, JHU, MS 1, series 1, box 40, folder 32, https://jscholarship.library.jhu.edu/handle/1774.2/43027.

52. Louisa was born in 1838, the eighth of nine children. While her given name was Louisa, she went by Louise and signed her name as such. Louisa died on 27 August 1922, at age 83.

53. Franklin, *Life*, 404.

54. Jameson diary, quoted in Hawkins, *Pioneer*, 104.

55. DCG to Louisa Gilman, 24 March 1880, quoted in Jones, *Elisabeth Gilman*, 72–73. Louisa was a gifted teacher and had some very unique classroom experience. The connection to the place where she taught—and her brother Daniel's involvement at the same institution years later—is most interesting. At the conclusion of the Civil War, Brigadier General Samuel Chapman Armstrong was appointed agent for the Freedmen's Bureau and superintendent of schools in Virginia. He persuaded the American Missionary Association to purchase 159 acres near Hampton, Virginia, as the site for a permanent school for African American and Native American students. The Hampton Institute officially opened in April 1868. It was incorporated by the state two years later and graduated its first class of men and women in 1871. One of the teachers the institute hired on a five-month contract in January 1869 was Louisa Gilman. She left her home in Norwich, Connecticut, and traveled five hundred miles south to Hampton, Virginia, for her teaching assignment. Nearly thirty years later, Daniel would speak—as a representative of the Slater Fund—at the school where Louisa had taught on the occasion of the grand opening of the Armstrong-Slater Trade School building. See "Principal's Report for the Year Ending June 30, 1897." Louisa's correspondence during this period of her life is housed at the University of Michigan and includes several letters to her sisters, including Harriett (or "Hattie," as she was known). The archives at the University of Michigan are under the name Louise Gilman.

Harriett Gilman had married George Lane, a very prominent New York City businessman and president of the chamber of commerce, in 1865. Their marriage lasted until Harriett's death in 1881. Louisa, the youngest surviving Gilman child at the time, then married Mr. Lane the following year. George died seven months later, on 30 December 1883, and Louisa would remain a widow until her death in 1922, living the entire time with her sisters and brother in Connecticut. "George William Lane Obituary."

56. Jones, *Elisabeth Gilman*, 72.

57. Jones, *Elisabeth Gilman*, 21.

58. Richards, *Skulls and Keys*, 115. William was not tapped for Skull and Bones and wrote to Daniel in June 1854 with details of some of the initiates: "Alexander, Barnes, Bumstead (codfish), Linus Child (buffoon) . . ." William Gilman to DCG, 26 June 1854, Gilman Papers, Yale, MS 582, series I, box 3, folder 179.

59. "Vast Forgeries Exposed."

60. "Gilman Compromise."

61. "W. C. Gilman Indicted."

62. "Story of Gilman."

63. See "William C. Gilman Sentenced."

64. "Gilman's Change of Prison."

65. "Business Troubles."

66. Catherine's name is sometimes written "Katherine," and she was referred to as "Katy."

67. "Pardon of Forgers."

68. Cynthia Davis, *Charlotte Perkins Gilman*, 11.

69. "Gilman, the Forger, Free."

70. The special collections at Yale have a folder of correspondence from Willie to Daniel with the following dates: 1850, 1852, 1854, 1862, 1868, 1902–3. Note the significant gap from 1868 to 1902. Gilman Papers, Yale, MS 582, series 1, box 3, folder 179.

71. DCG to William Gilman, 15 January 1903, Gilman Papers, Yale, MS 582, series 1, box 3, folder 179.

72. "William C. Gilman Obituary." No mention is made at all of his late wife, Catherine, or of his misdeeds.

73. Hawkins, *Pioneer*, 113.

74. Johns Hopkins University, *Third Annual Report*, 20.

75. French, *History of the University*, 46.

76. French, *History of the University*, 46–47.

77. Johns Hopkins University, *Third Annual Report*, 20–22.

78. Brent, *Charles Sanders Peirce*, 128.

79. Behrens, "Metaphysical Club," 338. The Hopkins trustees' minutes record the approval of a payment to Peirce of one thousand dollars "in consideration of all claims." Minutes of the Trustees, 1 December 1884, RG 01.001, Records of the Board of Trustees, JHU, series 2, 1:235. The reference to "all claims" was based on a rental arrangement Peirce had entered into. From assurances given by Gilman that he was in good standing with the university, "Peirce had contracted for a house for two years and had to sustain about a thousand dollars loss in order to free himself of it—a claim which was recognized by the trustees who paid him a thousand dollars compensation." Murphey, *Development of Peirce's Philosophy*, 292.

80. Hawkins, *Pioneer*, 117.

81. Johns Hopkins University, *Twelfth Annual Report*, 59.

82. Newcomb, "Abstract Science in America," 118–19.

83. French, *History of the University*, 51.

84. A proposal for the journal was presented by Gilman to the executive committee of the board and immediately approved on 14 April 1877. Executive committee minutes, 14 April 1877, RG 01.001, Records of the Board of Trustees, JHU, series 1, 1:41.

85. French, *History of the University*, 52.

86. Finkel, "History of American Mathematical Journals," 191.

87. French, *History of the University*, 52–53.

88. French, *History of the University*, 219.

89. Givler, "University Publishing in the United States," 108.

90. Charles Scribner, quoted in Hawes, *To Advance Knowledge*, 35.

91. In January 1891 Gilman invited Butler to Baltimore to give a lecture in a "pedagogical course" that Gilman was teaching at Hopkins. Butler obliged and wrote back to Gilman: "I

hope to reach Baltimore on the 28th or 29th, in order to spend two or three days there refreshing myself at the 'fountain head' that the Johns Hopkins affords." Nicholas Murray Butler to DCG, 15 January 1891, Gilman Papers, JHU, MS 1, series 1, box 7, folder 27.

92. Butler to DCG, 16 October 1890, Gilman Papers, JHU, MS 1, series 1, box 7, folder 27.

93. Hawes, *To Advance Knowledge*, 30.

94. Hawkins, *Pioneer*, 110–11; French, *History of the University*, 219.

95. Hawkins, *Pioneer*, 111.

96. Minutes of the Trustees, 1 December 1879, RG 01.001, Records of the Board of Trustees, JHU, series 2, 1:123.

97. French, *History of the University*, 219.

98. DCG to Thomas Davidson, 21 January 1884, quoted in Hawkins, *Pioneer*, 110; *Johns Hopkins University Circulars* 1 (December 1879): iii.

99. Hawkins, *Pioneer*, 110.

100. The quotation is from Macksey, *One Hundred Years of Scholarly Publishing*, 5. For a summary of Gilman's thoughts on the establishment of these journals, see Gilman, *Launching of a University*, 115–17. For a list of the publications, see *Johns Hopkins University Circular* 210 (November 1908): 115.

101. Johns Hopkins University, *First Annual Report*, 21.

102. Ira Remsen, quoted in Hawkins, *Pioneer*, 140.

103. De la Peña, *Empty Pleasures*, 18.

104. Feldman and Desrochers, "Truth for Its Own Sake," 115–16.

105. Stover, *History of the Baltimore and Ohio Railroad*, 155.

106. Crenson, *Baltimore: A Political History*, 300.

107. Sander, *John W. Garrett*, 291.

108. Hawkins, *Pioneer*, 5.

109. Sander, *John W. Garrett*, 299.

110. Gilman, *Launching of a University*, 35–36.

111. Sander, *Mary Elizabeth Garrett*, 186.

112. Thom, *Johns Hopkins: A Silhouette*, 89.

113. Hickey, "Pioneers of the New South," 1; see also Pumroy, "Bryn Mawr College."

114. Minutes of the Johns Hopkins Hospital Board of Trustees (hereinafter Hospital Board of Trustees minutes), 13 June 1870, 1:5–6, Chesney Medical Archives.

115. "His Life Crushed Out."

116. Hospital Board of Trustees minutes, 1 March 1873, 1:8–9, Chesney Medical Archives.

117. Chesney, *Johns Hopkins Hospital*, 1:12.

118. Chesney, *Johns Hopkins Hospital*, 1:14–15; see also Thom, *Johns Hopkins: A Silhouette*, 87–90.

119. Chesney, *Johns Hopkins Hospital*, 1:14.

120. Chesney, *Johns Hopkins Hospital*, 1:14.

121. Olson, *Baltimore*, 246.

122. Olson, *Baltimore*, 260.

123. Hospital Board of Trustees minutes, 13 April 1874, 1:18, Chesney Medical Archives.

124. Chalfant and Belfoure, *Niernsee and Neilson*, 108.

125. Hospital Board of Trustees minutes, 13 April 1875, 1:30, 32, Chesney Medical Archives.

126. Hospital Board of Trustees minutes, 18 January 1875, 1:25–26, Chesney Medical Archives. The Font Hill site remained in the hospital's possession until the board authorized its

sale to the Park Commission of the city of Baltimore for one thousand dollars an acre on 11 June 1907. Hospital Board of Trustees minutes, 11 June 1907, 1:21, Chesney Medical Archives.

127. Hospital Board of Trustees minutes, 24 February 1875, 1:27–28, Chesney Medical Archives.

128. Hospital Board of Trustees minutes, 9 November 1875, 1:35–36, Chesney Medical Archives.

129. Hospital Board of Trustees minutes, 18 September 1876, 1:40, Chesney Medical Archives.

130. Hospital Board of Trustees minutes, 19 February 1879, 1:47, Chesney Medical Archives.

131. Hospital Board of Trustees minutes, 13 October 1891, 1:187, Chesney Medical Archives.

132. Hospital Board of Trustees minutes, 18 September 1894, 1:248, Chesney Medical Archives. The trustees allocated $5,500 to purchase this land at their 12 March 1895 meeting.

133. Hospital Board of Trustees minutes, 11 February 1896, 1:271–72, Chesney Medical Archives.

134. Hospital Board of Trustees minutes, 8 February 1916, 2:307, Chesney Medical Archives. At this board meeting, President Cary and Secretary Parker, acting on behalf of the Board of Lady Visitors of the Colored Orphan Asylum (an entity established in 1875), officially resigned, "owing to the change in the character of the home which rendered their services no longer necessary."

135. The SEED School of Maryland, "About SEED Maryland."

136. The exact wording of Hopkins' letter of instruction is as follows: "I direct you to provide accommodation for three or four hundred children of this class [orphan colored children]; and you are also authorized to receive into this asylum, at your discretion, as belonging to such class, colored children who have lost one parent only, and in exceptional cases to receive colored children who are not orphans, but may be in such circumstances as to receive the aid of charity." Thom, *Johns Hopkins: A Silhouette*, 88. The 2018–19 requirements for admission to the SEED School of Maryland appear to align with what Mr. Hopkins outlined in 1873. See The SEED School of Maryland, "Are you eligible?"

137. Hospital Board of Trustees minutes, 11 May 1874, 1:20–21, Chesney Medical Archives. Niernsee's fee was three thousand dollars per year; he was paid monthly for his work.

138. Niernsee was born in Vienna, emigrated to the United States at the age of 22, and served as a major in the Confederate army during the Civil War. See Chalfant and Belfoure, *Niernsee and Neilson*.

139. Chapman, *Order Out of Chaos*, 109–10.

140. The physicians were, in addition to Billings, Dr. Norton Folsom, superintendent of the Massachusetts General Hospital; Dr. Joseph Jones, professor of chemistry and clinical medicine at the University of Louisiana; Dr. Caspar Morris, one of the founders and designers of the Protestant Episcopal Church Hospital; and Dr. Stephen Smith, designer of the Roosevelt Hospital and one of the founders of Bellevue Hospital Medical College. Brieger, "Original Plans for the Johns Hopkins Hospital," 519–20.

141. Johns Hopkins Hospital, *Hospital Plans*.

142. Harvey, "John Shaw Billings," 35. The Library of the Surgeon General's Office, later called the Army Medical Library, was the institutional medical literature repository of the US Army Surgeon General from 1836 to 1956. It was transformed into the National Library of Medicine, and Dr. Billings' portrait hangs in the reading room. National Library of Medicine, "John Shaw Billings Centennial."

143. Harvey, "John Shaw Billings," 38.

144. Griffith, "High Points," 326–27; see also Chapman, *Order Out of Chaos*, 57–74.

145. Hospital Board of Trustees minutes, 28 June 1876, 1:38–39, Chesney Medical Archives.

146. Johns Hopkins, "The Letter of Instructions Given by Johns Hopkins to His Trustees," 10 March 1873, quoted in Thom, *Johns Hopkins: A Silhouette*, 87.

147. John Shaw Billings, quoted in Porter, *Greatest Benefit to Mankind*, 528.

148. Billings to DCG, 11 November 1876, Gilman Papers, JHU, MS 1, series 1, box 4, folder 17, https://jscholarship.library.jhu.edu/handle/1774.2/41582.

149. Billings to Florence Nightingale, quoted in Grauer, *Leading the Way*, 10.

150. Kyle and Steensma, "John Shaw Billings," E46.

151. *Baltimore Sun*, 7 February 1877, 4.

152. Billings, "Hospital Construction and Organization," 4–5.

153. Hospital Board of Trustees minutes, 11 January 1877, 1:41, Chesney Medical Archives. Billings' report was subsequently published as *Reports and Papers Relating to the Construction and Organization, No. 3*. See https://collections.nlm.nih.gov/catalog/nlm:nlmuid-101718315-bk.

154. Billings, *Reports and Papers* [. . .] *No. 3*, 17.

155. Billings, *Reports and Papers* [. . .] *No. 3*, 18–19.

156. Flexner, *Daniel Coit Gilman*, 117.

157. Chalfant and Belfoure, *Niernsee and Nielson*, 108.

158. Billings' writings on the details of the design of the Johns Hopkins Hospital "became a kind of textbook on the subject of hospital construction and ventilation." See Oblensky, "John Shaw Billings," 288. Billings would remain active in hospital design and even assisted, from 1905 to 1908, with drafting plans for the Peter Bent Brigham Hospital in Boston. It is arguable that no American doctor held more sway or influenced more hospital design elements in the late nineteenth century than John Shaw Billings.

159. Billings' first estimate on the hospital project cost, submitted to the trustees in July 1876, came to $1,028,500. He also provided two estimates of what an individual ward might cost, one for a rectangular design ($24,063) and the other for an octagonal design ($25,137). His original estimate included two pay wards, twelve common wards, and 2 isolating wards. Billings, *Reports and Papers Relating to the Construction and Organization, No. 1*, 18–19.

160. Billings, *Reports and Papers* [. . .] *No. 3*, 18.

161. Gilman, *Launching of a University*, 122.

162. French, *History of the University*, 103–4.

163. Jameson, "Observations on Epidemic Cholera," 383. For Jameson's role in helping Baltimore address the cholera epidemic, see Pietila, *Ghosts of Johns Hopkins*, 43–47.

164. Thom, *Johns Hopkins: A Silhouette*, 51.

165. Minutes of the Trustees, 28 June 1876, RG 01.001, Records of the Board of Trustees, JHU, series 2, 1:236.

166. French, *History of the University*, 5.

167. Johns Hopkins, "Letter of Instructions," 10 March 1873, quoted in Thom, *Johns Hopkins: A Silhouette*, 90.

168. Sander, *Mary Elizabeth Garrett*, 189.

169. French, *History of the University*, 8.

170. President Eliot's remarks, 28–29.

171. Beeson, "One Hundred Years of American Internal Medicine," 437.

172. Gilman, "Inaugural Address," 63.

173. *Johns Hopkins University Circulars* 9 (March 1881): 117–19.

174. Gilman, *University Problems in the United States*, 230–31.

175. Gilman, "On medical education in the State University," 200.

176. Brieger, "California Origins of the Johns Hopkins Medical School," 352.

177. Billings, quoted in Billings and Chesney, "Two Papers," 313.

178. Billings, quoted in Billings and Chesney, "Two Papers," 315.

179. Harvey, "John Shaw Billings," 48.

180. DCG to Billings, 30 March 1876, Gilman Papers, JHU, MS 1, series 1, box 4, folder 1.

181. Billings to DCG, 31 March 1876, Gilman Papers, JHU, MS 1, series 1, box 4, folder 17.

182. Johns Hopkins University, *Second Annual Report*, 10.

183. Billings, *Medical Education*.

184. See Larkey, "John Shaw Billings and the History of Medicine." On the occasion of the opening of the fifteenth academic year at Hopkins in November 1890, Gilman announced that Professor Remsen's activities had necessitated his commandeering the hall—which had hosted all the dignitaries who had lectured at Hopkins to that point—for another purpose: "It is with real regret that we have decided to transform Hopkins Hall into a chemical lecture room." But such was life in the early Hopkins endeavor, as spaces were taken over and repurposed for the most pressing needs of the time. *Johns Hopkins University Circulars* 10, no. 83 (November 1890): 2.

185. William Osler, quoted in Silverman, "William Henry Welch," 236.

186. Billings to DCG, 1 March 1884, Gilman Papers, JHU, MS 1, series 1, box 4, folder 20, https://jscholarship.library.jhu.edu/bitstream/handle/1774.2/41585/01_04_20.pdf?sequence =1&isAllowed=y.

187. Johns Hopkins University, *Ninth Annual Report*, 10–11.

188. Minutes of the Trustees, 5 October 1885, RG 01.001, Records of the Board of Trustees, JHU, series 2, 1:249. At a meeting two weeks later, Welch was authorized to purchase "furniture, etc" in the "Autopsy Building of the Johns Hopkins Hospital." Minutes of the Trustees, 2 November 1885, RG 01.001, Records of the Board of Trustees, JHU, series 2, 1:251.

189. Flexner, *Daniel Coit Gilman*, 130.

190. First hired at Hopkins in 1886, Mall left for Clark University and then Chicago; he was recruited back to Hopkins in 1893.

191. Barry, *Great Influenza*, 38.

192. James K. Gilman, "Brief Military Career of Dr. William H. Welch."

193. Gilman Papers, JHU, MS 1, series 10, box 3, folder 2, "Opening Hospital (1888–89)."

194. Gilman Papers, JHU, MS 1, series 10, box 10.3, diaries 1889–97; Chaiklin, "Daniel Coit Gilman."

195. Letterpress book, "Director Johns Hopkins Hospital (January–August 1889)," Gilman Papers, JHU, MS 1, series 4, box 2.

196. DCG to Osler, 7 March 1889, letterpress book, "Director Johns Hopkins Hospital (January–August 1889)," Gilman Papers, JHU, MS 1, series 4, box 2.

197. DCG to Billings, 18 February 1889, letterpress book 7 (November 1865–March 1891), Gilman Papers, JHU, MS 1, series 4, box 2.

198. DCG to Billings, 28 February 1889, letterpress book, "Director Johns Hopkins Hospital (January–August 1889)," Gilman Papers, JHU, MS 1, series 4, box 2.

199. DCG to Angell, 3 June 1889, letterpress book, "Director Johns Hopkins Hospital (January–August 1889)," Gilman Papers, JHU, MS 1, series 4, box 2.

200. Angell to DCG, 7 June 1889, quoted in Chesney, *Johns Hopkins Hospital*, 1:127.

201. Johns Hopkins University, *Fourteenth Annual Report*, 9.

202. Griffith, "High Points," 328.

203. Billings, *Plans and purposes*, 19–20.

204. Hospital Board of Trustees minutes, 11 October 1892, 1:206–7, Chesney Medical Archives.

205. "Johns Hopkins University: President King."

206. Gilman Papers, JHU, MS 1, series 10, box 3, folder 2, "Opening Hospital (1888–89." See also Horowitz, *Power and Passion of M. Carey*, 233–34.

207. Chesney, *Johns Hopkins Hospital*, 1:193.

208. Jarrett, "Raising the Bar," 25. Gilman wrote years later of Charles Gwinn and his role throughout this process that "his unusual ability as a lawyer made him cautious. He looked at both sides of every question, and when he gave an opinion, it was sure to be based on careful consideration of the pros and cons. As his mind was exact, his pen was ready, and he was constantly called upon to draft such instruments as required precision." Gilman, *Launching of a University*, 121.

209. Rogers was active in many other Baltimore-area causes and left her entire personal estate (nearly $1 million) to Goucher College, whose library, bearing her name and constructed with funds bequeathed to the institution, was dedicated in 1952.

210. Chesney, *Johns Hopkins Hospital*, 1:292. For the full text of the circular, along with the complete roster of local committee members (cities included Baltimore, Philadelphia, New York, and Boston), see 1:291–94.

211. Jarrett, "Raising the Bar," 24–25.

212. Nancy McCall, "The Enduring Example of the Women's Medical Fund Campaign," 24 August 1984, Johns Hopkins University School of Medicine Founding Documents, Chesney Medical Archives, https://jscholarship.library.jhu.edu/handle/1774.2/44505.

213. Chesney, *Johns Hopkins Hospital*, 1:295–96.

214. Chesney, *Johns Hopkins Hospital*, 1:197.

215. DCG to Nancy Davis, 1 November 1890, Chesney Medical Archives, https://jscholarship.library.jhu.edu/bitstream/handle/1774.2/44541/1_b_2_16.pdf?sequence=1&isAllowed=y; see also Chesney, *Johns Hopkins Hospital*, 1:198–99.

216. Minutes of the Trustees, 5 November 1877, RG 01.001, Records of the Board of Trustees, JHU, series 2, 1:77.

217. Brown to DCG, 15 July 1881, Gilman Papers, JHU, MS 1, series 1, box 6, folder 16, https://jscholarship.library.jhu.edu/bitstream/handle/1774.2/41674/01_06_16.pdf?sequence=1&isAllowed=y.

218. Hawkins, *Pioneer*, 265. Interestingly, Brown would prove to be Gilman's closest confidant on issues related to the medical school endowment. Upon returning from his European sabbatical, Gilman wrote a proposed statement on behalf of the trustees, marked confidential, from Maine and dated 13 August 1890. He immediately sent a copy to Brown, who responded two days later in support of what Gilman had drafted, especially the condition that an endowment of five hundred thousand dollars be secured before the school opened its doors. And he believed that Gilman was the one who could raise it—no one else. In closing, Brown wrote: "I incline strongly to the opinion that an organized effort on the part of the Trustees to obtain the endowment fund from individuals would not be so likely to succeed as if the matter were undertaken by yourself personally and unofficially. I am under the impression that it was largely through the personal efforts of President Eliot and President [James] McCosh that the great endowments have been given to Harvard and Princeton, and I cannot help relying more upon the great work which you have accomplished in our University and which you are prepared to

carry forward to great results, than to any other agency." Brown to DCG, 16 August 1890, Johns Hopkins University School of Medicine Founding Documents, Chesney Medical Archives, https://jscholarship.library.jhu.edu/handle/1774.2/44559.

219. Brown to DCG, 16 August 1890.

220. Johns Hopkins University, *Fourteenth Annual Report*.

221. Gilman Papers, JHU, MS 1, series 10, box 3, folder 2, "Opening Hospital (1888–89)."

222. "W.W. Spence Dies at 100."

223. *Statements respecting the Johns Hopkins University*, 28–29.

224. Combined with her earlier gift to the fund, Garrett's total contribution to the medical school was $354,764.50, equivalent to nearly $7 million in today's dollars. McCall and Peterson, "Mary Elizabeth Garrett," 110.

225. Chesney, *Johns Hopkins Hospital*, 1:210–11. For a complete account of the negotiations around admission requirements and the Garrett gift, see 1: 203–21.

226. Chesney, *Johns Hopkins Hospital*, 1:218.

227. Osler to Welch, n.d., quoted in Cushing, *Life of Sir William Osler*, 388.

228. *Johns Hopkins University Circulars* 12, no. 102 (January 1983): 32–33; see also Chesney, *Johns Hopkins Hospital*, 1:298–302.

229. Minutes of the Trustees, 3 January 1893, RG 01.001, Records of the Board of Trustees, JHU, series 2, 1:457–58. The approved memoranda are included in the Hospital Board of Trustees minutes, 10 May 1893, 1:220–22, Chesney Medical Archives.

230. Chesney, *Johns Hopkins Hospital*, 2:468.

231. Flexner, *Medical Education in the United States and Canada*, 12.

232. Gilman, *University Problems in the United States*, 189.

233. Numbers and Warner, "Maturation of American Medical Science," 134.

234. Geiger, *History of American Higher Education*, 340.

### Chapter 7 · *The Slater Fund and Attempts to Integrate Hopkins*

1. "Address of President Daniel C. Gilman of Johns Hopkins University at The Inauguration of William Lyne Wilson as President of Washington and Lee University," 15 September 1897, Gilman Papers, JHU, MS 1, series 5, box 4, folder 3.

2. Elizabeth Dwight Woolsey Gilman, quoted in Rouse, "College Befriended," 77–87.

3. DCG to Benjamin Ewell, 28 May 1887, Gilman Papers, JHU, MS 1, series 1, box 14, folder 21, https://jscholarship.library.jhu.edu/handle/1774.2/42007.

4. Rowell to DCG, 23 November 1892, Gilman Papers, JHU, MS 1, series 1, box 40, folder 32, https://jscholarship.library.jhu.edu/handle/1774.2/43027.

5. Kargon and Knowles, "Knowledge for Use," 4.

6. Reverend Thomas B. Wells to DCG, 1 June 1880, Gilman Papers, JHU, MS 1, series 1, box 51, folder 16.

7. Kargon and Knowles, "Knowledge for Use," 4; see also Menand, *Metaphysical Club*, 257–58.

8. Huxley, "Impressions of America."

9. Crenson, *Baltimore: A Political History*, 322; on Baltimore's neighborhoods, see pp. 1–5.

10. Pietila, *Ghosts of Johns Hopkins*, 95.

11. H. L. Mencken to Abraham Flexner, 1935, quoted in Flexner, *Daniel Coit Gilman*, 13.

12. "Remarks of D. C. Gilman, President of the Johns Hopkins University, before the Charity Organization Society of New York, February 5, 1889," Gilman Papers, JHU, MS 1, series 1, box 63, folder 2, https://jscholarship.library.jhu.edu/bitstream/handle/1774.2/44160/01 _63_02.pdf?sequence=1&isAllowed=y.

13. "Johns Hopkins Returns Thanks."

14. John K. Wright, "Daniel Coit Gilman," 396. In 1908, then attorney general Charles J. Bonaparte said of Gilman, "By the wise choice of President Cleveland he aided in enlightening the foreign policy of our country, [and] in safeguarding the peace of the world" (397, Wright's brackets).

15. Fisher, *John F. Slater Fund*, 137.

16. Morrill to DCG, 28 January 1876, Gilman Papers, JHU, MS 1, series 1, box 32, folder 31.

17. Foner, *Reconstruction*, 170.

18. McFeely, *Yankee Stepfather*, 328.

19. Oakes, "Failure of Vision," 75.

20. Parker, *George Peabody: A Biography*, 111.

21. Du Bois, "Freedmen's Bureau," 354.

22. W. E. B. Du Bois, quoted in Gates, *Black Reconstruction in America*, 179.

23. Commission on Foundations and Private Philanthropy, *Foundations, Private Giving, and Public Policy*, 93–94.

24. Parker, *George Peabody: A Biography*, 117.

25. Peabody Education Fund, *Proceedings of the Trustees of the Peabody Education Fund*.

26. Du Bois, *Souls of Black Folk*, 71.

27. "Negro Question."

28. S. H. Howe, *Brief Memoir of the Life of John F. Slater*, 8.

29. Watkins, "Slater Fund," 2:582.

30. Will Alexander was the chief executive officer of the Commission on Interracial Cooperation and the first president of Dillard University. His 1933 address at the Hampton Institute commemorating the fiftieth anniversary of the establishment of the Slater Fund was published in the Fund's *Occasional Papers*. In his speech, Alexander recounted the friendship between John Fox Slater and Moses Pierce (whom he misidentified as Moses Payne). Will W. Alexander, *Slater and Jeanes Funds*, 4–5.

31. Veronica Alease Davis, *Hampton University*, 37.

32. Staley, *Norwich in the Gilded Age*.

33. Rubin, *Teach the Freeman*, 1:xix.

34. "Rev. L. W. Bacon Questioned."

35. Alexander, *Slater and Jeanes Funds*, 4.

36. Rubin, *Teach the Freeman*, 1:xix–xx.

37. Leonard W. Bacon to Rutherford B. Hayes, 26 December 1881, in Rubin, *Teach the Freeman*, 1:22–26.

38. Marion Lofton Smith, "Atticus Greene Haygood," 36.

39. DCG to William A. Slater, memorandum, August 1880, Gilman Papers, JHU, MS 1, series 1, box 43, folder 26, https://jscholarship.library.jhu.edu/handle/1774.2/43149.

40. DCG to Slater, memorandum, August 1880, Gilman Papers, JHU.

41. Haygood, *New South*, 7.

42. Haygood, *New South*, 10, 11.

43. Haygood, *New South*, 12.

44. Haygood, *New South*, 15–16.

45. Chace, "Enduring Benefactions," 4.

46. Haygood, *Our Brother in Black*, 181.

47. Emory University, "Atticus Greene Haygood."

48. Rubin, *Teach the Freeman*, 1:xxiii. Haygood and Hayes would remain close friends for

the rest of their lives. In a letter to Hayes dated 7 November 1892, Haygood would confess, "I have been on hard times. My effort to save Emory College pulverized me. *But I did it*" (2:264–65).

49. *Documents Relating to the Origin and Work of the Slater Trustees*, 23.

50. Slater trustees work documents, Gilman Papers, JHU, MS 1, series 1, box 43, folder 28, https://jscholarship.library.jhu.edu/handle/1774.2/43239.

51. Slater trustees work documents, Gilman Papers, JHU. When the Slater Fund was established, its founder was 67 years old and his philanthropy had been focused on the 1868 establishment of the Norwich Free Academy in his hometown, in addition to liberal support of the Park Congregational Church, to which he gave $33,000 for its construction. Fisher, *John F. Slater Fund*, xi. Demonstrating his broad commitment to access to education—and shortly after endowing his $1 million fund—Slater would give $16,000 to construct the Jewett City Library in Griswold, Connecticut, now named the Slater Library. "Notes about John A. Slater," Gilman Papers, JHU, MS 1, series 1, box 43, folder 27, https://jscholarship.library.jhu.edu/handle/1774.2/43154.

52. Staley, *Norwich in the Gilded Age*, 27.

53. Howe, *A Brief Memoir of the Life of John F. Slater*.

54. DCG, in *Addresses Delivered at the Dedication of the Slater Memorial Building*, 5.

55. Gilman, *Study in Black and White*, 7.

56. Anderson, *Education of Blacks in the South*, 36.

57. Haygood, *Pleas for Progress*, 129.

58. Anderson, *Education of Blacks in the South*, 91.

59. John Hope Franklin, "Jim Crow Goes to School," 232.

60. West, "Peabody Education Fund and Negro Education," 3.

61. Anderson, *Education of Blacks in the South*, 66.

62. Anderson, *Education of Blacks in the South*, 281.

63. Hayes to DCG, quoted in Rubin, *Teach the Freeman*, 2:251.

64. DCG to Morris K. Jesup, 25 May 1892, letterpress book 5 (1889–94), Gilman Papers, JHU, MS 1, series 4, box 2.

65. DCG to W. E. B. Du Bois, 13 April 1894, Gilman Papers, JHU, MS 1, series 43, box 29, folder 5, https://jscholarship.library.jhu.edu/handle/1774.2/43259.

66. Lewis, *W. E. B. Du Bois*, 383–85. Du Bois read his paper "Reconstruction and Its Benefits," at the AHA's December 1909 conference. He first appeared before the AHA eighteen years earlier, when he read his paper "The Enforcement of the Slave Trade Law" at the December 1891 annual meeting in Washington, DC. Guzman, "W. E. B. Du Bois—The Historian," 377.

67. Du Bois to Slater Fund trustees, quoted in Rubin, *Teach the Freeman*, 2:281.

68. Du Bois, *Education of Black People*, 89.

69. Lewis B. Moore to Hayes, quoted in Rubin, *Teach the Freeman*, 2:256.

70. Logan, *Howard University*, 112; see also Rubin, *Teach the Freeman*, 2:255.

71. Jesup to DCG, 21 March 1901, Gilman Papers, JHU, MS 1, series 1, box 25, folder 30.

72. Watkins, *White Architects of Black Education*, 148.

73. Watkins, "Slater Fund," 2:583. For a complete accounting of Slater Fund disbursements during the years 1882–91 and 1895–96, see Fisher, *John F. Slater Fund*, 134–47. Although the Slater Fund had granted thousands of dollars to Tuskegee over a period of many years, the institute's president, Booker T. Washington, expressed dismay over the lack of visits to the campus in Alabama. In a letter dated 31 December 1891, Washington wrote the following to President

Hayes: "It was a matter of great disappointment to us that you and Dr. Curry could not find it in your power to visit this institution in your recent Southern trip. We were very anxious to have you see what we are doing, especially were we anxious as no member of the Slater Fund Board has ever visited this school." Rubin, *Teach the Freeman*, 2:234.

74. J. L. M. Curry, "Slater Report 1901," quoted in Williams, *White Architects of Black Education*, 177–78.

75. See Curry, *Education of the Negroes since 1860*.

76. *Documents Relating to the Origin and Work of the Slater Trustees*.

77. Gilman, *Study in Black and White*, 4.

78. Howe, *Brief Memoir of the Life of John F. Slater*, 4.

79. *Occasional Papers, John F. Slater Fund Trustees, 1894–1935*.

80. Gilman Papers, JHU, MS 1, series 43, box 27, folder 18, "John Fox Slater meeting minutes," https://jscholarship.library.jhu.edu/handle/1774.2/43167.

81. James, James, and Boyer, *Notable American Women, 1607–1950*, 2:196.

82. Jones-Wilson et al., *Encyclopedia of African-American Education*, 1:428.

83. See Fisher, *John F. Slater Fund*, appendix G, for a listing of schools supported by the fund from 1882 to 1896, for example.

84. General Education Board, "Letter from the General Education Board."

85. Rockefeller Foundation: A Digital History, "General Education Board."

86. Gilman, *Study in Black and White*, 12.

87. Thom, *Johns Hopkins: A Silhouette*, 103.

88. W. D. Wright, "Thought and Leadership of Kelly Miller," 180.

89. Eisenberg, "Kelly Miller," 184; see also Miller, "Howard University."

90. Morgan, "Son of a Slave," 21. Howard University was named for the Civil War hero General Oliver Otis Howard, who founded the university in 1867, served as commissioner of the Freedmen's Bureau from 1865 to 1874, and served as president of the university from 1869 to 1874. McFeely, *Yankee Stepfather*, 2–9.

91. Morgan, "Son of a Slave," 21.

92. Campbell, *Biographical Memoir of Simon Newcomb*, 13.

93. "Miller, Kelly," RG 13.010, Office of the Registrar, subgroup 1, series 2, Ferdinand Hamburger Archives, JHU.

94. Morgan, "Son of a Slave," 21.

95. Robert Garrett II was the son of Johns Hopkins' best friend, John Work Garrett, former president of the B&O Railroad; Robert had succeeded to the presidency upon his father's death in 1884.

96. Morgan, "Son of a Slave," 22.

97. Morgan, "Son of a Slave," 22.

98. Thom, *Johns Hopkins: A Silhouette*, 103.

99. Morgan, "Son of a Slave," 22.

100. J. E. Rankin to DCG, 23 January 1890, RG 13.010, Office of the Registrar, subgroup 1, series 2, Ferdinand Hamburger Archives, JHU.

101. Simon Newcomb to DCG, 25 January 1890, RG 13.010, Office of the Registrar, subgroup 1, series 2, Ferdinand Hamburger Archives, JHU.

102. Meier, "Racial and Educational Philosophy of Kelly Miller," 122.

103. Kelly Miller to DCG, 17 March 1900, RG 13.010, Office of the Registrar, subgroup 1, series 2, Ferdinand Hamburger Archives, JHU.

104. Kelly Miller, *The Primary Needs of the Negro Race*, 15.

105. Edward R. Lewis to Isaiah Bowman, 23 November 1938, RG 13.010, Office of the President, Ferdinand Hamburger Archives, JHU; Bowman to Lewis, 25 November 1938, RG 02.001, Office of the President, series 1, file 73, "Negro Education."

106. Neil Smith, *American Empire*, 247. Broadus Mitchell had earned his PhD in economics at Hopkins in 1918 and taught there for twenty years. See also Jones, *Elisabeth Gilman*, 196–98. In her run for governor in 1930 Gilman had garnered just over 4,100 votes.

107. Johns Hopkins University, "Edward Lewis."

108. Irene M. Davis to Bowman, 11 January 1939, RG 13.010, Office of the Registrar, subgroup 1, series 2, Ferdinand Hamburger Archives, JHU.

109. Smith, *American Empire*, 246–47.

110. Smith, *American Empire*, 251.

111. Mitchell, "Excluded Because of Color."

112. Rodriguez, "All Quiet on the Southern Front"; see also Cook, "Broadus Mitchell, 95."

113. Gilman, *Study in Black and White*, 7.

114. "Nineteenth-Century United States President," 35.

115. Stimpert, "Johns Hopkins University," 138. See also Smith, *American Empire*, 247.

### Chapter 8 · *Allies, Not Rivals*

1. Hopkins faculty to DCG, 23 May 1896, quoted in Franklin, *Life*, 310–11.

2. DCG to Hopkins faculty, 28 May 1896, quoted in Franklin, *Life*, 311–12.

3. Jacob Cooper to DCG, 21 November 1900, Gilman Papers, JHU, MS 1, series 1, box 10, folder 2, https://jscholarship.library.jhu.edu/handle/1774.2/41833.

4. DCG to Cooper, 23 November 1900, quoted in Franklin, *Life*, 384–85.

5. Gilman, *Launching of a University*, 106.

6. White to DCG, 4 December 1900, Gilman Papers, JHU, MS 1, series 1, box 53, folder 3, https://jscholarship.library.jhu.edu/handle/1774.2/43628.

7. Franklin, *Life*, 384.

8. See Lagemann, *Private Power for the Public Good*, 7–9.

9. *Cornell Alumni News* 21:502. The first typhoid cases were reported in the fall of 1902, with the worst of the epidemic lasting through the spring of 1903. Twenty-nine Cornell students died. Prescott, "Sending Their Sons into Danger."

10. White, "University at Washington," 11.

11. White, "University at Washington," 6.

12. White, quoted in Rogers, *Andrew D. White*, 205–6.

13. See Benson and Boyd, *College for the Commonwealth*, 12–14.

14. Thomas, *Founders*, 33.

15. Washington, "Eighth Annual Message."

16. Washington, "George Washington's Last Will and Testament."

17. Another ardent supporter of a national university was John Wesley Hoyt. During a varied career that included teaching under Horace Mann at Antioch College, helping to reorganize the University of Wisconsin, and serving as both governor of the Wyoming Territory and the first president of the University of Wyoming, Hoyt advocated the national university idea from 1869 until his death in 1912. Thomas, *Founders*, 172.

18. Andrew Carnegie to White, 26 April 1901, quoted in Madsen, "Daniel Coit Gilman at the Carnegie Institution," 158.

19. Carnegie, "Wealth," 664.

20. Carnegie, "Best Fields for Philanthropy," 688.

21. George Atherton to Carnegie, 27 October 1895, quoted in Ris, "Education of Andrew Carnegie," 406.

22. Carnegie to J. B. Corey, 18 November 1896, quoted in Ris, "Education of Andrew Carnegie," 406.

23. Carnegie, *Empire of Business*, 79–80.

24. Atkinson, *On the Right Use of Books*, 11.

25. Hofstadter, *Anti-intellectualism in American Life*, 260.

26. Carnegie, quoted in Harlan, *Booker T. Washington*, 135.

27. Carnegie, quoted in Ris, "Education of Andrew Carnegie," 409.

28. Lester, *Forty Years of Carnegie Giving*, 21.

29. Lester, *Forty Years of Carnegie Giving*, 19.

30. White to DCG, 20 May 1901, Gilman Papers, JHU, MS 1, series 1, box 53, folder 3, https://jscholarship.library.jhu.edu/handle/1774.2/43628.

31. White to DCG, 20 May 1901, Gilman Papers, JHU.

32. Carnegie to White, 26 April 1901, quoted in Ris, "Education of Andrew Carnegie," 411.

33. Madsen, "Daniel Coit Gilman at the Carnegie Institution," 155.

34. White to DCG, 14 August 1901, Gilman Papers, JHU, MS 1, series 1, box 53, folder 3, https://jscholarship.library.jhu.edu/handle/1774.2/43628.

35. Gilman, *University Problems in the United States*, 318. It is interesting that Charles Walcott wrote to Gilman in 1899 requesting two more reprints of this article and stating that he was "more than delighted to find that I hold essentially the same view as yourself in regard to what should constitute the proposed National University. The only point we would differ in is that I think the necleus [sic] of the University should be around the National Museum rather than the Smithsonian." Walcott to DCG, 16 March 1899, Gilman Papers, JHU, MS 1, series 1, box 49, folder 21, https://jscholarship.library.jhu.edu/handle/1774.2/43532.

36. Gilman, *Launching of a University*, 106.

37. Mitchell and Garrison, *Biographical memoir of John Shaw Billings, 1838–1913*, 375–416.

38. *New York Evening Mail*, 1 June 1911, quoted in Chapman, *Order Out of Chaos*, 301.

39. Chapman, *Order Out of Chaos*, 324.

40. Franklin, *Life*, 392; see also Madsen, "Daniel Coit Gilman at the Carnegie Institution," 156.

41. Gilman, *Launching of a University*, 107.

42. Johnson and Malone, *Dictionary of American Biography*, 3:502.

43. Confusion persists to this day around the multitude of organizations and entities, all unaffiliated, that bear the Carnegie name, twenty-three total across the globe. The Carnegie Institution of Washington is the entity founded in 1902 and helmed by Daniel Coit Gilman. The name was changed in 2007 to Carnegie Institution for Science. The organization's website offers the best explanation as to why this occurred: "Our legal name, the Carnegie Institution of Washington, has led to confusion because four of our departments are outside Washington and because our legal name does not distinguish us from the other non-profits created by our donor. As a result, the institution adopted a new name in 2007—the Carnegie Institution for Science. The new name closely associates the words 'Carnegie' and 'science' and thereby reveals our core identity. The institution remains officially and legally the Carnegie Institution of Washington, but now has a public identity that more clearly describes our work." Under the title "Carnegie Confusion," the Carnegie Institution for Science lists all of the Carnegie-related entities and their addresses. Carnegie Science, "Andrew Carnegie's 23 Institutions."

44. Chapman, *Order Out of Chaos*, 323.

45. Madsen, "Daniel Coit Gilman at the Carnegie Institution," 156.

46. Madsen, "Daniel Coit Gilman at the Carnegie Institution," 159.

47. Gilman to White, 7 December 1901, quoted in Franklin, *Life*, 400.

48. Carnegie to Theodore Roosevelt, 28 November 1901, quoted in Ris, "Education of Andrew Carnegie," 412.

49. *New York Times*, 10 December 1901, 1.

50. DCG to White, 20 December 1901, quoted in Franklin, *Life*, 400.

51. At the request of Carnegie, the following trustees were elected by the incorporators of the institution. The ex-officio members included the president of the United States (Theodore Roosevelt); the president of the Senate (William Frye was serving as president pro tem of the Senate at the time); the Speaker of the House of Representatives (David B. Henderson); the secretary of the Smithsonian Institution (Samuel P. Langley); and the president of the National Academy of Sciences (Alexander Agassiz). Other members: John S. Billings, New York; Grover Cleveland, New Jersey; William E. Dodge, New York; William N. Frew, Pennsylvania; Lyman P. Gage, Illinois; Daniel C. Gilman, Maryland; John Hay, District of Columbia; Abram S. Hewitt, New Jersey; Henry L. Higginson, Massachusetts; Henry Hitchcock, Missouri; Charles L. Hutchinson, Illinois; William Lindsay, Kentucky; Seth Low, New York; Wayne MacVeagh, Pennsylvania; D. O. Mills, New York; S. Weir Mitchell, Pennsylvania; William W. Morrow, California; Elihu Root, New York; John C. Spooner, Wisconsin; Charles D. Walcott, District of Columbia; Andrew D. White, New York; Edward D. White, Louisiana; Carroll D. Wright, District of Columbia. In a letter to Secretary Walcott dated 9 January 1902, Cleveland expressed his inability to accept a position on the board. William Dodge, of New York, accepted on 29 January 1902, in Cleveland's place. See Carnegie Institution of Washington, *Proceedings of the Board of Trustees*, 10. This document has minutes from the 30 January 1902 meeting as well.

52. Carnegie Institution of Washington, *Articles of Incorporation*, 12. This small booklet includes all the legal documents and the roster of trustees, along with Carnegie's remarks at the inaugural board meeting as well as a letter from Secretary of State John Hay.

53. Gilman, *Launching of a University*, 109.

54. Carnegie Institution of Washington, *Articles of Incorporation*, 13.

55. Carnegie Institution of Washington, *Articles of Incorporation*, 11.

56. "Dr. Gilman Head of Carnegie Institution."

57. DCG to family, 2 February 1902, quoted in Franklin, *Life*, 401.

58. Carnegie Institution of Washington, *Proceedings of the Board of Trustees*, 11.

59. Franklin, *Life*, 399.

60. Madsen, "Daniel Coit Gilman at the Carnegie Institution," 161.

61. Ris, "Education of Andrew Carnegie," 412.

62. Reingold, "National Science Policy in a Private Foundation," 315.

63. Geiger, *To Advance Knowledge*, 63; see also Howard S. Miller, *Dollars for Research*, 166–81.

64. DCG, quoted in Madsen, "Daniel Coit Gilman at the Carnegie Institution," 163.

65. Reingold, "National Science Policy in a Private Foundation," 315.

66. Carnegie Institution of Washington, *Proceedings of the Board of Trustees*, 14–15.

67. Flexner, *Daniel Coit Gilman*, 159–60.

68. Gilman, *Launching of a University*, 110.

69. Madsen, "Daniel Coit Gilman at the Carnegie Institution," 164.

70. Reingold, "National Science Policy in a Private Foundation," 314.

71. For a roster of all these advisory committees, see Carnegie Institution of Washington, *Year Book No. 1, 1902*, xxxii–xxxiv.

72. Flexner, *Daniel Coit Gilman*, 160.

73. Madsen, "Daniel Coit Gilman at the Carnegie Institution," 165.

74. Carnegie Institution of Washington, *Year Book No. 1, 1902*, xxxv–xl.

75. Madsen, "Daniel Coit Gilman at the Carnegie Institution," 166.

76. DCG to Walcott, quoted in Madsen, "Daniel Coit Gilman at the Carnegie Institution," 166.

77. Daniel Coit Gilman, 1902 Diary, Gilman Papers, JHU, MS 1, series 10 personal, box 4, folder 4.

78. Carnegie to DCG, 27 October 1902, quoted in Franklin, *Life*, 401.

79. Madsen, "Daniel Coit Gilman at the Carnegie Institution," 167.

80. Carnegie Institution of Washington, *Year Book No. 1, 1902*, xli–xlii; see also Madsen, "Daniel Coit Gilman at the Carnegie Institution," 167.

81. Carnegie Institution of Washington, *Year Book No. 1, 1902*, xl.

82. Daniel Coit Gilman, 1903 Diary, Gilman Papers, JHU, MS 1, series 10 personal, box 4, folder 5.

83. Madsen, "Daniel Coit Gilman at the Carnegie Institution," 175–76.

84. White to DCG, 5 November 1903, Gilman Papers, JHU, MS 1, series 1, box 53, folder 3, https://jscholarship.library.jhu.edu/handle/1774.2/43628.

85. Carnegie Institution of Washington, *Year Book No. 3, 1904*, 17.

86. Gilman, *Launching of a University*, 112.

87. DCG, 8 December 1903, quoted in Carnegie Institution of Washington, *Year Book No. 3, 1904*, 17. Gilman's letter is in the Gilman Papers, Yale, MS 582, series 3, box 6, folder 3.

88. Henry Pritchett to Henry Higginson, n.d., quoted in Flexner, *Henry S. Pritchett*, 157.

89. For the revised bylaws as approved by the board, see Carnegie Institution of Washington, *Year Book No. 3, 1904*, 13–16; see also Flexner, *Daniel Coit Gilman*, 160–61.

90. For more on the trustees involved in the bylaw revision process, see Madsen, "Daniel Coit Gilman at the Carnegie Institution," 170–78.

91. Reingold, "National Science Policy in a Private Foundation," 315.

92. Carnegie Institution of Washington, *Year Book No. 4, 1905*, 15–33.

93. Charles M. Andrews, "Daniel Coit Gilman, L.L.D.," lxix.

94. Carnegie to Gilman, 10 December 1903, quoted in Franklin, *Life*, 402.

95. Eliot to DCG, 20 September 1885, Gilman Papers, JHU, MS 1, series 1, box 13, folder 43, https://jscholarship.library.jhu.edu/handle/1774.2/41983.

96. Gilman's introduction was for the 1862 version of de Tocqueville's work, translated by Henry Reeve and annotated by Francis Bowen.

97. American Bible Society, *Ninety-Third Annual Report*, 14–15.

98. Daniel Coit Gilman, "Centennial of the British and Foreign Bible Society," Gilman Papers, Yale, MS 582, series 2, box 5, folder 41.

99. DCG, 7 May 1889, quoted in Chesney, *Johns Hopkins Hospital*, 1:269. Gilman's speech, titled "Charity and Knowledge," was published in *Science* as well. See Gilman, "Charity and Knowledge."

100. Hart, "Protestant Enlightenment Revisited," 689.

101. Jones, *Elisabeth Gilman*, 29.

102. Arthur B. Kinsolving, quoted in Jones, *Elisabeth Gilman*, 237.

103. Sidney Hollander, quoted in Jones, *Elisabeth Gilman*, 234.

104. Daniel Coit Gilman, 1907 Diary, Gilman Papers, JHU, MS 1, series 10 personal, box 6, folder 2.

105. Daniel C. Gilman, "Europe" (1889–90), Gilman Papers, JHU, MS 1, series 10 personal, box 3, folder 3; see also Jones, *Elisabeth Gilman*, 44–52.

106. James Sylvester, quoted in Parshall, *James Joseph Sylvester: Jewish Mathematician*, 318.

107. Gilman recorded on 27 March 1908: "Paid Wh. Star $360 for three return tickets, Paris to New York." Daniel Coit Gilman, 1908 Diary, Gilman Papers, JHU, MS 1, series 10 personal, box 6, folder 4.

108. Gilman, 1908 Diary, Gilman Papers, JHU.

109. Gilman, 1908 Diary, Gilman Papers, JHU.

110. Peabody Education Fund, *Proceedings of the Trustees at their Fifty-Second Meeting*, 10–11.

111. Peabody Institute minutes, 27 October 1908, Gilman Papers, JHU, MS 1, series 1, box 9, folder 1, "Clippings, letters, re Gilman's death."

112. Davidson to DCG, 3 January and 22 May 1884, Gilman Papers, JHU, MS 1, series 1, box 11, folder 29, https://jscholarship.library.jhu.edu/handle/1774.2/41891.

113. Johns Hopkins University, *Seventeenth Annual Report*, 20.

114. Daniel Coit Gilman, biographical material, Gilman Papers, JHU, MS 1, vertical file, folder 1.

115. Butler, "Daniel Coit Gilman," 552.

### Conclusion

1. *Johns Hopkins University Celebration of the Twenty-Fifth Anniversary*, 62.

2. White, quoted in Franklin, *Life*, 326.

3. Gilman Papers, JHU, MS 1, series 8, "Tribute Volumes," box 8.1, 6. This gift from the Hopkins graduates to Gilman is housed in the Johns Hopkins University Special Collections, located in the Milton Eisenhower Library on the Homewood campus.

4. *Johns Hopkins University Celebration of the Twenty-Fifth Anniversary*, 43–44.

5. Mencken, "Daniel Gilman Is Forgotten Great Man."

6. Brubacher and Rudy, *Higher Education in Transition*, 181.

7. Gilman, *University Problems in the United States*, 55.

8. Flexner, *Daniel Coit Gilman*, 8.

Abbott, James Archer, Earle A. Havens, Bodil Ottesen, and Susan G. Tripp. *Evergreen: The Garrett Family, Collectors and Connoisseurs*. Baltimore: Johns Hopkins University Press, 2017.

Adams, Herbert Baxter. "Methods of Historical Study." *Johns Hopkins University Studies in Historical and Political Science* 2 (1884): 5–137.

*Addresses at the Inauguration of Daniel C. Gilman as President of the Johns Hopkins University, Baltimore, February 22, 1876*. Baltimore: John Murphy, 1876.

*Addresses Delivered at the Dedication of the Slater Memorial Building, at Norwich, Connecticut, Thursday, Nov. 4, 1886. By Professor John Putnam Gulliver and President Daniel Coit Gilman*. Cambridge, MA: University Press, 1887.

Agassiz, Louis. "Opinions of Professor Agassiz." In *Report of the Commissioner of Education for the Year 1872*. Washington, DC: Government Printing Office, 1873.

A.L. "The Late Professor Sylvester." *Journal of the Institute of Actuaries (1886–1994)* 33, no. 4 (1897): 345–49.

Alexander, Robert L. *The Architecture of Baltimore: An Illustrated History*. Baltimore: Johns Hopkins University Press, 2004.

Alexander, Will W. *The Slater and Jeanes Funds: An Educator's Approach to a Difficult Social Problem*. The Trustees of the John F. Slater Fund, Occasional Paper 28. Baltimore: Published by the Trustees, 1934.

Altschuler, Glenn C. *Andrew D. White: Educator, Historian, Diplomat*. Ithaca, NY: Cornell University Press, 1979.

American Bible Society. *Ninety-Third Annual Report of the American Bible Society, 1901*. New York: American Bible Society, 1909.

Anderson, James D. *The Education of Blacks in the South, 1860–1935*. Chapel Hill: University of North Carolina Press, 1988.

Andrews, Charles M. "Daniel Coit Gilman, L.L.D." *Proceedings of the American Philosophical Society* 48, no. 193 (September–December 1909): lxii–lxx.

Andrews, Matthew Page. "History of Baltimore from 1850 to the Close of the Civil War." In *Baltimore: Its History and Its People*, edited by Clayton Colman Hall, 151–237. New York: Lewis Historical Publishing, 1912.

Angell, James Burrell. *President Angell's remarks in Johns Hopkins University, Celebration of the twenty-fifth anniversary of the founding of the university and inauguration of Ira Remsen*. Baltimore: Johns Hopkins University Press, 1902.

"Are American Colleges of an Inferior Character?" *New York Times*, 7 August 1874, 2.

Arnold, James. *Shiloh 1862: The Death of Innocence*. Westport, CT: Praeger, 2004.

Association of American Universities. *Journal of Proceedings and Addresses of the Annual Confer-ence of the Association of Graduate Schools in the Association of American Universities, 1900–01.* Washington, DC: The Association, 1901.

Atkinson, William Parsons. *On the Right Use of Books: A Lecture.* Boston: Roberts Brothers, 1878.

Barker, Charles Albro. *Henry George.* New York: Oxford University Press, 1955.

Barnard, Henry. "California Educational Society." *American Journal of Education* 16 (1866): 785–90.

Barry, John M. *The Great Influenza: The Story of the Deadliest Pandemic in History.* New York: Viking, 2004.

Becker, Carl L. *Cornell University: Founders and the Founding.* Ithaca, NY: Cornell University Press, 1943.

Beeson, Paul B. "One Hundred Years of American Internal Medicine: A View from the Inside." *Annals of Internal Medicine* 105, no. 3 (January 1986): 436–44.

Behrens, Peter J. "The Metaphysical Club at the Johns Hopkins University (1879–1885)." *History of Psychology* 8, no. 4 (2005): 331–46.

Benson, Michael T., and Hal R. Boyd. *College for the Commonwealth: A Case for Higher Educa-tion in American Democracy.* Lexington: University Press of Kentucky, 2018.

Berkeley, George. *The Works of George Berkeley, D.D., Formerly Bishop of Cloyne: Including His Posthumous Works.* Edited by Alexander Campbell Fraser. Vol. 4. Oxford: Clarendon, 1901.

Billings, John Shaw. "Hospital Construction and Organization." In Johns Hopkins Hospital, *Hospital Plans.*

———. *Medical Education: Extracts from Lectures Delivered before the Johns Hopkins University, Baltimore, 1877–88.* Baltimore: William K. Boyle & Sons, 1878.

———. *The Plans and purposes of the Johns Hopkins Hospital.* Philadelphia: Medical News, 1889.

———. *Reports and Papers Relating to the Construction and Organization, No. 1.* Baltimore: Johns Hopkins Hospital, 1876. https://collections.nlm.nih.gov/catalog/nlm:nlmuid-1017 18313-bk.

———. *Reports and Papers Relating to the Construction and Organization, No. 3.* Baltimore: Johns Hopkins Hospital, 1877. https://collections.nlm.nih.gov/catalog/nlm:nlmuid-1017 18315-bk.

Billings, John Shaw, and Alan M. Chesney. "Two Papers by John Shaw Billings on Medical Education." *Bulletin of the Institute of the History of Medicine* 6, no. 4 (April 1938): 285–359.

Bishop, Charles C. "Teaching at Johns Hopkins: The First Generation." *History of Education Quarterly* 27, no. 4 (Winter 1987): 499–515.

Bishop, Morris, and Alison Mason Kingsbury. *A History of Cornell.* Ithaca: Cornell University Press, 1962.

Bledstein, Burton J. *The Culture of Professionalism: The Middle Class and the Development of Higher Education in America.* New York: Norton, 1976.

Bond, Allen Kerr. *When the Hopkins Came to Baltimore.* Baltimore: Pegasus Press, 1927.

Bonté, J. H. C. "Form of Release of Mortgage." *Annual Report of the Secretary to the Board of Regents of the University of California for the Year Ending June 30, 1891.* Sacramento: State Printing Office, 1890.

Boorstin, Daniel J. *The Americans: The National Experience.* New York: Knopf Doubleday, 2010.

Brechin, Gray. *Imperial San Francisco: Urban Power, Earthly Ruin.* Berkeley: University of Cal-ifornia Press, 2006.

Brent, Joseph. *Charles Sanders Peirce: A Life.* 2nd ed. Bloomington: Indiana University Press, 1998.

Brieger, Gert H. "The California Origins of the Johns Hopkins Medical School." *Bulletin of the History of Medicine* 51, no. 3 (Fall 1977): 339–52.

———. "The Original Plans for the Johns Hopkins Hospital and Their Historical Significance." *Bulletin of the History of Medicine* 39, no. 6 (November–December 1965): 518–28.

Briggs, Ward W., Jr., ed. *Soldier and Scholar: Basil Lanneau Gildersleeve and the Civil War.* Charlottesville: University of Virginia Press, 1998.

Brown, George William. *Baltimore, the 19th of April 1861: A Study of the War.* Baltimore: N. Murray, 1887.

———. *The Need of a Higher Standard of Education in the United States: An Address Delivered before the Philokalian and Philomathean Societies of St. John's College by George William Brown.* Baltimore: William Boyle, 1869.

———. *The Old World and the New: An Address Delivered by George William Brown before the Philocelan and Peithessophian Societies of Rutgers College, New Brunswick, New Jersey, at their Anniversary on the 22nd of July 1851.* New York: R. Craighead, 1851.

Browne, Gary Lawson. *Baltimore in the Nation, 1789–1861.* Chapel Hill: University of North Carolina Press, 1980.

Browne, John Ross. *Report of the Debates In the Convention of California: On the Formation of the State Constitution, In September And October, 1849.* Washington, DC: J. T. Towers, 1850.

Brubacher, John S., and Willis Rudy. *Higher Education in Transition: A History of American Colleges and Universities, 1636–1976.* 3rd ed. New York: Harper & Row, 1976.

Bryce, James. *The American Commonwealth.* Vol. 2. New York: Macmillan, 1924.

"Business Troubles: William C. Gilman's Debts." *New York Times,* 10 November 1877, 8.

Butler, Nicholas Murray. "Daniel Coit Gilman: Builder of Universities." *American Monthly Review of Reviews* 38, no. 5 (November 1908): 552–53.

———. "President Gilman's Administration at the Johns Hopkins University." *American Monthly Review of Reviews* 23 (January 1901): 49–53.

California Board of Commissioners. *Report Relative to Establishing a State University, made in accordance with a concurrent resolution passed at the fourteenth session of the legislature.* Sacramento: O. M. Clayes, 1864.

Calisphere. "Joseph Cummings Rowell, 1853–1938 [In Memoriam, 1939]." http://content.cdlib .org/view?docId=hb0m3n99bs&brand=calisphere&doc.view=entire_text.

Campbell, W. W. *Biographical Memoir of Simon Newcomb, 1835–1909.* National Academy of Sciences Biographical Memoirs, 17. Washington, DC: National Academy of Sciences, 1916.

Carnegie, Andrew. "The Best Fields for Philanthropy." *North American Review* 149, no. 397 (December 1889): 682–98.

———. *The Empire of Business.* New York: Doubleday, 1902.

———. "Wealth." *North American Review* 148, no. 391 (June 1889): 653–64.

Carnegie Institution of Washington. *Articles of Incorporation, Deed of Trust, Etc.* Washington, DC: New Era Print Company, 1902.

———. *Proceedings of the Board of Trustees, January 1902.* Washington, DC: Carnegie Institution of Washington, 1902.

———. *Year Book No. 1, 1902.* Washington, DC: Carnegie Institution of Washington, 1903.

———. *Year Book No. 3, 1904.* Washington, DC: Carnegie Institution of Washington, 1905.

———. *Year Book No. 4, 1905.* Washington, DC: Carnegie Institution of Washington, 1906.

Carnegie Science. "Andrew Carnegie's 23 Institutions." Accessed 1 May 2020. https://carnegie science.edu/andrew-carnegies-23-organizations.

Catton, William B. "The Baltimore Business Community and the Secession Crisis, 1860–1861." Master's thesis, University of Maryland, 1952.

Chace, William M. "Enduring Benefactions." *Emory Magazine* 73, no. 4 (Winter 1988): 4–6. http://www.emory.edu/EMORY_MAGAZINE/winter98/presmessage.html.

Chaiklin, Harris. "Daniel Coit Gilman: An Unrecognized Social Work Pioneer." Social Welfare History Project. http://socialwelfare.library.vcu.edu/people/gilman-daniel-coit/.

Chalfant, Randolph W., and Charles Belfoure. *Niernsee and Neilson, Architects of Baltimore.* Baltimore: Baltimore Architecture Foundation, 2006.

Chapman, Carleton B. *Order Out of Chaos: John Shaw Billings and America's Coming of Age.* Boston: Boston Medical Library, 1994.

Chernow, Ron. *Grant.* New York: Penguin, 2017.

Chesney, Alan M. *The Johns Hopkins Hospital and the Johns Hopkins University School of Medicine: A Chronicle.* Vol. 1, *Early Years, 1867–1893.* Baltimore: Johns Hopkins Press, 1943.

———. *The Johns Hopkins Hospital and the Johns Hopkins University School of Medicine: A Chronicle.* Vol. 2, *1893–1905.* Baltimore: Johns Hopkins Press, 1958.

———. *The Johns Hopkins Hospital and the Johns Hopkins University School of Medicine: A Chronicle.* Vol. 3, *1905–1914.* Baltimore: Johns Hopkins Press, 1963.

Clapp, Margaret Antoinette, ed. *The Modern University.* Ithaca, NY: Cornell University Press, 1950.

Clement, Richard W. "Library and University Press Integration: A New Vision for University Publishing." *Journal of Library Administration* 51, no. 5/6 (July 2011): 507–28.

Cole, Jonathan R. *The Great American University: Its Rise to Preeminence, Its Indispensable Role, Why It Must Be Protected.* New York: Public Affairs, 2009.

Commission on Foundations and Private Philanthropy. *Foundations, Private Giving, and Public Policy: Report and Recommendations of the Commission on Foundations and Private Philanthropy.* Chicago: University of Chicago Press, 1970.

Conable, Charlotte Williams. *Women at Cornell: The Myth of Equal Education.* Ithaca, NY: Cornell University Press, 1977.

Cook, Joan. "Broadus Mitchell, 95, Professor, Historian and Hamilton Authority." *New York Times,* 30 April 1988, 11.

Cooper, Jacob. *William Preston Johnston: A Character Sketch.* New Haven, CT: Yale University Press, 1878.

Cordasco, Francesco. *The Shaping of American Graduate Education: Daniel Coit Gilman and the Protean Ph.D.* Totowa, NJ: Rowman & Littlefield, 1973.

Council of the Society of Arts. *The Report of the Committee Appointed by the Council of the Society of Arts to Inquire into the Subject of Industrial Instruction with Evidence on Which the Report is Founded.* London: Longman, Brown & Green, 1853.

Cox, Richard P. *Civil War Maryland: Stories from the Old Line State.* Mount Pleasant, SC: Arcadia, 2008.

Crenson, Matthew A. *Baltimore: A Political History.* Baltimore: Johns Hopkins University Press, 2017.

Croft, Genevieve K. "The U.S. Land-Grant University System: An Overview." Congressional Research Service, R4589. 29 August 2019. https://crsreports.congress.gov/product/pdf/R/R45897.

Cummings, Martin M. "Dr. John Shaw Billings—Versatile Savant of American Medicine, 1974." In *In His Own Words: Martin M. Cummings and the NLM.* https://www.nlm.nih.gov/hmd/digicolls/cummings/index.html.

Cummins, Duane D. *Bethany College: A Liberal Arts Odyssey.* St. Louis: Chalice, 2013.

Curry, J. L. M. *Education of the Negroes since 1860.* The Trustees of the John F. Slater Fund, Occasional Paper 3. Baltimore: Published by the Trustees, 1894.

Curtis, Robert I. "Confederate Classical Textbooks: A Lost Cause?" *International Journal of the Classical Tradition* 3, no. 4 (Spring 1997): 433–57.

Cushing, Harvey. *The Life of Sir William Osler.* Vol 1. Oxford: Clarendon, 1925.

Davis, Cynthia. *Charlotte Perkins Gilman: A Biography.* Palo Alto, CA: Stanford University Press, 2010.

Davis, Veronica Alease. *Hampton University.* Mount Pleasant, SC: Arcadia, 2014.

"Death of Dr. James Carey Thomas." *Johns Hopkins University Circulars* 25–26, nos. 121–31 (December 1897): 37.

"Death of Galloway Cheston." *Johns Hopkins University Circulars* 10 (April 1881): 136.

"Death of Hon. Edward Tompkins." *Mariposa Gazette,* 22 November 1872, 2.

"Death of Johns Hopkins." *Baltimore American and Commercial Advertiser,* 25 December 1873.

"Death of Johns Hopkins." *Baltimore Sun,* 25 December 1873. https://www.newspapers.com/image/372398315/.

"The Death of Mr. Charles T. Child." *Electrical Review* 40 (28 June 1902): 857.

"Death of Professor Henry A. Rowland." *Johns Hopkins University Circulars* 20, no. 152 (May–June 1901): 63–68.

de la Peña, Carolyn. *Empty Pleasures: The Story of Artificial Sweeteners from Saccharin to Splenda.* Chapel Hill: University of North Carolina Press, 2010.

Denton, Lawrence M. *A Southern Star for Maryland: Maryland and the Secession Crisis.* Baltimore: Publishing Concepts, 1995.

De Pasquale, Sue. "Elisabeth Gilman Was a Fierce Advocate for Social Justice." *Hopkins Magazine,* Fall 2017. https://hub.jhu.edu/magazine/2017/fall/elisabeth-gilman-baltimore-socialist-firebrand/.

Diggins, John P. *Thorstein Veblen: Theorist of the Leisure Class.* Princeton, NJ: Princeton University Press, 1999.

Dilts, James D. *The Great Road: The Building of the Baltimore and Ohio, The Nation's First Railroad, 1828–1853.* Stanford, CA: Stanford University Press, 1993.

*Documents Relating to the Origin and Work of the Slater Trustees 1882 to 1894.* The Trustees of the John F. Slater Fund, Occasional Paper 1. Baltimore: Published by the Trustees, 1894.

Donald, David Herbert. *Lincoln.* New York: Simon & Schuster, 1995.

Donnelly, Ralph W. "Scientists of the Confederate Nitre and Mining Bureau." *Civil War History* 2, no. 4 (December 1956): 69–92.

Dorn, Charles. *For the Common Good: A New History of Higher Education in America.* Ithaca, NY: Cornell University Press, 2017.

Douglass, John Aubrey. *The California Idea and American Higher Education: 1850 to the 1960 Master Plan.* Palo Alto, CA: Stanford University Press, 2000.

———. *The Conditions for Admission: Access, Equity, and the Social Contract of Public Universities.* Palo Alto, CA: Stanford University Press, 2007.

———. "Creating a Fourth Branch of State Government: The University of California and the Constitutional Convention of 1879." *History of Education Quarterly* 32, no. 1 (Spring 1992): 31–72.

"Dr. Gilman Head of Carnegie Institution." *New York Times,* 30 January 1902, 2.

Du Bois, W. E. B. *The Education of Black People: 10 Critiques.* Edited by Herbert Aptheker. Amherst: University of Massachusetts Press, 1973.

———. "The Freedmen's Bureau." *Atlantic Monthly* 87 (1901): 354–66.

———. *The Souls of Black Folk*. With a critical introduction by Patricia Hinchey. Gorham, ME: Myers Education Press, 2018.

Duderstadt, James J. "Diversity." In *A University for the 21st Century*, 192–219. Ann Arbor: University of Michigan Press, 2000.

Dwight, Timothy. "Eighth Paper." In *The "How I Was Educated" Papers*, 78–90. New York: D. Appleton, 1888.

Dyer, Thomas G. *The University of Georgia: A Bicentennial History, 1785–1985*. Athens: University of Georgia Press, 1985.

Dykhuizen, George. "John Dewey at Johns Hopkins (1882–1884)." *Journal of the History of Ideas* 22, no. 1 (January–March 1961): 103–16.

Eisenberg, Bernard. "Kelly Miller: The Negro Leader as a Marginal Man." *Journal of Negro History* 45, no. 3 (1960): 182–97. doi:10.2307/2716260.

Eliot, Charles. "The New Education: Its Organization." *Atlantic Monthly* 23, no. 136 (February 1869): 203–20.

———. "President Eliot's Address." In *Addresses at the inauguration of Daniel C. Gilman*, 7–13.

Ely, Richard T. *Ground under Our Feet: An Autobiography*. New York: Macmillan, 1938.

Emory University. "Atticus Greene Haygood, Emory College President 1875–1884, Class of 1859." Accessed 9 February 2020. http://emoryhistory.emory.edu/facts-figures/people/presidents/profiles/haygood.html.

Feldman, Maryann P., and Pierre Desrochers. "Truth for Its Own Sake: Academic Culture and Technology Transfer at Johns Hopkins University." *Minerva* 42, no. 2 (June 2004): 105–26.

"Fenollosa, Ernest Francisco." Dictionary of Art Historians. http://www.arthistorians.info/fenollosae.

Ferrier, William Warren. *Henry Durant, First President, University of California: The New Englander Who Came to California with College on the Brain*. Berkeley: published by the author, 1942.

———. *Origin and Development of the University of California*. Berkeley: University of California Press, 1930.

Feuer, Lewis S. "America's First Jewish Professor: James Joseph Sylvester at the University of Virginia." *American Jewish Archives Journal* 36, no. 2 (1984): 152–201.

———. *The Scientific Intellectual: The Psychological & Sociological Origins of Modern Science*. New York: Basic Books, 1963.

Finacom, Steven. "Long on the move, Bishop Berkeley finds a home at Doe." *Berkeley News*, 2 February 2012. https://news.berkeley.edu/2012/02/02/bishop-berkeley-doe/.

Finch, Edith. *Carey Thomas of Bryn Mawr*. New Yorker: Harper, 1947.

Finkel, Benjamin F. "A History of American Mathematical Journals." *National Mathematics Magazine* 16, no. 4 (January 1942): 188–97.

Fisher, John E. *The John F. Slater Fund: A Nineteenth Century Affirmative Action for Negro Education*. Lanham, MD: University Press of America, 1986.

Flexner, Abraham. *Daniel Coit Gilman: Creator of the American Type of University*. New York: Harcourt, Brace, 1946.

———. *Henry S. Pritchett: A Biography*. New York: Columbia University Press, 1943.

———. *Medical Education in the United States and Canada: A Report to the Carnegie Foundation for the Advancement of Teaching, Bulletin Number Four*. Boston: D. B. Updike, 1910.

———. *Universities: American, English, German*. New York: Oxford University Press, 1930.

Foner, Eric. *Reconstruction: America's Unfinished Revolution, 1863–1877, Updated Edition.* New York: Harper Perennial, 2014.

Franklin, Fabian. *The Life of Daniel Coit Gilman.* New York: Dodd, Mead, 1910.

Franklin, John Hope. "Jim Crow Goes to School: The Genesis of Legal Segregation in Southern Schools." *South Atlantic Quarterly* 58 (Spring 1959): 225–35.

Franklin, John Hope, and Alfred A. Moss Jr. *From Slavery to Freedom: A History of African Americans.* 8th ed. New York: McGraw Hill, 2000.

French, John C. *A History of the University Founded by Johns Hopkins.* Baltimore: Johns Hopkins Press, 1946.

Fye, W. Bruce. "H. Newell Martin—A Remarkable Career Destroyed by Neurasthenia and Alcoholism." *Journal of the History of Medicine and Allied Sciences* 40, no. 2 (April 1985): 133–46.

———. "Profiles in Cardiology: H. Newell Martin." *Clinical Cardiology* 16 (1992): 631–32.

"The Gain of a Man." *Overland Monthly* 11, no. 1 (July 1873): 98.

Gates, Henry Louis, Jr. *Black Reconstruction in America: The Oxford W. E. B. Du Bois, Volume 6.* New York: Oxford University Press, 2007.

Geiger, Roger L., ed. *The American College in the Nineteenth Century.* Nashville: Vanderbilt University Press, 2000.

———. *The History of American Higher Education: Learning and Culture from the Founding to World War II.* Princeton, NJ: Princeton University Press, 2014.

———. "The Rise and Fall of Useful Knowledge: Higher Education for Science, Agriculture, and the Mechanic Arts, 1850–1875." In Geiger, *American College in the Nineteenth Century,* 153–68.

———. *To Advance Knowledge: The Growth of American Research Universities, 1900–1940.* New York: Oxford University Press, 1986.

Geiger, Roger L., and Nathan E. Sorber, eds. *The Land-Grant Colleges and the Reshaping of American Higher Education.* New Brunswick, NJ: Transaction, 2013.

General Education Board. "Letter from the General Education Board to John D. Rockefeller, Jr., 1902 March 08." *100 Years: The Rockefeller Foundation.* Accessed 29 April 2020. https://rockfound.rockarch.org/digital-library-listing/-/asset_publisher/yYxpQfeI4W8N/content/letter-from-the-general-education-board-to-john-d-rockefeller-jr-1902-march-08.

"George Peabody: The Funeral at Westminster Abbey, London—Observances in the United States. A British Man-of-War to Convey the Body to the United States." *New York Times,* 12 November 1869, 1.

"George Peabody Assailed," *New York Times,* 27 October 1866, 5.

"George William Lane Obituary." *New York Times,* 31 December 1883, 5.

Getman, Frederick H. *The Life of Ira Remsen.* Easton, PA: Journal of Chemical Education, 1940.

Gikandi, Simon. "Basil Lanneau Gildersleeve." Princeton & Slavery. Accessed 5 May 2020. https://slavery.princeton.edu/stories/simon-e-gikandi#ref-1.

Gildersleeve, Basil L. "The Creed of the Old South." *Atlantic Monthly* 69 (January 1892): 75–87.

———. *The Creed of the Old South.* Baltimore: Johns Hopkins Press, 1915.

———. *Letters of Basil Lanneau Gildersleeve.* Edited by Ward W. Briggs Jr. Baltimore: Johns Hopkins University Press, 1987.

———. "A Southerner in the Peloponnesian War." *Atlantic Monthly* 80 (September 1897): 330–42.

Gillman, Alexander William. *Searches Into the History of the Gillman Or Gilman Family, Including the Various Branches in England, Ireland, America and Belgium*. London: Elliot Stock, 1895.

Gilman, Daniel Coit. "Bishop Berkeley in America." *Hours at Home* 6 (June 1865): 115–22.

———. "Bishop Berkeley's Gifts to Yale College." *Papers of the New Haven Colony Historical Society* 1 (1865): 147–70.

———. "The Building of a University." In *The City's Voice: Pioneer Prose and Poetry from the Overland Monthly*, edited by Devorah Knaff, 302–11. Norco, CA: Santa Ana River Press, 2004.

———. *The Building of the University: An Inaugural Address Delivered at Oakland, November 7th, 1872*. San Francisco: John H. Carmany, 1872.

———. "Charity and Knowledge." *Science* 14, no. 335 (5 July 1889): 11–15.

———. "Humboldt, Ritter, and the New Geography." *New Englander* 18, no. 70 (May 1860): 277–306.

———. "The Idea of the University." *North American Review* 133 (October 1881): 353–67.

———. "Inaugural Address." In *Addresses at the Inauguration of Daniel C. Gilman*, 17–64.

———. "The Johns Hopkins University." *Cosmopolitan* 11, no. 4 (August 1891): 462–69.

———. *The Launching of a University, and Other Papers: A Sheaf of Remembrances*. New York: Dodd, Mead, 1906.

———. "On medical education in the State University." In *Transactions of the Medical Society of California, 1873*, by Daniel Coit Gilman, 194–201. Sacramento: T. A. Springer, 1873.

———. *On the Growth of American Colleges and the Present Tendency to the Study of Science. An Address Delivered at the Dedication of the Sibley College, of the Cornell University, June 21, 1871*. Ithaca, NY: Cornell University, 1872.

———. *On the structure of the earth with some reference to human history: A synopsis of twelve geographical lectures delivered before the senior and junior classes in the College of New Jersey. Feb. 1871. Printed for the students*. Princeton, NJ: Princeton University Press, 1871.

———. *Our National Schools of Science*. Boston: Ticknor & Fields, 1867.

———. "A Plea for the Training of the Hand." In *Monographs of the Industrial Education Association*, edited by Nicholas Murray Butler, 1:3–15. New York: Industrial Education Association, 1888.

———. "Scientific Schools in Europe: Considered in Reference to their Prevalence, Utility, Scope and Desirability in America." *American Journal of Education* 1 (1856): 315–28.

———. *The Sheffield Scientific School of Yale University: A Semi-centennial Historical Discourse, October 28, 1897*. New Haven, CT: Sheffield Scientific School, 1897.

———. *Statement of the Progress and Condition of the University of California*. Berkeley: University of California, 1875.

———. *A Study in Black and White: An Address at the Opening of the Armstrong-Slater Trade School Building, November 18, 1896*. The Trustees of the John F. Slater Fund, Occasional Paper 10. Baltimore: Published by the Trustees, 1897.

———. *University Problems in the United States*. New York: Century, 1898.

Gilman, Daniel Coit, Papers. Johns Hopkins University Special Collections.

Gilman, Daniel Coit, Papers. Yale University Special Collections.

Gilman, James K. "The Brief Military Career of Dr. William H. Welch." *Military Medicine* 182 (March/April 2017): 1831–34.

Gilman, Louise, Papers. William L. Clements Library Manuscripts Division. University of Michigan.

Gilman, William C. "Daniel Coit Gilman, 1831–1908." *Proceedings of the Washington Academy of Sciences* 10 (1908): 211–14.

"The Gilman Compromise." *New York Times*, 6 October 1877.

"Gilman's Change of Prison: His Transfer from Sing Sing to Auburn; Affecting Scene on the Train; the Prisoner on his Good Behavior." *New York Times*, 21 October 1877, 1.

"Gilman, the Forger, Free." *New York Sun*, 4 December 1879, 1.

Givler, Peter. "University Publishing in the United States." In *Scholarly Publishing: Books, Journals, Publishers and Libraries in the Twentieth Century*, edited by Richard E. Abel and Lyman W. Newman, 107–30. New York: Wiley, 2002.

Goldman, Eric F. "Importing a Historian: Von Holst and American Universities." *Mississippi Valley Historical Review* 27, no. 2 (September 1940): 267–74.

Goodwin, Cardinal. *The Establishment of State Government in California, 1846–1850*. New York: Macmillan, 1914.

Grant, Ulysses S. *The Personal Memoirs of General Ulysses S. Grant: The Complete Annotated Edition*. Edited by John F. Marszalek. Cambridge, MA: Harvard University Press, 2017.

Grauer, Neil A. *Leading the Way: A History of Johns Hopkins Medicine*. Baltimore: Johns Hopkins University Press, 2012.

———. "The Six Who Built Hopkins." *Johns Hopkins Magazine*, April 2000. https://pages.jh.edu/~jhumag/0400web/31.html.

Greene, Jack P. "The Johns Hopkins University." In "Four Universities: Founders' Visions and Today's Reality." *Academic Questions* 11, no. 2 (Spring 1998): 67–70.

Griffin, John Chandler. *A Pictorial History of the Confederacy*. Jefferson, NC: McFarland, 2008.

Griffith, Thomas Jefferson. "High Points in the Life of Dr. John Shaw Billings." *Indiana Magazine of History* 30, no. 4 (December 1934): 325–30.

Grimm, Robert T., Jr., ed. *Notable American Philanthropists: Biographies of Giving and Volunteering*. Westport, CT: Greenwood, 2002.

Guzman, Jessie P. "W. E. B. Du Bois—The Historian." *Journal of Negro Education* 30, no. 4 (Autumn 1961): 377–85.

Hamer, Marguerite B. "The Fate of the Exiled Acadians in South Carolina." *Journal of Southern History* 4, no. 2 (May 1938): 199–208.

Harlan, Louis R. *Booker T. Washington: The Wizard of Tuskegee, 1901–1915*. New York: Oxford University Press, 1983.

Harp, Stephen L. *A World History of Rubber: Empire, Industry, and the Everyday*. New York: Wiley & Sons, 2015.

Hart, D. G. "The Protestant Enlightenment Revisited: Daniel Coit Gilman and the Academic Reforms of the Modern American University." *Journal of Ecclesiastical History* 47, no. 4 (October 1996): 683–703.

Harvey, A. McGehee. "John Shaw Billings: Forgotten Hero of American Medicine." *Perspectives in Biology and Medicine* 21, no. 1 (Autumn 1977): 35–57.

Hawes, Gene R. *To Advance Knowledge: A Handbook on American University Press Publishing*. New York: American University Press Services, 1967.

Hawkins, Hugh. *Banding Together: The Rise of National Associations in American Higher Education, 1887–1950*. Baltimore: Johns Hopkins University Press, 2002.

———. "George William Brown and His Influence on the Johns Hopkins University." *Maryland Historical Magazine* 52, no. 3 (September 1957): 173–86.

———. *Pioneer: A History of the Johns Hopkins University, 1874–1889*. Rev. ed. Baltimore: Johns Hopkins University Press, 2002.

————. "Three University Presidents Testify." *American Quarterly* 11, no. 2 (Summer 1959): 99–119.

————. "University Identity: The Teaching and Research Functions." In Oleson and Voss, *Organization of Knowledge in Modern America*, 285–312.

Haygood, Atticus Greene. *Our Brother in Black*. New York: Phillips & Hunt, 1881.

————. *The new South: Gratitude, amendment, hope; A Thanksgiving sermon for November 25, 1880*. Oxford, GA, 1880. https://catalog.hathitrust.org/Record/100371989.

————. *Pleas for Progress*. Cincinnati: Cranston & Stowe, 1889.

Hickey, Damon D. "Pioneers of the New South: The Baltimore Association and New Carolina Friends in Reconstruction." *Quaker History* 74, no. 1 (Spring 1985): 1–17.

Hinsdale, Burke A. *A History of the University of Michigan*. Ann Arbor: University of Michigan Press, 1906.

"His Life Crushed Out." *Baltimore Sun*, 4 July 1902, 10.

Hofstadter, Richard. *Anti-intellectualism in American Life*. New York: Knopf, 1963.

Hofstadter, Richard, and Walter P. Metzger. *The Development of Academic Freedom in the United States*. New York: Columbia University Press, 1955.

Hofstadter, Richard, and Wilson Smith. "Gilman Recalls the Early Days of the Johns Hopkins, 1876." In *American Higher Education: A Documentary History*, 2:643–47. Chicago: University of Chicago Press, 1961.

Hollis, Ernest V. *Toward Improving Ph.D. Programs*. Washington, DC: American Council on Education, 1945.

Holloway, Laura C. *Famous American fortunes and the men who have made them: A series of sketches of many of the notable merchants, manufacturers, capitalists, railroad presidents, bonanza and cattle kings of the country*. New York: J. A. Hill, 1889.

Horowitz, Helen Lefkowitz. *The Power and Passion of M. Carey Thomas*. New York: Knopf, 1994.

Howe, Daniel Walker. *What Hath God Wrought: The Transformation of America, 1815–1848*. Oxford: Oxford University Press, 2007.

Howe, Mark Antony De Wolfe, and Henry C. Strippel. *The Life and Letters of George Bancroft*. Vol. 2. New York: C. Scribner's Sons, 1908.

Howe, S. H. *A Brief Memoir of the Life of John F. Slater of Norwich, Connecticut, 1815 to 1884*. The Trustees of the John F. Slater Fund, Occasional Paper 2. Baltimore: Published by the Trustees, 1894.

Howerth, I. W. "Natural Selection and the Survival of the Fittest." *Scientific Monthly* 5, no. 3 (September, 1917): 253–57.

Huxley, Thomas Henry. "Impressions of America." *New York Tribune Extra*, 25 August 1875, 2–3.

————. "University Education." *New York Tribune Extra*, 12 September 1876, 7–14.

"Huxley and Prayers." *Baltimore Sun*, 29 September 1876, 1.

"Important from Maryland: Secession Killed in the Legislature." *New York Times*, 30 April 1861, 1.

"Investigation of the Alleged Frauds in the Construction of the College of Letters—Testimony Taken by the Assembly Committee on Public Buildings and Grounds." In *Appendix to Journals of Senate and Assembly of the Twentieth Session of the Legislature of the State of California*, 4:1–464. Sacramento: State Printer, 1874.

Jacob, Kathryn A. "Mr. Johns Hopkins." *Johns Hopkins Magazine*, January 1974, 13–17.

James, Edward T., Janet Wilson James, and Paul S. Boyer, eds. *Notable American Women, 1607–1950: A Biographical Dictionary.* 3 vols. Cambridge, MA: Harvard University Press, 1971.

James, Henry. *Charles W. Eliot, President of Harvard University 1869–1909.* 2 vols. Boston: Houghton Mifflin, 1930.

James, I. M. "James Joseph Sylvester, F.R.S. (1814–1897)." *Notes and Records of the Royal Society of London* 51, no. 2 (July 1997): 247–61.

Jameson, Horatio G. "Observations on Epidemic Cholera, As It Appeared at Baltimore, in the Summer of 1832." *Maryland Medical Recorder* 3, no. 1 (July 1832): 283–430.

Jarrett, William H., II. "Raising the Bar: Mary Elizabeth Garrett, M. Carey Thomas, and the Johns Hopkins Medical School." *Proceedings of the Baylor University Medical Center 2011* 24, no. 1 (2011): 21–26.

———. "Yale, Skull and Bones, and the Beginnings of Johns Hopkins." *Proceedings of the Baylor University Medical Center 2011* 24, no. 1 (2011): 27–34.

Jensen, J. Vernon. "Thomas Henry Huxley's Address at the Opening of the Johns Hopkins University in September 1876." *Notes and Records of the Royal Society of London* 47, no. 2 (July 1993): 257–69.

———. "Thomas Henry Huxley's Lecture Tour of the United States, 1876." *Notes and Records of the Royal Society of London* 42, no. 2 (July 1988): 181–95.

"John Bates Clark Medal." American Economic Association. https://www.aeaweb.org/about-aea/honors-awards/bates-clark.

Johns Hopkins Department of Classics. "Gildersleeve." Accessed 7 May 2020. https://classics.jhu.edu/about/gildersleeve/.

Johns Hopkins Hospital. *Hospital Plans: Five Essays Relating to the Construction, Organization & Management of Hospitals, Contributed by Their Authors for the Use of the Johns Hopkins Hospital of Baltimore.* New York: William Wood, 1875.

"Johns Hopkins Returns Thanks: For the Naming of President Gilman on the Venezuela Commission." *New York Times,* 7 January 1896, 1.

Johns Hopkins University. "Edward Lewis." A History of African Americans at Johns Hopkins University. Accessed 13 February 2020. https://afam.nts.jhu.edu/people/lewis/lewis.html.

———. *Eleventh Annual Report of the President of the Johns Hopkins University, 1886.* Baltimore: Johns Hopkins University, 1886.

———. *First Annual Report of the President of Johns Hopkins University, 1876.* Baltimore: William K. Boyle & Son, 1876.

———. *Fifteenth Annual Report of the Johns Hopkins University, 1890.* Baltimore: Johns Hopkins Press, 1890.

———. *Fourteenth Annual Report the President of Johns Hopkins University, 1889.* Baltimore: Johns Hopkins Press, 1889.

———. *Fourth Annual Report of the President of Johns Hopkins University, 1879.* Baltimore: John Murphy, 1879.

———. Hard Histories at Hopkins. Accessed 1 January 2021. https://hardhistory.jhu.edu.

———. *Ninth Annual Report of the President of the Johns Hopkins University, 1884.* Baltimore: John Murphy, 1884.

———. Nobel Prize Winners. Accessed 30 March 2020. https://www.jhu.edu/research/milestones/nobel-prize-winners/.

———. "Reexamining Hopkins History." Hopkins Retrospective. Accessed 1 January 2021. https://retrospective.jhu.edu/our-initiatives/reexamining-hopkins-history.

————. *Second Annual Report of the Johns Hopkins University.* Baltimore: John Murphy, 1877.

————. *Seventeenth Annual Report of the Johns Hopkins University, 1892.* Baltimore: Johns Hopkins Press, 1892.

————. *Third Annual Report of the Johns Hopkins University, 1878.* Baltimore: John Murphy, 1878.

————. *Twelfth Annual Report the Johns Hopkins University, 1877.* Baltimore: Johns Hopkins Press, 1877.

————. *Twenty-Sixth Annual Report of the President of the Johns Hopkins University, 1901.* Baltimore: Johns Hopkins University, 1901.

"The Johns Hopkins University." *Baltimore Sun,* 4 October 1876, 2.

"The Johns Hopkins University: Opening Lecture by Professor Thomas Huxley." *Baltimore Sun,* 13 September 1876, 5.

"The Johns Hopkins University: Plans and Prospects of the New Institution." *Baltimore Sun,* 23 February 1876, 1.

"Johns Hopkins University: President King on the Medical School and Other Matters." *New York Times,* 6 May 1890, 1.

"Johns Hopkins University and Professor Huxley." *New York Observer,* 21 September 1876, 29.

*Johns Hopkins University Celebration of the Twenty-Fifth Anniversary of the Founding of the University and the Inauguration of Ira Remsen, L.L.D. as president of the University February Twenty First and Twenty Second 1902.* Baltimore: Johns Hopkins Press, 1902.

Johnson, Allen, and Dumas Malone, eds. *Dictionary of American Biography.* Vol 3. New York: C. Scribner's Sons, 1929.

Jones, Martha S. "The founder of Johns Hopkins owned enslaved people. Our university must face a reckoning." *Washington Post,* 9 December 2020. https://www.washingtonpost.com /opinions/2020/12/09/johns-hopkins-university-founder-enslaved-people/.

Jones, Ross. *Elisabeth Gilman: Crusader for Justice.* Salisbury, MD: Secant, 2018.

Jones-Wilson, Faustine C., Charles A. Asbury, Sylvia M. Jacobs, and Margo Okazawa-Rey, eds. *Encyclopedia of African-American Education.* 2 vols. Westport, CT: Greenwood, 1996.

Jordan, David Starr. *Leading American Men of Science.* New York: Henry Holt, 1910.

Kargon, Robert H., and Scott G. Knowles. "Knowledge for Use: Science, Higher Learning, and America's New Industrial Heartland, 1880–1915." *Annals of Science* 59, no. 1 (2002): 1–20.

Kelley, Brooks Mather. *Yale: A History.* New Haven, CT: Yale University Press, 1974.

Kerr, Clark. *Troubled Times for American Higher Education: The 1990s and Beyond.* Albany: State University Press of New York, 1994.

Key, Scott. "Economics or Education: The Establishment of American Land-Grant Universities." *Journal of Higher Education* 67, no. 2 (March/April 1996): 196–220.

Klepper, Michael, and Robert Gunther. *The Wealthy 100: From Benjamin Franklin to Bill Gates—A Ranking of the Richest Americans, Past and Present.* New York: Citadel, 1996.

Klynveld Peat Marwick Goerdeler LLP. "The Johns Hopkins University: Consolidated Financial Statements and Independent Auditors' Reports." Audit. Baltimore: KPMG LLP, 30 June 2017. http://www.govwiki.info/pdfs/Non-Profit/MD%20The%20Johns%20Hopkins %20University%202017.pdf.

Kyle, Robert A., and David P. Steensma. "John Shaw Billings: Civil War Surgeon, Medical Librarian, Founder of Index Medicus, and First Director of the New York Public Library." *Mayo Clinic Proceedings* 94, no. 3 (March 2019): E45–E46.

Krumpelmann, John T. "Basil Lanneau Gildersleeve Classicist and Germanist: South Carolina,

Virginia, Maryland." In *Southern Scholars in Goethe's Germany*, 104–33. Chapel Hill: University of North Carolina Press, 1965.

Kurtz, Benjamin P. *Joseph Cummings Rowell, 1853–1938*. Berkeley: University of California Press, 1940.

Ladd, Christine. "On the Algebra of Logic." In *Studies in Logic: By Members of the Johns Hopkins University*, edited by Charles S. Pierce, 17–71. Boston: John Benjamins, 1883.

Lagemann, Ellen Condiffe. *Private Power for the Public Good: A History of the Carnegie Foundation for the Advancement of Teaching*. Middletown, CT: Wesleyan University Press, 1983.

Lamb, Evelyn, "That Time It Took a Student 44 Years to Get Her Degree because She Was a Woman." *Scientific American*, 10 April 2020. https://blogs.scientificamerican.com/roots-of-unity/that-time-it-took-a-student-44-years-to-get-her-degree-because-she-was-a-woman/.

Lanier, Sidney. *Poems of Sidney Lanier*. Edited by Mary Day Lanier. New York: Charles Scribner's Sons, 1893.

Lanman, Charles Rockwell. "Daniel Coit Gilman (1831–1908)." *Proceedings of the American Academy of Arts and Sciences* 52, no. 13 (October 1917): 836–39.

Larkey, Sanford V. "John Shaw Billings and the History of Medicine." *Bulletin of the Institute of the History of Medicine* 6, no. 4 (April 1938): 360–76.

Leavitt, Judith Walzer, and Ronald L. Numbers. *Sickness and Health in America: Readings in the History of Medicine and Public Health*. 3rd ed. Madison: University of Wisconsin Press, 1997.

Leslie, Bruce W. "Dreaming Spires in New Jersey: Anglophilia in Wilson's Princeton." In *The Educational Legacy of Woodrow Wilson: From College to Nation*, ed. James Axtell, 97–121. Charlottesville: University of Virginia Press, 2012.

Lester, Robert M. *Forty Years of Carnegie Giving: A Summary of the Benefactions of Andrew Carnegie and of the Work of the Philanthropic Trusts Which He Created*. New York: C. Scribner's Sons, 1941.

Lewis, David Levering. *W. E. B. Du Bois: Biography of a Race, 1868–1919*. New York: Henry Holt, 1993.

Logan, Rayford W. *Howard University: The First Hundred Years, 1867–1967*. New York: New York University Press, 1969.

Lossing, Benson John, and Woodrow Wilson, eds. *Harper's Encyclopaedia of United States History from 458 A.D. to 1912*. Vol. 6. New York: Harper Brothers, 1912.

"The Loss of a Man." *Overland Monthly* 14, no. 4 (April 1875): 382.

Lowell, James Russell. *Letters of James Russell Lowell*. Edited by Charles Eliot Norton. Vol. 2. New York: Harper, 1894.

Lucas, Christopher. *American Higher Education: A History*. 2nd ed. New York: Palgrave Macmillan, 2006.

Ludmerer, Kenneth M. *Learning to Heal: The Development of American Medical Education*. New York: Basic Books, 1985.

MacMullen, Edith Nye. *In the Cause of True Education: Henry Barnard and Nineteenth-Century School Reform*. New Haven, CT: Yale University Press, 1991.

Macksey, Richard. *One Hundred Years of Scholarly Publishing: The Johns Hopkins University Press, 1878–1978*. Baltimore: Johns Hopkins University Press, 1978.

Madsen, David. "Daniel Coit Gilman at the Carnegie Institution of Washington." *History of Education Quarterly* 9, no. 2 (Summer 1969): 154–86.

Marsden, George M. *The Soul of the American University: From Protestant Establishment to Established Nonbelief*. New York: Oxford University Press, 1994.

Martin, Geoffrey J. *American Geography and Geographers: Toward Geographical Science*. Oxford: Oxford University Press, 2015.

Mayer, Milton. *Young Man in a Hurry: The Story of William Rainey Harper, First President of the University of Chicago*. Chicago: University of Chicago Press, 1957.

McCall, Nancy, and Elizabeth M. Peterson. "Mary Elizabeth Garrett." In Grimm, *Notable American Philanthropists*, 107–12.

McFeely, William S. *Yankee Stepfather: General O. O. Howard and the Freedmen*. New York: Norton, 1994.

"Medicine and Surgery in the Army and Navy." *New York Medical Journal* 108 (October 1918): 683–90.

Meier, August. "The Racial and Educational Philosophy of Kelly Miller, 1895–1915." *Journal of Negro Education* 29, no. 2 (Spring 1960): 121–27.

Menand, Louis. *The Metaphysical Club: A Story of Ideas in America*. New York: Macmillan, 2002.

Menand, Louis, Paul Reitter, and Chad Wellmon, eds. *The Rise of the Research University: A Sourcebook*. Chicago: University of Chicago Press, 2017.

Mencken, H. L. "Daniel Gilman Is Forgotten Great Man of This Nation." *Dayton Daily News*, 7 June 1925.

Mendenhall, Thomas C. *Biographical Memoir of Henry Augustus Rowland, 1848–1901*. Washington, DC: National Academy Sciences, 1903.

Miller, Howard S. *Dollars for Research: Science and Its Patrons in Nineteenth-Century America*. Seattle: University of Washington Press, 1970.

Miller, Kelly. "Howard University." In *From Servitude to Service: Being the Old South Lectures on the History and Work of Southern Institutions for the Education of the Negro*, 27–30. Boston: American Unitarian Association, 1905.

———. *"The Primary Needs of the Negro Race": An address delivered before the Alumni Association of the Hampton Normal and Agricultural Institute*. Washington, DC: Howard University Press, 1899.

Minor, Lloyd. "Gilman's Legacy: Ph.D. Education and the Making of the Modern University." Speech delivered at Johns Hopkins University Conference on the Future of Ph.D. Education, October 25, 2011. http://web.jhu.edu/administration/provost/reports_resources/speeches/111025_gilmans_legacy.

Mitchell, Braudus. "Excluded Because of Color." *Frontiers of Democracy* 6 (1939–40): 191.

Mitchell, Silas W., and Fielding H. Garrison. *Biographical memoir of John Shaw Billings, 1838–1913*. Washington, DC: National Academy of Sciences, 1917.

Morgan, Julia Bouvlitz. "Son of a Slave." *Johns Hopkins Magazine*, June 1981, 20–26.

Morrill, Justin S. *Speech of Hon. Justin S. Morrill, of Vermont, on the bill granting lands for agricultural colleges*. Washington, DC: Congressional Globe Office, 1858.

Murphey, Murray Griffin. *The Development of Peirce's Philosophy*. Cambridge, MA: Harvard University Press, 1961.

National Educational Association. *Journals of Proceedings and Address of the Thirty-Eighth Annual Meeting held at Los Angeles, California, July 11–14, 1899*. Chicago: University of Chicago Press, 1899.

National Library of Medicine. "John Shaw Billings Centennial." https://www.nlm.nih.gov/hmd/pdf/john.pdf.

National Science Foundation. "Rankings by total R&D expenditures." Accessed 28 March 2020. https://ncsesdata.nsf.gov/profiles/site?method=rankingBySource&ds=herd.

———. "Higher Education Research and Development Survey, Fiscal Year 2018." Table 23, "Federally financed higher education R&D expenditures, ranked by FY 2018 R&D expenditures: FYs 2009–18." Accessed 7 January 2022. https://ncsesdata.nsf.gov/herd/2018/html/herd18-dt-tab023.html.

"The Negro Question." *New York Times*, 24 April 1903.

Newcomb, Simon. "Abstract Science in America, 1776–1876." *North American Review* 122, no. 250 (January 1876): 88–123.

"The Nineteenth-Century United States President Who Was a Strong Advocate of Black Higher Education." *Journal of Blacks in Higher Education* 28 (2000): 34–36. doi:10.2307/2678680.

Noyes, William Albert, and James Flack Norris. "Biographical Memoir of Ira Remsen, 1846–1927." In *National Academy of Sciences of the United States of America: Biographical Memoirs, Vol. 14*, 207–57. Washington, DC: National Academies Press, 1931.

Numbers, Ronald L., and John Harley Warner. "The Maturation of American Medical Science." In Leavitt and Numbers, *Sickness and Health in America*, 135–42.

Oakes, James. "A Failure of Vision: The Collapse of the Freedmen's Bureau Courts." *Civil War History* 25, no. 1 (March 1979): 66–76.

"Obituary of Charles J. M. Gwinn." *Johns Hopkins University Circulars* 13, no. 110 (March 1894): 47.

"Obituary Record: Charles J. M. Gwinn." *New York Times*, 12 February 1894.

Oblensky, Florence. "John Shaw Billings—12 April 1838–11 March 1913: On the One Hundred and Twenty-Ninth Anniversary of His Birth." *Military Medicine* 132, no. 4 (April 1967): 286–91.

*Occasional Papers, John F. Slater Fund Trustees, 1894–1935*. Baltimore: Published by the Trustees. https://catalog.hathitrust.org/Record/000551472.

Oleson, Alexandra, and John Voss, eds. *The Organization of Knowledge in Modern America, 1860–1920*. Baltimore: Johns Hopkins University Press, 1979.

Olmsted, Frederick Law. *Report Upon a Projected Improvement of the Estate of the College of California, at Berkeley, Near Oakland*. San Francisco: Towne & Bacon, 1866.

Olson, Sherry H. *Baltimore: The Building of an American City*. Baltimore: Johns Hopkins University Press, 2007.

Osakwe, Danielle. "UGA professors and students discuss keeping or removing LeConte Hall portrait with racist past." *Red & Black*, 3 April 2019. https://www.redandblack.com/uganews/uga-professors-and-students-discuss-keeping-or-removing-leconte-hall/article_8a82941a-55b8-11e9-8182-ab9f47b11ccd.html.

Osler, William. *Aequanimitas*. London: P. Blakiston's Sons, 1904.

"The Pardon of Forgers: Gov. Robinson's Reasons for Refusing to Release Persons Convicted of Forgery." *New York Times*, 13 August 1879, 2.

Parker, Franklin. "George Peabody." In Grimm, *Notable American Philanthropists*, 242–46.

———. *George Peabody: A Biography*. Nashville: Vanderbilt University Press, 1971.

———. "George Peabody's Influence on Southern Educational Philanthropy." *Tennessee Historical Quarterly* 20, no. 1 (March 1961): 65–74.

Parshall, Karen Hunger. "America's First School of Mathematical Research: James Joseph Sylvester at The Johns Hopkins University, 1876–1883." *Archive for History of Exact Sciences* 38, no. 2 (1988): 153–96.

———. *James Joseph Sylvester: Jewish Mathematician in a Victorian World*. Baltimore: Johns Hopkins University Press, 2006.

———. *James Joseph Sylvester: Life and Work in Letters*. Oxford: Oxford University Press, 2013.

Parshall, Karen Hunger, and David E. Rowe. *The Emergence of the American Mathematical Research Community, 1876–1900: J. J. Sylvester, Felix Klein, and E. H. Moore*. History of Mathematics Volume 8. Providence, RI: American Mathematical Society, 1994.

Peabody Education Fund. *Proceedings of the Trustees at their Fifty-Second Meeting, 18 March 1909*. Cambridge, MA: University Press, 1909.

———. *Proceedings of the Trustees of the Peabody Education Fund, 1867–1914*. Vol. 2. New York: Wilson & Sons, 1881. https://catalog.hathitrust.org/Record/001735899.

Peirce, Bradford Kinney. *Trials of an inventor: Life and discoveries of Charles Goodyear*. New York: Carlton & Porter, 1866.

Pelfrey, Patricia A., and Margaret Cheney. *A Brief History of the University of California*. Berkeley: University of California Press, 2004.

Peterson, Kenneth G. "Joseph C. Rowell and California's Bacon Library." *Journal of Library History (1974–1987)* 17, no. 3 (1982): 278–90.

Pierson, G. W. "American Universities in the Nineteenth Century: The Formative Period." In Clapp, *Modern University*, 59–94.

Pietila, Antero. *The Ghosts of Johns Hopkins: The Life and Legacy That Shaped an American City*. New York: Rowman & Littlefield, 2018.

Pinney, G. W. "The New Education." In Pinney, Swinton, and Carr, *University of California and its relations to industrial education*. 77–107.

Pinney, G.W., William Swinton, and Ezra Carr. *The University of California and its relations to industrial education: as shown by Prof. Carr's reply to the grangers and mechanics; Prof. Swinton's testimony before the Legislature; the new education, by "Columella"; memorial to the Legislature by joint committee of the state Grange and Mechanics' deliberative assembly, and other documents*. San Francisco: Benjamin Dore, 1874.

Polos, Nicholas C. "A Yankee Patriot: John Swett, the Horace Mann of the Pacific." *History of Education Quarterly* 4, no. 1 (March 1964): 17–32.

Porter, Roy. *The Greatest Benefit to Mankind: A Medical History of Humanity*. New York: Norton, 1997.

Prescott, Heather Munro. "Sending Their Sons into Danger: Cornell University and the Ithaca Typhoid Epidemic of 1903." *New York History* 78, no. 3 (July 1997): 273–308.

"The Presidential Election." *Daily Exchange*, 12 November 1860, 1.

"Principal's Report for the Year Ending June 30, 1897." In *The Hampton Normal and Agricultural Institute*, 2–3. Hampton, VA: Normal School Steam Press, 1897.

"Professor Huxley in America." *New York Tribune Extra*, 23 September 1876.

"Public Libraries in the U.S." Accessed 6 July 2020. https://www.bridgespan.org/public-libraries.

Pumroy, Eric. "Bryn Mawr College." In *Founded by Friends: The Quaker Heritage of Fifteen American Colleges and Universities*, edited by John William Oliver, Charles L. Cherry, and Caroline L. Cherry, 147–62. Lanham, MD: Scarecrow, 2007.

Radcliffe, George L. P. *Governor Thomas H. Hicks of Maryland and the Civil War*. Baltimore: Johns Hopkins Press, 1901.

Rasmussen, Fred. "Charles A. Barker, scholar, pacifist led Hopkins history department." *Baltimore Sun*, 19 September 1993. https://www.baltimoresun.com/news/bs-xpm-1993-09-19-1993262045-story.html.

Reingold, Nathan. "National Science Policy in a Private Foundation: The Carnegie Institution of Washington." In Oleson and Voss, *Organization of Knowledge in Modern America*, 313–41.

Remsen, Ira. "Harmon Northrop Morse." *Proceedings of the American Academy of Arts and Sciences* 58, no. 17 (September 1923): 607–13.

"Report of Assembly Committee on Public Buildings and Grounds in Relation to the Construction of the College of Letters." In *Appendix to Journals of Senate and Assembly of the Twentieth Session of the Legislature of the State of California*, vol. 4. Sacramento: State Printer, 1874.

"Report of the Joint Committee of the Senate and Assembly Appointed to Examine into the Management of the University of California, including the Administration of the Trusts Confided to the Regents Thereof." In *Appendix to Journals of Senate and Assembly of the Twentieth Session of the Legislature of the State of California*, vol. 6. Sacramento: State Printer, 1874.

*Report of the President of the Johns Hopkins University, Baltimore, Maryland 1885.* Baltimore: Johns Hopkins Press, 1885.

*Report of the President of the Johns Hopkins University, 1891.* Baltimore: Johns Hopkins Press, 1891.

"The Rev. L. W. Bacon Questioned." *New York Times*, 13 November 1887. https://timesmachine.nytimes.com/timesmachine/1887/11/13/103150854.pdf.

Reynolds, Terry S. "The Education of Engineers in America before the Morrill Act of 1862." *History of Education Quarterly* 32, no. 4 (Winter 1992): 459–82.

Rhodes, Karl. "Founding America's First Research University." *Econ Focus, Third Quarter* 23, no. 3 (2018): 22–25.

Richards, David Alan. *Skulls and Keys: The Hidden History of Yale's Secret Societies.* New York: Pegasus Books, 2017.

Ris, Ethan W. "The Education of Andrew Carnegie: Strategic Philanthropy in American Higher Education, 1880–1919." *Journal of Higher Education* 88, no. 3 (2017): 401–29.

Rockefeller Foundation: A Digital History. "The General Education Board." Accessed 29 April 2020. https://rockfound.rockarch.org/general_education_board.

Rodriguez, Danton. "All Quiet on the Southern Front: The Bravery of Edward S. Lewis—A Look at the Policies and Politics Regarding Admission of African Americans to Johns Hopkins in the 1930's." Johns Hopkins University. Accessed 13 February 2020. https://www.yumpu.com/en/document/view/31116245/complete-the-history-of-african-americans-at-johns-hopkins-.

Rogers, Walter P. *Andrew D. White and the Modern University.* Ithaca, NY: Cornell University Press, 1942.

Ross, Earle D. *Democracy's College: The Land-Grant Movement in the Formative Stage.* Ames: Iowa State College Press, 1942.

Roth, Cecil. "The Jews in the English Universities." *Miscellanies (Jewish Historical Society of England)* 4 (1942): 102–15.

Rothberg, Morey, and Jacqueline Goggin, eds. *John Franklin Jameson and the Development of Humanistic Scholarship in America.* Athens: University of Georgia Press, 1993.

Rouse, Parke, Jr., ed. "A College Befriended: William and Mary in 1887." *Virginia Magazine of History and Biography* 1 (January 1986): 77–107.

Royal Commission for the Exhibition of 1851. Accessed 7 March 2020. https://www.royalcommission1851.org/.

The Royal Society. "Davy Medal." Accessed 7 May 2020. https://royalsociety.org/grants-schemes-awards/awards/davy-medal/.

Royce, Josiah. "Present Ideas of American University Life." *Scribner's Magazine* 10 (September 1891): 376–89.

Rubin, Louis D., Jr., ed. *Teach the Freeman: The Correspondence of Rutherford B. Hayes and the Slater Fund for Negro Education.* 2 vols. Baton Rouge: Louisiana State University Press, 1959.

Rudolph, Frederick. *The American College and University: A History (Introductory Essay and Supplemental Bibliography by John R. Thelin).* 1962. Reprint, Athens: University of Georgia Press, 1990.

Ryan, W. Carson. *Studies in Early Graduate Education: The Johns Hopkins, Clark University, the University of Chicago.* Boston: Merrymount, 1939.

Sander, Kathleen Waters. *John W. Garrett and the Baltimore and Ohio Railroad.* Baltimore: Johns Hopkins University Press, 2017.

———. *Mary Elizabeth Garrett: Society and Philanthropy in the Gilded Age.* Baltimore: Johns Hopkins University Press, 2008.

Saunders, Myra K. "California Legal History: The California Constitution of 1849." *Law Library Journal* 90, no. 3 (Summer 1998): 447–80.

"Scholars Without Money." *Time Magazine,* 23 March 1939.

The SEED School of Maryland. "About SEED Maryland." https://www.seedschoolmd.org/about.

———. "Are you eligible?" https://www.seedschoolmd.org/are-you-eligible.

SFGATE. "Verne A. Stadtman." Accessed 10 May 2020. https://www.legacy.com/obituaries/sfgate/obituary.aspx?n=verne-a-stadtman&pid=125095341.

Shaw, Wilfred B., ed. *The University of Michigan, an Encyclopedic Survey.* Vols. 8–9. Ann Arbor: University of Michigan Press, 1968.

Shils, Edward. "The Order of Learning in the United States: The Ascendancy of the University." In Oleson and Voss, *Organization of Knowledge in Modern America,* 19–47.

Shryock, Richard H. *The Unique Influence of The Johns Hopkins University on American Medicine.* Copenhagen: Ejnar Munksgaard, 1953.

Silliman, Benjamin. *The Truly Practical Man, Necessarily an Education Man: Oration Delivered at the Commencement of the College of California, June 5, 1867.* San Francisco: Towne & Bacon, 1867.

Silver, Daniel S. "The Secret History of Mathematicians." *American Scientist* 94, no. 6 (November–December 2006): 556, 558–59.

Silverman, Barry D. "William Henry Welch (1850–1934): The Road to Johns Hopkins." *Proceedings of the Baylor University Medical Center 2011* 24, no. 3 (2011): 236–42.

Slosson, Edwin E. *Great American Universities.* New York: Macmillan, 1910.

Smith, Edgar F. *Chemistry in America.* New York: D. Appleton, 1914.

Smith, Marion Lofton. "Atticus Greene Haygood: Christian Educator." PhD diss., Yale University, 1929.

Smith, Neil. *American Empire: Roosevelt's Geographer and the Prelude to Globalization.* Berkeley: University of California Press, 2003.

Somers, Wayne, comp. *The Encyclopedia of Union College History.* Schenectady, NY: Union College Press, 2003.

Sorber, Nathan M. "Creating Colleges of Science, Industry, and National Advancement: The Origins of the New England Land-Grant Colleges." In Geiger and Sorber, *Land-Grant Colleges and the Reshaping of American Higher Education,* 41–71.

———. *Land-Grant Colleges and Popular Revolt: The Origins of the Morrill Act and the Reform of Higher Education.* Ithaca, NY: Cornell University Press, 2018.

Spencer, Herbert. *Principles of Biology.* Vol. 1. New York: D. Appleton, 1897.

Stadtman, Verne A. *The University of California, 1868–1968: A Centennial Publication of the University of California.* New York: McGraw-Hill, 1970.

Staley, Patricia F. *Norwich in the Gilded Age: The Rose City's Millionaires' Triangle.* Charleston, SC: History Press, 2014.

*Statements respecting the Johns Hopkins University of Baltimore, presented to the public on the twentieth anniversary, 1896.* Baltimore: Johns Hopkins Press, 1896.

State of California. *Statutes of California.* Sacramento: O. M. Clayes, 1866.

Stave, Bruce M. *Red Brick in the Land of Steady Habits: Creating the University of Connecticut, 1881–2006.* Lebanon, NH: University Press of New England, 2006.

"St. Basil of Baltimore." *New York Times,* 21 October 1923.

Stemmons, Walter, and André Schenker. *Connecticut Agricultural College: A History.* Storrs: University of Connecticut Press, 1931.

Stevens, W. Le Conte. "Sketch of Professor John LeConte." *Popular Science Monthly* 36 (November 1889): 112–20.

Stimpert, Jim. "Johns Hopkins University." In *Founded by Friends: The Quaker Heritage of Fifteen American Colleges and Universities,* edited by John William Oliver, Charles L. Cherry, and Caroline L. Cherry, 125–46. Lanham, MD: Scarecrow, 2007.

Stokes, Anson Phelps. *Memorials of Eminent Yale Men.* Vol. 1, *Religion and Letters.* New Haven, CT: Yale University Press, 1914.

Storr, Richard J. *The Beginnings of Graduate Education in America.* New York: Arno, 1969.

"The Story of Gilman." *New York Times,* 13 October 1877, 4.

Stover, John F. *History of the Baltimore and Ohio Railroad.* West Lafayette, IN: Purdue University Press, 1995.

Summers, Festus P. *The Baltimore and Ohio in the Civil War.* New York: Putnam, 1939.

Sweetnam, George Kean. *The Command of Light: Rowland's School of Physics and the Spectrum.* Philadelphia: American Philosophical Society, 2000.

Swett, John. *Public Education in California: Its Origin and Development, with Personal Reminiscences of Half a Century.* New York: American Book Company, 1911.

Swinton, William. "Professor Swinton's Testimony." In Pinney, Swinton, and Carr, *University of California and its relations to industrial education,* 55–74..

Sylvester, James Joseph. *Address Delivered by J. J. Sylvester, F.R.S. (corresponding Member of the Institute of France), Professor of Mathematics, at Johns Hopkins University on Commemoration Day, February 22, 1877.* Baltimore: Cushings & Bailey, 1877.

Tappan, Henry Philip. *University Education.* New York: Putnam & Sons, 1851.

Tewksbury, Donald G. *The Founding of American Colleges and Universities Before the Civil War.* New York: Arno, 1969.

Thelin, John R. *A History of American Higher Education.* Baltimore: Johns Hopkins University Press, 2013.

Thom, Helen Hopkins. *Johns Hopkins: A Silhouette.* Baltimore: Johns Hopkins University Press, 2009.

Thomas, George. *The Founders and the Idea of a National University: Constituting the American Mind.* New York: Cambridge University Press, 2015.

Thursfield, Richard Emmons. *Henry Barnard's American Journal of Education.* Baltimore: Johns Hopkins Press, 1945.

Thwing, Charles Franklin. *The American and the German University: One Hundred Years of History.* New York: Macmillan, 1928.

Toews, Rockford E. *Lincoln in Annapolis, February 1865.* Introduction by Edward C. Papenfuse. Annapolis: Maryland State Archives, 2009.

Turner, James, and Paul Bernard. "The German Model and the Graduate School: The University of Michigan and the Origin Myth of the American University." In Geiger, *American College in the Nineteenth Century,* 221–41.

"The University and Its Management." *San Francisco Daily Evening Post,* 16 March 1874.

University of Cambridge: A Cambridge Alumni Database. "Sylvester, James Joseph (SLVR831JJ)." Accessed 1 May 2020. http://venn.lib.cam.ac.uk/cgi-bin/search-2018.pl?sur=&suro=w&fir =&firo=c&cit=&cito=c&c=all&z=all&tex=SLVR831JJ&sye=&eye=&col=all&maxcount=50.

University of Illinois Alumni Association. *Fortnightly Notes* 3, no. 3 (15 February 1915).

"Vast Forgeries Exposed: A Wealthy and Trusted Criminal." *New York Times,* 3 October 1877, 1.

Veysey, Laurence R. *The Emergence of the American University.* Chicago: University of Chicago Press, 1965.

Vozella, Laura. "Cheesecake on the tart side." *Baltimore Sun,* 15 December 2006. http://web .archive.org/web/20070320152617/http://www.baltimoresun.com/news/local/bal-md.vozella 15dec15,0,7196427.column?coll=bal-home-columnists.

Warren, Mame, ed. *Johns Hopkins: Knowledge for the World, 1876–2001.* Baltimore: Johns Hopkins University Press, 2000.

Washington, George. "Eighth Annual Message, December 7, 1796." The American Presidency Project. https://www.presidency.ucsb.edu/documents/eighth-annual-address-congress.

———. "George Washington's Last Will and Testament, July 9, 1799." In *The Papers of George Washington, Retirement Series, Vol. 4,* edited by W. W. Abbot, 479–511. Charlottesville: University Press of Virginia, 1999.

Watkins, William H. "Slater Fund." *Encyclopedia of African American Education.* 2 vols. Thousand Oaks, CA: SAGE, 2010.

———. *The White Architects of Black Education: Ideology and Power in America, 1865–1954.* New York: Teachers College Press, 2001.

Wayland, Francis. *Report to the Corporation of Brown University.* Providence, RI: G. H. Whitney, 1850.

"W. C. Gilman Indicted: He Promises to give Himself up Today." *New York Times,* 12 October 1877, 8.

Weber, Thomas. *The Northern Railroads in the Civil War, 1861–1865.* New York: Columbia University Press, 1952.

West, Earle H. "The Peabody Education Fund and Negro Education, 1867–1880." *History of Education Quarterly* 6, no. 2 (Summer 1966): 3–21.

"The West Point Graduates: Imposing ceremonies—Addresses by Professor Gilman and Secretary Belknap—The relative standing of the members." *New York Times,* 17 June 1875.

White, Andrew Dickson. *Autobiography of Andrew D. White.* 2 vols. New York: Century, 1905.

———. "Eleventh Paper." In *The "How I Was Educated" Papers,* 119–20. New York: D. Appleton, 1888.

———. "A University at Washington." *Forum Extra* 1, no. 5 (July 1890): 3–14.

"William C. Gilman Obituary." *Norwich (CT) Bulletin,* 31 March 1922, 5.

"William C. Gilman Sentenced." *New York Times,* 13 October 1877, 8.

Williams, Roger L. *The Origins of Federal Support for Higher Education: George W. Atherton and the Land-Grant College Movement.* University Park: Pennsylvania State University Press, 1991.

Wollenberg, Charles. *Berkeley: A City in History.* Berkeley: University of California Press, 2008.

Woods, Henry, Maurice Bloomfield, and Minton Warren. "Charles D'Urban Morris." *American Journal of Philology* 7, no. 1 (1886): 127–31.

Woody, Thomas. Review of *Daniel Coit Gilman, Creator of the American Type of University*, by Abraham Flexner. *Pennsylvania History: A Journal of Mid-Atlantic Studies* 14, no. 2 (April 1947): 168–69.

The World University Rankings. "The *Times Higher Education* World University Rankings 2022." Accessed 7 January 2022. https://www.timeshighereducation.com/world-university -rankings/2022/world-ranking#!/page/0/length/25/sort_by/rank/sort_order/asc/cols/stats.

Wright, John Henry. *The College in the University and Classical Philology in the College: An Address at the Opening of the Eleventh Academic Year of the Johns Hopkins University, October 7, 1886.* Baltimore: Johns Hopkins University, 1886.

Wright, John K. "Daniel Coit Gilman, Geographer and Historian, 1831–1908." *Geographical Review* 51, no. 3 (1961): 381–99.

Wright, W. D. "The Thought and Leadership of Kelly Miller." *Phylon* 39, no. 2 (1978): 180–92. doi:10.2307/274513.

"W. W. Spence Dies at 100: Baltimore Financier Celebrated Birthday on Oct. 18." *New York Times*, 4 November 1915, 7.

"YALE COLLEGE.; The Exercises of Presentation Week—Wooden Spoon Exhibition—The Class Oration and Poem—The De Forrest Prize." *New York Times*, 29 June 1864. https:// www.nytimes.com/1864/06/29/archives/yale-college-the-exercises-of-presentation-week wooden-spoon.html.

Yates, R. C. "Sylvester at the University of Virginia." *American Mathematical Monthly* 44, no. 4 (April 1937): 194–201.

Young, Arthur P. "Daniel Coit Gilman in the Formative Period of American Librarianship." *Library Quarterly: Information, Community, Policy* 45, no. 2 (April 1975): 117–40.

Young, John Russell. *Around the World with General Grant*. Baltimore: Johns Hopkins University Press, 2002.

Page numbers in *italics* refer to figures.

Abel, John Jacob, 202
academic freedom, x, 108–9, 155, 158–59
Academy of Music, 150, 163
Adams, Henry Carter, 174, 297n7
Adams, Herbert Baxter, 170, *171*, 172, 175, 214, 295n35, 297n7
admission requirements, 96, 102, 113, 157, 209
African Americans: education funds, 217–28, 234; Freedmen's Bureau, 218; Haygood on education of, 221–22; HBCUs, 218, 219; and industrial training, 224–25, 227, 228, 229, 232; at JHU, xiii, 229–34; orphanage plans, 8, 9, 190–92, 194, 211. *See also* Peabody Education Fund; slavery
Agassiz, Alexander, 166, 172, 313n51
Agassiz, Louis, 82–83, 91, 166, 276n59
Agricultural Act of 1890, 218
agricultural education: and Carr, 70, 72; and DCG, 28, 29, 30–31, 32, 40–42, 71, 73; experiment stations, 40, 41; and George, 72; Morrill on, 37–38. *See also* land-grant institutions
Agricultural, Mining and Mechanical Arts College (California), 44–45, 46, 50, 51
Albro, Alice, 278n128
Alexander, Will, 308n30
Allen, Eugene T., 169
Alvord, Benjamin, 53
American Association for the Advancement of Science, 162, 215
American Association of Universities (AAU), 174
American Association of University Professors, 299n39

American Bible Society, 253
*American Chemical Journal*, xii, 183, 185
American Chemical Society, 183
American Geographical Society, 35
American Historical Association, 226
*American Journal of Insanity*, 185
*American Journal of Mathematics*, xii, 125, 182, 185, 229
*American Journal of Philology*, 183, 185
*American Journal of Science*, 46, 117, 183
American Missionary Association, 300n55
American Oriental Society, 216
American Philological Association, xii, 180, 181
American Physical Society, xii
American Social Science Association, 216
American university system: Agassiz on, 82–83; in DCG addresses, 61–64, 152–60; influence of, viii; and Morrill, 37–38. *See also* classical curriculum *vs.* technical education debate
Ancient Languages: first faculty in, 53, 128–35, 143–47; as original department, 112, 264n19
Angell, James Burrill, *101*; advice by, 83–85, 100–104, 160; on Hurd, 203; on JHU, xi, 170; and research focus, ix, xi; writings, 269n3
animal experimentation, 141–42, 143
*Annual Report*, 184, 185
Archaeological Institute of America, 216
Archaeological Society, 181
Armstrong, Samuel Chapman, 224
Army Medical Library, 193
Association of American Universities, 215
Association of Land-Grant Colleges and Universities, 299n39

Atherton, George W., 239
Atkinson, William Parsons, 240

bachelor of arts degree: of DCG, 20; requirements for, 113; value of, 94
Bacon, Leonard Woolsey, 22, 220
Baker, Conrad, 60
Baldwin, William H., Jr., 228
Ball, Thomas R., 233
Baltimore: city charter, 215; and Civil War, 5; DCG's service to, 215–16; Great Fire of 1904, 190; as location, 99
Baltimore & Ohio Railroad, 3–6, 9, 187–88, 208, 231
Bancroft, Cecil Franklin Patch, 123
Barker, Charles, 68
Barnard, Henry, 28, 46
Bascomb, Florence, 158
Belgium, university model in, 29
Bellows, Henry Whitney, 54
Bergh, Henry, 141
Berkeley, George, 49, 64
Berkeley Club, 65
Bernays, Jacob, 131–32
Bigelow, Henry, 98
Billings, Frederick, 49, 66
Billings, John Shaw: and Carnegie Institution, 242–44, 247, 248; and cholera prevention, 196; and Civil War, 193; and hospital, xii, 192–96, 203–4; initial meeting with DCG, 115; lectures by, 199–200; and medical school, xii, 142, 192–96, 199–200
biology: Brooks lectures, 166; first faculty in, 139–43
Blair, Walter, 144
Blake, William Phipps, 45
Bonnycastle, Charles, 36
book collecting, 32–33, 49. *See also* libraries
Booth, Newton, 59, 66, 77
Bowman, Isaiah, 232, 233
Boyce, James P., 223
Breach, John S., 57
Bright, John, 21
British Guiana boundary dispute, 216
British university model: influence of, viii; and Jewish scholars, 120–21, 127; research by DCG, ix, 27, 30
Brooks, Chauncey, 3
Brooks, Phillips, 222

Brooks, William Keith, 166, 170, 172, 297n7
Brown, George William: and Civil War, 4; and classical *vs.* technical education debate, 110, 240; focus on graduate education, 12–13, 113; as initial trustee, 10, 11; and medical school endowment, 306n218; and salary negotiations, 123; and women's education, 208
Brown University, 36
Brush, George J., 57, 94–95, 111
Bryce, James, 174–75
Buchanan, James, 38
buildings and facilities: advice on, 88–89, 91, 96–97, 99; Angell on, 103, 170; Clifton estate, 9, 96, 103, 111, 157; DCG's approach to, 118–19, 153, 169; funding for, 112; Gilman Hall, *261*; Hopkins Hall, 157, *170*, *171*, 175, 200; hospital, 194, 195–96, 200; Huxley on, 165; initial, 111, 112, *170*, *171*; laboratories, 91, 118, 119, 136–37, 138, 140–41; modesty of, x, 96, 169–70
Bushnell, Horace, 43–44, 274n34, 277n101
Butler, Nicholas Murray, 168, 184, 257
Butterworth, Samuel F., 54, 69
Byerly, William Elwood, 95

California: constitution, 47–48; first visit to, 59; investigation of UC, 69–74; land-grant institutions debate, 44–47
California College of Pharmacy, 65
Calvert, George, 159
Cambridge University, 27, 61, 120–21, 127, 158, 208
career and work of DCG: as advisor, 213–14, 221, 256–57; for Barnard, 28–31; Carnegie Institution, xiii, 241–51; Connecticut State Board of Education, 34–35; Department of Education, 41, 58–59; for John Fox Slater Fund, 217–26, 228–29, 300n55; Goodyear, 23–24; as hospital director, 202–3; New York City public schools, 235; Peabody Education Fund, 216, 252, 255, 256; and retirement, viii, 235–37, 258; Sheffield Scientific School, 31–32, 33, 35–37, 57; University of Wisconsin offer, 42; US Legation to Russia, 21, 23, 24, 26; writing work, 25; Yale librarian position, 25, 26–27, 32–33; Yale presidency ambitions, 56, 58. *See also* presidency, Johns Hopkins University; University of California
Carnegie, Andrew, 9, 237–46, *245*, 249, 251